The Progressive Assault on Laissez Faire

THE PROGRESSIVE
ASSAULT ON
LAISSEZ FAIRE

*Robert Hale and the First
Law and Economics Movement*

BARBARA H. FRIED

Harvard University Press
Cambridge, Massachusetts
London, England

First Harvard University Press paperback edition, 2001

Library of Congress Cataloging-in-Publication Data

Fried, Barbara, 1951–
The progressive assault on laissez faire : Robert Hale and the
first law and economics movement / Barbara H. Fried.
p.   cm.
Includes bibliographical references and index.
ISBN 0-674-77527-9 (cloth)
ISBN 0-674-00698-4 (pbk.)
1. Right of property—United States.
2. Hale, Robert Lee, 1884–1969.
3. Free enterprise—United States.
4. Institutional economics.
5. Neoclassical school of economics.
6. Progressivism (United States).
7. Critical legal studies—United States.
I. Title.
HB701.F75   1998
330. 12′2—dc21   97-39972

CONTENTS

Contents

PREFACE

This book is a study of the work of Robert Lee Hale (1884–1969), a major figure in both the American Legal Realist movement and the looser association of institutional and progressive economists writing in the first part of the twentieth century. The book describes and assesses the lasting importance of Hale's contributions to legal theory and the nascent field of law and economics. Using Hale's work as a focal point, it also looks more generally at the progressive assault on laissez-faire constitutionalism and neoclassical economics from the 1880s through the 1930s.

Although Hale's work was highly regarded by many of his own contemporaries in both law and economics, it fell into relative obscurity after the 1940s. The sole exception was a thoughtful article in the early 1970s by the economic historian Warren Samuels, the first and (to date) only substantial study of Hale's work.[1] The last fifteen years have seen a substantial revival of interest in Hale, largely spurred by legal scholars in or sympathetic to the Critical Legal Studies movement, who have rightly identified Hale's writing as the logical precursor to their own work, and as the culmination of many of the most important strands of Realist thought.[2] Even among Hale enthusiasts, however, only a small portion of Hale's work is widely known. Moreover, it is fair to say that Hale remains unknown to a large number of scholars in legal theory, law and economics, political philosophy, and intellectual history, to whom his work is potentially of great interest. That is a significant loss. Even though among the least well-known of the Legal Realists and institutional economists, Hale produced over his lifetime a substantial body of work that represents, in many respects, the best of both fields.

Several recent intellectual developments make the current revival of interest in Hale's work particularly timely. The first is the resurgence in philosophical and legal circles of libertarian defenses of the minimal state, in the work of such figures as Robert Nozick, Eric Mack, Jeffrey Paul, and Richard Epstein, and the burgeoning literature on coercion since publication of Nozick's 1969 article on the subject.[3] Drawing on his extensive knowledge of law, economics, and political theory, Hale developed one of the most profound and elaborated critiques of libertarianism offered to date. Indeed, Hale's analysis of both coercion and natural property rights theory, along with the appropriate treatment of scarcity rents under a Lockean theory of entitlement, provides an uncannily close counterpoint to Nozick's arguments in *Anarchy, State and Utopia* and other works.

The second development is the emergence in the mid-1970s of what has aptly been called "the second great law and economics movement." The movement, which has grown to be a dominant force in legal academia, has developed largely unaware of the work of the institutional economists who made up the *first* great law and economics movement from the 1880s to the 1930s. Although preoccupied with a somewhat different set of concerns, the institutionalists offered a foundational analysis of the legal underpinnings of economic life that remains an important commentary on, and corrective to, the work of their successors. That is particularly true of Hale, whose work—alone among the institutionalists—reflects a sophistication about both law and economics that ranks it with the best of contemporary writing in the area.

Finally, as previously suggested, Hale's work is of enormous importance to contemporary legal scholars writing in what might loosely be termed the critical tradition, most notably the Critical Legal Studies movement. Along with law and economics, Critical Legal Studies has emerged as one of the more significant developments in legal scholarship in the past two decades, generating interest far beyond legal circles. Many of the best-known articles in the field have drawn explicitly on Hale's work. To that extent, the work is of obvious interest as a precursor to current thought. But only a small fraction of Hale's work has found its way into the literature. The balance— some of it never published—reveals a much more elaborate argument concerning the public roots of private rights than can be gleaned from his best-known articles taken alone, and one that should be of even greater interest to those writing in the critical tradition, and their critics.

In other respects, this project is an anachronistic one, or is at least swimming against the tide of recent historiography of the period. Recent accounts have tended to stress the conservative undercurrents in progressive politics; the progressive strains in the work of key conservative legal figures like Stephen Field, David Brewer, Christopher Tiedeman, and Thomas Cooley; and the relatively limited impact of laissez-faire ideology on judicial and legislative

decisions in the height of the so-called laissez-faire period in American constitutional law. The argument of this book returns to a simpler time, in which
progressives were progressive, conservatives were conservative, and the two
sides were joined in battle over the state's right to intervene in economic
affairs. My aim in reverting to a more traditional picture of American politics
of the period is not to take issue with the revisionist view that the motivations
of key players on both sides and the consequences of their acts were far
more complex than conventionally portrayed. Rather, my aim has been to
re-create faithfully the political landscape as its major antagonists would
have described it. Legal Realism and institutional economics were both born
in opposition to laissez faire. In that historical context, Hale et al. would
have had no trouble identifying Tiedeman, Field, et al. as the enemy, and
vice versa. That it turns out that they were less far apart than they thought
at the time would come as a (perhaps not unpleasant) surprise to both sides.
But one can make sense of the progressive response only by understanding
that they did not see it that way at the time.

Finally, a related note about terminology. What to call the positive, state
liberalism that united the British New Liberals, Social Democrats, and other
left-leaning social reformers in the years from the 1880s to the 1930s has
proved something of a dilemma. The term "progressive" having become
rife with embarrassments, contemporary historians have variously termed
it "democratic collectivism," "progressive liberalism," and "welfare state
liberalism."[4] Following James Kloppenberg's lead, for ease of exposition, I
have reverted to the old-fashioned term "progressive."[5] I do not mean
thereby either to limit inquiry chronologically to the Progressive Era, or to
take sides in the debates about whether progressivism constituted a coherent
political movement or whether many of the traditional progressive reform
programs had a decidedly conservative cast.[6] For purposes of this book,
"progressive" should be understood to refer broadly to that group of left-
liberal social theorists and reformers from the 1880s to the 1930s who believed
that the state had a critical role to play, through progressive tax and transfer
programs, labor legislation, and other welfare measures, in promoting a
social welfarist vision of the common good.[7]

This book is a long time in coming. Among the many pleasures of finishing
it, chief is having the opportunity at long last to acknowledge (if not retire)
the numerous debts I have incurred in the process. I am grateful to the
Columbia University Archives, which houses Hale's professional papers, the
Harvard Law School Library, and the Library of Congress, for permission

to consult and cite from Hale's correspondence and other papers. Special thanks go to the magnificent staff at the Stanford Law School library—in particular Dave Bridgman, Andy Eisenberg, and Paul Lomio—for their tireless and resourceful help. I have been privileged to work at an institution that has generously supported me throughout this process, materially and spiritually, and I am deeply grateful to Dean Paul Brest for his many efforts on both fronts. Research on the book was supported by grants from the Claire and Michael Brown Estate and the Deane Johnson Fund for Excellence in Teaching and Research.

Over the years, I have been blessed with a wonderful group of (extended) colleagues, who have contributed to this and other projects in immeasurable ways. Bob Gordon first piqued my interest in Hale's work almost ten years ago, in a casual hallway remark. His presence in these hallways is greatly missed. I am most grateful to Ian Ayres, Barbara Babcock, Joe Bankman, Guyora Binder, Markus Dubber, Lawrence Friedman, Bob Gordon, Tom Grey, Mark Kelman, Bob Rabin, Peggy Radin, Deborah Rhode, Dorothy Ross, John Henry Schlegel, Bill Simon, Rob Steinfeldt, Kathleen Sullivan; participants in faculty workshops at Buffalo, Columbia, Stanford, and Yale law schools; and three anonymous readers for Harvard University Press, for reading and commenting on various portions of the manuscript over the years. I have benefited from the able research assistance of a number of Stanford law students, including Alison Aubry, Frances Cook, Kim Hazelwood, Olga Hartwell, and Eric Pierson. I owe more indirect debts to Morton Horwitz and Frank Michelman, who—as teachers of mine many years ago at Harvard Law School—gave me my first inkling of the deeper possibilities of legal thought. Above all, thanks go to Joe Bankman and Mark Kelman, who have both been unstinting in their time and enthusiasm for this and other projects. Their critical judgment, (blessedly) corrupted by affection, has helped make my intellectual life at Stanford a very happy one.

My greatest personal debt is to Joe, for a thousand reasons too obvious or ineffable to name. This book is for him, and in memory of his dear, sweet dad, Jack.

The Progressive Assault on Laissez Faire

1

INTRODUCTION

In 1886, Christopher Tiedeman, a young law professor at the University of Missouri, published his famous treatise on the *Limitations of Police Power*.[1] Writing against the backdrop of increasing social unrest—"Socialism, Communism, and Anarchism," in Tiedeman's unsubtle formulation—he intended the treatise to show that the democratic majority's power to interfere in economic matters was severely constrained by a constellation of individual rights protected under the federal and state constitutions.[2] Chief among them, Tiedeman argued, were the individual's rights to liberty and to property, both enshrined in the due process clause of the Fourteenth Amendment.[3] Neither right, he conceded, could be without limits in a civilized society. But the limits could not exceed the legitimate police power of the state, which by human and natural law was "confined to the detailed enforcement of the legal maxim, *sic utere tuo, ut alienum non laedas*"—so use your own as not to injure others.[4] Tiedeman confidently construed "injury" for these purposes to encompass only that narrow band of conduct traditionally prohibited by criminal and tort law, together with a handful of other timeless offenses against the body politic, like having women run barrooms, billiard saloons, or other public resorts.[5] Among the things most assuredly not included, Tiedeman argued, was the right "to protect the weak against the shrewdness of the stronger, to determine what wages a workman shall receive for his labor, and how many hours daily he shall labor," to tell any man what he may charge for his wares or the use of his money, or any other manner of laws meant to promote greater economic security or equality.[6]

In the same year, the renowned economist John Bates Clark published an article entitled "The Moral Outcome of Labor Troubles."[7] The article contained the first glimmerings of his "marginal productivity" theory of distribution, which was not fully articulated until three years later. Not coincidentally, the article also marked the turning point in Clark's intellectual life from an outspoken critic of capitalism to one of its most influential champions.[8] Marginal productivity theory predicted that in a competitive market, each factor of production (labor, land, and other forms of capital) would be paid an amount exactly equal to the value of its marginal product. The theory, like Tiedeman's argument for limited police powers, was developed against the backdrop of increasing attacks from the left on the distributive justice of the market (including until very recently from Clark himself). Its relationship to those attacks was unmistakable. Although offering the theory as purely descriptive, from the start Clark took pains to underscore what he took to be its normative implications. What it implied, Clark argued, was that absent monopoly or other extreme interferences with its normal operations, the market would automatically reward labor and capital in proportion to the value each had generated, which Clark took to mean (self-evidently) in proportion to their just deserts. "To every man his product, his whole product and nothing but his product," as Clark put it in 1890.[9] That result, Clark argued, refuted dispositively not only Marxian theories of exploitation but all others as well. Initially presented in muted form, Clark's argument had developed into a full-blown apologetic for the distributive justice of unregulated capitalism by the publication of *The Distribution of Wealth* in 1899.[10]

Both Tiedeman's and Clark's arguments had considerable influence in their time. Together they forged what many contemporaries took to be a powerful rights-based defense of economic laissez faire. Tiedeman's constitutional argument for limited government was institutionalized in various state and federal court decisions limiting the permissible scope of economic regulation in the name of freedom of contract and private property.[11] Clark's philosophical argument for laissez faire had a more complicated fate. Few mainstream economists explicitly defended Clark's thesis, deeming its premises more properly in the realm of politics or philosophy than the science of economics. But his thesis had enormous appeal to a popular audience, shoring up a widespread intuition, going back at least to John Locke, that each person is entitled to the fruits of her labor, and by extension to whatever the market will pay her for relinquishing them.[12]

Beginning in the 1890s and continuing through the 1930s, progressive academics in law and in economics mounted parallel assaults on economic laissez faire. Two key objectives united the two camps of this "first great law and economics movement," to borrow Herbert Hovenkamp's apt phrase. The first objective was to show that Tiedeman's constitutionally protected sphere of economic life, like Clark's moral market, was constituted by a regime of property and contract rights that were neither spontaneously occurring nor self-defining, but were rather the positive creation of the state. What the state had made in one form, one was nudged to conclude, it could remake in another. Second, the particular configuration of contract and property rights embraced by late nineteenth- and early twentieth-century Anglo-American law had produced a distribution of wealth that was hard to square with any obvious intuitions of justice. What the state could remake, it therefore should. Robert Lee Hale, the principal subject of this book, was a key figure in both camps. His work constitutes perhaps their most important intellectual bridge.

Hale was trained both as a lawyer (LL.B., Harvard, 1909) and as an economist (M.A., Harvard, 1907; Ph.D., Columbia, 1918). Although a common marriage of interests in contemporary academia, it was unusual in Hale's time, and one that uniquely positioned him for what he took on as his central task: to educate lawyers, judges, and economists to the role of positive legal entitlements in shaping what were supposed the "natural" rights of ownership and the "natural" laws of distribution in a laissez-faire economy. His project immersed him in deconstructing the details of law, for which he had an impressive, Holmesian talent. But as Hale noted, he was more interested in political theory than in law, viewing law merely as the vehicle for allocating political power.[13] Hale's dissertation, published in 1918, marked the beginning of a lifelong interest in government regulation of public utilities as a model for the public control of all private property.[14] After a brief teaching stint in the Columbia economics department, Hale joined the faculty of Columbia Law School in 1919 at the invitation of the then Dean, Harlan Fiske Stone. Hale came initially under a joint appointment with the economics department and then full-time from 1928 until his retirement in 1949. His primary teaching was in the area of public utilities regulation and in a highly regarded course that he developed over many years called Legal Factors in Economic Society. The materials Hale prepared for the course, which were brilliant and quirky, offer the most comprehensive picture of Hale's legal philosophy. They formed the basis of his final work, *Freedom Through Law*, published in 1953.

During his lifetime, Hale wrote two books and about sixty articles, reviews, and commentaries, as well as leaving behind numerous unpublished manuscripts and course materials. He wrote in four principal areas: coercion, property rights, public utility rate regulation, and the normative implications of neoclassical economic theory. He is probably best known today for the first area, as a result of three widely cited and formative articles redescribing "free market" exchanges as a network of coercion.[15] The bulk of Hale's writing, however, was in the second and third areas—the general theory of property rights, and the theory as applied to the problem of public utility rate regulation. In addition to his dissertation and a leading casebook, *Cases on the Law of Public Utilities,* coauthored with two colleagues at Columbia, Hale wrote some twenty-five articles and reviews critiquing the Supreme Court's efforts to confine the scope and precedential significance of the government's power to regulate public utilities. In the area of economic theory, Hale wrote one article for publication as well as several unpublished manuscripts critiquing the claim that an "unregulated" market economy automatically achieved distributive justice (John Bates Clark's point) as well as allocative efficiency (that is, the allocation of resources to their most valuable uses).[16]

The division of Hale's work into distinct areas, however, is somewhat arbitrary and misleading. His arguments in the areas of coercion, property rights, and the distributive justice of the market not only share common themes. They are analytically dependent on one another, forming parts of a larger, comprehensive argument, developed over many years in his Legal Factors materials, detailing the legal conditioning of economic life.

Hale's intellectual preoccupations were, in many respects, typical of progressive social thought in the years from the 1880s to the 1930s. He shared with a wide range of humanists and social scientists of his time a methodological hostility to formalism, a preference for the inductive over the deductive method, and a belief that the overriding obligation of political life was to maximize collective welfare rather than to protect individual rights. Like John Dewey, Walter Lippmann, Herbert Croly, and other leading pragmatic social reformers of his time, Hale believed that the proper role of government was instrumental—to better the conditions of its citizens—and that in service to that end, government should be pushed to make its decisions both more conscious and more scientific. The main body of Hale's work—an assault on the twin bulwarks of classic liberalism, liberty interests and property rights—grew out of a long tradition of progressive thought. That tradition was sharpened for American progressives from the 1880s to the 1930s by the Supreme Court's invocation of both as constitutional bars to economic regulation. Like many economists of the nineteenth and early twentieth centuries, Hale believed that "[t]he paramount question of political economy to-day is the question of distribution."[17] His particular critique of the distributive justice of the market drew on a long tradition of leftist thought, originating with the early socialists, cast within the classical economic tradition. That tradition was transmuted by Henry George and the land-tax movement in the light of Ricardian economics, and finally reworked by the Fabian socialists, New Liberals, and others in the wake of the marginalist revolution in economics. His critique of the traditional liberal view that government held a monopoly on coercion was indebted to a complex web of leftist and progressive ideas, including the socialist attack on the coerciveness of labor contracts, Thomas Hill (T. H.) Green's "positive" conception of liberty, and the rise of the new sociology of Albion Small, Lester Ward, and others, stressing the interdependence of social life. Finally, Hale's argument that government power, rather than necessarily adding to private coercion, might actually ameliorate it, was advanced by most proponents of greater "social control," from T. H. Green to the supporters of the Wagner Act and other New Deal labor legislation.[18]

His closest intellectual ties, not surprisingly, were to the principal groups of progressive academics writing in economics and law respectively during those years: the institutional economists and Legal Realists. Hale's push to expose the legal underpinnings of the market can be seen as part of the larger project of the institutionalists to understand the social institutions that condition economic life. Those who were engaged in that project included Thorstein Veblen, Henry Carter Adams, Wesley Mitchell, Richard Ely, Edmund James, John Commons, Edwin Seligman, Simon Patten, Herbert Davenport, John Maurice Clark, Rexford Tugwell, Clarence E. Ayres, and Walton Hamilton. His attention to the details of those legal underpinnings—in particular private property and free contract—was central to the project of a number of Realists to show the social contingency of so-called natural rights. The work of Morris Cohen, Felix Cohen, Walter Wheeler Cook, Leon Green, Karl Llewellyn, Walton Hamilton, and Herman Oliphant, among others, comes to mind. Finally, Hale's choice to focus on public utility rate regulation was typical of his times as well. Historical accident had made railroads and public utilities the primary battleground for the legislatures and the courts to work out the appropriate limits of government control of private property. As a result, many of the most interesting progressive economists and legal theorists writing in the first part of the century turned their attention at one point or another to what may seem to contemporary eyes as the rather arcane field of public utilities regulation.

Hale's substantive agenda for political reform was also (at least in its broad outlines) typical progressive fare. He was, as he put it, centrally concerned with "the proper distribution of income," by which he and other progressives meant principally its redistribution from rich to poor.[19] Like many of his progressive colleagues, that concern grew partly out of utilitarian commitments and partly out of egalitarian ones, a philosophical tension substantially resolved for progressives by the Edgeworthian hypothesis that, all other things being equal, aggregate welfare would be maximized by an egalitarian distribution of wealth.[20] His notion of "proper" was, above all else, to create a decent standard of living for the working classes by raising their earning and spending power. As he stated simply in an early article, that goal would be accomplished by "adjustment of the worker's relations with those to whom he pays his dollar . . . [and] with those from whom he earns it."[21] The first half of that agenda immersed Hale in the Progressive-Era obsession with monopolies and other structural imperfections in the market that yielded supernormal returns to producers. The second half immersed him in the Progressive-Era obsession with labor relations. His solution in both areas was also typical progressive fare, although it was closest in its specifics not to the trust-busting or prounion wings of American progressivism, but to the British New Liberals.[22] In the area of consumer contracts, Hale supported efforts to curtail, through price controls and taxation, the power of corporations to extract a price in excess of a "fair return" on their investments. In the area of labor relations, he embraced what historians of the period would now describe as both corporatist and statist versions of liberal reforms, supporting the Wagner Act and other (corporatist) legislative and judicial efforts to increase the portion of the "national dividend" that was extracted by labor by boosting the bargaining strength of unions in private negotiations, as well as direct (statist) legislation mandating wages, hours, and other terms of employment.[23] More generally, he strongly supported that "quintessential progressive reform," a progressive tax-rate structure, the surplus from which would be used to finance government welfare programs to assure a social minimum for all citizens.[24]

As with many left-leaning social reformers of his time, it is not hard to detect a strong socialist influence on both the rhetoric and the substance of Hale's political agenda.[25] Hale's preoccupation with surplus value, like his preoccupation with the coerciveness of the private bargains by which it was distributed in the market, had obvious cognates in socialist theory. Moreover, the rhetoric of positive freedom that infused Hale's and other early twentieth-century progressives' writings echoes earlier socialist and protosocialist demands that "equal rights" must mean, at root, "equal means" to rights. But, again like most of his fellow progressives, Hale stopped short of advocating absolute equality of incomes or widespread government ownership of private property. He chose instead to steer what has been aptly termed "a middle way" between programmatic socialism and the possessive individualism of nineteenth-century laissez-faire liberalism.[26] Herbert Croly put it thus: "A democracy dedicated to individual and social betterment is necessarily individualist as well as socialist. . . There are two indispensible economic conditions of qualitative individual self-expression. One is the preservation of the institution of private property in some form, and the other is the radical transformation of its existing nature and influence."[27]

The progressives' motives for hewing to the middle way were complicated. In part, the choice reflected a genuine and surprisingly strong commitment to individual autonomy, but a commitment updated to reflect a new and more complex world of social interdependence. In this respect, the progressives stood apart not only from traditional Marxist socialists but from the Christian socialists and other communitarian idealists as well. They were Lockean individualists, but of a sort unrecognizable to traditional liberals, insisting on both a functional definition of autonomy and a more exacting separation of individual and social contributions to the social product. In part, the choice reflected the pragmatic, utilitarian belief that some degree of inequality was necessary to maintain incentives for productivity. Finally, the choice was pragmatic in a more personal sense, reflecting the high personal and professional cost of being labeled a socialist. Mindful of that cost, many progressives went out of their way to avoid prescriptions that smacked of class warfare and to distance themselves from some of the particulars of labor's cause. As discussed later, among the attractions of the particular prescription offered by Hale and others—what I have termed progressive rent theory—was that it framed the case for redistribution, at least formally, in nonclass terms.

In other areas, Hale stood on the more radical fringe of progressive politics. A reserved, intensely private man, Hale was a strong, behind-the-scenes activist in a number of politically explosive causes. Hale was part of a small committee of law professors and lawyers who worked during the summer of 1927 to reverse the conviction of Sacco and Vanzetti. Throughout the summer of 1927, Hale carried on an impassioned correspondence with his former teacher, A. Lawrence Lowell, head of the commission appointed by Massachusetts governor Alvan T. Fuller to review the convictions, in a futile attempt to persuade Lowell to recommend reversal of the convictions.[28] Two years later, he contributed to a collection of articles edited by Karl Llewellyn a scathing critique of the bullet testimony that had been crucial to the pair's conviction.[29] Throughout his adult life, Hale was also a strong supporter of racial equality long before such a position became popular. To that end, he assisted in litigating a number of important early desegregation cases and in developing the expansive theory of state action that underlay the landmark civil rights decision in Shelley v. Kraemer. In addition, he was a lifelong gadfly in his private correspondence, attacking establishment pieties on a wide range of matters from free speech for radicals to union-busting activities.[30]

To a considerable extent, then, Hale's work can be read as an exemplar of standard progressive preoccupations during the first part of the twentieth century. At the same time, Hale is a significant figure in his own right. Among his contemporaries, he was probably best known for his writings on public utilities rate regulation. His dissertation was one of the earliest and most sophisticated attacks on the fallacy of using the "fair value" of property as a rate base for rate-setting purposes. His argument, which was developed and refined in a number of articles in the 1920s and 1930s, was widely cited and relied on by other economists writing in the field. Of more significance from Hale's point of view, his argument was influential in the courts as well, partly as a result of Hale's close personal ties to several of the more liberal members of the Supreme Court. Hale remained close friends with his former dean and colleague, Harlan Fiske Stone, after Stone's appointment to the Supreme Court; in addition, he maintained an active correspondence with Justices Stone, Brandeis, Cardozo, Douglas, and Frankfurter concerning the rate regulation cases before the Court. Hale's critique of the "fair value" doctrine found its way into a number of concurring and dissenting opinions by the liberal minority on the Court in the 1920s and 1930s, and (with the change in Court personnel) into the Court's ultimate repudiation of the doctrine in the 1940s. The particulars of Hale's economic analysis of rate regulation have been incorporated and superseded by a field that has grown enormously more sophisticated since Hale's time. But his writings in the area remain of significant historical interest in understanding a dispute that took center stage in the fifty-year battle between the legislatures and the courts for supremacy in economic affairs.

Hale's most important contributions to legal theory, however, are his general writings on property rights, coercion, and the role of legal entitlements in structuring economic life. Not only did his writings in all three areas anticipate arguments now current in legal and philosophical circles; in many particulars, they remain the best treatments of the subjects to date. Hale's analysis of coercion, heralded in his own time by numerous figures including Roscoe Pound, John Dawson, John Dalzell, and John Maurice Clark, has since become standard in the legal literature, and has been important in the contemporary philosophical literature as well. In the area of property rights, Hale's careful analysis of the variable content infused into the empty idea of "ownership" represents the functional approach of Legal Realism at its best. His analysis of the legal underpinnings of economic life is the most comprehensive and astute offered to date. Hale was a better economist than either Richard Ely or John Commons, and, unlike either of them, had the benefit of both formal legal training and a strong analytical bent of mind.

As a consequence, his argument, worked out in a number of articles that finally culminated in *Freedom Through Law,* far outshines Ely's and Commons's respective, better-known efforts in *Property and Contract in Its Relation to the Distribution of Wealth* and *Legal Foundations of Capitalism.* One moral drawn from that analysis—that most so-called "private" rights derive from public authority through the government's articulation and enforcement of property and contract rules—has become a staple among contemporary legal scholars, who, in field after field of law, have attacked the enduring distinction between "public" and "private" spheres of action.

As this brief summary suggests, Hale's primary agenda was a critical one. He tried to show that the conventional distinctions and categories of thought ("fair value," "private" versus "public" spheres of action, "freedom" versus "coercion") that dominated legal and political discourse in the late nineteenth and early twentieth centuries had no functional content. That is to say, they were incapable of shedding any light on, let alone resolving, the difficult policy choices that confronted courts and legislatures when they were forced to decide between competing claims in society. The motivation for that critique was partly intellectual, partly political. Like Oliver Wendell Holmes (whose critical intelligence Hale in many ways shared) and many fellow Realists, Hale had an aesthetic abhorrence of the sort of sloppy, tautological thinking that characterized much legal discourse of his period. That abhorrence probably would have driven him to correction whether or not it served his immediate political ends. At the same time, "making our ideas clear" on these issues (in Charles Peirce's sense) by and large *did* serve Hale's political ends, by puncturing the Court's pretensions to deduce its conservative, political agenda from the inexorable commands of the Constitution itself. As Holmes had famously declared, dissenting in Lochner v. New York, "The Fourteenth Amendment does not enact Herbert Spencer's *Social Statics."* So also, Hale argued, there may be good and sound reasons not to regulate wages and working conditions in the interests of the working class, or not to control the rates that public utilities may charge their customers. But if so, those reasons were lodged in prudence, not in the Fifth and Fourteenth Amendments of the federal Constitution. The point was hardly an idle one, for if there were no constitutional principles at stake, such decisions were the legislature's and not the Court's to make.

There was, however, an affirmative part to Hale's agenda as well, one that drew on an important tradition in British progressive thought. Building on the insights of the marginalist revolution in economics, British political theorists on the left, beginning with the Fabian socialists in the 1880s and culminating with the writings of Leonard Hobhouse, John Hobson, and other

New Liberals in the 1900s through the 1920s, argued that even in well-functioning competitive markets, many producers realized surplus returns, or "scarcity rents," disproportionate to their actual sacrifice. The key to a just distribution of wealth, they argued, lay in the state's appropriating these rents through price controls and taxation, and then using the proceeds to benefit consumers and finance the general welfare state. Although rent theory played a significant role in British politics, it had relatively little influence in American thought, except in its narrower manifestation in the land tax movement spearheaded by Henry George. Hale was a notable exception. He was much taken with New Liberal rent theory, and his own prescription for allocating economic liberty in general and regulating public utilities in particular draws implicitly on that tradition. This aspect of Hale's work, long neglected, provides an invaluable look at this significant conjunction of neoclassical economic theory and progressive politics in the late nineteenth and early twentieth centuries.

Hale as Realist and Institutionalist

As previously suggested, Hale's closest intellectual ties were to the American Legal Realists and the institutional economists.[31] Indeed, in many ways Hale's work brought to fruition their shared intellectual and political project: as Hale put it, to expose "the function performed by the law in the production and distribution of wealth,"[32] in order to debunk the notion that the market was a natural (prepolitical) and neutral (apolitical) entity.

As noted before, Hale began his academic life as an economist. Although he severed any formal relationship to the Columbia economics department in 1928, he maintained strong ties to a number of important institutionalists through the 1930s. Wesley Mitchell, one of the most distinguished of the institutionalists, was on Hale's dissertation committee. Hale knew Commons's and Veblen's work well, and corresponded with Commons (who knew Hale's work as well).[33] He cotaught a course with John Maurice Clark at Columbia, and his work strongly influenced Clark's *Social Control of Business*.[34] Hale also worked closely with Walton Hamilton on public utilities rate regulation matters, and contributed an important article to Rexford Tugwell's 1924 *The Trend of Economics*, a sort of manifesto of the second wave of institutionalist economics.[35]

It is hard to come up with a definition of institutional economics that accurately captures the commonalities among its widely divergent members. Any group that contains both Thorstein Veblen and Rexford Tugwell is surely as unlike as it is like in its interests. What principally bound the institutionalists together was a shared distaste for the deductive methods of neoclassical economics, in which the institutions of modern capitalism were (in the words of Veblen, the institutionalists' intellectual forefather) "taken for granted, denied, or explained away."[36] They sought in their own work to surface those institutions and explicate their significance in economic life. By "institution," they meant roughly, in Walton Hamilton's words, "a way of thought or action of some prevalence and permanence, which is embedded in the habits of a group or the customs of a people."[37] Veblen's own writings display the enormous range of such institutions that caught their interest, from the psychological propensities that cast doubt on the simple hedonism underlying both Jeremy Bentham's felicific calculus and neoclassical economics, to labor unions, technology, and the institution of absentee ownership. Later institutionalists developed some of Veblen's suggestions and added others to the list, in the work of Robert Hoxie, Selig Perlman, John Commons, and others on trade unions;[38] of Commons on negotiable debt;[39] of Wesley Mitchell on the technical and psychological aspects of the money system and the business cycles that it produced;[40] and of Adolph Berle and Gardiner Means on the nature of the corporation and managerial capitalism.[41]

The institutionalists differed in their views of the permanence or desirability of particular institutions. Some, like Commons, at times espoused an evolutionary fatalism that was scarcely distinguishable from that of Herbert Spencer, William Graham Sumner, and other prophets of a minimal state.[42] But most followed Veblen in believing that institutions evolved over time; that the course of evolution could be affected by deliberate human intervention; and that there was no reason to privilege the status quo over what could be produced by such intervention.[43] Such beliefs, not surprisingly, were coupled with a strong reformist instinct. In the first wave of institutionalism, that instinct was evident in Henry Carter Adams's and Simon Patten's 1884 manifesto issued upon the founding of the predecessor to the American Economic Association, which called for a "progressive theory of legislation." The institutionalists' push for political reform ultimately culminated in the New Deal, staffed in significant part by the Realists and the second generation of institutionalists.[44]

Beginning with Adams's 1886 *The Relation of the State to Industrial Action*, a core group of institutionalists including Adams, Patten, Ely, Commons, Hamilton, and J. M. Clark focused particular attention on the legal institutions that underlay economic life, from the broad institutions of private property and right of contract, to the particular network of judge-made and statutory law governing labor relations. That interest put them on an obvious path of convergence with the Realists and led them to similar conclusions: that there was and could be no such thing as laissez faire, since the state (through its legal institutions) was unavoidably constitutive of economic life; and that one should make a virtue of necessity, by turning the government into a positive force in the economy. It is this strain of institutionalism to which Hale's work obviously belongs.

Hale's ties to the Legal Realists were more direct. He was originally brought to Columbia Law School at the prompting of two eminent Realists, Underhill Moore and Walter Wheeler Cook, to advance what Young B. Smith flatly described as "an economic interpretation of the law, expressed in scientific terminology."[45] Hale remained there until his retirement in 1949, through the heyday of Realism at Columbia. Throughout that period, Hale maintained professional and personal ties with a number of the most prominent Realists, including Karl Llewellyn, Herman Oliphant and Walton Hamilton (both members of the public utilities mafia), Underhill Moore, Charles Clark, and Jerome Frank, a friend and fan of Hale's.[46] Hale also participated in the curricular reform movement spearheaded by the Realists at Columbia.[47] Even though Llewellyn did not list Hale in his original catalog of Realists in his famous 1931 defense of Realism, he did include him in a longer list that he and Jerome Frank compiled and sent privately to Roscoe Pound, which detailed "Our [his and Frank's] notion of realists-in-part-of-their-work."[48] Llewellyn's own contemporaneous views are hardly determinative, in any event. Hale's work shared most of the recurrent strains of Realist thought: rejecting formalism for functionalism; abandoning the search for universal principles, in favor of particularized and contextualized fact inquiries; and denying that law could or should be distinct from politics, either in the narrow sense of partisan aims or in the broadest sense of the ethical life.

More than any other individual, Hale embraced and refined the Realist critique of law that tied together many of these strands. That critique insisted that the sorts of answers that courts were called upon to give could not be deduced mechanically from an abstract jurisprudence of rights, but emerged instead from the unexamined and unarticulated cultural and political assumptions of the judges themselves.[49] The Realist critique had obvious ties to Bentham's cynical, and the historicists' far more romanticized, view of the malleability of the common law.[50] But its greatest debts were to Holmes, whose own brand of pragmatism anticipated the core of the Realist argument, as well as to the logical positivists from Peirce to Wittgenstein, from whom Hale, Felix Cohen, and others borrowed their method.[51] As Holmes put it famously, "General propositions do not decide concrete cases."[52] Holmes's aphorism was fleshed out by Roscoe Pound and the succeeding generation of Realists in a number of important, and on occasion brilliant, articles.[53]

Their critique of "slot machine" jurisprudence, as Pound derisively termed it, was not anticonceptual in a nihilist sense. It was, in fact, strongly conceptual. But the critique insisted (in the logical positivist tradition) that the only concepts with meaning are those that can be defined "as functions of actual experience."[54] As Felix Cohen declared in the premier Realist manifesto of functionalism, "Any word that cannot pay up in the currency of fact, upon demand, is to be declared bankrupt, and we are to have no further dealings with it."[55] Much of Hale's career can be summarized in the list of words that he argued must be relegated to Cohen's trash heap of intellectual bankrupts, at least as those words were conventionally employed in legal discourse to limit the permissible scope of legislative action: "private" versus "public" realms of action, "coercion" versus "freedom," and "fair value."

Although the Realists have been most celebrated in recent decades for their methodological critique of formalism, for many a substantive agenda underlay that critique that was at least as significant: to debunk the notion of a freestanding, self-regulating market, by showing that the market was ineluctably constituted by the legal regime in which it operated.[56] That agenda was obviously closely tied to the work of institutionalists like Henry Carter Adams, Ely, Commons, and J. M. Clark. It is at this intersection of the Realist and institutionalist projects that Hale's work is situated.

The Realist and institutionalist critiques of an autonomous sphere of economic activity, like the Realist attack on formalism, displayed an intellectual radicalism that (as Robert Gordon has astutely noted) was often confused by its critics with political radicalism. As Gordon explains, "[O]ne can recognize that capitalist societies have a constructed and contingent legal constitution without actually wanting to change that constitution very much, or believing that it is politically feasible to change it more than a tiny bit. . ."[57] Hale, Llewellyn, Thurman Arnold, and other of the Realists helped to feed that perception by the irreverence, bordering occasionally on vituperation, with which they were wont to put their critique.[58] In fact, however, the political implications of their attack on laissez-faire liberalism were far from clear, beyond the immediate objective of getting courts out of the business of reviewing the constitutionality of economic regulation.

At the end of his own savaging of orthodox legal reasoning, Felix Cohen declared, "Fundamentally there are only two significant questions in the field of law. One is, 'How do courts actually decide cases of a given kind?' The other is, 'How ought they to decide cases of a given kind?' "[59] If one expands Cohen's notion of law beyond judicial decision-making to include all forms of lawmaking, his formulation accurately captures the two parts of the affirmative Realist project.

The Realists were best known in their own time for their attempt to answer the first of Cohen's questions, in the empirical studies of "law-in-action" called for and/or undertaken by Underhill Moore, Walter Wheeler Cook, Charles Clark, Herman Oliphant, Hessel Yntema, Jerome Frank, Karl Llewellyn, Joseph Bingham, Max Radin, and others. For a long time that branch of Realist inquiry was taken to stand for the whole, partly because of its resonance with trends in the other social sciences and partly because of the famous attacks on it by Pound, Morris Cohen, Lon Fuller, and others as amateur and nihilistic behavioral science gone berserk.[60] But as more recent historiography has argued (correctly in my view), the empirical wing of Realism, itself unfairly caricatured by contemporaries on the basis of its more extreme outcroppings, represented only one strain of the affirmative Realist project, and not the most important one.

Although like most progressives, Hale believed that knowledge of the world as it is must be the starting point for reform, he never identified with the empirical strain of Realism. He had no interest in the judicial process itself, a central focus of the empirical school. Unlike Karl Llewellyn, Arthur Corbin, and others who at least at times embraced their own version of a conservative historicism, he never believed that the answer to Felix Cohen's first question—what the law "is"—held the key to the second—what the law ought to be. Hale's real interest, like that of most progressive social theorists and reformers, lay in tackling Cohen's second question from a different starting assumption: how to promote pragmatic social reform through legislative change. For that branch of Realists, the moral of the shambles that they had made of conventional rights talk was that such talk had to be shucked off in favor of explicit policy analysis, in which alternatives were measured by their factual consequences, judged in the light of desired ends. As one commentator has astutely observed, where the Realists' critical (deconstructive) project was the natural forerunner of Critical Legal Studies, its pragmatic social reformer side was the natural forerunner of the (post–New Deal) legal process school, which viewed law as political, but with " 'politics' itself . . . re-translated from the notion of wide-open, subjective ideology to closed, determinate issues of technique."[61] But, unlike many of their successors in the legal process school, the Realists did not take a denatured, bloodless view of law as policy science. They were passionately committed to the view that facts were only an input to decisions, which ultimately had to be made by reference to some theory of the good life. As Hale expressed it, once economic study clarified a problem, "the final judgment on the issues is an ethical one."[62] Hale believed (perhaps deludedly) that he was educating students in that more complicated version of policy-making in his Legal Factors course.[63] As will be discussed later, he pursued that version more directly and successfully in his own proposals for cost-based rate regulation of public utilities as a model for reforming all property along rent-theory lines.

Storming the Citadel: Liberty and Property

In its broad outlines, the Realist critique of formalism was part of a larger intellectual revolt in the social sciences. However, its particulars were shaped far more directly by the twin pillars of laissez-faire constitutionalism that were erected by the Lochner-era Court: the right to preserve individual liberty (particularly as embodied in freedom of contract) and private property against government incursions.[64] The impress of the Court is clearly visible in the work of Roscoe Pound, Morris Cohen, Felix Cohen, Walter Wheeler Cook, Herman Oliphant, and numerous others. But it can be seen most clearly in Hale's work, the details of which are best understood as an elegantly elaborated response to the liberty-and-property dogma of the Lochner-era Court.

Most scholars trace the beginning of laissez-faire constitutionalism to the mid-1880s.[65] It hit its high-water mark in the 1900s through the 1930s, and was not finally interred until the 1937 decision in West Coast Hotel Co. v. Parrish, halfway through the New Deal.[66] Much has been written on the period, with more recent scholarship stressing the discontinuities and complexities of conservative legal and judicial thought and arguing the whole is not easily categorized as economic or political laissez faire.[67] The revisionist view undoubtedly offers a less distorted and more subtle reading of a number of figures formerly dismissed merely as conservative functionaries or prophets. However, it risks introducing distortions of its own. First, two of the areas in which courts unambiguously embraced laissez faire—curbing regulation both of the market return that owners could get for the use of their property and of the terms of labor contracts—represented a significant portion of the progressive agenda. Moreover, whatever contemporary historians may make of the period in retrospect, progressives themselves did not regard those two outcroppings of judicial laissez faire as self-contained sports. Second, the rhetorical power of laissez faire reached far beyond particular decisions of the courts. Its influence is most clearly revealed in the extent to which agonists across the entire political spectrum felt obliged to pay obeisance to the importance of preserving liberty and property rights. Elihu Root reflected the typical centrist/moderate reformer position, in stating that although the new social realities required a new role for the state, "I assume an agreement,

that the right of individual liberty and the inseparable right of private property which lie at the foundation of our modern civilization ought to be
maintained."[68] With the exception of doctrinaire socialists, reformers on the
left, whether out of expedience or conviction, were equally reluctant to take
on liberty and property directly. At the same time, for American progressives,
the traditional liberal version of liberty and property rights as embodied in
constitutional laissez faire stood in the way of any radical reform strategy.
A threshold question for any progressive reformer was how to subvert or
dismantle it.

There were a number of accommodationist strategies that progressives
repeatedly availed themselves of, strategies that left unchallenged the basic
constitutional claim to protected liberty and property interests but subordinated it to other countervailing powers of the government. Chief among them
were the right of the federal government to regulate interstate commerce, and
the right of federal and state governments under their general police powers
to regulate private activity in the interest of the common good. Instead,
Hale chose to attack directly the notion that there could or should be a
constitutionally protected sphere of liberty interests and property rights, at
least as conventionally understood.

The bulk of this book details Hale's assault on liberty and property. Before
presenting a summary of his argument, a word of caution is in order. The
book treats the fight over the soul of liberty and property separately, because
the arguments advanced are in some respects distinct, and also are elaborate
enough to require separate explication to do them justice. At the same time,
Hale's work is fully comprehensible only if one recognizes that the two are
intertwined in complex and often contradictory ways.

First, liberty has had a crucial and often contradictory relationship to
property in the western philosophical, rights-based tradition. At the risk of
gross oversimplification, one could describe that tradition as dominated by
two types of theories of property rights: those that justified property as the
foundation of liberty and those that justified it as the natural outgrowth or
consequence of liberty.[69] One might expect that the two theories implied
quite different ideal property arrangements. In fact, each has proved quite
pliable in that regard and (as will be discussed at length in the book) has
been enlisted at various times by both the right and the left to bolster their
respective political agendas. But in either case, liberty was inextricably linked
to the justification for property.

Second, "liberty" and "property" were functionally connected in the progressive critique of the market, as in the Marxist one. Contract terms, progressives argued, rather than being simple expressions of free will, were deter-

mined by each party's relative ability to hold out for more acceptable terms. That holdout power depended in significant part on the parties' relative wealth, which was itself in turn affected by the bargains that each party had the power to strike. In the Marxist view, that dynamic led inexorably to a world in which all capital devolved into the hands of the few, and the many were left to survive on whatever poor wage bargains they could strike in their necessitous state. Although progressives did not share Marx's determinist view, they did believe as an empirical matter that the normal operations of the market would tend to favor capital over labor, exacerbating existing disparities in wealth.

Finally, "liberty" and "property" were connected in narrow constitutional arguments through the doctrine of liberty of contract. As the dominant form of property rights shifted from possession and use to production for exchange, an owner's right to contract for the use or exchange value of her property was acknowledged to be an important part of the total economic value of that property. At the same time, as the courts broke free of their historical conception of property as a tangible thing, they began to view the resulting contract itself as a form of intangible property presumptively entitled to the full-blown protections accorded other forms of property.[70] Because "liberty of contract" was thus a melding of both liberty and property principles, courts invalidating price regulations in the labor or public utilities context under the rubric of liberty of contract could (and did) move with relative ease between the rhetoric of liberty and that of property.[71]

Chapter 2 is devoted to Hale's critique of liberty. In a series of important articles, Hale argued that traditional liberal thought had erroneously assumed that the government was the source of all legal coercion, because it defined coercion as the deprivation of free will by an overbearing force, on which the government generally had a legal monopoly. In fact, Hale argued (taking a cue from Holmes), coercion rarely took the form of direct compulsion that deprived individuals of all choice. Rather, it took the form of background constraints on the universe of socially available choices from which an individual could "freely" choose. Thus redefined, Hale argued, it was evident that coercion was present in the private sphere as well—in a form structurally indistinguishable from governmental coercion—in acts traditionally regarded as volitional. Chief among these acts were so-called voluntary market exchanges, in which each side coerced the other to relinquish its property or services by a (legally sanctioned) threat to withhold its own property or services if the demanded terms were not obtained in exchange. Moreover, such private coercion derived its force from public power, in the form of a legally created right to withhold property or services from exchange entirely, and the lesser included right to retain whatever price one could extract for agreeing to relinquish that right. That situation meant that when the government intervened in private market relations to curb the use of certain private bargaining power, it did not inject coercion for the first time into those relations; it merely changed the relative distribution of coercive power. Whether that change might actually *increase* net freedom in society was an empirical question, and one that could not be answered by recourse to abstractions like "freedom of contract."

Hale's redefinition of coercion as a background constraint on available choices allowed him to make three crucial and largely irrefutable points. First, as a purely descriptive matter, coercion (so defined) was ubiquitous, inevitable, and, to a considerable extent, desirable. Second, although coercion derives from a variety of sources (for example, natural necessity, legal conditions imposed directly by the state or indirectly by the state through the rules of property and contract), the functional differences between the resulting "unfreedom" experienced by the chooser were at most quantitative, not qualitative, ones. Third, given the foregoing, one could not (as the Supreme Court purported to do) condemn state interference with private choices merely on the ground that it was factually coercive. At a minimum, a sensible policy required some normative theory of what forms of coercive constraints society wished to prohibit and what forms to allow. Although no such theory was likely to be simple or uncontroversial, at least one thing was clear: the current de facto arrangement, in which the state by and large declined to intervene in the coercive effects of private bargaining power that itself derived from public authority, was hard to square with any coherent theory of liberty.

Hale's analysis of coercion drew on a rich tradition of critical thought, including Marx's and later socialists' argument about the coerciveness of labor contracts and progressives' preoccupation more generally with the role of bargaining power in allocating surplus social product; T. H. Green's insistence that liberty be given a "positive" and not merely "negative" meaning; and the pragmatists' and logical positivists' insistence, imported to law by the Realists, that abstractions like "liberty" be redefined in functional terms. Chapter 2 attempts to locate Hale's argument in this larger philosophical tradition, as well as to assess its lasting value.

Chapter 3 deals with Hale's attack on natural property rights theory—that is, the web of legal and economic arguments used to defend the sanctity of the existing property arrangements in late nineteenth- and early twentieth-century political debate. Chapter 4 deals with Hale's attempt to construct a new scheme of property entitlements along rent-theory lines. The laissez-faire defense of the existing, radically unequal distribution of wealth had been subject to a series of attacks since the mid-nineteenth century, most notably from utilitarian and Idealist camps. Although Hale's work reflects strands of both traditions, his principal argument (in my view) was internal to the natural rights tradition that it sought to undermine. Chapter 5 examines Hale's work on rate regulation of public utilities, as an example of applied (Halean) property theory.

The heart of Hale's attack on laissez-faire property was to show that whatever appeal a natural rights theory might have in the abstract, the existing regime of property rights could not be deduced from or reconciled with any plausible version of it. Hale's argument proceeded on two fronts. First, he argued, all rights to the possession, use, and exchange value of property are ineluctably creatures of the state, owing their existence to the government's willingness to articulate and enforce them through the rules of property and contract. In its broad outlines, Hale's argument for the public basis of private rights was a familiar one in Realist and progressive circles, and it had an older provenance in the legal positivism of Bentham and Austin, among others. But Hale's version of the argument was distinguished both by its analytic precision and by his characteristic inclination to push the point to its logical extreme, arguing that all exercises of private rights should be regarded as a delegation of public authority to "unofficial minorities." The doubt thereby cast on the classic distinction drawn between public and private spheres of activity has proved enormously fertile in contemporary legal thought. That doubt also had (in Hale's view) two immediate and significant political implications. It eliminated any constitutional bar to the state's revising the scope of existing property rights as it saw fit, on the ground that what the state of its own free will had given, it was free to take away. It also provided the lever to expand the so-called "state action" doctrine in constitutional law, in order to bring private discriminatory behavior within the ambit of the Fourteenth Amendment.[72]

Secondly, Hale argued, the particular assortment of rights that the liberal state had historically poured into the empty vessel of "ownership" was difficult to deduce from, or in some cases reconcile with, Lockean principles. Some traditional property rights could not be justified at all under a Lockean scheme. Chief among them were rights bestowed by the laws of inheritance, land grants, and government grants of monopoly privilege. This portion of Hale's argument was a familiar one in progressive and liberal thought, although Hale again pushed the point further than others were inclined to go, arguing that *all* private property rights should be regarded as a form of "monopoly privilege," as they endowed the owner with exclusive (that is, monopoly) authority over her property as against the world at large. Other property that the owner had acquired at least in part through her own sacrifice, Lockean principles would suggest she had a right to in some form. But, Hale argued, it was often impossible to deduce the precise form from those general principles. With respect to rights to the use value of such property, Hale argued, Lockean principles provided no guidance in choosing among conflicting uses of privately owned property. They also offered no guidance in choosing between private rights and the public welfare that the state was authorized to protect under its ill-defined "police powers." With respect to the right to the exchange value of such property, he argued, Lockean principles were equally indeterminate in fixing the extent of hold-up powers that an owner could exercise in setting the "market" price. Hale's development of the latter point in numerous articles over his career represents his most significant contribution to property theory, anticipating by several decades standard arguments in the contemporary law and economics and political philosophy literature about the significance of "property" versus "liability" rules of damages in fixing the meaning of property rights.

There were two essential morals to Hale's critique of the constitutional edifice of liberty and property rights. The first moral, and the one most closely connected to the Realist project, was that the edifice was built on words that could not sustain the burden that they were asked to carry. As Hale remarked, "[t]here may be sound reasons of economic policy to justify all the economic inequalities that flow from unequal rights." But if so, "these reasons must be more specific than a broad policy of private property and freedom of contract."[73] In area after area, Hale tried to show that concepts that had conventionally been thought to establish categorical limits on the constitutional exercise of legislative powers—coercion, state action, fair value, police powers, harm-based limits to private power embodied in the common-law injunction *sic utere tuo, ut alienum non laedas*—did no such thing. Some, like "fair value," invoked to limit rate regulation of public utilities, he showed to be arrant nonsense. Others, like "coercion," "state action," and private activity that harmed others and hence was regulable under the state's police powers, he conceded were not meaningless concepts. The problem, Hale argued, was that the concepts described to some extent all private action and hence could not categorically distinguish protected from unprotected private action. At most, they suggested relevant dimensions along which private actions might be sorted by degree. In this respect, Hale's work exemplified what numerous historians have noted was a typical progressive and Realist strategy: to turn all differences into differences of degree rather than of kind.[74] For the Realists, the strategy had an immediate political utility. If, for example, all uses that an owner might make of her property potentially harmed others, differing only in the degree of harm, the determination of which uses to prohibit and which to allow looked like one that was quintessentially the prerogative of legislatures, not constitutional courts, to make. The strategy, however, posed certain difficulties, a matter to be returned to in Chapter 6.

The second moral, and the one most closely connected to the institutionalist project, was that laissez faire was neither logically possible nor socially desirable. Economic life, like most other aspects of social life, was conditioned by formal and informal rules collectively devised. To that proposition, Spencer the sociologist, who recognized the interdependent complexity of society, might well have assented. However, most progressives parted company with Spencer and his followers over its implications for action. With few exceptions, they emphatically rejected what Herbert Croly termed the "optimistic fatalism" of the Spencerians, who believed that social forces progress most if left to evolve without conscious intervention by the state, and they embraced in its place a nonteleological historicism.[75] Where Spencer, Sumner, and others read the changeableness of social institutions over time as evidence of their adaptive (Darwinian) evolution toward perfection, most institutionalists and Realists read it as evidence of their serendipity. As Hale wrote in 1933, "alteration of our institutions must be discussed on its pragmatic merits, not dismissed on the ground that they are the inevitable outcome of free society."[76]

The conviction (as Croly put it) that "artificial selection" might best the results of "natural selection" was hardly a surprising one to find among social reformers.[77] But beginning with Lester Ward's attacks on Social Darwinism and his call for a new "sociocracy," progressives espoused with a quasi-religious fervor the Wardian conviction that "society and the social forces . . . constitut[e] just as much a legitimate field for the exercise of human ingenuity as do the various material substances and physical forces."[78] William James's and Oliver Wendell Holmes's different versions of pragmatism,[79] John Dewey's philosophy of instrumentalism,[80] and the various pitches made by the New Liberals, institutionalists, and Legal Realists to "substitut[e] . . . [social] control for the present chaos of the economic world"[81] all rejected the Social Darwinist apologia for what was (in Lippmann's famous trope) merely will-less "drift," in favor of a new "mastery." Indeed, the degree of fame achieved by Lippmann's rather vacant manifesto testifies to how deep a cord its rhetoric struck. Hale, writing his principal works in the heyday of progressive optimism about social control, shared that optimism, echoing Lippmann's belief that what was needed above all was (as Hale repeatedly put it) "[t]he substitution . . . of responsible for irresponsible government."[82]

The two morals together gave American progressives all the latitude that they needed to push their agenda for social reform through economic regulation. The legislature, not being bound by any constitutional strictures, was free to do as it saw fit; the plasticity of social institutions meant that their efforts would not be wasted. Hale, with the exception of his work on public utilities regulation, was somewhat vague on the shape that legislative reform should take. That omission will no doubt strike many readers as a serious limitation in his work. It is all very well to point out that "freedom of contract" is as coercive in its own way as state regulation of contract terms. Yet the question remains, what sorts of regulation should the wise legislature impose on private contracting? In Hale's partial defense, his vagueness reflected in part the Deweyian conviction shared by most progressives that the optimal form of economic regulation, like most questions of social policy, could be resolved only in the laboratory of democracy, through practical experimentation and collective choice.[83] In addition, Hale may have had the wisdom to know that his own intellectual tastes and talents lay in debunking the laissez-faire state, rather than in crafting the optimal patchwork of social controls and private initiatives that should stand in its place.[84]

Nonetheless, there is a consistent, affirmative agenda running throughout Hale's writings, one that was, in an important sense, internal to the liberal tradition that Hale was critiquing. The choice to co-opt traditional "natural rights" talk to its own political ends has had a long history on the left.[85] In the area of liberty, the two most significant assaults on classical liberalism in the nineteenth century—the socialists' recasting of the "free" labor contract as essentially coercive, and T. H. Green's rejection of the "negative" freedom of laissez faire in favor of a positive, functional freedom—both embraced, at least on a rhetorical level, the principle of individual autonomy. They simply urged a broader view of the threats posed to it in a modern, interdependent society. Hale's own analysis of coercion followed in that tradition. He presumed that political life should be organized to maximize liberty of the autonomous self of classical liberal thought, but he insisted that a functional definition of liberty and coercion be substituted for the formal categories that he demolished.

Co-optation of natural rights talk by the left was even more pronounced in the area of property rights. As noted before, the western philosophical rights-based (as distinct from utilitarian) tradition was dominated by two defenses of private property: that property was the foundation of liberty (the consequentialist view) and that it was the necessary outgrowth of liberty (the historical entitlement view). Through the mid-nineteenth century, the former view was largely harnessed to conservative political ends, by those who argued (in the Kantian tradition) that securing existing property rights was essential to the development of personality, and (in the Lockean libertarian tradition) that unfettered market exchanges of property were one important expression of freedom. In the late nineteenth and early twentieth centuries, the defense of property as the foundation of liberty was gradually usurped by political theorists on the left. They embraced the Kantian view, but argued that it implied that all citizens should possess at least the minimal property necessary for liberty.[86] And they attacked the libertarian defense of freedom of contract by recharacterizing market exchanges as coercive, and by arguing that in regulating such exchanges, the state could well increase overall freedom. Hale's critical writings on coercion trenchantly built on both of those leftist arguments. However, his affirmative proposals to reconstitute property as the servant of a true, functional liberty rarely got beyond the progressive commonplace that (all other things being equal) the government ought to redistribute property rights so as to maximize the aggregate, positive freedom in society.

As developed at some length in Chapters 4 and 5, the interesting portion of Hale's affirmative agenda lay in his reworking of the second strand of property theory—property as the necessary consequence of liberty. Locke's famous declaration that "*Labour* being the unquestionable Property of the Labourer, no Man but he can have a right to what that is once joyned to," was taken by his nineteenth-century conservative heirs—and indeed many more as well—self-evidently to justify a strong, laissez-faire property rights regime, in which what each person had created from nature or acquired by trade as a free moral agent, he had a right to keep.[87] But like the Kantian argument for preserving property as the root of personality, this argument too was gradually co-opted by social theorists on the left. They embraced in broad terms the Lockean premise that people are entitled to the fruits of their labor. But they parted company with Locke's conservative heirs over whether the market was the best means to achieve that end. The most famous attack, of course, came from the Ricardian, and later the Marxist, socialists. If taken seriously, they argued, the Lockean premise would require the entire value of property (ambiguously, use-value or exchange-value) to go to the factors of production that were responsible for generating it—by hypothesis under the socialist labor theory of value, to labor. Thus, the portion of exchange value that went to capital, in the form of interest or other profits, represented a theft of labor's product.[88]

The marginalist revolution in economics left in shambles the socialist labor theory of value, along with all other versions of cost-based value implicit in classical economic theory. In its place, the marginalists made three essential claims. First, value did not inhere in any property intrinsic to goods or services themselves but simply reflected the subjective value (utility) of the final product to the consumer. Second, all factors of production—labor, capital, and entrepreneurial skill—were "productive," meaning that they generated a portion of the value of the final product; and each factor was paid an amount equal to the marginal value that it contributed (John Bates Clark's "marginal productivity theory"). Finally, in competitive markets, the value of the marginal product to consumers would equal the cost to marginal suppliers, with the result that the market-clearing price would automatically compensate marginal suppliers for their costs, and no more.

Most mainstream economists were officially reluctant to draw any normative conclusions from the purely descriptive claims of marginalism, content to boot such matters out of the camp of economics altogether, and into that of ethics. But the more outspoken partisans of capitalism, who had been watching with nervousness the rising specter of socialism, pounced on the second of the three claims, Clark's so-called "marginal productivity theory," as a dispositive rejoinder to the socialist critique of the market. As Clark declared, marginal productivity theory meant that the market automatically distributes income to factors in accordance with the ordinary (Lockean) intuition of justice: "to each what he creates."[89]

As suggested at the outset, Clark's argument drew elaborate and various responses from progressives in the years from the 1880s to the 1930s. But unlike the generation of leftist critics that preceded them, whose analysis was rooted in classical economics, the progressives' critique by and large started from premises of neoclassical (marginal) economics itself. If one assumes that each factor of production was, as the marginalists claimed, paid the value of its marginal product by the market, why did that fact establish a moral entitlement to keep the value? Clark's purported explanation, Veblen, Hale, Herbert Davenport, and other progressive economists charged, was tautological, amounting to the assertion that people are entitled to the market value of what they produced because that is what the market paid them. A more satisfactory explanation required going back to first principles, to press on what Locke's notoriously ambiguous text might mean. The appealing intuition on which Lockean labor theory rested, progressives argued, and which accounted for its durability, was that personal sacrifice deserves reward—that is, that what we produce at some real cost to ourselves we are entitled to keep. If that principle was indeed the ethical core of the Lockean justification for private property, it explained why people had a right to retain the exchange value of their property or labor, to the extent that the value represented a fair return on their actual costs or sacrifice. But, progressives argued, as the marginalists' third claim implicitly conceded, exchange value was limited to a fair return on costs only for marginal producers in competitive markets. For inframarginal producers in those markets, and for all producers in noncompetitive markets, the return often far exceeded a fair return on costs. The excess (variously called "rents," "unproductive surplus," or "unearned increment") did not reflect any virtue on the part of the producers; it simply reflected the relative scarcity of the goods or services that they provided. Neither Lockean theory nor any other justification for ownership advanced by proponents of laissez faire explained why producers were entitled to benefit from that scarcity value.

The progressives' primary assault on "unproductive surplus" focused on monopoly rents, in which scarcity value was attributable to a naturally or artificially constrained number of producers. Alfred Marshall's version of neoclassical economics, which dominated economic thought well into the 1920s, acknowledged the problem of monopoly rents but argued that it was confined to a few industries. For the vast majority of industries, which Marshall assumed to be competitive in structure, he posited that the long-run equilibrium price paid to producers would tend to converge with the costs of production, eliminating all rents. Although Marshall himself declined to draw any normative conclusions from that fact, others did not, pointing out that it meant that the problem of rents was relatively contained.

The most prominent progressive line of attack on monopoly rents accepted Marshall's assumption of a bipolar economy, but argued that as the scale of production increased, more and more industries were gravitating to the former (monopolistic) pole. The view that monopolies were becoming the rule rather than a limited exception to an otherwise competitive market, although championed principally by the antimonopoly (trustbusting) wing of progressivism, was widely shared among centrist and even conservative economists and political theorists. Beginning in the 1920s, Joan Robinson, Edward Chamberlin, and other economists opened up a second line of attack on monopoly rents, arguing that the Marshallian model of a bipolar economy was itself erroneous and that most "real markets lie somewhere between the polar extremes of perfect competition and pure monopoly."[90] Chamberlin's and Robinson's 1933 books outlining different versions of monopolistic, or imperfect, competition made the argument famous. But variants of the argument had been advanced by numerous other economists in Europe and the United States in 1920s and early 1930s.[91] Although views differed as to the distributive implications of monopolistic competition, at least some models suggested that supernormal profits would persist in the long run in most markets.[92]

Hale and the other progressive rent theorists were sympathetic to the antimonopoly wing of progressivism. Had the theory of monopolistic competition been developed by the time that they were doing most of their writing, they undoubtedly would have found it congenial to their own ends as well. But, beginning with the Fabian socialists in 1870s, they launched a third, distinct attack on the distributive justice of the market. Like the antimonopolists, they largely took as given the Marshallian bipolar model of the economy; however, they focused instead on the pole of so-called perfect competition. As noted earlier, marginalist theory predicted that in competitive markets, the market-clearing price would equal the marginal cost to suppliers. But, the Fabians argued, extending the Ricardian analysis of land rents to all factors of production, the relative scarcity of certain inputs (land and other forms of fixed capital, human talents and know-how, and the like) meant that costs would rise as one approached the margin of production. As a result, even in so-called competitive markets, inframarginal producers would reap a surplus above a fair return on their true costs—that is, they would realize inframarginal rents. Marshall himself had acknowledged the possibility of inframarginal rents ("quasi-rents") in competitive industries in the short run, but he predicted that they would disappear in the long-run equilibrium, when the cost curve straightened out. The progressives argued, though, that it was the Marshallian short run, not the long run, that described reality. Thus, they concluded, inframarginal rents were a permanent and significant feature of even so-called competitive markets. That fact was irrelevant to most mainstream economists, whose predominant concern was to show that competitive markets would automatically reach optimally efficient output and pricing levels. But it was an embarrassment to those economists and political theorists who claimed that competitive markets would automatically achieve distributive justice as well. If surplus returns (in excess of cost) were morally unjustified in the case of monopolies, Hale and other progressive rent theorists argued, such returns were no more justified when paid to producers in so-called competitive industries in the form of inframarginal rents.

In its preoccupation with unearned surplus and its insistence that the market would allocate such surplus not by moral desert but in proportion to the relative bargaining power of the parties involved, progressive rent theory had strong and obvious ties to orthodox socialism. However, there were important analytical differences in the arguments, with important political implications. In Marxian economics, surplus value was created by the difference between the value of labor's input in the production of a given commodity, measured by the minimum wage that labor would demand to maintain some social minimum of existence, and the price paid for labor's output, the commodity itself.[93] Since the former measure seemed to approximate Lockean sacrifice, at least as the progressives understood it, the case for labor's retaining the surplus above that measure was not strictly Lockean in the progressive sense. Rather, the case was based on the assumption that as between labor, which produced value, and capital, which produced none, labor had a greater entitlement to the surplus. But, the Marxist socialists argued, given that capital holds a monopoly on the means of production and given a chronic oversupply of labor, capital can ensure that under the typical wage contract, it extracts all the surplus value of labor. Under Marx's inexorable law of the accumulation of capital, as capital increases, displacing more workers in the productive process, unemployment will increase and the bargaining power of remaining labor will decrease, until wage rates are driven below even a subsistence minimum. Thus, in Marxian economics, the coerciveness of the labor contract had a predictable, indeed inevitable, distributive result: it shifted all surplus value to capital.

In contrast, the inframarginal and monopoly rents that preoccupied Hale and other postmarginalist progressives could, in theory, accrue to any factor of production, labor as well as land and other forms of capital. That "law of three rents," as Sidney Webb termed it, meant that the existence of surplus value, like the coerciveness of the private bargains by which it was distributed, was an analytical observation devoid of necessary distributive implications. Where the socialist labor theory of value was a theory of expropriation of the Lockean rights of one group (labor) by another (capital), rent theory Lockeanism was formally evenhanded as between labor, land, and other forms of capital. As an analytic matter, any of the three could be a rentier— that is, could be the residual claimant extracting the surplus value from market prices above and beyond the costs of production. That conclusion had obvious attractions for progressives, who for reasons of political expediency, if nothing else, preferred not to frame the argument for redistribution in strict class terms. Moreover, labor had no more right to the surplus value that it generated over its own sacrifice than did capital. In all cases, that surplus value was the fortuitous result of the structure of the market, in which demand exceeded available supply at constant costs. As a result, surplus value represented (as Henry George said of land rents) "a value created by the whole community."[94] If anyone had a right to surplus value, the progressives argued, it was not any particular factor, but rather society at large, to do with as it saw fit to further the common good.

As suggested before, one can argue that progressive rent theory, like most forms of socialism, was consistent with the classical liberal (Lockean) premise that each person is entitled to the fruits of her own labor.[95] It merely insisted on a different and (progressives would have argued) more exacting account of the relative contributions made by individual and social factors than that offered by either socialists or proponents of laissez faire.[96] Nonetheless, progressives (not surprisingly) were led by their rent-theory version of Lockeanism to a very different set of policy prescriptions from their laissez-faire opponents. Those prescriptions, interestingly, converged with prescriptions that more liberal economists were drawn to on utilitarian grounds: that equality should be maximized, to the extent that such leveling did not sap the minimum return needed to preserve incentives to work or save. One of the particular devices proposed by Hale and other rent theorists for achieving that end—a tax levied on surplus above a supplier's minimum reservation price—was identical to so-called "optimal tax" proposals advanced by a number of economists, again on efficiency grounds.

This book is primarily a work of intellectual history—an attempt to excavate and restore in its historical context an elaborate and (in its time) seditious argument about the nature of law and legal rights. At the same time, the excavation was motivated in part by the conviction that Hale's argument retains force in the political and intellectual debates of our own day, particularly those concerning the proper role of government in economic redistribution. The book concludes, in Chapter 6, with an attempt to assess the durability of Hale's arguments.

2

THE EMPTY IDEA OF LIBERTY

Liberty is the fairest of all social Harmonies.

—Frederic Bastiat, *Harmonies of Political Economy*[1]

The world has never had a good definition of the word liberty, and the American people, just now, are much in want of one. We all declare for liberty; but in using the same word we do not all mean the same thing . . . The shepherd drives the wolf from the sheep's throat, for which the sheep thanks the shepherd as a liberator, while the wolf denounces him for the same act as the destroyer of liberty . . . Plainly the sheep and the wolf are not agreed upon a definition of the word liberty.

—Abraham Lincoln, Address at the Sanitary Fair, Baltimore, Maryland (April 18, 1864)

Liberty and Social Control

Throwing down the gauntlet in 1897, Richard Ely declared that "regulation by the power of the state . . . [is] a condition of freedom."[1] The declaration encapsulates a central political debate that raged in England and the United States from the 1880s through the 1930s about the appropriate role of the state in economic life. The case for a limited role was rooted partly in the utilitarian claim that the unregulated market would maximize aggregate welfare by maximizing individual gains from voluntary trades.[2] But its more important source was the philosophical libertarianism of Locke and Hobbes, which took liberty of action as an end in itself and which believed that the greatest threat to that liberty lay in the coercive power of government.[3]

Herbert Spencer was perhaps the most famous exponent of the view that, as Henry Carter Adams put it, "the dogma of non-interference . . . [is] identical with the principle of individual liberty."[4] Spencer stated the case most strongly in his 1884 *Man Versus the State*, the publication of which spurred a number of responses from progressives, including Adams's own epoch-making essay, "Relation of the State to Industrial Action." "Liberal-ism," said Spencer with approval, has "habitually stood for individual free-dom *versus* State-coercion."[5] By the end of the nineteenth century, as one historian has noted, "Individualism" was a term of art, referring not to any affirmative theory of selfhood but to a theory of the appropriate limits of state action.[6]

The limits that Spencer himself thought appropriate were notoriously ex-treme. He acknowledged a legitimate role for the government in enforcing property and contract rights and in national self-defense ("anarchy plus the constable"), thereby differentiating himself from the radical individualist anarchists. But he brooked little else, rejecting (among other roles for the government) public education, public health measures, public works, public postal service, public charity for those unable to care for themselves, and government regulation of currency.[7] Few of Spencer's followers on either side of the Atlantic went that far. In the United States, for example, where Spencer's influence was considerably greater than in his native England, most proponents of laissez faire acknowledged a legitimate role for government in supplying a wide range of public goods. They focused their attacks on what they saw to be illegitimate efforts by government to bestow special privileges through tax policies, protective tariffs, land grants, and labor laws and other forms of economic regulation.[8] However, all shared with Spencer the assump-tion that "an increase in the power of the state always meant a decrease in the liberty of the citizen."[9] Indeed, the rhetorical trope that less state action should be the rule to which one recognized exceptions only as necessary was widely adopted by more progressive liberals as well, although (not surprisingly) they tended to find necessity with far more frequency than did their individualist counterparts. "State interference is an evil, where it cannot be shown to be a good," declared Oliver Wendell Holmes in 1881, echoing John Stuart Mill's sentiment expressed thirty years earlier.[10]

Proponents of laissez faire shared as well Spencer's view that the core liberty to be protected against government interference was liberty of con-tract, by which they meant liberty in economic affairs.[11] In 1921 Harvard economist Thomas Carver expressed the Spencerian argument in this way:

> The most important characteristic of the economic life of civilized people is its freedom from compulsion. Nearly every economic act of the average individual is one which he does voluntarily. Even when he is under compulsion, it is usually found to be for one of a very few reasons. It may be to prevent him from using violence or fraud against someone else. It may be to compel him to carry out an agreement into which he

has voluntarily entered . . . The striking fact about all these and all other cases of compulsion which are tolerated by civilized people is that they are all exercised by the government. Among all free people one private citizen is forbidden to exercise compulsion over any other. That is a work which is reserved exclusively for the government through its officers. "Compulsion is mine; I will compel," says the government.[12]

Carver's bland self-assurance in describing private economic activity as a bastion of freedom is somewhat breathtaking, considering the fact that a mere four years earlier a revolution in Russia had been successfully waged, at least in part, on the opposite claim. But his position accurately reflects how deeply ingrained in late nineteenth- and early twentieth-century British and American thought was the view that the market was the province of freedom, and the government the province of coercion.

How much practical effect such sentiments had on politics in either England or the United States has been much debated. Recent historiography has taken a generally skeptical view, arguing that the mid-nineteenth century—the supposed heyday of legislative laissez faire—was in fact characterized by widespread government intervention in both England and the United States, in the form of direct economic legislation and a burgeoning government bureaucracy; and that the period from the 1880s through the 1930s—the supposed heyday of judicial laissez faire in the United States—in fact rarely saw courts overturning economic legislation on any ground.[13] Moreover, recent revisionist scholarship has argued that, with the possible exception of labor legislation, those few instances in which courts did overturn economic legislation were more frequently explained by hostility to class legislation or other special interest legislation than by any broad enthusiasm for laissez faire.[14]

However limited its practical impact, the rhetoric of liberty, and in particular the assumption that less interference by the state in private economic affairs necessarily meant more freedom for its citizens, had two extraordinarily important effects for present purposes. First, that rhetoric framed political debate in the years from the 1880s to the 1930s, setting the terms in which opponents and proponents of economic regulation put their respective cases. Why laissez faire in its unadulterated form should have played so prominent a role in public discourse when it possessed so little political clout is something of a mystery.[15] But as a matter of intellectual history, its public rhetorical role commands attention in its own right. Second, at least in the United States, the rhetoric of liberty arguably had a practical effect as well in the one arena in which constitutional laissez faire—and, in particular, liberty of contract—took hold: the so-called "labor question."[16] Here, too, historians have been skeptical that judicial appeals to liberty of contract were anything more than a pretext for judges to enforce their own views of policy, frequently derived from class self-interest.[17] Whether talk of a constitutional right to liberty of contract was the source of, or merely pretext for, judicial decisions, the generation of American progressive legal thinkers writing from 1890 to the 1930s took the talk seriously enough to refute it at length.

The beginnings of a constitutional doctrine of "liberty of contract" are usually traced to a series of state court decisions in the mid-1880s, culminating in the 1886 decision of the Pennsylvania court in Godcharles v. Wigeman, striking down a state act that prohibited payment of wages in scrip.[18] Over the next twenty years, a number of state and federal courts followed suit. They elevated "liberty of contract" to a constitutional right protected under the due process clauses of the Fifth and Fourteenth Amendments, and then invoked that right to strike down a variety of state and federal laws, virtually all of which sought to regulate the terms of labor contracts.[19] The struggle between the courts and the legislatures in the United States over "liberty of contract" came to a head in a series of notorious cases in the first two decades of the twentieth century, in which the Court struck down various prolabor measures that (along with antimonopoly legislation) were the centerpiece of progressive legislative reform.[20] The stage was set by the Court's famous (or infamous) 1905 decision in Lochner v. New York.[21] The Court in Lochner struck down a New York statute setting maximum hours for bakers, asserting that it was an unconstitutional infringement of the "liberty of person and freedom of contract" of "master and employe[e]" alike.[22] Three years later in Adair v. United States, the Court invoked the rationale of Lochner to strike down an 1898 act of Congress, which (among other things) had made it unlawful for a railroad to discharge an employee solely because of his membership in a union.[23] "It was the right of the defendant to prescribe the terms upon which the services of [the employee] would be accepted," declared the Court, "and it was the right of [the employee] to become or not, as he chose, an employe[e] of the railroad company upon the terms offered to him."[24] In 1915 in Coppage v. Kansas, the Court struck down a statute prohibiting employers from requiring employees to sign so-called "yellow-dog contracts," under which, as a condition of employment, employees agreed not to join a union at any time during their employment.[25] Although Coppage was a symbolic victory for employers, it was not until two years later that yellow-dog contracts assumed much practical importance, when the Court held in Hitchman Coal and Coke Co. v. Mitchell that a union's efforts to organize employees who had signed a yellow-dog contract with their employers constituted a tortious interference by a third party with contractual relations, and on those grounds could be enjoined.[26]

Together, the triumvirate of *Adair, Coppage,* and *Hitchman* came to symbolize the evils of judicial laissez faire for the generation of American progressives writing between the two world wars.[27] For progressives sympathetic to an expanded role for the government in economic affairs, the first order of business was to neutralize the claim, on which all three cases ultimately rested, that any increase in economic regulation by the state necessarily diminished individual liberty. At least in the political arena, one could have conceded the point, but argued the loss was insignificant when measured against the gains in material well-being for the less privileged that such regulation could secure. That was the position taken by orthodox socialists, and, as time went on, increasingly by the Fabian socialists as well, who came to regard such notions as "liberty" as just a form "of outdated sentimentality which obstructed the realization of [the] ideal" of bureaucratic efficiency on behalf of equality.[28] So also progressives could have found shelter in some form of "official Socialism," as Leonard Hobhouse came to call it.[29] Ultimately, most of them chose not to. They embraced the goal of greater liberty, but argued that it was best achieved through greater equality, realized by (in what became a catchphrase of the left in opposition to individualism on the right) greater "social control."[30]

The decision to clothe the case for equality in the mantle of liberty might seem ironic at this distance. Surely it did to Ludwig von Mises, reviewing Hale's version of the argument in 1953.[31] In its time, however, the choice was understandable, indeed predictable. In the world of late nineteenth-century political discourse, the invocation of liberty was trumps.[32] As a result, anyone hoping to fire the popular political imagination in support of increased social control had to find a way to pry "liberty" loose from its historical link to a minimal state. For American progressives like Robert Hale, Richard Ely, Roscoe Pound, T. R. Powell, and Morris Cohen, who were trying to frame the case for social control within a legal regime that had raised liberty to a constitutionally protected status, the pragmatic arguments for the choice were even more compelling. Pragmatic considerations may have counseled that choice on a more personal level as well. As Stefan Collini notes, "Hobhouse knew whereof he spoke when in 1897 he referred to the 'obloquy' incurred in calling oneself a Socialist."[33] In the United States, Henry Carter Adams, John Commons, Richard Ely, and others, all of whose careers were jeopardized by charges of socialism, could likewise testify to that obloquy firsthand.[34]

But for most progressives, political expediency coincided with deep conviction. Although they all embraced in one form or another the socialist ideal of greater state intervention on behalf of equality, they parted company with "official" socialism over whether equality was an end in itself, or only a means to greater personal liberty. The labels they adopted—New Liberalism, Liberal Socialism, Social Democracy—to put distance between themselves and official socialism signaled their conviction that the concern for equality manifest by their new versions of collectivism had to accommodate the values of individual autonomy and democracy represented by an older liberalism. The labels signaled as well their insistence that increased state action was a means of implementing a higher individualism, not socialism.[35] As Henry Carter Adams put it, his intellectual mission was to find "a principle . . . adequate to bridge over the chasm between the purpose of individualism and the criticisms of socialism."[36] Here, as in many other areas, John Stuart Mill was the most important spiritual forebear of the progressives, epitomizing in the philosophical leap from the classic liberalism of *On Liberty* to the socialistic yearnings of the later editions of *Principles of Political Economy* the fervent hope that the causes of liberty and equality might coexist.[37] Leonard Hobhouse described his own aspirations to heal that breach as follows:

> If . . . there be such a thing as a Liberal Socialism . . . it must clearly fulfil two conditions. In the first place, it must be democratic. It must come from below, not from above . . . It must engage the efforts and respond to the genuine desires not of a handful of superior beings, but of great masses of men. And, secondly, and for that very reason, it must make its account with the human individual. It must give the average man free play in the personal life for which he really cares. It must be founded on liberty, and must make not for the suppression but for the development of personality.[38]

After an early flirtation with a more programmatic socialism (part Fabian, part Marxist), Hobhouse came to distrust its tendency "to hail any and every extension of State authority, whatever its principle or its object as a triumph for Socialism."[39] John Hobson began his political life as a more committed socialist than was Hobhouse. But by 1909, he insisted that his proposed conception of the state "is not Socialism, in any accredited meaning of that term," and did not involve "any violent breach of continuity with Liberal traditions."[40] John Dewey spent the greater part of his professional life working out the conditions necessary for individual "self-realization," through participation in a community that did not subsume or transcend its members.

Thorstein Veblen's most important contribution to modern thought—sketching the descriptive limits of individual rational choice—reflected more than passing agreement with radical individualists like Carl von Menger, F. A. Hayek, Ludwig von Mises, Lionel Robbins, and Karl Popper that the moral significance of human life lies in purposive choice.[41] Richard Ely, although strongly influenced throughout his life by the collectivist ideals of the closely linked Christian Socialist movement and Historical School in Germany, ultimately espoused allegiance to the middle way. "I condemn alike that individualism which would allow the state no room for industrial activity, and that socialism which would absorb in the state the functions of the individual."[42] John Commons called for increased government in the service of increased individualism, not socialism.[43] Even T. H. Green, for whom the pull toward an idealist (Hegelian) vision of the state was strongest, never lost the conviction that individuals and not the state were the final repository of value, and that the end of all state action was to guarantee the conditions necessary for self-development of the individual personality.[44] George Bernard Shaw, an irrepressible apostate even to his own cause, characteristically put best the case for liberty. Commenting on the case of the Russian subject who in 1888 left Russia, where he worked thirteen hours a day, to work in England eighteen hours a day "because he felt freer here," Shaw remarked as follows:

> It brings to mind the story of the American judge who tried to induce a runaway slave to return to the plantation by pointing out how much better he was treated there than the free wage-nigger of the Abolitionist states. "Yes," said the runaway; "but would you go back if you were in my place?" The judge turned Abolitionist at once. These things are not to be reasoned away . . . Like the Russian, [man] will rather be compelled by "necessity" to *agree* to work eighteen hours, than ordered by a master to work thirteen. No modern nation, if deprived of personal liberty or national autonomy, would stop to think of its economic position. Establish a form of Socialism which shall deprive the people of their sense of personal liberty; and, though it double their rations, and halve their working hours, they will begin to conspire against it before it is a year old. We only disapprove of monopolists; we *hate* masters.[45]

There were exceptions, of course. But most progressives regarded the problem of liberty with a seriousness that matched that of the most fervent individualists. They shared with Spencer the conviction that the fundamental end of politics was to develop character. One could say (almost without irony) that they differed from him only as to means.[46]

Robert Hale was typical in this regard. Unlike many of his progressive contemporaries (Veblen, Dewey, Davenport, Lippmann, Croly, and Hobhouse), he showed little interest in the particulars of individual subjectivity or individual choice. Although he acknowledged in passing society's role in shaping individual preferences and the doubt that cast on the ethical significance of choice, in his own writing he took those preferences, and the desirability of maximizing them, largely as given.[47] He eschewed a Deweyian romantic fervor for a reconstituted self, in favor of a grimmer, more materialistic notion of freedom, one that is closer, at least in tone, to Marx than to Dewey. All these attitudes must cast some doubt on how seriously he weighed the "liberty" side of the progressive program. But throughout his career, he at least purported to take seriously the proposition that government's ultimate duty was to maximize positive liberty, in the sense of power to effect one's desires. One of his central, unifying intellectual missions was to show that such a goal was more likely to be reached by greater, not less, government control—to show, as Hale put it in a letter in 1923, that "the antithesis between 'socialism' and 'individualism' [is] . . . meaningless."[48]

In a series of important articles and course materials written over the course of his career, summed up in his aptly titled *Freedom Through Law,* Hale argued that proponents of laissez faire could maintain that the government held a monopoly on the legitimate use of coercive force only because they defined coercion in a way that was hopelessly muddled and changeable, and that persistently confused whether an act was coercive in fact with whether it was either legal or desirable. Hale's response was to reformulate the problem of coercion, to show that under any coherent definition of coercion, the sphere of private, "voluntary" market relations was indistinguishable from direct exercises of public power. As Hale said, "We live, then, under two governments, 'economic' and 'political,'" the second public and hence visible, the first private and hence invisible.[49] That reality meant that when the government intervened in private market relations to curb the use of certain private bargaining power, it did not inject coercion for the first time into those relations. Rather, it merely changed the relative distribution of coercive power. Whether in any given case that redistribution would increase or decrease the aggregate liberty of its citizens was therefore an empirical and not an analytical question, and one that could not be answered by reference to abstract (constitutional) rights. Thus, concluded Hale, "[t]here is no *a priori* reason for regarding planned governmental intervention in the economic sphere as inimical to economic liberty, or even to that special form of it known as free enterprise."[50]

In its broad outlines, Hale's analysis was squarely within the progressive tradition. Among other strands of progressive thought, the analysis drew on the socialist characterization of the labor contract as coercive; on T. H. Green's redefinition of liberty as the positive "power to act as one wishes"; and on the work of Holmes, Wesley Hohfeld, and their successor Legal Realists in redefining abstract legal rights in terms of the functional relationships that they created. It reflected as well the broader conviction, shared by most progressives, that laissez-faire philosophy was at root (as one historian has put it) an avoidance of the realization that "economic power is as real and public in nature as political power,"[51] and that the most important fighting ground for freedom in modern industrial society was economic rather than political equality. But Hale's analysis of the problem of coercion survives the particular legal and political controversies that gave rise to it. It remains among the best treatments of the problem to date, gaining renewed interest in recent years as scholars have resurrected the problem of coercion for serious philosophical and legal inquiry.[52] This chapter will look briefly first at the traditions out of which Hale's analysis grew, before turning to that analysis in more detail.

New Wine in Old Bottles: The Progressive Reworking of Liberty

"Rightly understood . . .," declared Hobhouse in 1909, "socialistic legislation appears not as an infringement of the two distinctive ideals of the older Liberalism, 'Liberty and Equality.' It appears rather as a necessary means to their fulfilment."[53] Over the years, progressives defended that provocative claim with two different rhetorical strategies. First, following the lead of John Stuart Mill, they embraced the traditional liberal definition of liberty as freedom from formal constraint or compulsion by other human beings. But they argued that it was mere historical accident, not logical necessity, that had led liberals to think that the minimal state was the best means to achieve that freedom. Once liberals understood how far unbridled private rights in modern society might interfere with the liberty of others, they would understand as well that government action might be the best friend that old-style liberty had.

Second, following the lead of T. H. Green, progressives reformulated the concept of liberty to offer, at least on a rhetorical level, a cleaner break with the past. In place of the old definition of liberty as freedom from arbitrary, human interference with choice—what T. H. Green termed "negative liberty"—they argued for a "positive" notion of liberty that measured the individual's power to effect his or her desires.[54] Embracing the socialist premise that the primary source of power was wealth, progressives argued that the state, by promoting greater economic equality through various compulsory redistributive programs, was in fact championing the cause of liberty. As Hobhouse stated, "[T]he struggle for liberty is also, when pushed through, a struggle for equality."[55]

The two arguments were rarely as distinct as Green's contrast suggests, and most progressives embraced both at different points. Indeed, both strains were important to Hale's reformulation of the problem of coercion. But the latter strain came to dominate debate in the early part of the twentieth century, as progressives turned increasingly to a straightforward redistributive agenda more comfortably accommodated by the rhetoric of positive liberty.

Recasting the Problem of Negative Liberty. Whether one perceives progress to be most threatened by individual or by collective action, declared Dewey, depends largely on what abuses one is reacting against.[56] Two factors, progressives argued, explained why eighteenth- and early nineteenth-century liberals perceived the greater threat to lie in collective action. First, at least in England, the most conspicuous form of government action during the period was special interest legislation on behalf of landowners and mercantile classes. But, progressives argued, that particular form of abuse had been largely eliminated by the mid-nineteenth century, through the success of the radical reform movement in securing the repeal of the Corn Laws, the passage of the Free Trade Tariff in 1860, and the reform of Parliament. As a result, declared T. H. Green in 1881, "[t]he popular jealousy of law, once justifiable enough, is . . . out of date."[57]

Second, progressives argued, in the preindustrial society of the eighteenth century, one could reasonably have believed that individual action posed little threat to others' liberty. But, in what came to be a stock progressive story, they argued that the increased physical proximity and economic interdependence of all people, along with increasing concentrations of wealth, all brought on by the industrial revolution, had rendered that atomistic view of social life obsolete.[58] Dewey described it thus: "[T]he non-social individual is an abstraction arrived at by imagining what man would be if all his human qualities were taken away. Society, as a real whole, is the normal order, and the mass as an aggregate of isolated units is the fiction."[59] The change wrought in social relations required a radical change in legal relations. What we were accustomed to call natural rights, Rexford Tugwell argued, were on second thought revealed to be merely socially created rights that were indulged because "their exercise has not seemed sufficiently antagonistic to others to call for repressive action from the group. In a pioneer society liberties are allowed the individual which cannot be allowed when civilization is further advanced."[60]

The argument that interdependence required a new, "social" freedom—the freedom to choose only among those lines of activity that do not unduly injure others—got almost universal assent when it came to controlling monopolies and trusts.[61] But its implications, progressives insisted, extended far beyond that. All the traditional prerogatives of ownership—the right to use one's property for private purposes as well as to sell it for whatever price the market would bear—carried with them the potential to injure others.[62] Faced with this new reality, one could justify an increased role for the government even within the purely Hobbesian (minimalist) conception of the nightwatchman state. As Hobhouse explained in *Liberalism*, the paradigmatic defense of social control in the name of liberalism, "[I]ndividualism, when it grapples with the facts, is driven no small distance along Socialist lines."[63] Echoing that sentiment, J. M. Clark argued, "It is not a question whether our great-grandfathers were right or wrong; the thing they defended no longer exists. Individualism and control are both new, and the case for both needs to be completely restated."[64] Those arch-individualists like Spencer, who anachronistically persisted in championing the minimal state as the means to maximize freedom, were dismissed as eighteenth-century men commenting on nineteenth-century facts.[65] The more influential and pragmatic voices of laissez faire—Adam Smith, Jeremy Bentham, and James Mill—progressives argued, had never intended the presumption against governmental interference to extend beyond its demonstrated usefulness. "Had we lived in 1776," declared Edwin Seligman, "we would certainly have been followers of Smith: did Smith live in 1886, he would no less have been in the vanguard of the new school."[66] Echoing and amplifying that sentiment forty years later, J. M. Clark added that had history permitted Adam Smith the last word, Smith probably would have thrown his support behind the current proposals for increased social control, as representing "democratic and humanitarian control in the interest of just the classes which mercantilism neglected."[67]

Thus pried loose from its historically contingent connection to the minimal state, the classical liberal ideal of "negative liberty" could accommodate most of the progressive agenda. J. S. Mill and Henry Sidgwick, two important forerunners to the early twentieth-century progressives, went to great pains to sell their programs for expansive government as the salvation of individual liberty. One historian has described Sidgwick's *Elements of Politics* as the "best and most careful demonstration" that progressive legislation meant to insure a social minimum was consistent with individualism.[68] The more famous demonstration, however, was provided by J. S. Mill in Book V of *Principles of Political Economy.* "Laisser-faire," declared Mill, "should be the general practice; every departure from it, unless required by some great good, is a certain evil,"[69] and then proceeded to enumerate the many great goods to be accomplished by broad government control of economic life. Like much of *Principles,* Mill's dazzlingly slippery argument lent succor to all sides of the debate over laissez faire. Roscoe Pound attributed the growth of laissez-faire doctrines in part to the fact that "Chapter XI of Book V of Mill's *Political Economy* . . . was studied by every liberally educated lawyer of the last fifty years."[70] Yet growth of opposition could as easily be laid to the same text. As his progressive heirs recognized, Mill's "unless" was capacious enough to hold their entire reform agenda. Henry Carter Adams's 1887 essay, "The Relation of the State to Industrial Action," for example, a blueprint for later progressive arguments for government control of the economy, defended state regulation as necessary to achieve the "benefits of free competition," while "guarding society from the evil consequences of unrestrained competition."[71] As time went on, that strategy was abetted by a growing consensus among economists that monopoly was widespread and that even most so-called competitive markets had monopolistic tendencies. J. M. Clark expressly drew on both Sidgwick and Mill for his own fourteen-point justification for far-reaching governmental powers to regulate the economy, "arising out of the fact that the conditions necessary to successful individualism are lacking."[72] In 1926, commenting with more ironic detachment on progressives' tendency to defend social control as a piecemeal corrective in special cases in which individualism "works badly," Clark noted that "the volume of these special cases has swollen so inordinately . . . that one wit has defined a liberal as 'one who believes that this is the best of all possible worlds, and that almost everything in it is an unfortunate exception.' "[73]

Positive Liberty.   However broad its reach in other respects, the progressives' revised version of negative liberty did not comfortably justify what became the dominant focus of progressive legislative efforts: redistributive measures designed to improve the position of the working and lower classes through Poor Laws, a progressive income tax, and certain forms of paternalistic legislation.[74] For those efforts, some more radical reworking of the notion of liberty was required. In his influential 1881 lecture, "Liberal Legislation and Freedom of Contract," T. H. Green provided it. In place of the classical liberal notion of liberty as freedom from formal "restraint or compulsion," which Green termed "negative freedom," he urged embrace of a "positive freedom," which he defined as the "positive power or capacity of doing or enjoying something worth doing or enjoying."[75] Green's reformulation of the problem of liberty found an enormously receptive audience. By the turn of the century, Green's invocation of "positive liberty" had become a standard rhetorical trope in public discourse, extending far beyond the narrow circle of progressive intellectuals. Woodrow Wilson recounted it thus in his famous declaration in *The New Freedom:* "[T]o let [the individual] alone is to leave him helpless as against the obstacles with which he has to contend. . . . Freedom to-day is something more than being let alone. The program of a government of freedom must in these days be positive, not negative merely."[76]

Green's reformulation of freedom worked two significant changes to the classical notion of liberty. It replaced freedom as formal license to pursue one's desires with freedom as the functional power to achieve them—the "power to act according to choice or preference";[77] and it limited the universe of choices worth protecting to those that sought a worthy end. In short, freedom was the actual power to do what one ought to do. In Green's view, one ought to do only one thing: to act in such a fashion as to make "contributions to a common good."[78]

The latter change, as Green acknowledged, reflected a teleological (idealist) notion of the will with close ties to the Hegelian and Kantian, as well as Christian, traditions.[79] By shifting the meaning of freedom from the mere exercise of the will, to the right to will things worth willing, Green justified reform efforts to guarantee a social minimum to all citizens as a means of maximizing freedom. But as later critics rightly complained, he accomplished that end only by transforming the word "freedom" beyond recognition.[80] As Dewey said of Mill, whose life's work presents its own version of that equivocation, a "thoroughly socialized ideal of happiness is the most charac-teristic feature of Mill's ethics. It is noble, but it is not hedonism."[81]

The teleological strain in Green's work is strongly detectable in the work of many of the later progressives. Dewey, an early admirer of Green, built his own brand of individualism around the maintenance of one's capacity for continuous growth towards self-realization, in which the needs of the community shaped one's individual desires. Hobhouse, like Dewey, argued that freedom of choice was fundamental to self-development, but he made clear that he meant choice not as mere "self-assertion," but rather as rational judgment founded on the common good: "[T]he fundamental importance of liberty rests on the nature of the 'good' itself. . . ."[82] So also did Henry Carter Adams, John Hobson, Richard Ely, Walter Rauschenbusch, J. M. Clark, Sidney Webb, Roscoe Pound, Charles Horton Cooley, Herbert Croly, and numerous others call in one way or another for a new form of individual-ism that "soften[ed] the ideal of maximum self-assertion to maximum self-realization."[83] They shared with Green the belief not only that the value of will depends upon the value of what is willed but also that what ought to be willed was that which would promote the common good. As Hale said, quoting Justice William Johnson with approval, " '[T]he rights of all must be held in subserviency to the good of the whole.' "[84]

But it was the first shift in meaning—from negative to positive freedom—that proved politically more significant. When Anatole France proclaimed with undisguised contempt that "[t]he law in its majestic equality, forbids the rich as well as the poor to sleep under bridges," he provided the refrain for a generation of progressives, who insisted that liberty be measured not by the absence of formal constraints on the pursuit of one's desires but instead by the presence of power to effect them.[85] Jean Jaurès, echoing France's sentiment as well as his sarcasm, stated that "To conceive of freedom only in its negative aspect" would make the inhabitant of Constantinople "not subject like the Parisians to regulations over hygiene and roads, not forced to send his children to school, a free citizen, while we are the victims of tyranny."[86]

The shift to a positive definition of liberty, which reflected a more general revolt against formalism in the social sciences, had a number of important philosophical and political implications. First, while "negative liberty" had been construed (wrongly, Hale and others argued) to create a categorical preference for less government, "positive liberty" suggested that the state had the right, indeed the obligation, to use its own power to increase the effective power of its citizens. As Hobhouse succinctly stated, "The function of State coercion is to override individual coercion . . ."[87] Applying that principle to liberty of contract itself, T. H. Green argued thus: "To uphold the sanctity of contracts is doubtless a prime business of government, but it is no less its business to provide against contracts being made, which, from the helplessness of one of the parties to them, instead of being a security for freedom, become an instrument of disguised oppression."[88]

Second, when harnessed to the progressives' belief that the root of func-tional power in society was economic wealth, positive freedom provided all the justification required for a radically redistributive agenda. "[L]iberty without equality is a name of noble sound and squalid result," declared Hobhouse, echoing Anatole France.[89] That belief obviously had close kin-ship to Marx's brand of materialism. Indeed, critics charged with some justification, "positive freedom" was nothing more than a stand-in for eco-nomic wealth.[90] But progressives offered a more moderate version of the

Marxian critique, one that at least in theory could coexist with a liberal democracy. Unlike Marx, they did not believe that the maldistribution of wealth was an inevitable by-product of capitalism, and most stopped short of calling for abolition of private property or enforced equality as a cure. Instead, following T. H. Green's lead, they embraced the radical individualist claim that private property was the "bulwark of liberty" but drew a vastly different moral from it. Rather than requiring strong protections of existing property rights (as Kant and others had assumed), it required the state to redistribute wealth to ensure to each citizen the minimum necessary for economic and moral autonomy. As Hobhouse put it, if property is "the basis of a harmonious and rational development of personality," it requires "the condemnation of a social system in which property of the kind and amount required for such development of personality is not generally accessible to all citizens . . . A society which should accept this principle, could not tolerate anything like the existing distribution of wealth, could not permit those methods of accumulation which concentrate wealth in the hands of the few, and leave the many—so far as the practical object of earning their living is concerned—as naked as they were born."[91] Thus it is, Hobhouse concluded, that the conception of property as an instrument of personality, "[c]herished as a Conservative principle, . . . has in it the seed of Radical revolution . . . Ethical individualism in property, carried through, blows up its own citadel."[92]

Hale's account of the problem of coercion drew on both traditions in British progressive thought—the Millian reworking of negative liberty and the Greenian abandonment of it entirely in favor of positive liberty. But it took a somewhat different tack, reflecting the different political realities that Hale and other American progressives faced. Great Britain, not having a written constitution, lacked a textual justification for the judiciary to override the legislative will. As a consequence, at least by the mid-nineteenth century, Parliament was left relatively free to legislate as it saw fit without constitutional constraints. As noted at the outset, the political situation in the United States was quite different. Seizing on the presence of "liberty" and other grand words in the federal and state constitutions, beginning in the 1880s, courts claimed authority to set aside social legislation that they deemed to transgress constitutionally protected liberty interests. That situation meant that while British progressives could concentrate their arguments for greater social control on Parliament, their American counterparts first had to deal with the courts. For that task, American progressives could not rely on the broad, philosophical appeals to positive liberty and equality that might suffice to move the body politic. They had instead to meet the argument on its own terms—that is, in the stylized, legally cognizable argot of (American) constitutional law.[93]

American progressives had available a number of accommodationist strategies to achieve that end, strategies that allowed them to pay rhetorical deference to the existing constitutional edifice even as they dismantled it. Chief among them was the doctrine of "police powers." Even the staunchest defenders of liberty of contract conceded that individuals' constitutional right to "negative liberty" from governmental control had to cede to the greater right of the government to control private actions for the public good under its implied police powers. As the conservative majority in *Adair* said, "[T]here [is] no disagreement as to the general proposition that there is a liberty of contract which cannot be *unreasonably* interfered with by legislation."[94] The question, of course, was what was "unreasonable." Given the indeterminacy of the answer and the courts' own inconsistent responses,[95] it is hardly surprising that the most famous constitutional battles concerning social legislation were nominally waged over the appropriate limits of the state's police powers.[96] With varying success, progressives commonly defended prounion legislation as simply a straightforward exercise of police powers, arguing that the state had determined that what was good for the unions was also good for America, or, alternatively, that protecting workers from economic injury resulting from their unequal bargaining position was itself a legitimate object of the police powers.[97]

Hale happily lent support to the "police powers" strategy when it seemed politically prudent. But he launched a more radical attack on the notion of negative liberty itself. T. H. Green and his philosophical heirs had attacked the notion of negative liberty—the freedom from formal restraint—as morally impoverished, at least in a world of scarcity, where those who did not already possess property might well be unable to obtain the minimal resources necessary for a decent life. Hale, unable to rely on moral appeals alone in the face of supposed constitutional authority, argued instead that the concept was analytically incoherent, and hence useless in interpreting constitutional limits to government control. Hale first sketched out his argument in a 1912 letter to Secretary of the Interior Walter Fisher. He presented it in more extended form in two articles written in 1920, "Law Making by Unofficial Minorities" and an unpublished manuscript on economic nationalism.[98] Hale developed the argument fully for the first time in his 1923 article, "Coercion and Distribution in a Supposedly Non-Coercive State."[99] Although Hale reworked the argument somewhat in different versions written throughout his life and made it the organizing principle of several courses that he taught, his basic argument remained unchanged from the 1923 article.[100]

The occasion for "Coercion and Distribution" was a scathing review of Thomas Nixon Carver's *Principles of National Economy*, published in 1921.

Carver was in many ways an unlikely choice as stand-in villain for the *Lochner*-era Court. A rather undistinguished economist at Harvard, Carver had done graduate work with Richard Ely at Johns Hopkins, and maintained close contacts with many of the leading progressives of the time, including Lippmann, Croly, Beard, and Dewey.[101] His economic program, though not radical, was hardly the standard fare of laissez-faire economics. Notwithstanding Hale's description of Carver as of the school that thinks "[t]he practical function of economic theory is merely to prove to statesmen the wisdom of leaving [economic] matters alone,"[102] Carver envisioned his *Principles of National Economy* as a blueprint for achieving "a fair distribution of the products among all classes, to the end that all may share in the national prosperity," a fact that he thought required a somewhat self-congratulatory apology in the introduction.[103]

Carver's *Principles* was a disjointed hodgepodge of homilies and exhortations, intermixed with more technical economic analysis on a dazzling array of topics, and ending with a summary presentation of Carver's six-point program for "the complete abolition of poverty." The program, which he called "Constructive Liberalism," was developed at greater length in Carver's 1915 *Essays in Social Justice*. It advocated combining direct government controls (what Carver termed "voting" programs) on income distribution, with indirect government intervention (what he termed "balancing-up" programs) to raise the equilibrium prices for unskilled labor by lowering its supply through immigration restrictions, programs to encourage lower birth rates among unskilled labor, vocational education, and so on. Although various of Carver's proposals were, to Hale's mind, ill-conceived and internally inconsistent,[104] Carver's ultimate sin was not the substance of his program; indeed, the program embraced, and even anticipated, many of the standard progressive reform proposals.[105] The sin was his rhetorical insistence, in terms so simpleminded and hyperbolic that they would have given even the *Coppage* Court some pause, on equating the existing regime of property and contract rights with freedom, and equating direct government intervention to alter the terms of either with compulsion. Even though conceding that some amount of direct government intervention was necessary to achieve greater equality, Carver argued that such intervention would always result in a net increase in coercion, in contrast either to doing nothing, or to altering incomes through his "balancing-up" program. Thus, as to any proposed intervention, he argued, one must always ask, "Are the results of repression or regulation worth as much as they cost?"—cost, that is, in individual liberty.[106]

The task that Hale set for himself was to show that Carver, and by extension the Supreme Court and other opponents of state control, had posed the wrong question. They believed that the government held a monopoly on coercion because they fundamentally misconceived the nature of coercion. When properly understood, Hale argued, coercion would be seen to be ubiquitous in the private sphere—in a form indistinguishable in nature and origin from governmental coercion—in acts traditionally regarded as volitional. Chief among such acts were so-called voluntary market exchanges. Rather than the unfettered expression of will that laissez-faire proponents imagined, such exchanges were in fact coerced by the common-law right of property owners and would-be laborers to withhold their property and labor, respectively, except on such terms of exchange as they demanded. That state of affairs meant that in intervening in private contracts to limit one side's right to dictate the terms of exchange, the government was indeed constraining that side's liberty, as laissez-faire proponents had argued. But it was simultaneously enlarging the sphere of choices, and hence liberty, of the other side.[107] Thus, as Hale wrote to Arthur Hadley, in the first instance "[t]he question raised by any proposed equalizing scheme 'is a question of liberty against liberty, not liberty against equality.' "[108]

Hale's argument demolished as an analytical matter not only the old laissez-faire notion of negative liberty but also the updated progressive version. As Hale noted, once all schemes of rights were recognized to constrain others' liberty to act as they wished, "it would then be plain that to admit the coercive nature of [any given scheme] would not be to condemn it."[109] The choice among possible schemes was a choice among liberties; the question for society was how, as a policy matter, it wished to choose.[110] Hale ventured at least a tentative answer to that question, one that was consistent with the typical progressive (social welfarist) response: rights should be assigned so as to maximize the aggregate real (positive) freedom enjoyed by society as a whole. The most likely means to that end, he argued, again echoing the traditional progressive line, was to increase the options available to the least well-off people in society, subject only to preserving adequate incentives for the richer members of society to be productive. But the particular answer was less important to Hale than showing that it required a calculus that was quintessentially the legislatures' and not the courts' to make.

Hale's argument obviously drew on a long tradition of social criticism from the left. The observation that the world of so-called "voluntary" contractual arrangements was in fact a "system of *Machtoekonomie*"[111] figured prominently in socialist doctrine. Socialists had charged that in a capitalist economy, those with capital used the necessity of the laborer to strike a wage bargain that paid the laborer only his or her minimum survival wage, transferring labor's surplus value to themselves. As Rodbertus put it, "although the contract of labourer and employer has taken the place of slavery, the contract is only formally and not actually free, and Hunger makes a good substitute for the whip."[112] The same observation shows up in a politically more muted form, in the almost ubiquitous assertion among progressives in the 1880s to the 1930s that the working classes were economically subordinated to owners of capital. In the political arena, it figured prominently as well in early twentieth-century battles over labor legislation. Indeed, the description of the employment relationship as a locus of coercion was a progressive commonplace in legal, economic, and political circles, as was Hale's overarching analogy between political and managerial power. Progressives repeatedly defended—in rhetoric that replaced the socialist charges of exploitation with softer talk of "unequal bargaining power"—prounion and proworker legislation as necessary to counterbalance the force of concentrated capital.[113]

But Hale, along with a number of other Legal Realists, including Walter Wheeler Cook, Thomas Reed Powell, Morris Cohen, Roscoe Pound, and Wesley Hohfeld, and fellow institutionalists Henry Carter Adams, Richard Ely, and John Commons, put that progressive commonplace in analytic form, generalizing its reach beyond labor contracts, and cleansed it of its necessary (socialist) distributive implications.[114] Whereas socialists had assumed that economic coercion worked in only one direction—coercing labor to transfer the surplus value that it had generated to capital—Hale's analysis showed that in every exchange, coercion was exerted *formally* by both sides. Hale, like other progressives, also went out of his way to acknowledge that the balance of *substantive* coercive power at times lay with labor as well.[115]

Markets as a Network of Coercion

The Structure of Coercion: "Volitional" versus "Voluntary" Choice

Writing in 1953, to take Hale to task for his assertion that coercion was ubiquitous in the private as well as the public sphere, Ludwig von Mises argued that a "state or a government is an apparatus of coercion and compulsion. Within the territory that it controls, it prevents all agencies, except those that it expressly authorizes to do so, from resorting to violent action. A government has the power to enforce its commands by beating people into submission or by threatening them with such action. An institution that lacks this power is never called a government."[116] What von Mises did not add, but clearly implied, was that an institution that lacks this (authorized) power is also never called coercive.

Von Mises, like Carver, transfixed by the Weberian observation that the government alone had a legal monopoly on violent force, concluded that the government held a legal monopoly on coercion.[117] The conclusion followed only if one assumed that for an act to be coercive, it must take the form of direct force that overbears the will of the coerced party. In fact, as Hale noted in a 1943 article, courts reviewing allegations of coercion routinely made that assumption: "The notion lingers on that coercion necessarily implies that the party to whom it is applied has no volition, as does the converse notion that where he has volition, or the ability to make a choice, there is no coercion or duress."[118] The assumption was simply wrong, Hale argued at length. What most people identified as coercion rarely took the form of direct physical compulsion that deprived individuals of all choice. Rather, it operated as background constraints on the universe of socially available choices from which an individual might "freely" choose. In a number of well-known judicial opinions, Holmes had made the same observation about coercion between private parties. In the classic example of private coercion trotted forth in the common law—the individual who is "compelled" to turn over his money when a gunman threatens "Your money or your life"— Holmes pointed out, the victim's will is not overborne by a force that deprives him of all choice. The robber's threat literally leaves him with at least two choices. The more real the threat of the latter ("your life"), the more eagerly the victim opts for the former. More generally, as Holmes noted, "It always is for the interest of the party under duress to choose the lesser of two evils. But the fact that a choice was made according to interest does not exclude duress. It is a characteristic of duress properly so called."[119]

What Holmes had shown to be true of the classic examples of private coercion, Hale argued, was true of almost all forms of government coercion. Some of the sanctions that the state had at its disposal—infliction of death or imprisonment, the seizure of property in satisfaction of judgments—*if imposed*, did in fact make obedience a physical necessity.[120] But in most cases, Hale argued, the government got its way in the first instance not by imposing such sanctions but instead by extracting voluntary compliance by threatening to impose them. Thus, when the government "compels" someone to carry out a contract into which he has voluntarily entered, it does so customarily not by forcibly seizing property that is the subject of a contract but instead by persuading the person to turn over the property "voluntarily" lest it be seized. As long as the person "has the physical power to disobey," noted Hale, "his obedience is not a matter of physical necessity, but of choice"—that is, it is volitional.[121]

Moreover, Hale argued, most of the state's mandates do not even nominally take the form of absolute commands. They take the form of restrictions, rewards, or penalties, conditioning one out of the total universe of available choices. Thus, when the government passes a minimum wage law, it does not (to focus for the moment on the employer's perspective) demand that the employer relinquish a portion of its wealth to its workers or else suffer a penalty. The government merely states that *if* the employer chooses of its own free will to employ a given worker, it must pay at least minimum wage. That is to say, it reduces the universe of the employer's legally available choices by one, by eliminating the choice to employ a worker but at a subminimum wage. However, it leaves the employer "free" to choose among the remaining alternatives. So also do the anti–yellow-dog laws at issue in *Adair* and *Coppage:* they do not require that an employer hire anyone at all. They merely state that if an employer chooses voluntarily to hire someone, it may not require the person to sign a yellow-dog contract as a condition of employment. The same observation held, Hale argued, with income taxes, or taxes levied on particular commodities: "When the government, for instance, levies a thirty cent tax on a $3.00 theatre ticket, a person is not literally compelled to pay either the tax or the price. He always has the option of not attending the theatre."[122]

That the individuals in all these cases acted out of volition does not mean that their acts were not in some important sense coerced. After all, as Hale noted, "Even a slave makes a choice. The compulsion which drives him to work operates through his own will power. He makes the 'voluntary' muscular movements which the work calls for, in order to escape some threat . . ."[123] Nevertheless, no one would deny that the servitude was "involuntary." But the coercion did not take the form of an overbearing force that eliminated all choice. Rather, it took the form of circumstances that narrowed a person's available universe of choices to a set of relative evils, excluding the choice that he or she would have preferred. In the case of the robber, for example, the preferred choice excluded was to keep one's money and one's life; in the case of *Adair* and *Coppage*, it was to employ someone *and* require him or her to sign a yellow-dog contract; in the case of the theater tax, it was to purchase the ticket without paying the tax.[124]

Markets as a Network of Mutual Coercion

When Carver, Spencer, and others extolled the market as a sphere of freedom, they focused only on the moment of choice, embodied in the contract, to give up what one already had in favor of a greater advantage to be secured by trade. But from that vantage point, the choice of the slave to work rather than to starve or be beaten; the choice of the victim to hand over money rather than to be killed; the choice to work and remit a portion of one's earnings to the government as tribute rather than not to work at all, were equally voluntary choices to improve one's position over what it would have been in the absence of that choice. Once one understood that coercion operated as background constraints on socially available choices, not as the deprivation of all choice, Hale argued, it would be evident that the sphere of so-called voluntary market exchanges—no less than slavery, extortion, and taxation—was really a complicated network of mutual coercion, in which the "choice" to accede to the other side's terms was coerced by the fact that the money, goods, or services that one obtained in exchange were unavailable on more favorable terms. The reason that they were unavailable—and hence the source of the coercion—was not natural necessity. Instead, it was the state itself, which, through its laws of liberty, property, and contract, gave owners the right to withhold property and services from others absolutely, and the power to waive that right upon payment of the price demanded. Hale described the situation thus:

> Adam Smith's "obvious and simple system of natural liberty" is not a system of liberty at all, but a complicated network of restraints, imposed in part by individuals, but very largely by the government itself at the behest of some individuals on the freedom of others, and at the behest of others on the freedom of the "some" . . . . What in fact distinguishes this counterfeit system of *"laissez-faire"* [the market] from paternalism is not the absence of restraint, but the absence of any conscious purpose on the part of the officials who administer the restraint, and of any responsibility or unanimity on the part of the numerous owners at whose discretion the restraint is administered.[125]

Hale's argument was the natural extension of a radical reconceptualization of property and contract begun in the nineteenth century. Traditional Lockean liberals had grounded property in the ownership of one's self. From that, they argued, flowed liberty to act as one wished and to own that which one created or wrested from nature by one's own labor. The resulting scheme of ownership was embodied in the private, common-law regime of property and contract rights. The beauty of that regime, liberals argued, was that it protected the natural rights of owners without limiting the natural liberty of others. Property created nonoverlapping, vertical relationships between individuals and the things that they owned. Contracts, in turn, created voluntary, horizontal relationships between otherwise independent jural equals. As a result, both sets of relationships were private—that is to say, the state was not a party to them except as enforcer—and neither set imposed dominion over other people.[126] Into this paradise of freedom, coercive force was thought to insinuate itself in only one of two forms: force or fraud by other individuals, transgressing the natural, consensual boundaries of property or liberty; and prohibitions or edicts by the government.[127] The former, it was argued, was severely constrained by the criminal and tort laws, which proscribed such "violent interference" by private individuals except in the case of clear justification or excuse.[128] That circumstance left only the latter, giving the government close to a monopoly on the legitimate exercise of coercive force.

That traditional liberal view, progressives argued, fundamentally misconceived the nature of property. Property was not a vertical relationship of people over things, as theorists like Carver had imagined, transfixed by the picture of property as a thing that one physically possessed. Rather, property was a horizontal relationship between people, made up of a complicated network of reciprocal rights and duties with regard to particular economic interests. As a result, property rights bestowed on owners not merely power over inanimate objects but also power over others with respect to those objects. Among social theorists, the transformation in the conception of property arguably began with the early socialists' recharacterization of property as power. It was carried forward and generalized by Lester Ward, Hobhouse, Dewey, and other late nineteenth- and early twentieth-century apostles of social interdependence, who insisted (in Hobhouse's words) that "[t]here is no true opposition between liberty as such and control as such, for every liberty rests on a corresponding act of control."[129] As a result, as Hobhouse stated in language very close to Hale's, the question posed by social control was "not of increasing or diminishing, but of reorganizing, restraints."[130] Among legal theorists, the transformation of property had an even older provenance, in the observations of Jeremy Bentham and others that all rights, and in particular property rights, abrogate the liberty of others.[131]

Hale's analysis, however, had more immediate roots in the early, functionalist strand of Legal Realism developed by Holmes, Wesley Hohfeld, Arthur Corbin, and others. In "Privilege, Malice, and Intent" and other brilliant, anticonceptualist writings, Holmes deconstructed abstract legal concepts like the right to compete, or the privilege to abstain from contracting with others, into the complicated functional relations that they embodied.[132] In two important articles published in 1913 and 1917, Yale law professor Wesley Hohfeld formalized Holmes's basic insight, offering a more systematic and precise vocabulary to describe the range of functional relations created by legal rights.[133] What are loosely referred to as "rights," Hohfeld argued, in fact comprehend a number of quite distinct legal capacities or entitlements conferred on the holders. Hohfeld categorized those capacities into four groups: "right," "privilege," "power," and "immunity." In the Hohfeldian scheme, "right" denoted a "claim" that the holder had to make others act in particular ways with respect to the rights-holder. "Privilege" denoted the liberty to act in a certain manner without being interfered with by others. "Power" denoted the ability to alter one's own or others' legal capacities. "Immunity" denoted freedom from having one's own legal capacities changed by others. In each case, Hohfeld argued, the scope of the capacity is defined by a correlative incapacity put on the relevant universe of non–rights-holders. Hohfeld denoted those correlative incapacities as "duty," "no-right," "liability," and "disability," respectively.

Hohfeld's complicated typology of jural correlatives potentially applied to the entire universe of legal relations. In his original article, Hohfeld himself had suggested a wide range of applications in the areas of trusts, property, and contracts. Arthur Corbin, an early Hohfeld fan, picked up on Hohfeld's suggestions to reconceptualize the meaning of "offer" and "acceptance" in the area of contracts.[134] Walter Wheeler Cook, another early fan, had used Hohfeld's typology most famously to redescribe the nature of labor relations in the wake of the *Hitchman* case, as well as (more obscurely) the nature of equity jurisdiction and the alienability of contracts, debts, and other choses in action.[135] But its most important application was in the area of traditional property rights. Take the typical landowner, said Hohfeld, who holds a fee simple in a tract of land (call it Blackacre). What we are accustomed to think of as a unitary right is, in fact, a complicated bundle of rights, privileges, powers, and immunities. Thus the landowner has the right to insure that others (the "duty-holders") do not enter onto Blackacre, do not cause physical harm to it, and so on. The owner also has an indefinite number of privileges with respect to Blackacre, including the privilege to enter onto it or to harm it within certain limits set by public policy, without having others (the no–rights-holders) restrict him. So also the owner has the power to alienate some or all of his legal interests in Blackacre to another—for example, by giving someone a life estate in the property or a license to use it for certain purposes, or by selling the fee simple outright. Finally, the owner has a number of immunities from others' attempts to alter his legal capacities with respect to Blackacre without his consent—for example, immunity from having others alienate his interests to a third party, or from extinguishing his own privileges with respect to Blackacre.[136] What that situation meant was that a property right did not, as the classical system had assumed, establish a vertical relationship between people and things. It established instead a series of horizontal relationships among people, in which each capacity in the owner's entire bundle of rights imposed a correlative incapacity on nonowners. Arthur Corbin summed up the Hohfeldian revolution with a certain undigested enthusiasm in this way: "Our concept of property has shifted; . . . . 'Property' has ceased to describe any *res*, or object of sense, at all, and has become merely a bundle of legal relations—rights, powers, privileges, and immunities."[137]

Despite the air of musty scholasticism that hung about Hohfeld's scheme, many of the Realists were quick to see its seditious implications.[138] First, Hohfeld's logical positivist method implicitly reoriented legal thought away from abstract, free-floating notions of entitlement and toward the sort of pragmatic, consequentialist view of law that was naturally more congenial to the Realists' philosophical and political ends.[139] Second, by deconstructing supposedly unitary concepts like "property" and "liberty" into their component, functional relations, his method implicitly underscored how intricate and changeable those relations were, thus undermining the "givenness" of whatever set of relations happened to exist at any time.[140]

Third, and of more immediate relevance here, the Hohfeldian scheme made clear that no existing legal entitlement had any formal meaning except in relation to reciprocal legal infirmities placed on others. As Holmes had noted, even the prohibition on battery, the most apparently nonredistributive of all legal rules, sacrificed the would-be batterer's "gratification of ill-will" to the other side's right to be free from pain.[141] Hohfeld's scheme showed that the same was true of all legal rights, in particular the "right" to exclude the world at large from use of one's property, and the "power" to waive that right on payment of the sum demanded. That reality meant that the existing scheme of private property and contract rights itself constrained the liberty of others, and any attempt by the state to rearrange rights merely substituted one form of constraint for another. Bentham, Dewey, Hobhouse, and others had made that point as a functional matter. Hohfeld's analysis gave to the Legal Realists a vocabulary to show that it was necessarily true as a formal matter as well. Finally, Hohfeld's analysis underscored a point, again anticipated by both the socialists and the Benthamites, that it was the state itself, through its complex scheme of property and contract rules, that created the horizontal relationships among individuals embodied in those rules.

John Commons, reading Hohfeld through his own peculiar, rose-tinted lenses, concluded that the lesson of Hohfeld was that the basic unit of all economic and political activity is not "a mass of disconnected individuals" but "a set of relations, habits, transactions, or customs of associated individuals." In short, Hohfeldianism overthrew the "anarchistic" view of economic life as a collection of individual wills, in favor of economic life as "a going concern."[142] Hale drew a less romanticized moral from it. If, as laissez-faire advocates seemed to believe, "liberty" is the absence of government constraint, Hohfeld's analysis showed that the existing regime of private property rights could not be reconciled with liberty, since the essence of property rights was to impose (through the agency of the state) correlative restraints on the universe of nonowners.[143]

Redescribing the so-called "voluntary" labor contract from that perspective, Hale argued, the typical choice to work for wages should be understood as follows.[144] A man (our hero) must eat to survive. "While there is no law against eating in the abstract, there is a law which forbids him to eat any of the food which actually exists in the community—and that is the law of property." Owners have the power (in Hohfeldian terms) to remove our hero's legal duty not to consume their food, but the privilege not to do so unless he agrees to their terms. Those terms are likely to include the payment of money, equal to the market price of the food. Alternatively, our hero can try to produce his own food. Again, there is no law to prevent him from doing so in the abstract. But "in every settled country there is a law which forbids him to cultivate any particular piece of ground unless he happens to be an owner. This again is the law of property." Again, owners of property have the power to lift that legal duty, but again they are unlikely to agree to do so, unless he agrees to pay the market price of the land.

Assuming that our hero has some money, he can obtain either the food he needs or the land on which to produce it, provided that he is willing to part with his money, under the (legal) threat by the owners to withhold their food or land unless he agrees to do so. Suppose, however, that he has no money to acquire food or land on which to produce it. He could try to make money by producing and selling goods. But he is unlikely to be able to produce things in quantities sufficient to keep him alive "except with the use of elaborate mechanical equipment. To use any such equipment is unlawful, except on the owner's terms." If our hero lacks the money to persuade the owner to sell him the equipment, he will usually be able to obtain access to it only by becoming an employee of the owner, on terms enforced by the owner by threatening not to employ our hero at all unless he consents to them. Those terms not only will require that our hero relinquish his constitutional right to remain idle. They also will usually require that our hero abandon any claim of title in the products that he produced, accepting as recompense whatever hourly wage the employer will consent to pay. "In short," concluded Hale, "if he be not a property owner, the law which forbids him to produce with any of the existing equipment, and the law which forbids him to eat any of the existing food, will be lifted *only* in case he works for an employer. It is the law of property which coerces people into working for factory owners . . ."[145]

Just as the law of property secures workers' labor for the owners of factories by coercive force, so also, Hale argued, it secures the revenue that such owners derive from their customers by coercive force. "The law compels people to desist from consuming the products of the owner's plant, except with his consent; and he will not consent unless they pay him money." Like our hero from whom money is demanded for food or the means to produce it, the owner's customers "can escape, of course, by going without the product. But that does not prevent the payment from being compulsory, any more than it prevents the payment of a government tax on tobacco from being compulsory. The penalty for failure to pay, in each case, may be light, but it is sufficient to compel obedience in all those cases where the consumer buys rather than going without."[146]

The summary of Hale's argument up until this point focuses only on the coercive power of capitalists to compel exchanges on terms that they will consent to, on threat of withholding their capital or products of their capital from those who require them. But, as Hale took pains to point out, that describes only one half of the exchange. In each case, the other side—labor or consumers—brings a counterforce of its own to bear on the capitalist, under a legally sanctioned threat to withhold needed services or money. In the case of the wage contract, the capitalist, to make productive use of his capital equipment, must acquire workers. The laws that give people ownership of themselves—that is, laws against slavery—give each would-be worker the right to refuse to work, and also the power to waive that right upon receipt of a satisfactory wage. Thus, the laborer "induces the employer to pay him his wage by *threatening* not to work for him, and then not carrying out his threat."[147] So it is also with the consumer, who has the law-given right to withhold needed money from the producer, as well as the power to waive that right upon receipt of the goods in return.[148]

Thus, Hale concluded, although the particular rights and duties created by a contract are "created at the initiative of private individuals,"[149] without any explicit requirement of law that they do so, their "freedom to decline to do so is nonetheless circumscribed."[150] Each party "makes the contract in order to acquire certain legal rights he does not now possess, or to escape certain legal obligations with which he is now burdened. Were his liberty not restricted by these obligations imposed on him by the law and enforced in the ordinary courts, he might never submit himself to the new obligations of the contract. Thus in a sense each party to the contract, by the threat to call on the government to enforce his power over the liberty of the other, *imposes* the terms of the contract on the other."[151]

In redescribing the market as a network of mutual coercion, Hale was making a formal, or structural, point. As he emphasized repeatedly, his analysis implied nothing about the *extent* of coercive force exerted by a particular threat to withhold. That was an empirical question, the answer to which depended, as Hale put it, upon the strength of one's "desire to escape a more disagreeable alternative."[152] In the language of economics, it depended on the marginal (surplus) value added by the goods or services offered over the next best, socially available, alternative.[153] Take a typical sale of goods, said Hale—the purchase of a bag of peanuts for five cents. "[T]he consequence of abstaining from a particular bag of peanuts would be, either to go without such nutriment altogether for the time being, or to conform to the terms of some other owner. Presumably at least one of these consequences [actually, both] would be as bad as the loss of the five cents, or the purchaser would not buy; but one of them, at least, would be no worse [at least for the marginal consumer], or the owner would be able to compel payment of more."[154] So also, in the case of labor, the coercive force exerted by an individual laborer taken alone would be limited to his marginal productivity—that is, "the extent to which production would fall off if [he] left and if the marginal laborer were put in his place—by the extent, that is, to which the execution of his threat of withdrawal would damage the employer."[155] Commons, seizing on the same point, argued that the basic unit of every market transaction was not two parties but five—buyer (B), seller (S), next best buyer (B'), next best seller (S'), and the state, devising the working rules (including property rights and rules of contracting) according to which any disputes will be resolved.[156]

The preceding analysis focused only on the incremental coercive power possessed by a given individual in the market. In the paradigmatic competitive market, where perfect substitutes were readily available at marginal cost, such incremental power was zero: no seller could coerce a price in excess of market price, and no buyer could coerce a price that was lower. But the same analysis could be applied to measure the coercive power possessed by buyers or sellers *as a class,* a perspective obviously more congenial to the political concerns of the progressives and socialists.[157] From that perspective, whether buyers and sellers exert coercive force on each other depends on how disagreeable the other side would find life absent the class of contracts at issue—or, to put it in the affirmative, on the surplus such contracts generated for each side. At one extreme, Hale noted, one could imagine situations in which constraints imposed on one's rights to use others' property or labor were painless, because they thwarted no desire—for example, one's duty to go without a would-be employer's wages of a dollar a day when one owned enough property to pay for all one desired.[158] At the other extreme, where the rights held by one side were vastly superior in strategic importance to those possessed by the other, "the other party may in effect be compelled to submit by contract to almost any terms imposed by the stronger party." Consider, for example, Hale argued, a propertyless inhabitant in a company town without even the money for a railway ticket out, whose only option to gain food, lodging, and other necessities was a bargain with the company: "Under such extreme circumstances it is literally true that the company can make rules which the inhabitants will be forced by the governmental authorities to obey . . ."[159] At such an extreme, Hale argued, threatening to "withhold a mess of potage from a hungry Esau . . . [may] prove[ ] no less effective than threatening to shoot [him] as a means of relieving him of his birthright."[160]

Hale's argument also said nothing about the desirability of coercion. By redescribing coercion as the background constraint on available choices, Hale had shown coercion to be ubiquitous and, to a large extent, inevitable. As Hale declared in his review of Mortimer Adler's *The Idea of Freedom*, contrary to Adler's mistaken belief that with respect to the enactment of a particular wish, people generally "enjoy complete freedom or [are] completely deprived of it,"[161] in fact such freedom is always constrained to some extent. In economic matters in particular, Hale argued, absolute freedom is "out of the question. The most we can attain is a relative degree of freedom, with the restrictions on each person's liberty as tolerable as we can make them."[162] In particular, Hale's argument said nothing about the desirability of the coercive force exerted by private property rights. The point is worth stressing, since Hale was so frequently misunderstood on this point by his own contemporaries and later scholars. In many of his writings, Hale acknowledged the necessity of private property, as well as the importance of price as a "method of regulating consumption" and rewarding the producer for the costs of production.[163] He acknowledged as well that the inequality in rewards that results from most private property regimes, reflecting inequality in productivity, might well lead to increased material freedom for all members of society, and that in many cases the benefits of that increased wealth would outweigh the coercion entailed in individual bargains.[164]

What Hale's argument was meant to suggest, however, was that the choice among competing claims of freedom could not be resolved by constitutional abstractions like a "right to liberty."[165] Decisions like *Coppage*, Hale insisted, illustrated the incoherence of such attempts. The Court frequently made the baffling assumption, said Hale, "that a statute which strikes down an impediment to a vital liberty, by restricting the less vital liberty to maintain that impediment, is itself a curtailment of liberty in general."[166] Echoing Holmes's frequent refrain, Hale argued that the choice had to be made as a matter of policy—that is, as a conscious decision to tolerate some forms of coercion but not others for the good of society. One could make that choice by any number of criteria: minimizing overall coerciveness; eliminating the most extreme forms of coercion; or permitting those forms of coercion that were exerted by rights that we wished to privilege because they created an important incentive for productivity, or because we deemed the rights-holders' claims particularly meritorious. As discussed later, Hale had his own thoughts on what criteria should be used. But his central point was a simpler one: the choice was a quintessential legislative choice. Instead of acknowledging that fact forthrightly and retreating from the field, Hale argued, courts had smuggled their own unarticulated notions of policy in the back door, by inconsistently discovering coercion-in-fact as it suited their ends. The resulting scheme of privileged liberties, Hale charged, might be logically incoherent, but it was not politically incoherent. Courts by and large invoked the constitutional right of liberty "to protect the more powerful against legislative attempts to limit *their* power to restrict the liberty of those less richly endowed by the law with property rights."[167]

Hale's argument, which appeared to put all sources of coercion on an equal footing, was intensely annoying to many of his contemporaries. As Carver protested to Hale, "[I]n describing the ordinary wage contract or the ordinary contract of purchase and sale [as coercive] . . . [t]he opponents of liberalism have been deliberately trying to confuse the issue . . . in order to make it appear that the extension of government authority does not involve an increase of coercion, but at most it involves a change in the form of coercion."[168] Benjamin Cardozo, sounding a less sectarian note, protested nonetheless against the argument that any motive or temptation for action was coercive: "The outcome of such a doctrine is the acceptance of a philosophical determinism by which choice becomes impossible."[169] It remains annoying to many—on philosophical if not political grounds—who continue to intuit a difference between, for example, demanding $1,000 to pull a drowning man out of a pool and demanding $1,000 to sell him a Picasso drawing once he is up on dry ground.

Hale did not mean to suggest that there was no difference. But he wished to get others to see that it was no easy thing to articulate what the relevant difference was, and that most proffered explanations failed to do the job. That cautionary note retains force some sixty years later, when debates about the meaning of coercion still rage in legal and philosophical circles. Hale's attacks on then conventional theories of coercion, once he went beyond his critique of the market as a sphere of freedom, never amounted to a serious, sustained philosophical treatment of the problem. But many of his observations still shed light on current debates over the nature of coercion. Chief among these observations was his repeated insistence on what is referred to in contemporary legal and philosophical circles as the "baseline" problem—the fact that finding an offer coercive is always parasitic on a prior, implicit determination either that the coerced party had a baseline entitlement to be free of such pressure or that the coercer had a baseline duty not to impose it. Talk of coercion as a freestanding moral problem thus merely distracted attention from what was the real issue: what baseline entitlements and duties do we wish, as a moral or legal matter, to establish? In addition, Hale's observations help illuminate what Hale himself thought to be one promising baseline: that the coercer had no right to profit unjustly from exploiting the coerced party's constrained set of choices. For all these reasons, Hale's observations repay attention.

Separating the Sheep from the Goats

Threat versus Promise. The distinction most often suggested in Hale's time, as well as in contemporary philosophical debates, between offers that were coercive and those that were not, was that the former threatened to worsen someone's situation, whereas the latter promised to improve it. As Justice Harlan Fiske Stone said, rejecting the argument that federal payments to farmers to restrict output were coercive, "Threat of loss, not hope of gain, is the essence of economic coercion."[170] Elaborating that argument, in rejecting the claim that the federal government was coercive in conditioning its grants-in-aid to a state on the state's compliance with various federal standards, Justice George Sutherland thus opined: "[T]he statute imposes no obligation but simply extends an option which the State is free to accept or reject . . . Nor does the statute require the States to do or yield anything. If Congress enacted it with the ulterior purpose of tempting them to yield, that purpose may be effectively frustrated by the simple expedient of not yielding."[171] On the other side, courts defended the prohibition on blackmail and other typical forms of common-law duress on the ground that such conduct impermissibly threatened loss as a way of extracting payment: "A person has no right to demand money . . . as a price of abstaining from inflicting unpleasant consequences upon a man."[172]

Whatever other relevance the distinction might have, Hale argued, it did not (as proponents seemed to think) help distinguish conduct that was coercive-in-fact from that which was not. In either case—whether one is paying to improve one's position or to prevent it from being worsened—one has at least a nominal choice: the choice to forgo the gain in the former case, and to bear the loss in the latter.[173] At the same time, in either case the decision to accept the "offer" is coerced, in the sense that it is made only because it is the lesser of evils in the universe of available choices. There is no a priori reason to think that the coercion operating in the latter case is stronger than that operating in the former. Consider, for example, Hale argued, the state's imposing a $1,000 tax on people doing X, versus paying people a $1,000 bribe not to do X. In both cases, the choice not to do X is coerced by the state, in the sense that people stand to be $1,000 poorer if they do X than if they do not. If people systematically experience the tax as more coercive than the bribe, it is only because they anticipated having to bear the greater evil in the second case (going without the state's bribe) and not in the first (paying the tax). Indeed, in many situations, action taken to insure a prospective gain could be occasioned by fear rather than hope if the gain "is essential to avert hardship, or even disappointment." Conversely, a "threatened loss of money may merely diminish a hope of enjoying it, without inspiring fear." The answer in any particular case, Hale argued, "would seem to depend on psychological factors which vary from case to case."[174]

More plausibly, Hale suggested, the distinction was meant to identify not all behavior that was coercive-in-fact, but that subset of such behavior that was morally objectionable. Here, too, however, Hale continued, there were difficulties. First, the distinction between threat of loss and promise of gain was ambiguous, with the characterization of many "offers" depending upon mere verbalisms. For example, at first blush, all contracts for the sale of goods or services seem to be on the right (noncoercive) side of the line, since the seller extracts money in exchange for the promise to improve the position of the buyer by providing needed goods or services. However, by redescribing the money paid as the "price [demanded for] abstaining from inflicting the unpleasant consequences of doing without the property or services," one could convert the offer to sell into a threat of harm, and thus appear to make "any sale of property, or any acceptance of a salary or wage, a felony."[175] Some courts, Hale suggested, tried to avoid that clearly unintended result by further stipulating that by threat of harm, they meant a threat to inflict harm by an affirmative act rather than by a mere failure to act.[176] But even with that qualification, Hale argued, the distinction failed to explain the outcome in numerous cases. We permit many offers that clearly constitute threats to inflict affirmative harm unless paid—for example, a landowner who demands payment from the neighbors *not* to build a house on the landowner's own property that would be an eyesore to the neighbors; a tradesperson who demands payment from would-be competitors *not* to open up a shop in their locality.[177] On the other side, we forbid many offers that clearly constitute promises to do an affirmative good if paid—for example, the promise to perform those acts that one is already required to perform under a contract.[178]

In fact, Hale argued, a more accurate, though still unsatisfactory, account of what distinguished "coercive" from "noncoercive" offers in the preceding cases was that for those offers deemed "coercive," the offeror had a preexisting legal or moral duty to do the thing (acting or abstaining) that the offeror now offered to do only upon payment of money.[179] Even that distinction did not explain the outcome in all cases. Holmes may have been correct in his famous assertion that "As a general rule, . . . what you may do in a certain event you may threaten to do, that is, give warning of your intention to do in that event, and thus allow the other person the chance of avoiding the consequences."[180] But the rule was subject to numerous exceptions. For example, the fact that someone who had a de facto monopoly on necessary goods could refuse to sell the goods entirely did not mean that she could threaten not to sell them except on payment of an extortionate amount. Another example dear to Hale was the arcane legal doctrine known as "unconstitutional conditions," which held that under certain circumstances, the government's offer to grant certain privileges to which the recipient had no preexisting legal right, on condition that the recipient waive other legal rights, was unconstitutionally coercive.[181]

More important, Hale argued, was that the definition was circular, like the pronouncement (to use Felix Cohen's waggish example swiped from Molière) that opium "puts men asleep *because* it contains a dormitive principle."[182] Calling an offer "coercive" follows automatically from one's prior conclusion that such a threat was legally or morally unjustifiable—that is to say, from a decision that the offeree was entitled to be free of such pressure and that the offeror had a duty not to impose it. It does not help resolve which threats *are* unjustifiable—that is, what baseline entitlements to bestow to begin with. As Hale described the circularity that such an inquiry inevitably seemed to invite, "One is likely . . . to have a vague feeling against the use of a particular form of economic pressure, then to discover that this pressure is 'coercive'—forgetting that coerciveness is not a ground for condemnation except when used in the sense of influence under pain of doing a morally [or legally] unjustifiable act. And obviously to pronounce the pressure unjustified because it is an unjustified pressure is to reason in a circle."[183]

Necessity of the Offeree. Alternatively, some suggested, what made an offer coercive was that the offeree was not in a position to refuse it. Carver, for one, had urged that distinction on Hale in responding to Hale's criticism of him in "Coercion and Distribution." Take the classic example of a coercive offer, said Carver: a passerby's offer to save a drowning man, in exchange for a substantial amount of money. What made the offer coercive in most people's minds, Carver argued, and distinguished it from Hale's preposterous examples of normal market transactions, was that the drowning man's necessity made the offer irresistible.[184] But, Hale responded, the irresistibility of the offer explained neither when courts intervened nor how. Necessity might be equally present in a so-called "normal" market transaction. "The services of a wrecking truck or a salvaging vessel or, for that matter, of a physician, are required only because of necessities; but not every contract to pay for such services will be annulled." The only thing that distinguished the drowning man's case from the others was that in the former case, the offeror had used that necessity to extort a price for his services in excess of what the courts deemed "fair."[185] That the remedy in such cases usually took the form of forcing the offeror, ex post, to disgorge excess profits supported Hale's view that it was the excessive price extracted by the offeror and not the necessity of the offeree that offended the courts. Thus, said Hale, "The test of validity is not compulsion (which is always present), but the quantitative reasonableness of the terms."[186] As Walter Rauschenbusch described that intuition, commenting on a more famous necessitous offer: "When Jacob made his tired and hungry brother Esau sell his birthright to get some of the pottage that stood steaming and savory before him, he charged what the market could bear, but he did a shabby thing. It is not to the credit of those who have taught us christian conduct that our judgment still fumbles about the moral nature of unearned profit."[187]

Subjective Experience of the Offeree. As Hale noted, popular feeling sometimes distinguished between coercive and noncoercive offers on the basis of whether the offeree subjectively experienced the offer as coercive. It is true, Hale acknowledged, that one was likely to feel coerced (for example) by the legal requirement to pay taxes, but not by the practical need to sell one's services for money.[188] But, he argued, that difference in subjective reaction does not indicate the strength of coercive force or whether it is justifiable. The difference often results solely from social convention, which leads one in the second case but not in the first to "accept[ ] the lesser evil gladly, only because [one] takes for granted the alternative of the greater evil."[189]

Motive or Intent of the Offeror.   Popular thought also sometimes distinguished between coercive and noncoercive offers on the basis of the motive or intent of the party making the offer. As Hale summarized the argument, "If I plan to do an act or to leave something undone for no other purpose than to induce payment, that might be conceded to be a 'threat.' But if I plan to do a perfectly lawful act for my own good, or to abstain from working for another because I prefer to do something else with my time, then if I take payment for changing my course of conduct in either respect, it would not be called a threat." Thus, "[i]f a man pays me to keep out of a particular business, or if he pays me to work for him (when I am not legally bound by contract to do so), then it seems absurd to many to say that he paid me under threat of coercion—unless, in the first case, my sole motive in entering the business was to bring him to terms, and unless in the second I preferred working for him to any other occupation of my time, and my sole motive in abstaining was again to bring him to terms."[190]

Courts at least on occasion looked to the offeror's motive in determining whether an offer was lawful.[191] But as with the distinction between a "threat" and a "promise," the offeror's motive was irrelevant to whether the offer was coercive in fact—that is, whether the offeree felt under compulsion to accept it. As Hale noted, criticizing Holmes for confusing intent with effect in distinguishing between a tax and a dollar penalty of equal amounts, the effect on the paying party in the two cases is identical.[192] It was relevant, if at all, only in determining whether such coercion as the offeror applied was justified.[193] On that point, Hale argued, "motive" *should* be weighed seriously—motive not in the customary sense of malice or other affective states motivating the offeror, but meaning whether payment was demanded as recompense for real sacrifice incurred. As discussed later, "motive" in the latter sense was critical to Hale's affirmative proposal for limiting economic coercion along rent theory lines, and persists in contemporary arguments on blackmail and other forms of coercion that seek to distinguish "good" from "bad" demands for payments on the basis of whether they were made in return for "productive" or "unproductive" services.[194] However, the use of the word "coercion" to denote only those demands that were in this specialized sense "unjustified," Hale urged, could only confuse discussion.[195]

The preceding arguments sought to distinguish among the universe of offers on broad descriptive or philosophical grounds. Critics aimed two additional arguments more specifically at Hale's assertion that the economic coercion of the marketplace was *legally* comparable to other forms of coercion, in particular to economic regulation by the state.

Presence of State Action. In the conventional view, the coercive force exerted by private parties to a bargain was purely private in origin—that is, it arose from the strategic advantages possessed by each of the parties. The coercive force exerted by the government through economic regulation was quintessentially public—that is, it rested on state authority, which was backed by state force. That difference did not negate Hale's central point that so-called private coercion was indistinguishable in its *effects* from government regulation. But it arguably made it easier legally to justify courts' intervening in the latter and not the former case.

As noted before, the *Lochner*-era courts found authority to strike down anti–yellow-dog statutes, minimum wage statutes, and other forms of economic regulation in the due process clauses of the Fifth and Fourteenth Amendments of the U.S. Constitution. By their terms, the clauses apply only to acts committed by the federal and state governments respectively, not to acts committed by private parties.[196] This so-called "state action" requirement built into the Fifth and Fourteenth Amendments had two important consequences in Hale's time. First, the requirement was interpreted to mean that *courts* had no authority to interfere with private bargaining power, at least under the due process clauses.[197] That circumstance did not prevent courts from intervening on other, nonconstitutional grounds—for example, because the terms of the bargain were against public policy, or because the bargaining tactics that were employed violated one of the numerous common-law tort prohibitions customarily invoked against labor organizers beginning in the 1890s.[198] But the result was still to give courts greater authority over state than over private actions. How much greater depended in practice upon how broadly courts construed the due process rights guaranteed by the Fifth and Fourteenth Amendments. When the New Deal Court in the late 1930s severely cut back the reach of "due process" to purely procedural guarantees, it eliminated the disparity between state and private action by freeing *both* from substantive constitutional scrutiny. However, when Hale formulated his theory of coercion in the height of the substantive due process analysis of the earlier *Lochner* era, the disparity still was significant.

Second, and of more importance for Hale's purposes, when conjoined to the broad reading of "due process" adopted by the *Lochner*-era courts, the state action requirement limited both *Congress's* and *state legislatures'* authority to regulate private bargaining conduct. The problem typically arose with legislation that curbed the power of one private party over another—most often, as in *Adair* and *Coppage,* the power of employers over employees. The coercive power that the legislation itself exerted over employers in such cases, being state action, was subject to due process requirements; but the coercive power that employers exerted over employees (which power the legislation was intended to counteract) was not. The consequence of that asymmetry, at least in the hands of the *Lochner*-era courts, was to license courts to strike down any economic legislation they might choose, since the unconstitutionality (under a substantive due process analysis) of the governmental coercion that was inherent in such legislation would always trump the legislature's otherwise legitimate desire to control private coercion on policy grounds. In fact, although that line of argument had a potentially limitless reach, it was employed only rarely by the courts to invalidate social legislation. Nevertheless, the few occasions on which it was employed—cases like *Adair* and *Coppage*—were stinging enough to give bite to the "state action" requirement. As a consequence, the "state action" requirement, separating "private" from "state" acts, created a significant obstacle to Hale's program to treat private and state coercion as equivalent for policy purposes.[199]

Hale's response to the "state action" problem was adumbrated earlier. Hale, along with a number of other Realists, argued that the so-called private power exerted by private parties to a bargain was in fact public power, delegated by the state through its laws of property and contract. Such laws granted individual owners (in Hohfeldian terms) the right to withhold property entirely and the privilege to waive that right on condition that others meet the demanded price, and these laws were ultimately backed up by state force. Private contracts were thus, in Hale's memorable phrase, a form of "law-making by unofficial minorities."[200]

Hale's argument, carried to its logical extreme, obliterated the constitutional distinction between public and private acts, thereby rendering the state action requirement irrelevant. The ramifications of that argument are explored in more depth in Chapter 3. As Hale noted, although the argument outraged many of his contemporaries, it was not entirely novel. Courts had held private action to be state action in other cases "where the state's delegation [to private parties] has taken some novel legislative form."[201] If they failed to recognize it here—in everyday exercises of property and contract rights—Hale argued, it was because "[t]he blinding light of familiarity seems to obscure from observation the details of what goes on beneath it."[202]

Hale's expanded view of state action suggested that public and private coercion should be subject to the same due process requirements, but it left open what those requirements ought to be. The answer that one normally would have expected from progressives of Hale's time was that there were no substantive due process requirements at all—a position that would have rendered Hale's broad "state action" argument irrelevant, at least in this context, by taking economic regulation (public or private) entirely out of the scope of the Fifth and Fourteenth Amendments. After all, progressives (including Hale) had fought bitterly to get courts out of the business of reviewing economic legislation under a substantive due process analysis. The last thing in the world that they wanted was to get courts back in that business, by urging an expansive view of substantive due process that applied to public as well as private acts. Hale, however, took a slightly different tack. He embraced in principle a constitutional substantive due process requirement that applied to public *and* private exertions of power; but he argued that courts, out of deference to the legislatures' greater institutional competence, ought to decline jurisdiction over the issue, leaving it to state and federal legislators to vindicate the "spirit" of that requirement through legislation that would maximize liberty interests "taken as a whole": "[Private] power permeates the entire economic system, and attempts to alter it may have repercussions that require more comprehensive treatment than a court is capable of giving; they may also involve conflicts of interest that can be resolved better by legislative means."[203]

It seems fair to suggest that Hale was trying to have it both ways here, in arguing that freedom from undue economic coercion might rise to a constitutional right, but that the final arbiters of that right were the legislatures and not the courts. However doctrinally or politically untenable that solution might have been, it did mean that Hale's broad reading of state action was not irrelevant. His argument that all private action was ultimately state action was addressed simply to the legislatures rather than to the courts, in effect instructing legislators that as they sought to regulate economic relations for the public good, the Constitution obliged them as much to counteract undue pressure from private sources as to avoid undue pressure from public ones.

Jural Equality.   Hale's Hohfeldian reformulation of coercion acknowledged that the coercion exerted by parties to a bargain was at least formally reciprocal. Just as an employer pressured would-be workers to accede to its terms by threatening to withhold access to its capital, so also would-be workers pressured employers to accede to their terms by threatening to withhold their labor. Seizing on the same point, the Court in *Adair, Coppage,* and *Hitchman* argued that the state's only obligation was to treat citizens as formal (jural) equals. The state had done that, the Court argued, in giving each party the right not to enter the contract except on terms that the party assented to, and the obligation, once it was entered into, to "forego, during the time and for the purpose covered by the agreement, any inconsistent exercise of his constitutional rights."[204] As the Court conceded, any bargain—in particular the labor contract—may be asymmetrically coercive in fact. But since the state did not create those inequalities, it had no obligation to remedy them. Moreover, the Court argued, those inequalities are the inevitable outcome of the free operation of any scheme of liberty and property interests.[205] As a result, the state could not remedy the inequalities without creating an (indefensible) jural inequality between unions and employers, by vindicating the freedom of contract and property rights of the former but not the latter.[206]

The argument sounded a familiar note, going back at least to the Kantian case for jural equality, and embraced by Herbert Spencer in vindicating freedom of contract under his "law of equal freedom."[207] Progressives had a number of rejoinders. First and of most importance, they rejected outright the premise on which it rested: that the state's job was to promote formal, as opposed to substantive, fairness. With Anatole France's pronunciamento, they had banished jural equality to that "heaven of legal concepts" that lived in pure ether, blessedly ignorant (as Felix Cohen put it) of "terrestrial human affairs."[208] Second, even assuming some sympathy for the goal of jural equality, the Court itself, they noted, did not consistently pursue it. The majority in *Hitchman*, for example, while defending the employer's choice to withhold jobs from union members as a simple exercise of its freedom of contract, concluded that union members' concerted withholding of labor through a strike was coercion that required courts to intervene to protect employers' constitutional rights.[209] Moreover, as Hale noted, the argument made no sense on its own terms. When the legislature outlawed yellow-dog contracts, it not only prevented employers from buying labor but also prevented employees from selling it, under a contract that waived the employees' right to join a union. As a formal matter, then, *both* sides were equally restricted in their freedom to contract. Indeed, the Court itself had argued as much in *Lochner* and *Adair*, when it struck down labor legislation as an unconstitutional infringement of the liberty of "master and employe[e]" alike.[210] If all that was required of the state was formal evenhandedness, it met that obligation as much in a regime that regulated the terms of contracts as in one that did not. Finally, Hale insisted, it was simply untrue that the so-called unregulated state *was* formally evenhanded in its treatment of citizens. Through its laws facilitating the formation of corporations, land grants, grants of monopoly privileges, and numerous other acts of de jure favoritism, the state had helped create a world in which wealth and power were unequally distributed.[211]

The Positive Theory of Freedom

Hale's primary aim in attacking the conventional notion of coercion was to get courts out of the business of liberty-mongering by showing that the proper distribution of liberty in society could not be resolved by an abstract theory of rights. That still left the question of what the legislature ought to do about the matter, when left to its own devices. Hale, like most other progressives, was somewhat vague on the programmatic implications of promoting freedom *through* law. While skeptical about the conventional distinctions drawn between desirable and undesirable forms of coercion, Hale thought that the two could be distinguished coherently. His own suggestions followed closely his more general proposal for maximizing welfare by redistributing wealth along rent-theory lines. That proposal will be discussed in detail in Chapter 4. In brief, Hale argued that at the first cut, the legislature ought to distribute coercive bargaining power so as to maximize the aggregate positive freedom that people experienced, in the sense of "power to exercise one's will."[212] He assumed that, all other things being equal, that end would be accomplished by equalizing the coercive power to which private parties were subject—an assumption supported only by unplumbed analogy to F. Y. Edgeworth's hypothesis of the declining marginal utility of material wealth.[213] Thus, in the case of labor contracts, if one concurred in the general progressive view that the current balance of bargaining power strongly favored employers over labor, a government policy directed towards maximizing freedom would use its own coercive weapons to tilt the balance of power more towards labor. As Hale noted, the government had a variety of weapons at its disposal to accomplish that end, including bolstering the legal rights of labor unions; restricting the terms of bargain directly (for example, through minimum wage laws); creating greater demand through government plans to bolster employment (for example, public works, government enterprises, and deficit financing); or subjecting the profits of employers to a progressive income tax, the proceeds of which could be redistributed to labor or others whose "bargaining weapons are weak."[214]

That presumptive rule of equality, however, Hale believed, had to bend to two important considerations. First, virtually all progressives acknowledged that individual rights implied *some* entitlement to property produced by one's own labor that could not be overrun by collectivist ends—what Jean Jaurès called the "legitimate and essential" property rights.[215] The difficulty lay in articulating what those rights were. The distinction offered by Hobhouse and others between property for use and property for exchange or power was imprecise. Other formulations offered were little better.[216] Second, all believed that inequalities in bargaining power, and the resulting inequalities in wealth that they produced, must be tolerated to the extent that they functioned as a necessary spur to productivity.

As Hale argued at length in developing his rent-theory version of distributive justice, both objectives would be satisfied if individuals were allowed to benefit from any disproportionate coercive power that they possessed only to the extent of a just reward for the sacrifice their efforts entailed. In fact, Hale argued, precisely that impulse, only half-articulated, explained the actual outcome in the most perplexing coercion cases. The easy coercion cases involved threats to do that which, if done, would be illegal. If a robber, for good and sufficient reasons of policy, may not kill or forcibly seize property, no separate justification is required to explain why he may not threaten either result unless his victim "voluntarily" turns over the property. The hard cases to explain involved threats to act, in which the action itself would not be illegal. Take the classic hard case, the problem of blackmail. People are generally privileged to expose an unpleasant truth about another person. If so, why should it be illegal to threaten to expose that truth unless payment is made? One possible answer to that conundrum, suggested Hale, is that the privilege to disseminate true but damaging information about others is a privilege bestowed "for the protection of the public." Threats to disseminate such information made solely to extract a payoff *not* to disseminate it thus "subvert[] the purpose for which the privilege is accorded," turning a public service into a purely private gain, unnecessary to protect the public interest and unearned through meritorious effort.[217] In short, the problem with blackmail is not the suffering to the blackmailed party (who has no privilege against having painful secrets revealed), but the reward to the blackmailer, which is disproportionate to personal desert.

The intuition that the problem in many so-called "coercion" cases was at root a problem of just price, Hale argued, may also explain the result in cases like Carver's hypothetical of the passerby extorting a substantial sum to save a drowning millionaire. In such cases, unlike blackmail, the right to withhold (or to threaten to withhold) one's services or property from others *was* bestowed for the private benefit of the would-be withholder. When courts nonetheless invalidate the resulting contract because it was extracted under duress, Hale argued, it is because they implicitly conclude that such rights, although meant for private advantage, may not be used to extract "abnormal private advantage."[218] Thus it appears, Hale concluded, "Courts will not always permit a person to realize on the full nuisance value of his rights and privileges, even those rights and privileges which it accords to him for his private benefit."[219]

In the end, then, Hale's prescriptive analysis of coercion was subsumed in his larger program for revising property rights along rent-theory lines. That raises the question whether freedom ultimately had any political importance to Hale and his fellow progressives except as a rhetorical stand-in for material wealth. For those like Holmes and Brandeis, who engaged directly with the problem of freedom of speech and other expressive freedoms, the answer is clearly yes. Their eagerness to have courts defer to legislatures on economic matters while jealously guarding personal liberties posed a recurring dilemma: how to justify as a matter of constitutional doctrine harsher judicial review of legislation that curbed expressive freedoms than that which curbed economic freedoms.[220] But for most of the others, including Hale, the answer may well be no. That is hardly surprising, given the historical context in which they wrote, where the meaning of freedom was battled out in the context of market exchanges, and where what progressives perceived to be extreme inequalities in material well-being overshadowed in their minds all other conditions of freedom. Thus, Hale's excursion into the meaning of freedom and coercion was, in the end, probably largely tactical: an effort to dismantle constitutional obstacles, erected in the name of freedom, to a more egalitarian distribution of wealth. But in the process, Hale offered a clear-eyed analysis of the problem of coercion that endures beyond its historical task.

3

THE EMPTY IDEA OF PROPERTY RIGHTS

Against an unplanned and undirected industrialism, and its imminent hazards to life, liberty, and property, we have no constitutional rights. But thanks to John Locke—or to the thinkers, statesmen, warriors, business men, and jurists who put the punch in his words—we have adequate safeguards against the resort by any state to the kind of stuff the Stuart kings used to pull.

—Walton H. Hamilton, "Property—According to Locke"

By redefining coercion as a constraint on the background universe of available choices, Robert Hale showed it to be ubiquitous in the private sphere of so-called voluntary market relations. That argument bolstered the familiar progressive claim that by intervening in market relations by admittedly coercive means in order to counteract the coercive effects of private power, the state could actually *enlarge* the scope of individual liberty. If so, Hale and others argued, the mere fact that "liberty" interests might be in some sense constitutionally protected posed no obstacle to greater government intervention in the economy. But any legislative proposals along those lines faced two further, serious objections. The first was that inequalities in private coercive power derived from unequal property holdings that were themselves constitutionally protected from usurpation by the state. The second was that some inequality was necessary to preserve incentives to productive activity that benefited nonowners and owners alike.[1]

Like most progressives, and indeed virtually all political philosophers and economists, Hale took the latter, essentially utilitarian, concern quite seriously. In his work on public utilities, he concluded that it argued for protecting property values at least to the extent of a fair return on the owner's actual investment. In his discussions of property incomes in general, Hale routinely acknowledged the need to protect incentive incomes.[2] But it was the former, rights-based objection with which the progressives ultimately had to contend. Hale, paraphrasing Veblen, declared, "[I]n accordance with the theory of 'natural rights,' . . . 'natural liberty' did not include liberty to transgress 'prescriptive rights' of ownership."[3]

As discussed at length in Chapter 2, in responding to the argument that the right to *liberty* barred economic regulation by the state, virtually all progressives felt constrained to embrace the classical ideal of individual liberty, quibbling only as to definition and means. But the English utilitarian tradition traceable to Hume, Bentham, and, more ambiguously, John Stuart Mill, had long since lent intellectual respectability to the position that any natural right to *property* was, as Bentham famously put it, nonsense on stilts.[4] Freed from conventional pressures to adhere to some form of natural property rights theory, many progressives turned their backs on it entirely.

Some found an alternative principle of distributive justice in the (Benthamite) utilitarian premise that wealth should be distributed in accordance with the greatest good of the greatest number. Hume, Bentham, and Mill had concluded that end would best be served by preserving most of the existing scheme of property rights. But later progressives, armed with the Edgeworthian hypothesis that transferring an incremental dollar from richer to poorer would *increase* aggregate well-being, found in utilitarianism all the justification required for a radically egalitarian redistribution of wealth.[5]

Others found justification in the neo-Hegelian idealist view of property as the creature of the state, with private property rights protectible only insofar as they serve the public good. In modern Anglo-American thought, the tradition originates in large part with T. H. Green. Among English progressives, its impress is evident in the work of Leonard Hobhouse, John Hobson, and the other New Liberals, as well as (in a more attenuated form) the Fabian socialists. Among Americans, it is evident in the arguments of Richard Ely, Walter Rauschenbusch, John Commons, John Dewey, and (again in a more attenuated form) Herbert Croly, Walter Lippmann, and others, for the publicness of all private property.[6] Ely tried (no doubt for public relations purposes) to package his version of social property as "conservative," on the ground that it assumed an *ethical* state and a theory of social welfare, with the institution of private property "bent and shaped to meet the exigencies of the social situation."[7] But it was clearly radical in any sense that mattered. If all private property was held in trust for the public, any redistributive scheme was permissible if judged to further the common good. In practice, the radicalism latent in the idealist view of property was tempered by Green's view, shared by his successors, that the public good would be furthered by preserving at least some of the incidents of private ownership, to foster moral self-development or productivity. However, like Bentham's

utilitarian defense of private property, that self-imposed restraint on redistribution was only as durable as the particular conception of the public good
on which it rested. As Hobhouse cautioned, "[W]hatever tenderness we
show to the interests of individuals, remember that we do this, too, in the
name of the common welfare."[8]

The utilitarian and idealist visions of distributive justice were grounded in
radically different philosophical traditions. But, as Hobhouse noted, quoting
Green back-to-back with Mill, the two traditions converged in the belief that
"[a] right is nothing but what the good of society makes it. If it were well
for society as a whole to destroy every right of private property to-morrow,
it would be just to do so . . . If, therefore, any right to any form of property
or freedom no longer serves a good social purpose, it must go."[9] Moreover,
to the considerable extent that what the idealists judged to be good for society
was the distribution of wealth in accordance with the greatest good of its
aggregate members, the two traditions converged on a prescriptive program
as well. Under the circumstances, it is hardly surprising to find the two
strands existing side by side, and indeed frequently impossible to disentangle,
in progressive attacks on the traditional natural rights defense of private
property.

Although one can detect traces of the idealist tradition in Hale's work,[10]
utilitarianism exerted the stronger pull on him. Hale frequently espoused
an unadulterated utilitarianism in his unpublished writings.[11] Moreover, his
program to revise property rights to secure the maximum equality consonant
with maintaining adequate incentives to produce, mirrored the conclusions
that many of his contemporaries reached by a straightforward application of
post-Edgeworthian utilitarianism.[12] But whether from conviction, intellectual
predilections, or a prudential judgment about what would prove most persuasive to the unconverted, Hale's argument for a wholesale revision of
property rights rarely relies on either premise. Instead, it is largely internal
to the natural rights tradition that it critiques, grounded on the Lockean
imperative that people have an exclusive right to that which they have
created with their own labor. The argument, developed in numerous articles
written during Hale's career and in the materials for the Legal Factors course
and predecessor seminars that he taught for over thirty years at Columbia,
had two parts.

The first part was an essentially negative claim. Granting the legitimacy
of a "natural right" to property roughly along Lockean lines, Hale argued,
the existing property arrangements that laissez-faire advocates sought to
protect were not deducible from, and in some instances wholly irreconcilable
with, Lockean premises. This portion of Hale's argument was most closely

allied to the institutionalist and Realist projects that aimed to show that economic life was rooted in law, and that the particular makeup of laws that characterized late nineteenth-century Anglo-American society was histori-cally contingent and normatively indeterminate. In its broad outlines, Hale's argument is squarely within the conventional critique of natural rights emerg-ing from both camps. However, he developed the argument more fully than any of his contemporaries and pushed its implications for legal theory further than anyone since has done. The balance of this chapter will be devoted to exploring the argument and Hale's contribution to it.

There was also, however, an affirmative part to Hale's argument, critical to defending the state's right to regulate the exchange value of property. The laissez-faire argument against such state regulation assumed that if one had appropriated property by just (that is, Lockean) means, one necessarily owned the right to exchange it for whatever the market would bear. But Locke's theory of property rights was at root a theory of sacrifice: that which a person had produced by her own labor became, by virtue of her sacrifice, her own. Rather than supporting an entitlement to whatever price the market might set, Lockean theory (taken seriously) suggested that sellers were enti-tled only to that portion that compensated them for the cost of supplying the goods or services. Any surplus over that cost reflected an economic "rent" that the seller was able to extract from buyers merely because fortuities of natural and social circumstances had produced a market price in excess of the seller's cost. If anyone had "created" that surplus value, it was not the individual producer, but the community at large. In Leonard Hobhouse's words, "[A]ll that is known as 'economic rent' . . . is due not so much to the exertions of any assignable individual as to the general growth and energy of the community."[13]

Whereas classical (Ricardian) economics had predicted that the incidence of rents would be limited to payments for the use of more fertile land, the marginal revolution in economics showed that the Ricardian analysis would hold true for any factor of production (labor, capital goods, and pure capital, as well as land) that was not readily reproducible at constant costs. Spurred by the empirical prediction of marginalism that economic rents were ubiquitous, many progressive economists and political theorists at the turn of the century took the normative implications of a strict Lockeanism very seriously indeed. In England, by the 1890s virtually all economists and political theorists sym-pathetic to socialist goals had abandoned the Marxian version of Lockeanism embedded in a labor theory of value. Many substituted in its place what one might call "rent-theory Lockeanism." Individuals had a moral right only to that portion of income that compensated them for the costs of production;

any unearned surplus above that amount was the moral property of the community, which it could appropriate and redistribute as it chose. By the early 1900s, theory had been translated into practice, as the Liberal Party under Lloyd George's guidance adopted a series of budgets that restructured British fiscal policy along rent-theory lines. In the United States, the influence of rent theory on politics and political thought was more attenuated, although the narrower version of rent theory embodied in Henry George's land tax movement enjoyed popular support for some time. Hale, however, whose work shows clearly the impress of the British progressive-socialist tradition, was a notable exception. The theory of just distribution that underlies his work both in property rights and coercion is best understood as a species of rent theory.

In principle, rent-theory Lockeanism, like the more generous version of individual property rights embraced by conservatives and ascribed—wrongly, in the view of most progressives—to Locke, rests ultimately on individualistic premises. Both assert the moral claim of the individual, as against the state, to what she has created. Rent-theory Lockeanism merely insists on a more exacting separation of the individual and social components in the creation of wealth. As Simon Patten and Edmund James put it in their manifesto for the precursor to the American Economic Association, "The state is a positive factor in material production and has legitimate claims to a share of the product."[14] Elaborating on the argument two years later, James described the state as the great "'silent partner' in every business enterprise," which takes its rightful share through taxation: "To test the relative productivity of the state and the individual, compare the fortune accumulated by Cornelius Vanderbilt in America with what he might have accumulated had he been adopted when an infant by a family of Hottentots."[15]

For at least some of its supporters, most notably Henry George, the revised individualism reflected in rent theory presented a moral imperative, as compelling as utilitarianism or idealism was to their respective adherents. Hale's position is more ambiguous. It is difficult to tell whether he embraced rent theory out of conviction, or merely as a means to enlist the individualistic impulse behind laissez-faire economics in a program that he found more palatable on strictly utilitarian or (less likely) idealist grounds. In the end, it was not necessary for him to choose, as rent-theory Lockeanism led him to the same conclusion that he likely would have reached by either of the other routes. That portion of income that compensated individuals for the sacrifice entailed in the production of wealth ought to be protected from government incursion; any remaining value was the moral property of the community, to be appropriated and redistributed as it saw fit in the interests of the common good. The development of a rent-based theory of just distribution, and Hale's application of it to public utilities regulation, will be explored in Chapters 4 and 5 respectively.

The Naturalness of Natural Rights

The natural rights tradition against which Hale was writing assumed, first of all, the *naturalness* of rights. That is to say, its proponents assumed that the rights of ownership that they sought to protect from the state existed independent of the state.

In law, that assumption translated into the claim that rights of ownership had chronological precedence, and hence moral sovereignty, over any rights of the state.[16] Although the claim was most strongly identified in the nineteenth and early twentieth centuries with Locke, there is reason to doubt that Locke himself would have endorsed it, at least in its pure modern form.[17] For present purposes, however, the answer is immaterial. As the Legal Realist Walton Hamilton stated, the historical importance of Locke to modern thought attaches "not to what [he] meant, but to what was made of his words."[18] What was made of his words by laissez-faire proponents in the past two centuries is clear enough. "Individuals have rights," as the most famous recent exponent of the minimal state has put it.[19] The clear implication of that statement is that, whatever the content of those rights, they existed long before there was a state threatening to transgress them. Maintaining that private property rights were, as J. M. Clark put it, found "ready-made" by the state may not have been necessary to defend their sanctity against state incursions.[20] But at least in the strict contractarian view of state power, it was sufficient. Those rights that individuals possessed prior to the formation of the state and that they did not expressly relinquish as part of the social contract, they necessarily retained.[21]

In political economy, the naturalness of ownership rights translated into the argument, dominant in economic thought at least since Adam Smith, that the laws governing the distribution of wealth had the same natural status usually accorded the laws governing production. That is to say, distribution was the inevitable result of natural economic forces beyond human control. As a result, any moves to alter the existing distribution of wealth were doomed, not (as in the natural rights tradition in law) because they were morally objectionable but because they were physically impossible.

The Realists and institutional economists undertook parallel assaults on the claim of naturalness, the Realists training their sights primarily on natural rights, and the institutionalists primarily on the natural laws of distribution.

In both cases, they argued, the "tendency to find an ideal, super-social and humanly uncontrollable foundation of property"[22] resulted from the failure to recognize the constitutive role of law in the distribution of wealth. Some laissez-faire proponents, they maintained, had suppressed the role of law entirely, treating property rights as self-generating. Others had acknowledged its role in a general way but had treated as inevitable the particular configuration of rights that resulted. Veblen summarized the institutionalist critique with characteristic causticity: "So the institution of ownership is taken into the inquiry not as a factor of growth or an element subject to change, but as one of the primordial and immutable facts of the order of nature . . . Property, ownership, is . . . conceived to be given in its finished (nineteenth-century) scope and force. There is no thought either of a conceivable growth of this definitive nineteenth-century institution out of a cruder past or of any conceivable cumulative change in the scope and force of ownership in the present or future."[23]

Of course, the institutionalists and Realists were hardly the first to note the legal foundations of wealth. Among legal thinkers, Hume and Blackstone had explicitly argued that property rights are the positive creation of the state, and Bentham had long since famously declared this, to a very different end: "Property and law are born and must die together. Before the laws there was no property: take away the laws, all property ceases."[24] Mill, developing Bentham's general observation at some length in the famous Book V ("On the Influence of Government") of *Principles of Political Economy*, detailed the government's pervasive role in constructing even so-called laissez-faire economies. The resulting catalog served as a bible for later generations of progressives, both for its suggestive contents and for the powerful imprimatur of Mill. More significantly for Hale and the other institutionalists, Mill was the first economist to see what Bentham's observation implied for traditional economic theory. It meant that the laws governing the distribution of wealth were distinct from those governing its production, and—unlike the latter—were mutable.[25] Mill accepted the traditional view that the laws governing the production of wealth were determined by technical conditions (including the properties of matter, the state of knowledge and humans' inherent physical and mental makeup), and that hence they partake at any given time of the "character of [immutable] physical laws."[26] But, in a passage that served as a blueprint for the institutionalist argument, he insisted that the same could not be said of laws governing the distribution of property:

> [T]he Distribution of wealth . . . is a matter of human institution solely. The things once there, mankind, individually or collectively, can do with

them as they like. They can place them at the disposal of whomsoever they please, and on whatever terms. Further, in the social state, in every state except total solitude, any disposal whatever of them can only take place by the consent of society, or rather of those who dispose of its active force. Even what a person has produced by his individual toil, unaided by any one, he cannot keep, unless by the permission of society. Not only can society take it from him, but individuals could and would take it from him, if society only remained passive; if it did not either interfere *en masse*, or employ and pay people for the purpose of preventing him from being disturbed in the possession. The distribution of wealth, therefore, depends on the laws and customs of society. The rules by which it is determined are what the opinions and feelings of the ruling portion of the community make them, and are very different in different ages and countries; and might be still more different, if mankind so chose.[27]

The moral of Mill's account could scarcely be clearer: the distribution of wealth, a product of human choice, is subject to human alteration at any time. If only society would channel its energies into choosing wisely, Mill argued, it could advance human welfare far more than through any technical improvements in production: "It is only in the backward countries of the world that increased production is still an important object: in those most advanced, what is economically needed is a better distribution."[28] The institution most ripe for study and change, concluded Mill, the one on which "the economical arrangements of society have always rested," was "the institution of individual property."[29]

But despite its formidable sponsorship, Mill's argument went largely unheeded. As Ely remarked, Mill was the notable exception among English writers, who, since Smith, had treated property as a "'natural' institution . . . natural as to specifics as well as the general proposition of private ownership."[30] Hale, canvasing contemporary economics textbooks, concluded that the typical book ignored entirely the role of property law in economic distribution. Although it might discuss the pros and cons of private ownership of different sorts of things, it typically failed to consider the possibility that ownership could be qualified in any respect.[31] The institutionalists and (to a lesser extent) the Realists undertook to detail Mill's argument with sufficient specificity to make the point irresistible. Their project is self-evident in the titles of their principal works: Ely's *Property and Contract in their Relations to the Distribution of Wealth,* Commons's *Legal Foundations of Capitalism* (a title that Hale said he himself would have used for *Freedom*

Through Law, had Commons not preempted it),[32] and J. M. Clark's *Social Control of Business.*[33] But the materials that Hale developed for the Legal Factors course and predecessor seminars, supplemented by numerous articles, offer the most thorough and subtle presentation of the argument. Ely and Commons lacked not only Hale's legal training but also his (Holmesian) taste and talent for discerning the functional relations buried in the intricacies of legal doctrine. Of the various efforts at detailing the legal conditioning of economic life, J. M. Clark's *Social Control of Business* comes closest in breadth and depth to Hale's analysis, and indeed shows Hale's clear influence.[34]

All income, Hale argued, ultimately rests on legal rights.[35] Far from being "natural" (that is, existing independent of the state), such rights depend on the willingness of the state not only to enforce them but also to articulate them in the first instance. Hale's first point—the state's role in enforcing private rights—obviously has close kinship to the familiar Realist observation that without a remedy, there is no right. The observation was articulated most famously in Holmes's prediction theory of law, which insisted that a legal right is no more than the mere hypostasis of a prediction that if you do X, courts will do Y.[36] For most of the Realists, Holmes's argument served as a homey piece of practical advice to those who would know the precise scope of a right (and its correlative duty) to keep their eyes on the ball. J. M. Clark put it thus, with a lack of sentimentality worthy of Holmes: "[W]hat are rights? Legally, they are those interests which society chooses to protect. Which reduces our proposition to a very simple form: those injuries are forbidden which the law forbids; those interests are protected which the law protects."[37]

Although Hale was hardly indifferent to that positivist moral, the state's role as enforcer had a normative significance for him as well. It meant that all so-called private property rights ultimately derived from public power, in the form of a promise by the state to refrain from interfering with an owner when she exercises any right of ownership, and to force the correlative Hohfeldian duty-holders (all nonowners) to desist from any interference with those rights without the consent of the owner. That fact was lost on extreme advocates of laissez faire, suggested Hale, who failed to see that if the state is precluded from intervening in the economy, it is precluded from enforcing the private property rights that are the root of their cherished laws of "supply and demand": "Heaven save the institution of property from its friends!"[38]

Among Realists, Hale invested the state's role in enforcing rights with unusual normative significance. But he ultimately rested the case for the publicness of private property rights on his second point: the state's role in articulating the scheme of property rights to be enforced. Hale's line of attack began in an important way with Holmes's famous 1897 article, "The Path of the Law." Throwing down the gauntlet to those who failed to see that in interpreting the law, judges actually made it, Holmes wrote, "You always can imply a condition in a contract. But why do you imply it? It is because of some belief as to the practice of the community or of a class, or because of some opinion as to policy, or, in short, because of some attitude of yours upon a matter not capable of exact quantitative measurement, and therefore not capable of founding exact logical conclusions."[39] In the area of contract law, Holmes's point was picked up and carried on in Arthur Corbin's quietly revolutionary articles and treatise, deconstructing contract doctrine into its positivist, component parts,[40] and culminated in the most durable Realist analysis of contracts rights, Lon Fuller and William Perdue's "The Reliance Interest in Contract Damages."[41] Developing the same point in the context of property law, Hale contrasted property rights with physical attributes, ownership of which, he argued, could rightly be said to be a natural endowment, not the creation of positive law. By contrast, a particular car is known to be, say, Jones's car—and hence to impose on all the world except Jones a duty not to use it without Jones's permission—only because the law has so designated it:

> The statement that each person has a duty not to make unauthorized use of another's property, and that each person has a right not to have others make unauthorized use of his property, and a privilege to use it himself, is an incomplete statement of the duties and rights of each. The requirement that I refrain from striking another man's face is a complete statement of my duty in the matter. The law does not have to make a further statement defining what his face is. But the statement that I must not make use of Jones's automobile does not suffice to tell me whether I have a duty, and Jones a right, which will be violated if I drive off without Jones's permission in a particular car which is parked in the street. Before concluding that my act violates Jones's right, the law must furnish another premise in addition to the major premise that I may not use Jones's property without his permission. It must also furnish a minor premise that the particular car in which I drove was Jones's property. It is Jones's property only by virtue of the law, whereas Jones's face which I may have struck is known to be his face without any legal definition.[42]

Hale's argument was more than Austinian positivism reworked. That is, he was insisting not merely that property rights are what the state says they are. He was insisting as well that until the state says something, in its official or unofficial guise, property rights are (conceptually) nothing at all.

In the area of inheritance rights, for example, Hale noted that opponents of an estate tax routinely asserted that the right to transfer property to one's heir was a "natural" incident of ownership, existing apart from the state. "Natural heirs take from their ancestors or relatives, not from the State," declared a 1919 *New York Times* editorial.[43] Not so, said Hale. "It is of course true that heirs take from their ancestors or relatives (or from their testators). But they do so only by virtue of what the state does. If the ancestors or relatives die intestate (that is, without having left a will), it is the state intestacy laws that determines who shall inherit. . . And if the deceased made a will, it is only by virtue of [the] law [of testamentary disposition] that the title passes to those named in the will as beneficiaries."[44] Moreover, as Mill had noted, the state's role is not limited to the binary decision whether or not to delegate to individuals the right to make testamentary dispositions as they wish. In most legal regimes (including those championed by natural rights proponents), the state has qualified that right in a variety of ways, for example, by removing it from those deemed to lack "testamentary capacity," requiring equal divisions among all children, and limiting the testator's ability to place restrictions on future use of the property.[45]

So also, Hale and other progressives argued, the more general right to exclusive possession of any property depends first on the law's decision whether to privatize it at all—that is, whether to create the right to invoke the state's powers to exclude others from its use—and if so, on the limits it sets on that right. In the United States, for example, even a fee simple in property bestows rights that fall far short of complete exclusivity, subordinating the owner's claim to, among other things, the government's superior rights of eminent domain, taxation, public easements, and actions to prevent waste, as well as private rights to have noncompatible uses protected under nuisance law.[46]

But the most hotly contested prerogative of ownership at the turn of the century was not the right to use or transfer one's property by gift or inheritance; rather, it was the right to obtain its market value in a voluntary exchange. Hale's insistence on the positive roots of all property rights was worked out in its most interesting form in this connection.

The laissez-faire defense of an owner's right to the market value of her property raised a preliminary definitional problem. As Hale noted, in one sense it is merely a truism that every voluntary exchange is at market value: "In one sense, the price at which any sale takes place *is* its market value—the value for which the property or service is exchanged on the actual market in which the buyer and seller participate."[47] Conservative economists like (the later) John Bates Clark had embraced a version of that truism as an argument *against* any government intervention in the market, on the ground that because the price of all goods and services automatically reflected their social value, all exchanges were putatively fair.[48] But as Hale saw, the argument could as easily be turned around to justify all such interventions. For example, responding to the argument that minimum wage laws deprive employers of the right to obtain labor at its "just equivalence," Hale argued that if opponents meant by that its equilibrium price, they were by definition wrong, as the minimum wage would automatically become the new equilibrium price.[49]

Presumably, then, what opponents of price regulation had in mind by "just equivalence" was what the equilibrium price would have been in the absence of the offending regulation. But, Hale argued, contrary to customary laissez-faire assumptions, there was no "economic reason for supposing that there [was] something 'sacred' or even 'natural' (i.e., not law-made) in the pre-existing exchange value" of the commodity in question.[50] It too was the product, at least in part, of "persistent and powerful, though subtle and obscure, governmental intervention" in the workings of the market.[51] Hale's argument on this point was part of a larger assault by the institutional economists on the static conception of market equilibrium that dominated orthodox economic thinking in the late nineteenth and early twentieth centuries. Neoclassical economists could treat equilibrium prices as naturally occurring phenomena, they argued, only by taking as given currently existing supply and demand functions, and ignoring entirely the existence of bargaining—the " 'higgling of the market' "—as "a negligible disturbing element not capable or worthy of receiving scientific study."[52] On the supply side, among the questions omitted from that static conception of economics were the effects of government subsidies, taxation, investments in the economic infrastructure, tariffs, and antitrust laws on the supply of various goods;[53] of government investments and usury policies on the interest rate;[54] and of education policies, immigration laws, and labor laws on the supply of labor.[55] On the demand side, it omitted (among other things) any consideration of the effect of income distribution policies,[56] the social and psychological factors conditioning human preferences,[57] and expectations about whether the law would protect various attributes of ownership. On this last point, Hale, Commons, and other progressive economists dwelt on the fundamental economic insight that the exchange value of property is nothing more than the capitalized value of its expected future earnings stream, in part to drive home the social and legal construction of value. If the future earnings stream of any property depended on the precise legal rights that its owner had to exploit it, the value that the market placed on such property at any moment was nothing more than (to press Holmes's bad man of law into service as a bad man of economics) an hypostasis of a prediction about what rights of exploitation future courts and legislatures would recognize, and what risks of erosions in value they would protect against.[58]

Although Hale devoted little space in his published work to the government's pervasive influence on supply and demand, his course materials surveyed the territory in detail.[59] At the extreme, Hale suggested, such influence had an enormous effect on equilibrium prices. One striking example that he used in the Legal Factors materials to illustrate that fact, no doubt hoping that its extremity and strangeness would force a self-consciousness usually lacking with respect to more familiar (indigenous) examples, was the efforts of the governments of South Africa and Kenya indirectly to coerce natives to supply cheap farm and mining labor by dispossessing the natives of their own land, applying head taxes that natives could feasibly pay only by selling their own land and working for others, and prohibiting natives from growing certain crops.[60] Although stopping short of legalized slavery, such measures were scarcely less effective in driving down the market price of labor to close to what slavery would in any event require—a subsistence wage sufficient to keep workers alive.

But Hale's real interest and contribution lay in the legal conditioning of the bargain itself. As J. M. Clark noted in his fine overview of distribution theories from the classical economists through the 1930s, the preoccupations of Hale, Ely, and Commons with "the effects of property and contract in their varying specific forms on production and distribution" and with the coercive elements in the economic system make them the logical successors to the earlier school of "bargain theorists" (Sismondi, Duhring, and Tugan-Baranovsky). In contrast to the static neoclassical view, Clark argued, all of the foregoing "treat the market not as a passive machine whose function is limited to the registering of results rigidly predetermined by the independent forces of supply and demand but as an institution whose behavior may itself have some influence on the result."[61]

At the most general level, Hale, by redefining the market as a system of mutual coercion, hoped to show that the ability to extract *any* price for one's goods or services depended upon the legal right to withhold them from others.[62] As a result, said Hale, it was not possible to defend any "particular income . . . merely because it is the result of 'free bargaining.' The coercion in which it originated is not necessarily less 'artificial' or 'arbitrary' or even 'confiscatory' than that which would take it away in whole or in part. The justification of each income must rest on some other ground than that the recipient has 'produced' it."[63]

Faced with that argument, most economists would have readily conceded that the law's willingness to make property both appropriable and exchangeable was a prerequisite to creating exchange value. But they would have insisted that society faced a simple, binary choice of endowing property with those characteristics or not. As a consequence, while the legal right to withhold or exchange one's property was a necessary precondition to the property's having *any* exchange value at all, it had no effect on what that exchange value would be. In response, Hale refined the argument in a number of articles to show that by altering the particular configuration of property or contract rights (and hence the extent of owners' holdout powers) in bilateral monopoly situations, the state not only could, but routinely did, alter the equilibrium price within limits. Those limits were set at the low end by the cost to the seller, and at the high end by the intrinsic value to the buyer, measured by the highest price that the buyer would pay (the buyer's so-called reservation price).

Among the more interesting examples that Hale examined was the effect of liability rules on market prices in *in*voluntary exchanges. The argument is a familiar one to contemporary legal audiences, in the context of the differential effects of so-called "property" versus "liability" rules of tort damages.[64] Anticipating that analysis in its broad outlines by several decades, Hale argued that the price at which a nonowner is allowed by law to liquidate a property interest without the consent of the owner (i.e., in an involuntary exchange) sets the outer limit on its *voluntary* exchange value. He worked through the analysis in a number of contexts, including eminent domain, trespass claims, and (the one most familiar to contemporary audiences), nuisance claims. All of his analyses repay close reading, but for present purposes two will more than suffice to make the point.

In a 1931 article on valuation of property in cases of taking by eminent domain,[65] Hale argued that the seemingly straightforward task of ascertaining "market value" to be paid to property owners in such cases involved extremely complicated decisions by the government that in effect created the market value to be "ascertained." The problem, said Hale, is that the market price of any piece of property depends (among other things) on the pool of potential buyers, which in turn depends in significant part on the extent of potential buyers' legal rights to circumvent the market. In constructing a hypothetical sales price in eminent domain proceedings, for example, the court must implicitly decide whether to include the taker in the hypothetical market of potential buyers, and if so, whether to endow the taker with the power of eminent domain. If the taker is excluded from the hypothetical market entirely, or (what amounts to the same thing) is included but given the power of taking by eminent domain at a market value determined without regard to the taker's presence in the market, the market-clearing price should reflect none of the property's idiosyncratic value to the taker, but only the value to the owner (in the form of the lower of reproduction costs or intrinsic value).[66] If, on the other hand, the taker is included in the hypothetical market and deprived of the power of eminent domain, the market-clearing price should reflect part or all of that idiosyncratic value. In short, in the former case, the court has not only "abrogat[ed] . . . the right to withhold the property from the government altogether" in upholding the government's right to condemn by eminent domain. It has also "abrogat[ed] . . . the economic advantage which would flow from the existence of that right," by precluding the owner from "obtaining compensation amounting to more than what the market value would be in the absence of the peculiar needs of the condemning party."[67] In doing so, the court has altered the hypothetical equilibrium price of the property.[68]

Thus, concluded Hale, courts seeking a scientific answer to the value of property taken by eminent domain are engaged in a futile search. The "exchange value of the right to own the . . . property [is] ambiguous, depending on the hypothesis chosen under which the . . . property would be exchanged at all."[69] The obvious implication for Hale was that the choice among conceivable hypotheses was a decision of policy, not a determination of fact.[70]

In the portion of the Legal Factors materials dealing with liability rules for trespass and nuisance, Hale extended the analysis to the effect of legal entitlements on equilibrium prices in private exchanges. As a prime example, Hale chose Vincent v. Lake Erie Transp. Co., a case that has continued to fascinate legal scholars, for reasons that Hale was the first to point out.[71] The defendant in Vincent had damaged plaintiff's dock after tying his boat to it during a storm without plaintiff's permission. Finding that necessity justified defendant's mooring his boat to the dock without the owner's consent, the court nonetheless held defendant liable for the loss in value to the dock. As Hale noted, as in the eminent domain cases, this decision not only deprived plaintiff of the absolute right to exclude the defendant but also deprived plaintiff of the right to exact whatever defendant would have paid for the right not to be excluded. "The abrogation of the absolute power to exclude in view of the emergency abrogates likewise the power to take advantage of the shipowner's special needs, just as the power to appropriate property by eminent domain denies the owner the opportunity to take advantage of the taker's special needs."[72]

As Hale noted, the abrogation here—limiting the ex post involuntary "rental" fee to plaintiff's out-of-pocket costs—was actually far more stringent than in eminent domain cases. Were this case treated as "an exceptional instance of a *private* power of eminent domain [with] the shipowner appropriating one night's use of the dock," the dock owner should be entitled to fair rental value of the dock for the night, measured by a market including all potential renters (except the defendant) on the night of the storm in question.[73] The resulting price would therefore permit defendant to capture the transitory monopoly profits created by necessity, but only to the extent of the highest reservation price of would-be renters *not including* the defendant. Suppose, said Hale, that the normal rental fee for the dock was $25; on the night of the storm, a vessel owner other than defendant would have paid $10,000 to dock there, and defendant would have paid $15,000. An unqualified property rule of damages would give plaintiff up to $15,000 (the highest price he could have extracted from defendant had he been left free to bargain). The normal rule in eminent domain cases would give plaintiff $10,000 (the equilibrium price in a market not including defendant). The court in *Vincent* awarded none of these figures, but instead gave plaintiff an amount equal to the loss from damage to his dock. At first blush, any other result seems antithetical to the announced aims of tort law. In theory, in tort cases the owner is entitled only to the cost of what was taken; in contracts and eminent domain cases, to the market value. The two measures would converge, however, if opportunity costs (equal to the price the owner could have charged for what was unilaterally taken) were included in out-of-pocket losses to the owner in tort cases. The question that the courts faced was, in effect, whether opportunity costs ought to be included. As Hale noted (along with later generations of law and economics scholars), the effect on all subsequent *contractual* arrangements of not including opportunity costs in damage calculations is to limit the market price that potential (informed) emergency dockers will be willing to pay ex ante to the amount required to liquidate their tort liability after the fact—the actual damage done to the dock.[74] In short, by making clear that property rights do not include the right to exclude nonowners in emergencies, courts have altered the equilibrium price for negotiating for such property use ex ante.[75]

For Hale, the state's ineluctable role in creating private wealth had two morals. The first, already anticipated in the discussion of coercion, was addressed primarily to the courts. All private rights over property, Hale argued, are merely a delegation of public authority to "unofficial minorities." In Hale's view, the public basis of private rights implied two things for constitutional law. The one that is relevant for present purposes concerned how far the constitution protected private property. Since private individuals hold property as agents of the state, Hale argued, they must do so at the sufferance of the state. As a constitutional matter at least, then, any rearrangement of existing property rights would not constitute a redistribution of natural rights, but simply a different, and conscious, distribution of state-created rights, the "substitution . . . of responsible for irresponsible government."[76] That radically positivist view of rights obviously stands in some tension to any form of Lockean rights, even Hale's strict rent-theory Lockeanism. But the two views are not irreconcilable. Hale's view merely insists that one acknowledge that such "rights" are created by an internal and revocable decision of society about the most just arrangement of its affairs, and that they do not exist as a prior (external) constraint on permissible arrangements.

The other implication for constitutional law concerned the scope of the so-called "state action" doctrine. A number of provisions in the federal constitution protect individuals against certain actions by the state (such as abridgment of speech and unequal protection under the law). Such provisions raise the threshold question, what constitutes "state action"? In 1932, the Supreme Court held in Nixon v. Condon that the decision of the executive committee of the Texas Democratic Party to exclude blacks from voting in the Democratic Primary was a form of state action, and hence it was unconstitutional under the equal protection clause.[77] Three years later, the Court held in Grovey v. Townsend that the same action taken (in the wake of Nixon) by the party convention rather than the executive committee did not constitute state action, because it was merely an act of self-determination by its membership.[78] This was not a distinction likely to recommend itself to anyone, except those happy with victory in any way that they could get it. But Hale went further. Including both cases in the Legal Factors materials, he argued that all exercises of private rights constitute state action, since they rely for their efficacy on either state enforcement or "voluntary" cooperation extracted from others under the implicit threat of state enforcement. As Hale noted with some sarcasm, when the Court decided otherwise, holding (for example) in the 1880s public accommodations cases that proprietors of inns, theaters, and railroads who refused to serve blacks were acting as private parties and hence were not in violation of the Fourteenth Amendment, it "did not inquire how the proprietors would have been able to exclude the negroes without the authority of state law for the exclusion of trespassers."[79]

Hale's radical expansion of the state action doctrine, like his argument for the ubiquity of coercion and the positivist basis of all rights, was not meant to answer what the state should do about any particular act of private discriminatory conduct. It is conceivable, said Hale, that we might conclude that the benefits of private autonomy—for example, in excluding unwanted members from a private club—argue for giving individuals *greater* latitude in exercising their delegated rights than we would extend to the state in exercising those rights directly. But if so, it would not be because there is no discriminatory state action. It would be "because such state discriminatory action as there is, is thought reasonable, being in furtherance of a policy to permit private clubs to choose their own members."[80] In most cases of racial discrimination, Hale believed, no policy at all supported holding individual actors to a less stringent standard than the state itself. Consonant with that belief, he participated in drafting the briefs for Shelley v. Kraemer and companion cases that tested the constitutionality of private covenants restricting homeowners from reselling their homes to racial minorities.[81] He saw his views substantially vindicated in the Court's decision in *Shelley*, which held that the state's enforcement, through the normal judicial process, of private, racially restrictive covenants constituted state action for purposes of the Fourteenth Amendment.[82]

The second moral that Hale drew from the state's role in creating private wealth, this one addressed to both courts and economists, was that the particular arrangement of rights articulated by the state at any point was contingent. For constitutional doctrine, as Hale suggested (being only a little bit cute), such contingency implied that the Court could preserve whatever natural rights might exist while altering the distribution of wealth, simply by reaffirming their formal existence but redefining their content: "There may be sound reasons of economic policy to justify all the economic inequalities that flow from unequal rights. If so, these reasons must be more specific than a broad policy of private property and freedom of contract. With different rules as to the assignment of property rights, particularly by way of inheritance or government grant, we could have just as strict a protection of each person's property rights, and just as little governmental interference with freedom of contract, but a very different pattern of economic relationships."[83] For economics, such contingency implied, as Hale's comments suggest, that the existing distribution of wealth was not the inexorable result of natural economic laws, but rather (as Mill had argued) the product of innumerable changeable decisions of government policy. As Henry Carter Adams had described the matter in an early and influential statement of one of the central tenets of institutional economics, "[T]he industrial weaving of society is largely determined by its legal structure . . . Every change in law means a modification in rights; and when familiar rights are changed, or, what amounts to the same thing, when new duties are imposed, the plane of action for all members of society is adjusted to a new idea."[84]

Given the constitutive role of legal rules in the economic order, the conclusion was unavoidable, argued Hale, that laissez faire does not now exist: "The distribution of wealth at any given time is not exclusively the result of individual efforts under a system of governmental neutrality."[85] Moreover, it never could exist. That, said Hale, was the major point he wished to make in *Freedom Through Law*: "[I]n curbing economic power, government is faced with choosing between different policies as to how wealth should be distributed, and . . . it is making a choice even when it does nothing."[86] That moral absorbed, said Hale, "the next step is to . . . realize that the question of the maintenance or the alteration of our institutions must be discussed on its pragmatic merits, not dismissed on the ground that they are the inevitable outcome of free society."[87]

But none of these points foreclosed the possibility that the particular array of rights that the state had chosen to articulate and enforce mirrored shared notions of a just order.[88] In the area of inheritance rights, for example, when all was said and done, there remained a choice between some form of rule permitting transfers to designated heirs and one requiring transfer to the state. Hale's and others' arguments are unlikely to have dissuaded many from the intuitive sense—egged on by familiarity, if nothing else—that in opting for the former rule, the state was vindicating a natural right in property, not creating a normatively arbitrary one. A similar rejoinder could be made to the predicament of Hale's hypothetical car-owner, "Jones." It is true, as Hale argued, that Jones "owns" his car only by virtue of legal rules that declare him owner. But if those legal rules merely codify a shared moral judgment that Jones ought to be able to call any car his own that he has, for example, purchased with his own money in a voluntary exchange; and further that such ownership ought to carry with it the right to prohibit the world from using the car in any fashion and the right, when he decides to sell it, to collect whatever price the market will bear, why shouldn't the state be regarded as merely the agent for enforcing private, prepolitical, communally shared norms? So, at least, one would expect the laissez-faire argument to go. For Hale, like most progressives, the ultimate question to be faced was therefore the *rightness* of that odd assortment of rights collected by late nineteenth-century society under the rubric of "private property."

The Rightness of Natural Rights

For most laissez-faire proponents at the turn of the century, the argument for private ownership of property rested on what they took to be the self-evident Lockean premise that each person has a right to what he has produced with his own labor. As Mill paraphrased the argument (suggesting for the moment his own assent), "Nothing is implied in property but the right of each to his (or her) own faculties, to what he can produce by them, and to whatever he can get for them in the fair market; together with his right to give this to any other person if he chooses, and the right of that other to receive and enjoy it."[89]

The question was whether one could deduce from that general principle of distributive justice the particular assortment of rights that laissez-faire advocates sought to protect. Economists of the German Historical school had hoped, by demonstrating the changeableness of rights over time, at least to cast doubt on whether one could trace any particular configuration back to universal principles.[90] One detects a similar motivation at work when Mill notes at some length in *Principles* the variability of inheritance rules across countries and over time.[91] Use of the historical approach to destabilize current practice had considerable influence on the first wave of institutionalists, notably Richard Ely, E. R. A. Seligman, and John Commons.[92] But Hale chose instead to attack the claim more directly by showing the formal impossibility of deducing the existing scheme of property rights from Lockean premises. As Mill, an at least sometime-Lockean, put it,

> The laws of property have never yet conformed to the principles on which the justification of private property rests. They have made property of things which never ought to be property, and absolute property where only a qualified property ought to exist . . .
>
> Private property, in every defence made of it, is supposed to mean the guarantee to individuals of the fruits of their own labour and abstinence. . . To judge of the final destination of the institution of property, we must suppose everything rectified which causes the institution to work in a manner opposed to that equitable principle, of proportion between remuneration and exertion, on which in every vindication of it that will bear the light it is assumed to be grounded.[93]

If the alternative were private property as currently constituted (i.e., without such correctives) or communism, said Mill in a burst of rhetorical high flourish, "all the difficulties, great or small, of Communism would be but as dust in the balance."[94] Hale, like most progressives, writing at a time when communism looked both more imminent and less attractive, and public support of it politically more costly, would not have gone that far. But by demonstrating that the existing scheme of property rights failed to conform to a Lockean ideal, Hale could shift onto its proponents the burden of finding some other ground to oppose revising property rights along more egalitarian lines.

Hale's attack on the rightness of private property was part of a larger progressive assault on all differential advantages, including native talents and social opportunities, that produced inequalities in wealth unrelated to individual merit. Mill, for example, took as given the injustice of rewarding individuals based on their talents.[95] Richard Tawney, Frank Taussig, and others insisted with equal fervor that it was unjust to reward individuals on the basis of differential social opportunities.[96] Although Hale was clearly sympathetic to both arguments,[97] his own writings focused on the injustice of privilege that was legally, rather than naturally or socially, bestowed. Hale's argument had three distinct strands. First, he argued, the state had (as Mill put it) made property of things that under a Lockean labor theory of rights ought never to have been property at all. Second, he argued, there were other things over which an owner might have some special claim under a Lockean theory of rights. But the theory frequently offered no basis—at least on the general level on which it was invariably articulated—for choosing between the owner's claim on the one hand, and the conflicting claims of the state or nonowners on the other hand, all of which seemed equally compelling under Lockean principles. Finally, the Lockean rationale didn't seem to explain at all why ownership rights should extend to the right to receive (and retain) the unregulated exchange value of one's property. The first two arguments will occupy the balance of this chapter. The third argument—by far the most important to Hale—will be considered at length in Chapter 4.

Rights as Grants of Special Privilege: Land Grants, Monopolies, and Inheritance

Chief among the things, progressives argued, that ought never to have been property in a true Lockean scheme was the one thing that had given Locke himself so much trouble: the right to land and other natural resources. In a passage that Hale quoted frequently, Mill stated the following: "Nor is the function of the law in defining property itself so simple a thing as may be supposed. It may be imagined, perhaps, that the law has only to declare and protect the right of every one to what he has himself produced, or acquired by the voluntary consent, fairly obtained, of those who produced it. But is there nothing recognized as property except what has been produced? Is there not the earth itself, its forests and waters, and all other natural riches, above and below the surface?"[98] A Lockean labor theory of property rights could justify giving owners the value of the land to the extent of the value added by their own labor. But, progressives argued, it was hard to see how it justified anything beyond that. As Lockean socialists had long argued, it did not self-evidently explain why landlords had a right to rents generated principally by the labor of others. Moreover, it also did not explain why those who own *and* work the land have a right to that portion of its value, realized in the form of higher profit on produce from the land or higher resale value of the land, that reflects the scarcity of land rather than the labor mixed in with it.[99]

It has been suggested that Locke himself found an answer to that dilemma in his essentialist view of property. Believing that in mixing one's own labor with God's land, one created an entirely new object, Locke could believe as well that "there is not a thing which persists through making and altering and from which one would have to subtract the value added by the labourer."[100] But few of Locke's nineteenth-century successors would have embraced that essentialist premise. Indeed, Herbert Spencer offered a scathing attack on it in the first edition of *Social Statics*, arguing that by the same logic, if you wander by a dilapidated and empty house and repair it with the intention of living in it, you have a claim for title as against its rightful owner who shows up after the work is completed. At most, said Spencer, in both cases you should have "an equitable title to compensation . . . [for the] extra worth which your labour has imparted to it."[101]

Assuming that one rejects an essentialist view of property, the state's gift of land to private individuals will be unproblematic under a Lockean scheme, Hale argued, only so long as it is valueless. As Hale noted, a strong interpretation of Locke's proviso that "enough, and as good" of like resources be left for all latecomers would satisfy that condition by requiring that any land given to private owners not be scarce, and hence have no value.[102] But, Hale and others argued, that proviso had long since ceased to be met in land-poor England. By the late nineteenth century, it was met less and less frequently in the more developed portions of the United States as well. As a result, Hale argued, what began (under programs like the Homestead Act) as a gift equally open to all ripened into a de facto grant of special privilege available only to early comers, in the form of economic rents that could be extracted from the community, in exchange for the use or products of owners' (now) scarce property.[103] The principle may be illustrated very simply, said Hale, by considering the case of passengers in a day (railway) coach:

At the beginning of the journey there are less than a quarter as many passengers as there are seats. At that time a rule which permitted each passenger to reverse the back of the seat in front of him and occupy both seats to the exclusion of other passengers would operate equally. Any passenger excluded from the seats I occupy suffers no hardship; he can occupy two other seats by himself. But the same rule obviously causes disproportionate hardship to some the moment the car begins to fill up. If the early arrivals are still permitted to exclude others from the extra seats that are occupied, the latter will either have to stand up, or pay the first passengers for the privilege of occupying even one seat. And such payments, even though no greater than the value of sitting down, would not reward the recipients for any affirmative acts of service, but simply for not forcing the person who pays to stand up.

So also with new immigrants to a community in which the land is already parcelled out to its inhabitants. "Many arguments can be made in favor of the resulting inequalities in legal treatment" between old and new comers, concluded Hale, "but it is difficult to see how it can be denied that they *are* inequalities."[104] Moreover, as is implicit in the preceding, it is difficult to see how any of the arguments could rest on Lockean premises. As Hale argued, the increments in value that accrue to the owner as a result of scarcity no more "reflect the values of any affirmative services performed by them" than does "the reward which the passerby demands for tossing the life preserver to the drowning millionaire."[105]

The attack on private ownership of land had enormous support across a wide spectrum of political groups in the latter part of the nineteenth and early part of the twentieth centuries.[106] To most progressives and socialists, it represented an indefensible usurpation of public wealth for private purposes.[107] To many on the right, private ownership of land—at least absent a strong Lockean proviso—was inconsistent with the demand for "a fair field and no favour" as a precondition for competitive individualism.[108] As Herbert Spencer, a onetime eloquent proponent of that view, averred, the "Law of Equal Freedom" requires that if one person shall have the right to possess land, then all shall have it. Since scarcity will make that impossible, if not now then for future generations, "[the law of equal freedom] . . . does not permit property in land."[109] Hale, summing up what he took to be the devastating implications of government land policy, wrote this in 1922: "The dependence of present economic conditions, in part at least, on the government's past policy concerning the distribution of the public domain, must be obvious. *Laisser-faire* is a utopian dream which never has been and never can be realized."[110]

The task for progressives was to show that there was nothing unique about land—to show, that is, that if private ownership of land was unjustified under Lockean premises, so also was any special privilege conferred by the government unequally on its citizens, in the form of franchises to railroads, public utilities, and other formal monopolies, general corporate franchises, and the like. As John Hobson said, "The slow education which the land question has conducted upon the nature of monopoly and socially created values, was bound in time to bear fruit in a growing recognition of similar elements of monopoly and social values inherent not only in liquor licenses and other legalised monopolies but everywhere throughout the indus-trial[ized] system where competition is impeded or estopped."[111] Thus, Hale argued, any occupation pursued under an express grant of monopoly is "like a public office," and restrictions imposed on the citizen's actions are "no more a restr[ictio]n on his liberty than is a similar require[men]t as to the postmaster."[112] As applied to public utilities, Hale concluded, that fact meant that although the prudence of any given government restriction on utilities might be open to debate, the government's *right* to impose it was not. Any restriction placed on public utilities and railroads merely represented a condition placed on the grant of monopoly privilege.[113]

Although Hale put the point more forcefully than many others, his position was hardly eccentric. Henry Sidgwick, writing in 1891, expressed the growing hostility of old liberals to all forms of monopolies. They were, he declared, "the most deep-seated weakness and most formidable danger of Individual-ism," which created a strong prima facie case for state control.[114] Railroads and public utilities in particular were perceived to exemplify Richard Ely's "social side" of property. As Mill stated, "[A] government which concedes such monopoly unreservedly to a private company does much the same thing as if it allowed an individual or an association to levy any tax they chose, for their own benefit, on all the malt produced in the country, or on all the cotton imported into it."[115] Harleigh Hartman, encapsulating that view in legal terms, argued that utilities hold "but the naked title of a trustee" with respect to land and other privileges granted by the state, and thus "the [title] reverts to the public as *cestui que trust*."[116] Although antimonopolist sentiment remained strong among progressives through the early years of the twentieth century, it was not limited to them. In the United States, the Supreme Court, divided for some sixty years on the extent of the government's power to regulate railroads and utilities, never disputed that that power was greater than with other property, because of the government's role in creating the owners' monopoly power. That view was endorsed across the political spectrum. Many commentators extended the argument beyond the monopoly franchise to *all* state-bestowed privileges that enabled some enterprises to earn greater profits than others. Herbert Knox Smith, for example, the first head of the federal Bureau of Corporations, commenting on the general corporate franchise, reflected widespread, if not universal, sentiment when he declared in 1910 "That some degree of control should be exercised by the Government over corporate operations seems to me entirely justifiable." In establishing corporations, the community gave them "great and peculiar powers and exemptions not granted to the individual." Being therefore responsible for any resulting evil, the community was "entitled to restrain and limit its creatures."[117] As Hobhouse correctly prophesied, once the attack on land monopolies was carried to its logical end, it would "lead the individualist who was in earnest about his principles to march a certain distance on parallel lines with the Socialist enemy."[118]

But Hale pushed the moral of the land question further, arguing that *all* private property rights are, technically speaking, a grant of formal monopoly privilege to use and dispose of the property in question.[119] Where that formal right acquires a functional value through scarcity, he argued, such value is as much a form of government largesse as is the income from an exclusive franchise to operate a public utility or railroad, or indeed from any of the litany of governmental interferences with the free market that Adam Smith, taking a broad view of the problem, had lumped under the designation "monopoly."[120] As Hale well knew, the obvious rejoinder was that, unlike public utilities franchises, land grants or any other direct grant of scarce wealth, the *institution* of private ownership was equally open to all (or in not so remote history, all white males of suitable age). Thus, ownership was at least formally a general right of citizenship, not a special one reserved for a select few. But, as Hale (the Realist) argued, that so-called right was not a right in the technical, Hohfeldian sense: "[W]hat is the nature of a 'right to acquire property?' It is not an enforceable right. One cannot get a decree of conveyance against anyone else on the mere ground that the plaintiff has a 'right to acquire property.' Nor is it a permissive right, a 'privilege' in the Hohfeldian sense; one who goes about acquiring property without regard to anyone else will soon find that he had a duty not to do so." What it means, at most, is that "one may acquire property by consent of a previous owner." To the anticipated rejoinder that "the consent of previous owners is obtainable by all on equal terms—by paying the market price," Hale offered the typical progressive response. It was the substantive and not the formal right that mattered, and only those possessed of sufficient money to pay the market price have the power to obtain that consent. Self-consciously echoing Anatole France's famous statement that the law in its majestic equality forbids the rich and poor alike to sleep under the bridges or on the park benches, Hale elaborated thus:

> One owner, as the result of the entire net-work of restrictions inherent in property rights, gets the benefit only of finding that liberty to use a particular ragged suit of clothes will not be interfered with by the acts of non-owners. Another owner gets the liberty of wandering over a large estate and using a large number of automobiles without the interference of others. A third gets an income from his ownership which frees him from the interferences which the property rights of others would impose . . . The benefits conferred by these rights are not equal in any important sense. They are equal at most in the sense that the manner of their enforcement may be the same, if even this is true.[121]

The point was one that Hale held to strongly throughout his life. In helping draft an amicus brief in Sweatt v. Painter (a school desegregation case predating Brown v. Board of Education), for example, Hale apologetically requested of his coauthors that they qualify the statement that the Fourteenth Amendment establishes absolute "equality before the law," to say equality based on race. "There ain't no such animal" as equality before the law, wrote Hale. "We don't have equal rights. Each of us has his own unique set of property and contract rights, and they aren't equal in any significant sense . . . I'm sorry to be so fussy, but I . . . hate to add vitality to the notion that our 'free enterprise' system is based on legal equality, which would be upset by any form of 'statism.' "[122]

At the extreme to which Hale and other progressives pushed the argument for property as publicly bestowed privilege, its implications were scarcely distinguishable from a thoroughgoing idealist social conception of property. *All* wealth was common wealth held in the "public trust," not (as in the idealist version) because the state had a transcendent moral claim that trumped individual Lockean rights, but because the preconditions of just Lockean appropriation had not been met. Commons embodied that thought in the argument that each person is a "public utility" to the extent that "public powers are employed in his behalf against others."[123] Hale, translating the metaphor into public policy, argued that any forms of taxation or regulation that the government sees fit to impose on individual property rights are merely "conditions attached to a privilege."[124] A tax disproportionately affecting the rich might appear monstrous, said Hale, until one realizes that the tax collected is just " 'change' for the [disproportionately large] property rights given by the government."[125] In an analogy he was particularly fond of, Hale argued that looking only at the payments made to the government and ignoring those received in return would be "like comparing the amount of change handed by a street-car conductor to various passengers, without taking account of how much he has left from their payments after giving them the change. The payment of $4.95 to one and of five cents to another would seem to be unjustified discrimination if we leave out of account the fact that the former had paid the conductor a five-dollar bill and the latter a dime."[126] Similarly, he argued, we should no more assume that property owners have the right to retain money that they have extracted, as agents of government through the lawmaking power delegated to them by the laws of private property, than that IRS agents have the right to retain moneys that they collect on behalf of the government.[127]

The not-too-subtle implication of Hale's analogy—a common one in progressive circles—was that property was a form of theft. Although more cautious in his later writings, Hale drew out that implication explicitly in his early correspondence.[128] Many old-style liberals were willing to follow the progressives' attacks on monopoly privilege pretty far, but not that far. Their resistance is understandable. It is one thing to argue that the state violated Lockean principles when it appropriated unequal holdings for some individuals out of the common pool of assets. It was quite another to argue that it violated those principles whenever it enforced unequal holdings, however they were come by. If one could show that one's disproportionately greater property was the result of disproportionately greater labor, a classical Lockean, at least, would be satisfied.

Finally, there was the problem of inheritance. Of all legal institutions, said Hale (echoing general progressive sentiment), this accounts for the greatest part of economic inequality in American life. "Inequalities which flow from other sources, such as unequal grants of privilege or lands, or the unearned increment of land values, or from unequal abilities, would last only during the lifetimes of those who benefit from them, were it not for the power to perpetuate them through the operation of the law [of inheritance]."[129] Bentham, otherwise inclined to leave the system of property rights more or less intact, made an exception for inheritance, proposing severe limits on the power to dispose of property by will and on the right of succession.[130] Mill, declaring unrestricted inheritance the single most important evil in the private property system, "prevent[ing] all from starting fair in the race," argued for an absolute upper limit on the amount any person should be allowed to inherit, or (alternatively) a highly progressive inheritance tax.[131] In England, such sentiment ultimately led to enactment of a mildly graduated death duty in 1894, made more steeply progressive in 1914.[132] In the United States, the

1884 publication of Charles Bellamy's *The Way Out,* advocating a (Millian) cap on the amount that any individual could receive by inheritance or bequest, launched the progressive attack on inherited wealth. Over the next two decades, most progressive economists and political theorists joined the call for a graduated inheritance tax.[133] By 1902, twenty-six states had enacted some form of inheritance or estate tax; by 1916, the number had grown to forty-two.[134] As Hale began writing in the 1910s, Congress was considering a permanent federal estate tax (finally enacted in 1916). Periodic proposals thereafter to increase rates of the estate tax triggered heated debates well into the 1930s.[135]

Opponents of an inheritance tax had argued that such a tax violated the principle of equality of opportunity, by depriving those who had success-fully exploited those opportunities of the right to transfer their accumulated wealth at death.[136] In response, Hale and other progressives suggested that fairness cut the other way. Whatever the other merits of the institution of inheritance, said Hale, clearly it results in "legal inequalities as between those who inherit much and those who inherit little or no property."[137] It is no answer to the charge of inequality, said Hale with barely contained sarcasm, to say that "everybody had the same right to be born the son of an intestate millionaire."[138] It is equally evident that those inequalities "have nothing whatever to do with inequalities in the services rendered . . . [by] those who inherit"—that is, with anything that would justify the inequality on Lockean grounds.[139]

It is obvious, at least in retrospect, that the two sides to the dispute were not talking about the same thing. Progressive proponents of an inheritance tax (implicitly) treated inheritance as a right that attaches (if at all) to the recipient. From the recipient's perspective, inheritance is property bestowed by a stroke of good fortune, which, like an unequal endowment of native talent, is unearned and hence undeserved. Opponents of an inheritance tax, like Andrew Mellon, viewed inheritance as a right that attached to the giver. As Mill put it, while nonetheless proceeding to support limitations on the power of bequests, "[T]he power of bequeathing is as much a part of the right of property as the power of using; that is not in the fullest sense a person's own, which he is not free to bestow on others."[140] From that perspec-tive, the lucky heirs' failure to do anything to earn their fortunes was irrele-vant. They were merely the fortuitous beneficiaries of their ancestors' choice to bestow justly acquired property on them. But the latter view, progressives suggested, presupposed the very proposition that opponents of an inheri-tance tax had to defend: that ownership of property during one's lifetime entitled one to dispose of it as one chose at death. As J. M. Clark put it,

"The principles of individualism do not dictate any particular system [of inheritance]."[141] One could surely imagine a conception of the individual self under which all of one's legitimate interests (including interests in property) would terminate upon death. Indeed, the Supreme Court took precisely that view in its 1898 decision in Magoun v. Illinois Trust & Savings Bank,[142] upholding a progressive inheritance tax against an equal protection claim on the ground that since inheritance itself was a special privilege conferred by the state, the state was free to condition it as it saw fit.

Viewed together, Hale argued, all these forms of government largesse—land grants, grants of monopoly privilege, and rights of inheritance—took on an enormous significance. They meant that the existing inequalities in wealth were attributable in large part *not* to differences in exertion, but to inequalities in legal status.[143] Not only, then, was an economy free of government intervention an impossibility. The particular form that government intervention had taken, at least in recent history, tended to favor the rich over the poor.[144]

Conflicting Rights of Use

Obviously, though, not all private wealth was the gift of the state, or (with the state's permission) of one's ancestors. As even the most ardent opponent of natural rights would have conceded, some portion of wealth was actually produced by its owner's efforts—although, they would have hastened to add, rarely by those efforts alone. But even with respect to *that* portion of wealth, those defending existing property rights on Lockean grounds faced a further difficulty: how to move from the observation that one had in some general sense produced the property in question, to a specific and unique set of protectible rights with respect to that property. As one contemporary (sometime) natural rights advocate has acknowledged, a "natural" scheme of property rights requires "that we have a very clear sense of what counts as individual rights," and correlatively as transgressions against those rights.[145]

Proponents of laissez faire had traditionally dismissed the problem out of hand, arguing that property rights were self-defining once the state (through criminal, tort, and contract law) protected property against dispossession by force or fraud. Thomas Carver stated the "force" half of the argument in this way: "It cannot be too much emphasized that . . . the essence of property exists instantly, automatically and necessarily, as soon as violence is repressed. Nothing but force or violence either destroys private property or seriously limits it. Practically every limitation that exists or ever can exist in the absolute right of property is due either to the failure of the group to protect the individual against some infringement or to the exercise of force or authority by the group itself to limit the individual's power over his possessions. If we once get this point clearly in mind, and never forget it, it will save us from much confusion of thought later on."[146] Carver may have put the point more strenuously than many; in fact, though, his optimism reflected a widespread assumption that it was a trivial task to define the state's proper role in protecting property rights and enforcing contracts.

In a series of notes and articles, Hale argued that assumption could not survive a close look at the rights of possession and use actually protected under the common law. Such a look revealed two things. First, any workable scheme of property rights had to accommodate conflicting uses of other property (what Hale referred to as horizontal constraints on use), as well as limitations imposed by the state in the name of public welfare (what he called vertical constraints). As a result, such a scheme would have to stop considerably short of the absolute dominion over possessions that the rhetoric of natural rights suggested. Second, Hale suggested, it would be an astonishing coincidence if the odd assortment of lines actually drawn by the common law between conflicting private uses and between private use and public welfare—"the law's more or less blind and haphazard distribution of favors and burdens"[147]—could be deduced from a Lockean ideal. Given the inherent conflicts that the state was forced to resolve, it was equally implausible that any alternative set of lines could be deduced from such an ideal, or indeed from any other strong intuitions of natural justice. As a result, Hale argued, it would inevitably fall to the state to draw the boundaries as it saw fit, in accordance with its notions of the common good. As Hale had suggested in his writings on coercion, that de facto power gave progressives the latitude to effect most of the reforms that they sought within a nominally Lockean scheme. But the franker conclusion to be drawn was that the Lockean ideal had no clear operational meaning at all.

Horizontal Constraints on Use. In the classic formulation of the laissez-faire ideal, each person was assumed to have complete dominion over the things she produced, subject only to compliance with the ancient maxim, *sic utere tuo ut alienum non laedas*—that the property be used so as not to harm others. The function of the ideal minimal state was simply to police that injunction. As Spencer put it in his famous "law of equal freedom," "Every man is free to do that which he wills, provided he infringes not the equal freedom of any other man."[148] Hale described the resulting pattern of income distribution in the ideal laissez-faire state as follows: "Each person's wealth will then consist of (1) what he has himself produced; [and] (2) what other producers have voluntarily transferred to him. In the process of producing and exchanging, [an individual] will be neither hampered or aided by gov[ernmen]t except that others will be forced not to *hinder* him, and he will be forced not to force them to help him and not to conduct his producing at their expense."[149]

As Hale noted, the formulation raises the central question, "what is meant by 'at their expense' "?[150] The typical response, exemplified by Carver's comments mentioned earlier, was that it meant only physical destruction or dispossession of property by force or fraud.[151] Hale argued that limited view of injury might make sense in defining rights to use land and other tangible assets in conditions of relative unscarcity. In such cases, the formal reciprocity of rights and duties described by Hohfeld still held. As a result, any rights granted to the owners formally would impose corollary duties on all nonowners, limiting their liberty interests and (potentially) property rights as well. But in practice, the correlative burdens were largely devoid of bite, since they left nonowners with "enough, and as good" (to use Locke's formulation) to exploit for themselves:

Under simple conditions, practically everybody had, or could easily acquire, a piece of land and the requisite tools and materials with which to produce his livelihood. The rights of other owners did not defeat his interest in living, nor did they compel him to give up his interest in personal independence in order to live. Whatever interest the rights of other owners defeated was not a very vital one. It took special laws of slavery or serfdom to deprive people of independence. While the interests which private property defeated under such conditions were not very vital, the interests were much more vital which they promoted—the interests which owners had in their own independence.[152]

As a result, under such conditions, one could imagine something close to a self-executing rule of property rights that protected owners' "personal unmolested use thereof" against wrongful transgressions.[153] As Hale stated, "The law has only to recognize each family's property right in its farm and its products, and protect that property from interference."[154]

But in a nascent Coasian analysis that took its cue from Holmes, Hale argued that as a result of increased economic development, many of the uses of property traditionally thought to be protected now conflicted with each other.[155] The point had been made in a general way by T. H. Green, Hobhouse, Dewey, and others, in noting that the rise of social interdependence had rendered obsolete the notion of an "unsocial"—that is to say, purely self-regarding—freedom.[156] In a world where the plurality of individuals are living in mutual contact, Hobhouse concluded, it is possible to have "unsocial freedom" only if everyone's desires are automatically attuned to social ends. Absent that happy coincidence of personal choice and social utility—what Alexander Pope had optimistically described as the world of Nature's God where "true [s]elf-love and [s]ocial are the same"[157]—it fell to the state to choose between conflicting preferences, according to some larger notion of the common good. Translating that sociological insight into legal terms, Hale argued that any workable scheme of property rights had to stop considerably short of the absolute dominion that the rhetoric of natural rights suggested. As Hale noted, the common law had conceded that fact implicitly in the doctrine of *damnum absque injuria,* under which tort penalties were imposed only where the plaintiff could show both actual harm *and* legal liability—a frank enough acknowledgment (at least in translation) that the law did not purport to reach all uses that inflicted injury.[158] The central challenge facing natural property rights proponents, said Hale, is to show that the "distinction between injury and damnum absque injuria [is] susceptible of being tested by laissez faire economic principles"[159]—to show, that is, that the particular subset of factual injuries that give rise to legal liability under the common law is deducible from a coherent theory of natural rights.

Hale, like many later property theorists, found in the case of Miller v. Schoene the clearest disproof of that proposition.[160] The facts of *Miller* posed a classic example of what economists now would describe as the "joint costs" of Coasian noncompatible uses. Growing on two neighboring parcels were apple orchards and cedar trees, with the latter harboring a fungus that endangered the former. The state, to preserve the more valuable apple orchards, ordered destruction of the cedar trees. Forced to choose between competing claims of ownership, the Court upheld the state's decision. Hale seized on the case in part to illustrate the impossibility of government nonfeasance in the face of any set of conflicting rights. As Justice Stone noted in a passage of the opinion that Hale frequently quoted with approval, "It would have been none the less a choice if, instead of enacting the present statute, the state, by doing nothing, had permitted serious injury to the apple orchards within its borders to go on unchecked."[161] But the particular facts of the case also pushed into high relief a further problem for laissez-faire advocates: the unlikelihood that any normative theory of rights could illuminate the choice between two conflicting uses that, along any conceivable dimension, seemed to have equal intuitive appeals to justice. The Supreme Court, implicitly conceding that fact, did not even attempt to resolve the question under a rights-based analysis of traditional nuisance law, upholding the statute instead under an essentially utilitarian calculus, the warrant for which it located in the doctrine of police powers.[162]

Miller v. Schoene was perhaps the most striking illustration that it was impossible to choose between horizontally conflicting rights of use except on grounds of public policy. But Hale argued that it was equally, if less obviously, impossible in all situations of conflicting rights. Hale's argument on this point had been anticipated by Holmes in "Privilege, Malice, and Intent," an article of great importance to Hale.[163] In it, Holmes had pointed out that every tort case in which the defendant's act was not illegal per se presented a problem of conflicting property or liberty interests—at the extreme, merely the "general one of letting men do what they want to do."[164] Thus, the function of tort law could not be simply to proscribe all conduct that was factually harmful to others; it had to decide which forms of harmful conduct would be privileged and which not. As Holmes noted, the external theory of tort liability that he had labored so hard to establish created a general privilege for harmful acts when the harm caused was not foreseeable. However, that general privilege did not begin to exhaust the list of harmful acts immune from legal liability. Setting up a shop in a small village that can support but one of its kind, intending thereby to ruin a deserving widow who is established there already; building a house on one's land in such a position as to spoil the view from a neighbor's far more valuable house; giving honest answers to inquiries about a servant, with the intention thereby to prevent the servant's getting a job, all involved conduct from which there ensued harm that was not only foreseeable but also intentional.[165] The defendants were nonetheless privileged in each case knowingly to inflict the damage complained of. Why?

As Holmes argued, the answer is suggested by the common law doctrine of "prima facie torts," which states that one is liable for intentionally inflicting damage to another's property or trade only if it is "done without just cause or excuse."[166] But that response merely pushes the answer down one level: what is a just cause (privilege) in each case? That answer, Holmes famously declared, cannot be deduced "from empty propositions like *sic utere tuo ut alienum non laedas*" (which teaches nothing but a benevolent yearning for a world where nonconflicting uses were the norm), or "although there is temporal damage, there is no wrong" (Holmes's paraphrase of *damnum absque injuria*), when "the very thing to be found out is whether there is a wrong or not, and if not, why not."[167] Rather, it comes down in each case to "a proposition of policy of a rather delicate nature" as to whether the advantages to the community from permitting such harms outweigh the costs. As Holmes expressed it, in a sentence that Hale could have written,

"It seems to me desirable that the work should be done with express recognition of its nature."

In the Legal Factors materials and his article on "Prima Facie Torts, Combination, and Non-feasance," Hale elaborated Holmes's argument that the choice of which harms to permit was legislative in nature.[168] For Hale, like most progressives in the early part of the twentieth century, the most glaring instance of the Court's legislative line-drawing under the guise of determining preexisting rights occurred in labor cases. Building on Holmes's observation that intentionally inflicted competitive harms are pervasive, Hale noted that given the (Halean) insight that all bargains result from "mutual threats to damage the other party in his property or trade unless he will accede to the terms offered," a court could extend the prima facie tort doctrine to virtually any commercial transaction simply by determining that the threat to withhold "lack[s] just excuse."[169] But in fact, in the late nineteenth and early twentieth centuries, courts had routinely constrained the use of bargaining weapons in one context only: workers' concerted efforts to withhold, or threaten to withhold, labor through strikes or union boycotts. In all other contexts, including employers' antiunion actions, parties were generally held privileged to use any bargaining tactics that they wished in order to obtain more favorable contract terms, provided that their actions were not per se criminal.[170]

The most infamous pair of cases navigating that tricky line between employee and employer privilege were the Supreme Court's decisions in Coppage v. Kansas[171] and Hitchman Coal & Coke Co. v. Mitchell.[172] The Court held in Coppage that an employer could threaten to discharge an employee who would not sign a yellow-dog contract, notwithstanding that the effect of such threat was to coerce employees to give up their right to belong to the union, because the employer was merely exercising a right of its own. Two years later, it held in Hitchman that a union could not coerce an employer to give up his right to run a nonunion shop by threatening financial loss, because the damage inflicted on the employer lacked "a just cause or excuse." As Hale noted, the different results in the two cases could not be explained by logical deduction from any evenhanded theory of rights. Whichever side capitulated on the issue of running a nonunion shop, it would thereby waive the right to refuse to agree to a contract on the other side's terms, with its waiver extracted by a threat of an even greater evil of no contract at all.[173] Echoing Holmes, Hale argued that the different results could be explained only by the Court's implicit determination that intentionally inflicting harm on the other side was justified as a matter of policy in one case but not in the other.[174]

Vertical Constraints on Use. Wherever courts or legislatures drew the lines between conflicting, private uses of property, the resulting scheme of private property rights was further constrained by the government's residual authority to regulate private rights in the interest of the "public welfare." That authority, the state's so-called "police powers," took on increasing importance in the courts in the second half of the nineteenth century, and it became a chief battleground between progressives and conservatives in the period from the 1880s through the 1930s. As both groups saw from the start, the police powers doctrine was potentially capacious enough to house almost any interference in private economic affairs that the legislature might see fit to undertake.[175] Progressives, cheered by that prospect, heralded the police powers doctrine as the "greatest unwritten clause of our Constitution,"[176] while conservatives denounced it as merely a legal cover for "the radical experimentations of social reformers."[177]

Given that the "public welfare" was just another name for the aggregate interests of all citizens, the police powers doctrine could be thought of as merely imposing another form of horizontal constraint on owners, this one to take account of the conflicting interests of the world at large, rather than the more limited group of individuals seeking to exercise their own noncompatible rights. The conservative treatise writer, Christopher Tiedeman, argued as much in his 1886 *A Treatise on the Limitations of Police Power,* insisting that the police power of government—like its powers under tort and contract law—should be "confined to the detailed enforcement of the legal maxim, *'sic utere tuo, ut alienum non laedas.'"*[178] However, little turned on the verbal characterization of the doctrine one way or the other; the only question of any interest was how the doctrine was to be applied in practice.

The courts' answer over time bore out conservatives' worst fears. Although late nineteenth-century courts made some effort to confine the doctrine to uses that endangered the "public health, safety and morals"—a generous enough standard in its own right—by the early twentieth century, they abandoned even that limitation, at least intermittently permitting the state pursuant to its general police powers to restrict the exercise of any rights deemed injurious to "the public welfare."[179] Even the requirement of "injuriousness" provided little guidance or check on the government's powers. Under traditional legal doctrine, what differentiated the state's police powers from its right to take property under eminent domain only upon payment of just compensation was that under its police powers, the government curtailed private rights in order to prevent public harm; under its powers of eminent domain, it curtailed those rights to create a public benefit.[180] Later commentators have cast doubt on the philosophical basis of that distinction.[181]

But the focus of progressive attacks was on its logical coherence. As Holmes's and Hale's careful analyses of legal rights implied, the distinction between withholding a benefit from the public and doing the public positive harm is not factual but legal. The distinction depends solely on the parties' preexisting legal rights. Consider the example of Miller v. Schoene, which itself arose as a police powers case: by leaving their fungus-infested cedar trees standing, the owners harmed their neighbors, rather than merely failing to bestow a benefit upon the neighbors, only if their neighbors had a preexisting right to be free of the noxious effects of the fungus. Or, to take an example dearer to Hale, charging what the market will bear is a harm to the public rather than a failure to bestow a larger benefit on the public through trade, if the public has a preexisting right to purchase such property at a lesser price. If it does have such a right, the seller's refusal to provide the property at that lower price leaves the public worse off than it has a right to be. If the public does not have the right, the same refusal merely fails to leave it better off than it has a right to be.[182]

Given the inherent malleability of the police powers doctrine, Hale and other progressives argued in their familiar trope, adjudication under that standard could not be anything but a bald policy determination, with the courts' seeking to balance the benefits to public welfare from the proposed prohibitions against the harm that the prohibitions would inflict on individual liberty and property interests. It was inconceivable that a court inclined to uphold any given restriction on property rights could not justify its decision under that broad cover. As Morris Cohen put it, "[T]he significant question is not whether you are for or against private property, but rather where you will draw the line between public and private things and affairs."[183] Teddy Roosevelt expressed the general progressive sentiment about where the line should be drawn, in declaring, "We are face to face with new conceptions of the relations of property to human welfare. . . [P]roperty [is] subject to the general right of the community to regulate its use to whatever degree the public welfare may require it."[184]

The police powers doctrine in practice thus allowed progressives to recast virtually the entire reform program implied by the idealist "social conception" of property into the "harm"-based exception built into the Lockean rights tradition. The Court, in applying the doctrine in the area of particular interest to Hale—rate regulation of businesses—had tried for some sixty years to limit its scope to those businesses deemed to be "affected with the public interest." But, as Hale and others argued, given that any business affected the public in innumerable ways, the limitation was as open-ended as the notion of "public welfare" itself. As a result, the limitation could not ultimately contain the expansion of state rate-setting authority to all businesses, a view that the Court itself somewhat reluctantly came to by the 1930s.[185]

The moral of the mainstream progressive assault on the rightness of property rights was clear. Some of the most significant rights of possession, gratuitous transfer, and use could not be justified at all under the broad Lockean justification given for creating private ownership in the first place. As to other rights, the most that laissez-faire proponents could hope to show was that the existing scheme was not inconsistent with Lockean premises. They could not show that the scheme was the *only* one that was consistent with those premises, or indeed even the best one. Given the essentially legislative nature of the choice that had to be made between the existing scheme and an infinite number of alternative schemes equally consistent with the broad principle that people were entitled to use the fruits of their labor as they saw fit, provided that they did no injury to others, Hale and others argued, the choice was properly left to the legislatures and not to the courts.

Hale reserved his real fire on the subject of the rightness of so-called natural rights, however, not for the right to possess or to use the property, but to retain its exchange value. In a series of articles written over his career, Hale argued that the right to retain the full market value extracted in a voluntary, unregulated exchange—a key tenet of laissez-faire politics—was not just not logically entailed by Lockean principles. It was irreconcilable with them. As suggested earlier, the argument had a complicated history in economic and political thought. That history, and Hale's contribution to it, are the subject of Chapter 4.

4

A RENT-THEORY WORLD

Suppose that there is a kind of income that constantly tends to increase, without any exertion or sacrifice on the part of the owners: those owners constituting a class in the community, whom the natural course of things progressively enriches, consistently with complete passiveness on their own part. In such a case it would be no violation of the principles on which private property is grounded, if the state should appropriate this increase of wealth, or part of it, as it arises. This would not properly be taking anything from anybody; it would merely be applying an accession of wealth, created by circumstances, *to the benefit of society, instead of allowing it to become an unearned appendage to the riches of a particular class.*

—John Stuart Mill, *Principles of Political Economy*

The story of modern economics is the story of "rent," that is, of unearned surplus due to scarcity conditions of one kind or another.

—Henry Allen Overstreet, "The Changing Conception of Property"

Like most of his contemporaries, Hale believed that changes in the mode of production had dwarfed the economic significance of rights to possess and use property. With the rise in mass production, most property was no longer produced for personal use, but rather for exchange.[1] The shift from production for personal consumption to production for exchange meant that rights of ownership were determined in the first instance by bargains between factors of production. As a result, Hale and other progressives argued, once entitlements were initially distributed through the nonmarket mechanisms of inheritance, government grant, or Lockean appropriation, it was "prices and price relationships," not the right to "personal unmolested use" of property, that decided the subsequent distribution of wealth.[2]

Not surprisingly, that academic observation mirrored political realities. The most pressing political question facing Hale's generation was whether the state and federal governments had the right to alter the distribution of wealth resulting from exchange relationships, by means of wage and price regulations, factory legislation, and other direct controls on the terms of exchange, or progressive taxation of the income generated by an otherwise unfettered exchange.[3]

In the constitutional arena, boosters of a "free" market usually treated as sacrosanct those prices that were determined by the market without "governmental interference specifically directly towards price control."[4] They generally tolerated various other forms of government intervention (e.g., curtailing uses of property and imposing other nonprice regulation under the state police power, increasing costs of production by imposing tariffs on imports of raw materials, taxing gains from sale) that were equally likely to decrease the value of property realizable by exchange or exploitation.[5] In the legislative arena, the arguments for a "free" market had a broader reach, targeting progressive taxation and a wide array of nonprice regulations, along with wage and price controls. In all cases, however, the laissez-faire argument against government intervention rested on essentially the same claim: that the right of ownership in one's labor or one's property should necessarily carry with it the right to the profits from its "unregulated" exchange. As Thorstein Veblen paraphrased the argument, the natural right of property included the "freedom to buy and sell, limited only by the equal freedom of others to buy and sell."[6]

Unlike rights to use property, one could not defend that proposition even in a general way by invoking the common law maxim, *sic utere tuo ut alienum non laedas*—you may use your property as you wish, provided that you do no injury to others. The purpose of bargaining over price was to divide the joint gains that both sides expected to realize from their exchange. That meant that any advantage given to one side was not only formally at the expense of the other (as Hohfeld argued with respect to *all* rights), but functionally as well. In redescribing the bargain as an act of mutual coercion, Hale meant to make that point, among others. Commons's graphs and matrices showing the division of joint gains from trades was meant to drive it home in a graphic way.[7] Instead, as Hale noted, the laissez-faire argument for unfettered exchanges usually rested on the (undefended) assumption that "in some manner the [owner] has 'produced' these earnings, and that some 'natural law' forbids the government to deprive people of what they have produced," except perhaps by a scheme of taxation that has a motive other than simple redistribution.[8] Defending that principle with respect to labor income in his Law of Conduct and Consequence, Herbert Spencer argued that justice requires that "each man should receive benefits proportionate to his efforts,"[9] a result automatically obtained if each "obtains from his fellows such payment for his service as its value, determined by the demand, warrants"—that is, its market price.[10] Defending the same principle with respect to income from capital, the conservative treatise writer Thomas Cooley wrote, "[T]he capability of property, by means of the labor or expense or both bestowed upon it, to be made available in producing profits, is a potential quality in property, and as sacredly protected by the constitution as the thing itself in which the quality inheres."[11]

Despite the strong Lockean flavor to that assumption, progressives—many of them assiduous students of Locke's works—argued that Locke himself did not embrace it. Hobhouse, typical in this regard, pounced on the two restrictions that Locke himself had imposed on the natural right to appropriate property: that one may appropriate only "[a]s much as anyone can make use of to any advantage of life before it spoils,"[12] and (in his famous Proviso) that "enough, and as good" be left for all others.[13] Given that Locke believed that laws and government ought to accommodate themselves to natural law and not the other way around, Hobhouse concluded, "it seems clear that Locke might be led, if he were living now, to somewhat radical conclusions" as to the appropriate arrangement of property rights in the modern industrial state.[14]

As more conventional readings of Locke make clear, construing Locke as a proto–Social Democrat poses a number of difficulties, historical and textual. But whatever Locke himself might have made of the laissez-faire argument for unlimited rights of exchange, Hale undertook to show that the argument was inconsistent with Lockean premises as Locke's laissez-faire heirs conventionally understood them. The first part of Hale's argument—his attack on the "naturalness" of unregulated prices—has already been discussed in Chapter 3. Contrary to what laissez-faire advocates implicitly assumed, Hale argued, one did not "produce" the price fetched by one's goods or services in anything remotely like the sense in which one could be said to have physically produced the goods or services themselves. Whereas the labor that brought forth the goods or services was a necessary prerequisite to exchange, the actual exchange value at any time was the product of myriad legal and social forces in which the typical producer (as a "price taker") played virtually no role. Thus, society's intervention in that exchange, whether brought about directly by regulating the terms of the exchange or indirectly by taxing the proceeds, merely substituted one socially created price for another.

What that meant, Hale argued, echoing his arguments about coercion and use rights, was that one could not establish a baseline entitlement to any given equilibrium price on the ground that it was natural (that is, that it arose without the aid of the state). But Hale's argument was at most a partial truth. For some range of goods or services, the government likely had little direct effect on equilibrium price. Moreover, even where its influence was great, the state could simply have created what justice independently required. The extensive debates over distributive justice that preoccupied political thought at the turn of the century thus ultimately reduced to the question, Why should justice be thought to require an entitlement to whatever price one's property or services happened to fetch on the market? The debates reduced, that is, to the rightness of the claimed natural right to the exchange value of property.

If (as its adherents assumed) the Lockean labor theory of property rights was a desert theory of entitlement, it justified ownership of that portion of exchange value that represented a fair price for the sacrifice actually incurred. But, Hale argued, contrary to the frequent assumption of laissez-faire advocates, the theory justified no more than that. Society had acknowledged as much in regulating prices charged by formal or de facto monopolies, as well as the transitory monopolies present in necessity and duress cases. But, argued Hale, if the justification for regulating monopoly profits was that the producer had realized a gain disproportionate to his sacrifice, the same logic would argue for appropriating that portion of gain in competitive markets that reflected returns in excess of true costs. As Hobhouse stated, "Locke's doctrine would then amount to this, that the social right of each man is to a place in the economic order, in which he both has opportunity for exercising his faculties in the social service, and can reap thereby a reward proportionate to the value [meaning cost] of the service rendered to society."[15] That argument, which formed the basis of Hale's and other progressives' proposals to reform property rights along strict rent-theory lines, is the subject of this chapter.

It is useful as a preliminary matter to narrow the terms of the debate. By definition, the value to the marginal purchaser put a ceiling on exchange price. As Hale noted, countering the argument that minimum wage laws set the price of labor higher than it was "worth," all those who voluntarily purchase labor at the minimum wage (or, by extension, any other price above it) must value labor at least as much as the price that they paid, or they would not have purchased it.[16] At the other end, whatever he might have made of a rights-based claim to that portion of exchange price equal to the seller's costs, virtually no progressive economist or political philosopher disputed the purely utilitarian need to protect whatever portion would provide the minimum incentive necessary to induce the desired level of labor or capital investment.[17] As a practical matter, that objective meant protecting a return sufficient over the long run to generate at least a fair return on the expected costs to the producer, including future investments in increased productivity.[18] Thus, what was at stake in the debate was the proper distribution of joint consumer and producer surplus from the trade—the difference between the buyer's reservation price and the seller's costs.[19] As Hobson put it, "The only true bone of contention, the only valid cause of conflict between capital and labour, land, ability, is the unproductive surplus."[20] The question then, rephrased, was whether any factor of production—capital, land, or labor—had a natural right to whatever distribution of surplus the market (in the absence of direct price regulation) happens to produce.

In the case of monopolies, the answer, at least since Adam Smith, was that they had no such right. As Frank Knight remarked in 1934, regarding the social and ethical justification for private appropriation of monopoly gain, "there has been virtually no difference of opinion, and the only problem has to do with practicable methods of prevention."[21] To the extent that monopoly profits were deemed objectionable solely because they were derived from a formal grant of privilege, it was entirely consistent to extol government controls on monopoly prices while condemning all other government intervention in price relationships.[22] But Adam Smith himself had defined monopoly far more broadly, to include in a category of "enlarged monopolies" corporate franchises, apprenticeship laws, import duties, and all other laws that had the tendency to restrain competition in particular employments "to a smaller number than might otherwise go into them."[23] John Stuart Mill had urged the government to take control of all natural monopolies, either by nationalizing them or by making conditional grants to private companies to run them in the best interest of the public.[24] By the end of the nineteenth century, there was a growing consensus in both England and the United States that the government ought to regulate natural and legal monopolies in some form, a sentiment crystallized in the almost universal support for either regulation or outright public ownership of public utilities.[25] By the early twentieth century, all but the strongest probusiness forces agreed that it was appropriate for the government to intervene in any business that was in the position to administer prices.[26]

As Hale noted, courts had implicitly reached the same conclusion in "salvor" cases that were the contract law counterpoint to tort "necessity" cases like Vincent v. Lake Erie.[27] The typical case involved a contract for goods or services in which one party had exploited what amounted to a transitory monopoly position to extract terms extremely favorable to itself. The classic example—which Thomas Carver put to Hale as an illustration of "real" coercion (in contrast to Hale's preposterous inclusion of normal market transactions), and which, as Hale told Carver, Hale had used frequently in his own writing—was that of the drowning man who agrees to pay a passerby a substantial amount of money for the relatively trivial effort involved in saving him.[28] Under the rubric of "duress," "necessity," or "unconscionability," courts frequently intervened in such cases ex post to reform the contract terms to conform to the "normal" market price—that is, to "what the property *would* sell for in a hypothetical 'normal' market, in which other parties might have made bids, had not the buyer or seller been prevented by ignorance or pressing necessity from seeking them out."[29] Such decisions, Hale argued, in effect required disgorgement of monopoly profits. Unlike eminent domain cases (or trespass or nuisance cases in which injunctive relief against the would-be transgressor is denied), the "extorting" party remains free not to provide the goods or services in question, assuming that the other side could not or did not expropriate them unilaterally. But if he chooses to provide them, it will have to be at a judicially determined fair price that gives him only that portion of joint consumer/producer surplus from the trade that normal market prices would have afforded.[30]

As Hale noted, the effect of such a rule is to prevent parties from exploiting the necessity peculiar to one buyer or seller, but not that which—shared by all such would-be buyers or sellers—is reflected in the normal market value of the service. "[Courts] will not inquire, apparently, into whether the normal market value itself, resulting from the mutual coercion of buyers and sellers of the service, is so high or so low as to give an undue advantage to one side or the other."[31] As John Dawson concluded, commenting on a similar limitation in the German Civil Code of 1900, "a rule of law whose implications were revolutionary was thus deprived of all subversive effects and brought into harmony with basic assumptions of a competitive economy."[32] But, Hale argued, that limitation made no sense if—as courts suggested—the reason for intervening in duress or other monopoly cases to begin with was that the price charged was excessive when measured against the sacrifice involved.[33] If so, the same logic would justify regulating that portion of the normal market value that generated an excess return (as measured against cost).

But, in the most technical economics piece that he published, Hale argued that classical economics had obviated the need to resolve how far the rationale of monopoly regulation should extend. It obviated it by assuming that in competitive markets, the long-run equilibrium price of any commodity would equal the cost of purchasing the factors (land, labor, and capital) that went into producing the commodity, where costs, with the notable exception of land, were equal to the sacrifice of those who provided them.[34] Thus, one could defend the distributive effects of the market on either a utilitarian or a Lockean basis. Classical economists were free to pick their ground according to their philosophical preferences, and for the most part, they moved casually between the two.[35] But, Hale argued, the purely descriptive claim on which the argument rested—that price *would* converge with cost in a competitive market—was undone by the neoclassical (marginal) revolution. The marginalists showed that, contrary to classical assumptions, in a competitive market the equilibrium price of a good or service would equal the marginal cost of the last item produced, not the average costs of all items produced.[36] That outcome meant that even in situations of competition, whenever supply could not be expanded at constant costs, the "owners of the superior resources" in the form of land or capital equipment acquired for lower than reproduction cost—so-called "inframarginal producers"—would realize a surplus return ("economic rent") in excess of costs.[37] Utilitarian considerations might still counsel against widespread intervention in market-based distribution, if the government could not deprive inframarginal producers of rents without disrupting the return to marginal producers as well. However, such intervention could no longer be thought to be precluded on strictly Lockean grounds. As James Bonbright wrote in 1936, summarizing the lessons of the preceding generation, "In orthodox economics, the only intelligent excuse for the profit system is, not that it results in a 'fair' distribution of wealth—for no sane modern economist could maintain that absurd thesis—but rather that profits furnish an incentive necessary to get the work of the world accomplished."[38]

The argument, a fair summary of an enormously complicated and confused history of economic thought, forms the core of Hale's assault on the justice of market-based distribution and lays the groundwork for his affirmative reconstruction of property rights along rent-theory lines. To understand both halves of his argument fully requires at least a brief digression into economic history.

Classical Theories of Distribution

As a preliminary matter, some clarification of terms may be helpful. In conventional economic terminology, which the following discussion adopts, "value theory" refers to the theory of how prices of final commodities (that is, commodities sold to end-users) are determined. "Distribution theory" refers to the theory of how prices of the factors—labor, pure capital, and capital goods (including land)—that go into producing final commodities are determined. Thus, "distribution theory" in the context of production has a different and more technical meaning than what is customarily meant by "theories of income distribution." Distribution theory refers *not* to how society's total income or wealth is distributed (by the market or the government) among individuals but rather to how that income is distributed by the market among the various productive sectors of society. Obviously, however, the two meanings are closely related.

In general, the classical economists adhered to a "cost of production" theory of value, which held that a commodity's "natural price" (that is, its long-run equilibrium price in a competitive market) would equal the sum of the cost of factors that went into producing it. Smith, the first to offer a comprehensive version of the argument, identified the three factors as labor, capital, and land. Their costs, he argued, would equal the "natural rates of wages, profit, and rent," respectively, which he defined as the "ordinary or average" rate of wages, profit, or rent prevailing at any given time.[39] Mill, following David Ricardo's lead, excluded land rents as a cost of production, thereby reducing it to a two-factor (wages and profits) model, the version that remained standard until the marginalist revolution in the 1870s.[40]

So far, the "cost of production" theory says nothing more than that the prices of final commodities are supply-driven—that is, they are determined solely by the prices that their producers must pay for the factors that go into them.[41] To fashion a Lockean justification for the resulting income paid to factors, one would have to show further that the prices paid for various factors are commensurate with the cost, or sacrifice, incurred by those who provided them. That showing requires two things: a normative theory about what constitutes "cost" for each factor; and an empirical claim that prices paid to factors in fact tend to converge with costs so defined. What follows—in effect an attempt to piece together a classical theory of distribution to the factors of production (labor, capital, and land)—does more than the classical economists ever themselves purported to do. As has frequently been remarked, none of the classical economists had a coherent theory of distribution.[42] In the absence of such a theory, a "cost-of-production" theory of value is really, as Cairnes remarked of Mill, nothing more than an *expense* of production theory of value, from the partial and limited vantage point of the capitalist employer. That is to say, it merely asserts that the price of final products equals the sum of the expenses incurred by the capitalist employer in producing them, in the form of wages, profits, and rents.[43] The theory says nothing about how wage rates, profits, and rents themselves are set, either on the demand side or (of particular relevance here) on the supply side. To put it another way, the "cost" in such "cost of production" theories is just an opportunity cost from the vantage point of the capitalist employer, and not a "real cost" (sacrifice) from the vantage point of the ultimate providers of labor, capital, or land.

Notwithstanding the foregoing, all of the classical economists offered at least a partial theory of distribution, implicitly or explicitly. Of more importance for present purposes, they were *construed* as having offered such a theory by a wider, nontechnical audience, who relied on what they understood it to be in formulating a philosophical (largely Lockean) defense of the distributive effects of an "unregulated" economy. What follows, then, should be understood as an attempt to reconstruct the logic of that defense, rather than to describe classical theories of distribution in terms that are most faithful to their authors' own intent.[44] Also, in drawing out the Lockean implications of classical distribution theory, I do not mean to suggest that the classical economists themselves necessarily would have cared about those implications. As noted earlier, most classical economists defended property rights on a confused mixture of Lockean and utilitarian principles, moving between them largely unselfconsciously as it suited their immediate purposes. A chief aim of this discussion is to show that such casualness was sustainable largely because classical distribution theory suggested that in a competitive economy, where price would reflect cost, the two principles would point to the same conclusion.

Wages. In the case of labor, the Malthusian "Iron Law of Wages" (strongly embraced by Smith and Ricardo, and with some greater skepticism by Mill) appeared both to define the costs of providing labor and to predict that wage levels would tend to converge with those costs.[45] Malthus predicted that any increase in the wage level above subsistence would induce workers to reproduce at a greater rate, until the resulting increase in supply of workers drove wages back down to subsistence level.[46] As a result, all wages would tend in the long run towards subsistence level, unless workers could somehow be persuaded to resist their natural impulse to increase population in response to a rise in the standard of living. Malthus recognized that wages might temporarily rise above that level in response to any increase in demand, as a result of a time lag in increasing supply. Smith and Ricardo, taking the point one step further, argued that the surplus could be permanent in the case of a constantly growing economy, since the supply of labor might lag perpetually behind demand.[47] But with that exception, the strong version of Malthusianism predicted wage levels equivalent to the bare minimum required to sustain the physical capacity to work. Neither Malthus, Smith, nor Ricardo went that far. All three believed that the level of consumption that reflects minimal subsistence "depends on the habits and customs of the people"—that is, it is a social, rather than a physical, minimum of existence— and in many countries is considerably higher than that required to sustain the mere physical capacity to work.[48] Nevertheless, even that higher (variable) figure would yield incomes that converged with costs for all workers, provided that one regarded the cost of inducing each generation to produce the next generation of workers as an ongoing cost of labor, and that one further assumed that the inducement required was constant among all participants in a given society, even if it varied across societies.

As Smith acknowledged, Malthus's "Iron Law of Wages" seemed at first blush to be refuted by persistent, observable differences in wage rates that could not be explained simply as temporary dislocations in the labor market. But, Smith argued, further reflection would reveal that the nominal differences in wage rates were merely compensating for the disparate levels of disutility involved in different occupations. That disparity was produced by five variable factors: the agreeableness or disagreeableness of the employment, the ease or difficulty of learning the trade, the constancy of the employment, the degree of responsibility attached to the employment, and the degree of uncertainty of success.[49] After one accounted for that "difference in sacrifice, present or past," it was clear, Smith argued, that different nominal wage rates yielded equal "net advantages" to all workers.[50]

While both the Malthusian and the Smithian accounts of wages implied that wages would converge with the costs of labor, the two rested on different notions of cost. Malthusianism, at least in its strong version, assumed the cost of labor to equal the payment required to sustain the labor physically. Wages in this sense, Hobhouse graphically argued, are like coal stoking an engine. They must be sufficient to keep the laborer "physically efficient"— that is, to repay him for the "muscular energy" that he puts out in the day—and ensure beyond that that he is "able to support children to replace him, and the wife that brings them up," so that the "national industry [can] be maintained as a going concern without loss."[51] Smith's corrective to Malthus, on the other hand, assumed the cost of work to equal the subjective disutility that the work imposed on workers, as compared with less irksome work or (implicitly) leisure. That definition of cost, equal to the minimum payment demanded for forgoing available alternatives, more closely paralleled the definition used by classical economists with respect to interest.[52] In either case, it was at least debatable whether as an ethical matter, costs so defined should be treated as sacrifices generating a Lockean entitlement to wages. In the case of strict Malthusianism, while payment of the minimum required to keep current workers working as well as to induce them to produce the next generation of workers represents a necessary cost from the employers' perspective, it does not necessarily measure the sacrifice entailed in working from the laborers' perspective. They might well be willing to work for nothing, were they physically able to. Moreover, even a subsistence wage arguably generates surplus for them, in the form of (a well-nourished) life in nonworking hours. Thus, in some admittedly extreme, strict Lockean sense, minimum subsistence wages arguably may *overcompensate* some workers for the cost to them of labor. Smith's version, which measured the incremental disutility of work, did not present that difficulty. But it presented other difficulties, in its undefended assumption that the five sorts of psychic disutility that Smith identified ought to be treated as a real sacrifice for which compensation was (in the Lockean sense) justly paid. For most (if not all) of those factors, that assumption was at least disputable.[53] Classical economists and their contemporaries, however, by and large overlooked such nice questions. They regarded Malthus and Smith together as having shown that wages received were merely the payment due for the real (Lockean) sacrifices of labor.

Interest. It is somewhat harder to reconstruct the classical theory of costs with respect to capital than to labor. As a result, it is also harder to evaluate capitalists' Lockean claim to the income generated by their capital under classical economic assumptions.[54] For most classical economists, the justification for profits reduced to the justification for interest.[55] "Interest" in this sense referred not (as in common parlance) to the return on money loans per se, but to the return on any investment in physical capital. Since in the time of the classical theorists most physical capital was in the form of tangible goods, the term "interest" most commonly referred to the (net) return on a stock of capital goods, whether retained by the self-financing businessperson as his profit or paid over to his lender as a return on the loan.[56]

Smith and Ricardo both treated interest as a cost to the borrower/producer of capital-intensive goods, and hence a determinant of the value (price) of those goods. But, unlike labor, neither had a well-developed theory about what determined the interest rate, and in particular (the relevant point for present purposes) about whether the lender incurred a cost in providing the capital.[57] It was Nassau Senior and John Stuart Mill who provided the missing supply-side argument.[58] In *Outlines of the Science of Political Economy*, the essentials of which were delivered in his 1825 to 1830 Oxford lectures on political economy, Senior propounded his theory of profit as a reward for "abstinence," that is, for the "deferral of enjoyment." Capital owes its existence and preservation, he argued, solely to the willingness of its owners to abstain from the pleasure of present consumption in favor of saving. That willingness is induced by the prospect of payment for deferral in the form of interest.[59] In short, "[a]bstinence . . . stands in the same relation to Profit as Labour does to Wages," both representing the underlying "real cost," or sacrifice, to providers for which profit and wages, respectively, are the demanded compensation.[60] As Malthus assumed for labor supply, so also Senior assumed for savings, that the subjective cost (here, of deferral) was constant.[61] That is, to translate the argument into modern terms, he assumed that the supply curve for capital was perfectly horizontal (elastic) across its entire range. Given Senior's assumptions, the Lockean case for profits seemed strong, at least at first blush: the entire payment to all savers merely compensated for the sacrifice endured in deferring consumption.

Mill, incorporating in *Principles* Senior's theory of interest as the wages of abstinence,[62] altered it in one important respect that increased its usefulness in justifying income from capital. Senior had defined abstinence to include only sacrifice incurred by "the *original constructor*" of capital assets in creating capital rather than in using the wealth for current enjoyment. He expressly excluded those who, having received (by gift or inheritance) capital that others had created, forbore from consuming it currently. It was not a distinction that would appeal to a utilitarian (at least a utilitarian trying to induce savings in a world in which the right to transfer property by gifts and inheritance is taken as given), and it is clear that Senior embraced it on purely Lockean grounds.[63] But as Mill rightly saw, once one accepts forbearance from spending to be a real cost, Senior's objection really goes to the Lockean justification for allowing transfers of property by inheritance and gift to begin with, rather than to the right of the recipients (once transfer is permitted) to be compensated for the disutility of abstaining from spending money that is now rightly theirs. Thus, Mill argued, he would curtail inheritance and gift "as much as is consistent with justice to those who thought fit to dispose of their savings by giving them to their descendants." But for any transfers that are permitted, the lucky recipients' forbearance from current consumption of that wealth is as real a cost to them as to those who had created it.[64]

Thus amended by Mill to include *any* forbearance to consume one's capital, Senior's theory of interest as the "wage of abstinence" appeared to do for interest what Malthusianism did for labor wages. It predicted that interest rates will tend to the minimum level necessary to remunerate "abstinence." Like the Malthusian theory of wages, however, the "abstinence" theory of interest raised a number of problems. The first problem concerned Senior's assumption of a constant subjective cost of abstinence. In comments that anticipated by some forty years Marshall's marginalist analysis of savings behavior, Mill suggested that the amount required to induce savings differed not only from society to society but also from individual to individual. As a result, the prevailing rate of interest will inevitably pay those persons "in whom the effective desire of accumulation is above the average," more than they require to save, and will pay those in whom it is below the average, less. Translated to marginalist terms, Mill was, in effect, arguing that the supply curve of savings was not flat, but positively sloped, with price determined by the cost of abstinence to the marginal saver.[65] The consequence was to yield a surplus to inframarginal savers over the disutility that they suffered in deferring consumption—precisely the result that Ricardo would predict with respect to land.[66]

The second problem with the abstinence theory of interest was that neither Senior nor Mill explained what they meant by a "time preference" for present over future consumption. Without that explanation, one could neither test the existence of the preference nor assess the normative claim that by forgoing present consumption, savers incurred the sort of sacrifice that created a (Lockean) entitlement to compensating payments in the form of interest. As a result, contemporary critics charged, the abstinence theory was nothing more than a tautological assertion that profit was the reward for sacrifice.[67] Viewed in the most cynical light (which was the light in which Marx and later socialists were inclined to view it), that assertion was simply a cover for what in fact amounted to pure exploitation of labor by capital. But, for the most part, these objections took hold only later. At the time that it was offered, "abstinence" theory was taken by most people to rebut the rising charge that interest amounted to nothing more than theft of the rightful produce of labor.[68]

Land Rents.   It was with respect to land rents that the classical scheme, with its implied equation of sacrifice and price, came under attack.[69] Comments throughout *Wealth of Nations*, preshadowing later Ricardian rent theory, suggest that Smith viewed land rents as a pure surplus to landlords for providing the (to them) costless bounties of nature. Under that view, land rents were purely price-determined. That is to say, landlords would be paid whatever was left after wages and profits were subtracted from the price of goods sold.[70] But Smith lacked the conceptual apparatus to reconcile that view with his (correct) belief that land rents were a true cost of production (that is, were price-determining), in the sense that land not receiving the going rate of rent would be shifted to more profitable uses.[71]

The key lay in the theory of differential rent, independently put forth by David Ricardo, Thomas Malthus, Sir Edward West, and Robert Torrens in 1815.[72] Widespread investigations into the recent history of grain price movements during the Napoleonic War revealed that as the population grew and more soil was cultivated to meet the growing demand for grain, the price of grain rose. The explanation for that phenomenon, all four concluded, lay in the law of diminishing returns. Each (equal) increment of labor and capital applied to equal quantities of land yields diminishing returns. This is true, whether the incremental cultivation is through intensive means (undertaking increasingly more expensive cultivation per unit of output of land already under cultivation) or extensive means (bringing increasingly inferior soil under cultivation). In either case, farmers will continue to increase cultivation of land, at higher and higher costs per incremental unit of crop produced, until the labor and capital cost of producing that unit exactly equals the price at which it sells. From that explanation, all four deduced classical (Ricardian) rent theory. The price of wheat produced under conditions of diminishing returns will be set by the least favorable circumstances under which cultivation is carried on—in modern terminology, by marginal cost, equal to the cost of labor and capital to the farmer cultivating no-rent land at the intensive or extensive margin.[73] As a result, each time an increase in demand causes incrementally inferior land to be brought under cultivation, the price of wheat rises, because the cost of labor and capital employed in producing the last unit of wheat rises as well.[74] But that price will be obtained for wheat produced on more fertile land (and thus with less labor and capital) as well as for that produced on marginal land. Anticipating marginal productivity theory, all four argued that capital and labor as the variable input will obtain their marginal product—that is, will be paid an amount exactly equal to the value that they added to production. The surplus, they concluded, will be paid as rent to the landlord holding inframarginal (that is, superior) land.

Two things followed from that argument, both of which were critically important for the future development of value and distribution theory. First, rent does not enter into the value (that is, price) of final products, because such price will be determined by the costs of production on marginal (no-rent) land. As Marshall averred, Ricardo thereby discovered "the deepest and most important line of cleavage in economic theory: . . . the distinction between the [rents] which do not, and the profits which do, directly enter into the normal supply prices of produce for periods of moderate length."[75] Second, the amount of rent paid to any individual landlord bore no necessary relation to the landlord's costs. Rather, the amount was purely price-determined—that is, it was determined by the price at which wheat sold, which was in turn determined solely by the quantity of labor and capital required to produce the wheat at the no-rent margin.[76] In Ricardo's terms, "[c]orn is not high because a rent is paid, but rent is paid because corn is high."[77] Or as Sir Edward West declared, at somewhat greater length,

[O]n any increased demand for corn, the capital [meaning wage advances and any additional capital] . . . which is laid out to meet this increased demand is laid out to less advantage. The growing price, therefore, of the additional quantity wanted is increased, and the actual price of that quantity must also be increased. But the corn that is raised at the least expense will, of course, sell for the same price as that raised at the greatest, and consequently the price of all corn is raised by the increased demand. But the farmer gets only the common profits of stock on his growth, which is afforded even on that corn which is raised at the greatest expense; all the additional profit, therefore, on that part of the produce which is raised at a less expense, goes to the landlord in the shape of rent.[78]

As a result, not only was rent (as Smith had acknowledged) a return for nature's bounty rather than human effort. It also grew larger as nature's bounty grew more scarce, driving up the marginal price of agricultural production, and hence the surplus to inframarginal landowners.[79] The former observation was sufficient to condemn all rents on Lockean grounds, as Ricardo, Mill, and Smith all acknowledged.[80] But the latter observation, containing the first appearance of marginalism in economic analysis, pointed the way to a more generalized rent theory that progressives would seize on in attacking the justice of all market-based distribution. The larger implications of rent theory, however, eluded Ricardo, West, Torrens, and Malthus, in part because they believed that only agricultural land was scarce, and in part because they believed that all commodities other than agricultural produce were produced under constant returns to scale, where marginal cost was therefore equal to average cost, generating no rent for any factor.[81] As a result, all four concluded that the problem of rent could be solved simply by repealing protectionist legislation (the infamous Corn Laws) that kept lower-priced foreign grain out of British markets except in years of extreme famine.[82] Repeal, argued Ricardo and others, would lower rents to landlords by taking out of use marginal (less fertile) lands at home.

Hale, summarizing the political implications of the classical scheme, concluded that the instructions of classical (Ricardian) political economists to statesmen were therefore beguilingly simple: If you "merely abolish all laws [including Corn Laws and other government-made monopolies] which interfere with economic processes," (1) production will automatically be channeled into areas where it will satisfy the most wants; and (2) (the point relevant for present purposes) the distribution of wealth will automatically be in accordance with sacrifice, as prices will (in the absence of government interference) tend to equal costs of production, including a fair profit and interest.[83] In short, the "free" market will automatically achieve allocative efficiency and distributive justice.[84]

The Land Tax Movement

The Ricardian preoccupation with land rents survived in the next generation in the work of John Stuart Mill and the single taxers, for whom the most famous spokesman was Henry George. The Ricardians had assumed that only agricultural land could command rents, and then only for its greater fertility. But the increasing urbanization and industrialization of Great Britain and the United States during the mid- and late-nineteenth century created a demand for land that was valued for its proximity to growing urban centers, rather than its fertility. In the United States, where agricultural land had never been scarce, urban rents presented the first large-scale incidence of land rents.[85] In Britain, by the end of the nineteenth century, urban rents made up the vast majority of land rents, reflecting both an increase in urban land values, and a decrease in agricultural rents in the wake of free trade in agricultural produce.[86]

If Lockean principles were hard to reconcile with private ownership of agricultural rents, they were equally at odds with private ownership of urban rents. Such rents, progressives argued, resulted solely from the growth of society, which caused demand for urban lands to outstrip supply, and not from any effort of landowners. The rents were, in short, a social and not an individual product.[87] The question was how best to attack those rents. The Ricardian solution—in effect increasing the supply of fertile land under cultivation by capturing the fruits of equally fertile foreign lands—was successful in reducing agricultural rents. But one could not eliminate the locational advantage of urban lands simply by manipulating supply. As political interest in the rent question revived in the second half of the nineteenth century, largely spurred by Mill, attention focused instead on depriving landlords of the benefits of that advantage by taxation.[88] Mill proposed exempting the present value of all land from such a tax, to avoid having to ascertain what portion of the increase in value to date was attributable to improvements made by the landlord and what to its scarcity value; and taxing any future increase in value in the property, at an unspecified rate.[89] The proposal had strong political appeal in England throughout the balance of the century. A version of it was eventually enacted in the Budget of 1909, which imposed a 20 percent tax on future "unearned increments" in urban lands not used for building purposes, a measure that was extended in 1947 to the future increments in all lands.[90]

Henry George was the more famous, although ultimately less successful, apostle of a land tax. Whereas Mill regarded land rents as only one of a number of incomes that the state presumptively had a moral claim on through taxation or other means, George thought that they occupied that position uniquely. In *Progress and Poverty*, his wildly popular manifesto of what became known as the "single-tax" movement, George proposed not only imposing a sweeping land tax but also simultaneously repealing all other taxes. Unlike Mill's proposal, George's land tax was not limited to the future unearned increments in the value of property. It would have levied a 100 percent tax on all pure ground rents (that is, rents on the portion of land value attributable solely to the undeveloped site), whether they reflected value that accrued before or after enactment of the tax, leaving untaxed any rents attributable to improvements on the land.[91] The proposal—which in effect expropriated the economic value of land—thus amounted, as George acknowledged, to "a simpler, easier, and quieter way" to attain the same end as abolishing private property in land entirely.[92] George candidly stated his proposal as follows: "[l]et the individuals who now hold [land] still retain, if they want to, possession of what they are pleased to call *their* land. Let them continue to call it *their* land. Let them buy and sell, and bequeath and devise it. We may safely leave them the shell, if we take the kernel."[93]

George himself was influenced as much by the individualist tradition impelling Herbert Spencer's initial opposition to private land ownership as by the collectivist tradition impelling Mill's. But it was Mill's successors rather than Spencer's who took George to heart.[94] The single-tax movement had enormous popular appeal in England and the United States in the twenty years after *Progress and Poverty* was published.[95] But other than George, the movement garnered little professional support within the then-burgeoning American economics establishment, most of whose members regarded its underlying theory as hopelessly amateurish.[96] Unlike Mill's proposal in England, it also had no significant legislative success in either country.[97] It may, however, have had indirect influence in a number of areas, including spurring local communities to rely more on a nonconfiscatory property tax (albeit on both land and improvements), to tax vacant land at higher rates, and to adopt rent control ordinances limiting the capital base on which allowable rents were computed to the landlord's actual investment in land and improvements.[98]

The most significant influence of the land-tax movement, however, was the fuel that it lent to broader progressive and socialist movements for distributional reform.[99] As John Hobson stated in 1897, in a thoughtful assessment of George's significance, "The real importance of Henry George is derived from the fact that he was able to drive an abstract notion, that of economic rent, into the minds of a large number of 'practical' men, and to generate therefrom a social movement."[100] Once the idea of rent, or surplus, as the key to distributional justice was planted in the public imagination, in time it naturally expanded beyond land, to economic rents in any form. In this respect, Hale was typical. He early on flirted with a Millian version of a land tax, arguing in a 1912 proposal to the Department of the Interior that when the government makes agricultural land grants, it ought to insert a condition in the grant "to the effect that if after the expiration of say 25 years the land should be more valuable for other than agricultural purposes, the government might condemn it by eminent domain proceedings, paying therefor the value of any improvements made by the owner plus a small bonus, but *not* the increased value of the land, except for such increase as was due to the owner's own cultivation." The result, said Hale, would be that "[t]he honest applicant for agricultural land would have every benefit he now gets from such land, *except* the speculative benefit which is not part of the incentive which induces him to farm; and depriving him of that will be of immense benefit to the rest of the community in the course of 25 years."[101] In addition, Hale qualifiedly supported the single-taxers in his early correspondence,[102] and some of his proposals for regulating the return of public utilities retain a strong Georgian flavor.[103] But like most progressives attracted to Georgian rent theory, Hale ultimately rejected the Georgians' single-minded focus on land, in favor of a broad-based attack on unearned incomes in any form.[104]

The Marginal Revolution

Had the single-tax movement ever achieved its political objectives, as a practical matter it might well have effected a radical redistribution of wealth. But as a theoretical matter, its analysis was wholly within the Ricardian tradition, which—with the notable exception of land—left unquestioned the claim of pre-Ricardian classical economics that the competitive market would automatically achieve distributive justice.

That claim was shaken by the advent of marginal analysis in the latter part of the nineteenth century, which revolutionized classical theories of value and distribution. In the 1870s, William Jevons, Carl von Menger, and Léon Walras independently put forth a new theory of value. It asserted that in a competitive market, the prices of products and services would be determined not by the cost of factors that go into their production (as classical economists had believed), but rather by their value to the marginal consumer (their so-called "marginal utility"). That is to say, prices would be determined by marginal demand, reflecting the subjective value of goods or services to the marginal consumer, rather than by supply, reflecting the cost of production.[105]

In the 1880s and 1890s, John Bates (J. B.) Clark, Philip Wicksteed, and Knut Wicksell extended the central insight of marginal utility analysis to distribution theory, through the development of so-called marginal productivity theory.[106] Just as the price of final goods is determined by their utility to marginal consumers, Clark and the others argued, the price of each factor is determined by its contribution to value for the marginal purchaser (its so-called "marginal productivity"), assuming all other factors are held constant. The effect was to generalize Ricardian rent theory to all factors of production—land, labor, and capital—under conditions of competition.[107] Ricardo, in effect, had argued that if one holds the amount of land constant and applies increasing doses of capital-and-labor to it, capital-and-labor will earn its marginal product, equal to the value of crops that it will generate on no-rent land. Land will earn the surplus in the form of rent, equal to the difference between the average and marginal productivity of the variable product. Wicksteed, Wicksell, and Clark saw that one could extend the analysis to each factor of production, holding all others constant. Thus, for example, when land is the variable factor and labor-and-capital is held constant, "the margin [meaning rent paid for land] will be a no-wage, no-interest margin,"[108] and the residual surplus will be equal to interest and wages.[109]

By generalizing Ricardian rent theory, marginal productivity analysis provided what classical supply-side explanations of distribution could not: a means, as Wicksteed put it, by which all the laws of factor pricing could "be expressed in common terms."[110] In conjunction with marginal utility analysis, marginal productivity analysis produced a unified theory of value and distribution, in which all prices (for factors as well as the final product) were driven by the demands of marginal consumers. That is, the marginal utility of a final product to consumers determined the price of the product; the price of the product in turn determined the prices of factors that went into it, in accordance with their marginal contribution to its value.[111]

But of more importance for present purposes, marginal productivity analysis provided the basis for generalizing Ricardo's theory of differential land rents to all factors of production. As Wicksteed, Wicksell, and J. B. Clark saw, Ricardian land rents were just a special case of the general principle that rents will accrue to the more productive (that is, inframarginal) units of any factor that is not reproducible at constant costs.[112] Thus, Ricardo's assumption of an absolutely fixed supply of land was just "a limiting case of the infinite array of possible supply elasticities."[113] As Hale maintained, whenever supply cannot be readily altered at costs that do not increase with quantity, the "owners of superior resources," in the form of scarce land or capital equipment acquired for lower than reproduction cost, will realize a surplus return in excess of costs.[114] While early marginalist analysis concentrated on rents accruing to land and other forms of concrete capital, the same logic suggested that rents should accrue to labor and pure capital as well. In Marshall's terms, there will be a "worker's surplus" or "saver's surplus" whenever one is remunerated for work or waiting, respectively, at a price (determined by the marginal productivity of one's labor or capital) that exceeds the minimum amount that one would have demanded to provide it—in short, whenever one is an inframarginal supplier.[115]

By the 1890s, marginal analysis had established complete dominance in economic analysis. Hale was typical of his generation of economists, in declaring it in 1924 "the more sophisticated of accepted theory."[116] Its influence was enormous on the generation of political theorists and socially minded economists writing from the 1880s through the 1920s, who set about to rethink, in light of its lessons, the classical economists' claims that the market would automatically achieve allocative efficiency and distributive justice. For present purposes, it is the latter claim that is relevant. But as the former claim also attracted significant attention from the institutional economists, it is worth a brief excursion.

Allocative Efficiency

Marginalism strengthened considerably the classical claims that the "unregulated" market would achieve allocative efficiency, by supplying the mechanism by which it might be supposed to do so. Marginalist value theory predicted that final goods would automatically be priced proportional to their marginal utility. Marginalist distribution theory predicted that factors going into producing those final goods would automatically be priced proportional to their marginal productivity. The two principles together (both illustrations of the so-called "equimarginal principle"), when built up into Walras's general equilibrium theory, predicted that the market automatically allocated resources to ends that would generate the greatest aggregate utility.[117]

At the same time, marginal analysis achieved that synthesis by a single-minded focus on exchange value, taking as given a host of social, psychological, and institutional factors that conditioned that value. Mainstream economists understandably regarded that narrowing of focus as indispensable to the considerable analytical progress that neoclassical economics had made. As Schumpeter declared, marginal analysis lifted "the logical core of the economic process above the ground of the institutional garb in which it is given to observation," thereby making logical generality possible.[118] But to at least some of its institutionalist and progressive critics, what marginalism thereby left behind cast serious doubt on the significance of what remained.[119] The most vociferous attacks came from Thorstein Veblen.[120] Aiming his fire at marginal analysis in general—the method of inference, declared Veblen, "by which an individual is presumed invariably to balance pleasure and pain under given conditions that are presumed to be normal and invariable"[121]—and in particular at the "static" model that formed the basis of J. B. Clark's economics,[122] Veblen charged that both accounts omitted virtually all that was of interest in economic life. Included in that list were the way in which preferences came to be created,[123] the influence of cultural phenomena (in particular contract and private property ownership) on all facets of the economy,[124] and the "phenomena of growth and change[,] . . . the most obtrusive and most consequential facts observable in economic life."[125] The result, Veblen suggested, was a theory so daft in its aspirations to universality as to be merely comical: ". . . so that, *e.g.*, a gang of Aleutian Islanders shushing about in the wrack and surf with rakes and magical incantations for the capture of shell-fish are held, in point of taxonomic reality, to be engaged on a feat of hedonistic equilibration in rent, wages, and interest. And that is all there is to it."[126]

But numerous others joined the fray, including Hale, John Maurice (J. M.) Clark, C. E. Ayres, John Commons, John Hobson, Leonard Hobhouse, and Frank Knight. First, they argued, the claim that the unregulated market will automatically allocate resources to ends that generate the greatest aggregate happiness rests on the dubious equation of choice and utility. The assumption that people choose what gives them utility had come under fire without the prompting of marginalism, in the arguments of Thomas Hill Green and others for state paternalism in the service of positive freedom—the freedom to do not what one wanted, but what the "best" version of one might want.[127] However, the prominent role of utility in marginal analysis gave new urgency to the question of whether transitory human preferences as reflected in price measurements were an adequate measure of individual (and hence in the aggregate, societal) well-being. Figures as diverse as J. M. Clark, John Commons, Wesley Mitchell, Frank Knight, Walter Lippmann, Leonard Hobhouse, Alfred Marshall, Arthur Hadley, and Simon Patten all raised doubts on this score, pointing inter alia to the power of custom, advertising, inadequate information, and self-destructive impulses to shape preferences in directions that had little to do with the rational calculation of self-interest envisioned by most economists.[128] The pioneer social psychologist Charles Horton Cooley expressed that skepticism with particular force: "It would be fatuous to assume that the market process expressed the *good* of society. The demand on which it is based is a turbid current coming down from the past. . . To accept this stream as pure and to reform only the mechanisms of distribution would be as if a city drawing its drinking-water from a polluted river should expect to escape typhoid by using clean pipes."[129]

In response to such attacks, mainstream economists abandoned entirely the hedonistic notion of utility, current in one form or another since Bentham's felicific calculus, in favor of revealed preferences (that is, choice), measured by the marginal rate at which consumers substituted one commodity for another.[130] Neoclassical economics thus met objections that its theory of demand was inadequate by banishing the theory from the realm of welfare economics altogether. The result was a claim that was tautologically true: choice always equated with utility, because utility was redefined to mean nothing but choice. But that analytical victory, progressives charged, was achieved at the cost of relinquishing any claims to the social significance of choice. As J. M. Clark stated: "In the hedonistic form of the marginalist theory 'product' meant a social gain, a creation of utility. With the general abandonment of utilitarian psychology . . . it has seemed to some that the product which governs rewards must be defined as anything that commands a price, with no implications of a social character."[131] Or as he put it more succinctly elsewhere, the theory of marginal utility was simply a way of saying that one buys what one buys.[132]

Second, even if individual choice approximates individual welfare, the assumption that maximizing individual choice will maximize *social* welfare, progressives argued, ignores the fact that many of those choices will impose external costs on others in current and future generations.[133] As Herbert Davenport asserted, with Veblenesque sarcasm, it is hard to believe that private exchange transactions reflect social utility, when a football coach is accorded a salary of $1,000 a month and an instructor of economics $1000 a year, or a lawyer can get rich by advising clients how legally to do illegal things. Surely the social organism that would countenance such a result, suggested Davenport, ought to be put in "a social insane asylum."[134] James Bonbright, more skeptical that the "economic heretics" who attacked orthodox economics for its failure to develop a theory of social value would be able to generate a plausible theory themselves, nonetheless concluded that "the abandonment [of the attempt] would mean the bankruptcy of economics as a guide to social action."[135]

Finally, the marginalists' claim, at most, was that *given* an initial set of preferences and endowments and a fixed state of technology, the market would automatically allocate resources so as to maximize the satisfaction of those preferences—in more familiar contemporary terminology, that it would achieve Pareto optimality.[136] The limited nature of that claim naturally raised the possibility that by altering any of those givens, the state could generate a new set of Pareto-optimal equilibrium prices that increased aggregate utility. For the institutionalists, like most of the other progressives, that possibility was presented acutely by the hypothesis, popularized by Edgeworth at the end of the nineteenth century, that the utility of each additional dollar declines as one's overall wealth increases. At the extreme, Edgeworth's hypothesis suggested that any contributions that the market could make to aggregate utility by achieving a Pareto optimal state *given* an initial distribution of wealth were swamped by the utility gains from a radically egalitarian redistribution of that wealth.[137] That politically explosive suggestion was ultimately derailed by mainstream economists' almost universal skepticism, crystallized by Lionel Robbins in 1935, whether one could make the comparisons among individuals' utilities that such a prescription required.[138]

Hale incorporated the preceding critiques in his work.[139] In an unpublished manuscript written around 1915, entitled "Defects of the Marginal Utility Measure of Service," he also explored the possibility that the government could increase aggregate consumer surplus over the results of the unregulated market by rechanneling resources from goods that generated low consumer surplus to inframarginal purchasers to those that could potentially generate high surplus to (new) inframarginal purchasers.[140] But the central question for Hale, like most other progressives, was the light shed by the marginalist revolution on the distributive justice of the market.

Distributive Justice

The classical claim that the market would automatically achieve distributive justice had come under vociferous internal attack throughout the nineteenth century in the exploitation theory advanced (among others) by Sismondi, Rodbertus, Lassalle, and finally Marx.[141] Building on suggestions of a pure labor theory of value in Smith and Ricardo, they argued that the exchange value of goods is determined solely by the quantity of labor required for their production. That is to say, labor alone produced value. But to realize that value in an industrialized society, labor required access to the means of production, which (under the system of private property) had come to be owned exclusively by a small group of capitalists. The only way for workers to obtain access was thus to sell their labor to capitalists through a wage contract. By exploiting the necessitous conditions and weak bargaining position of workers (made weaker over time, in Marx's account, by inexorably increasing unemployment), capitalists were able to negotiate terms for the wage contract that allowed them to retain most of the surplus value produced by labor, over and above subsistence wages.

The first wave of marginalism in the 1870s dealt what most contemporary critics regarded as a fatal blow to exploitation theory.[142] By demonstrating that the value of all goods and services reflected their utility to marginal purchasers rather than their cost of production, it appeared to refute definitively the classical economists' descriptive labor theory of value. If that descriptive claim was wrong, so also was the normative Marxian claim that followed from it, that the distributive share paid to capital in the form of interest or other profits was merely a theft of a portion of labor's product, made legal by the extortive rights attached to private property. While thus (deliberately or otherwise) interring Marx's critique,[143] most of the marginalists purported to offer no alternative view on whether the market was distributively just. As Marshall described that intellectual diffidence, "the Laws of Economics are statements of tendencies expressed in the indicative mood, and not ethical precepts in the imperative."[144] To this extent, marginal analysis represented a partial (albeit ironic) triumph for Mill's and Sidgwick's plea to separate production and distribution (distribution, that is, in the sense of the distributive shares that went to individuals, not the pricing of factors). They were separated not as Mill had done by treating the two questions as of separate but equal weight, but by banishing distribution from the realm of economics altogether, and into that of ethics.

Within the first generation of marginalists, the notable exception was John Bates Clark.[145] In his 1899 book, *The Distribution of Wealth*, Clark argued that the theory of marginal productivity—which predicts that "free competition tends to give to labor what labor creates, to capitalists what capital creates, and to *entrepreneurs* what the coordinating function creates"—means that the market will automatically distribute income to factors in accordance with the ordinary intuition of justice: "to each what he creates."[146] Although Clark declined to pass judgment on that intuition one way or the other, consigning such questions to the realm of "pure ethics,"[147] it is clear throughout *Distribution* that he regarded it as self-evidently right.

The result was a thoroughgoing apologetic for the distributive results of free-market capitalism. Clark thereby completed the work begun by Senior in extending the Lockean justification for property from labor to capital. If there is some doubt about the political motivation behind marginal utility analysis, there is none about Clark's marginal productivity theory.[148] *The Distribution of Wealth* is replete with comments reflecting Clark's belief that the greatest threat to society lay in the socialist charge that free competition in a capitalist society exploits the laboring classes by robbing them of a portion of their rightful product.[149] If the allegation were true, Clark said, "every right-minded man should become a socialist."[150] As he put it portentously, "[M]ore hinges on the truth of [the natural law of distribution] than any introductory words can state. The right of society to exist in its present form, and the probability that it will continue so to exist, are at stake."[151] By demonstrating that each factor of production was automatically rewarded on the basis of its respective contribution to the final joint product, Clark's version of marginal productivity purported to dispose not merely of Marxian exploitation theories—a job already accomplished in most people's minds by marginal utility analysis when it discredited the labor theory of value—but of all other theories of exploitation as well. Clark's (aptly named) *Social Justice Without Socialism*, published in 1914, contains a particularly stark example of the quasi-religious fervor with which Clark embraced marginal productivity analysis as the moral salvation of capitalism. The natural law of distribution implied by marginal productivity, he argued,

> tends in the direction of a fair division of products between employer and employee, and if it could work entirely without hindrances, would actually give to every laborer substantially what he produces. In the midst of all prevalent abuses this basic law asserts itself like a law of gravitation, and so long as monopoly is excluded and competition is free . . . its action cannot be stopped . . . If there are "inspirational points" on the mountain-tops of science . . . this is one of them, and it is reached whenever a man discovers that in a highly imperfect society the fundamental law makes for justice, that it is impossible to prevent it from working and that it is entirely possible to remove the hindrances it encounters . . . Nature is behind the reformer . . . To get a glimpse of what it can do and what man can help it do is to get a vision of the kingdoms of the earth, and the glory of them—a glory that may come from a moral redemption of the economic system.[152]

Although Clark's particular brand of naive apologetics was a source of embarrassment for most mainstream economists,[153] it nonetheless attracted a significant following among economists and noneconomists alike, becoming, as Seligman noted, "a byword for devotees of the *status quo*."[154] Not surprisingly, it was a prime target of progressive economists in the first two decades of the century. The most heated debate concerned whether, as a descriptive matter, it was possible to measure the marginal product of any factor in isolation, given that the factors of production are complements.[155] The argument, of course, was not purely academic. If, for example, as Hobson argued, the output specifically attributed to the last worker really resulted from the cooperation of the total number of workers and capital equipment, why should the particular division of that joint product arrived at by the market be inherently "just"? As Veblen said, any claim that it is reduces ultimately to a tautology: "By a dialectical conversion of the terms, this metaphysical dictum [that ownership of property goes to the workman who has produced it], is made to fit the circumstances . . . by construing acquisition of property to mean production of wealth; so that a businessman is looked upon as the putative producer of whatever wealth he acquires. . . . His acquiring a defensible title to it makes him the putative producer of it."[156]

Hale's predominant attack, however, was on the internal logic of Clark's normative argument. Granting for the sake of argument that the market price paid to each factor correctly isolated that factor's marginal product, it did not follow that the resulting distribution of wealth was just. The "marginal product," Hale argued, formally measured the value to the purchaser of a given input, not the cost to the supplier of providing it. In fact, Clark's marginal productivity theory contained no theory of costs at all. As Hale remarked, "the basis of distribution on this theory has shifted from the earlier basis of 'sacrifice' to that of 'imputed productivity,' a basis which Clark expressly approves as 'ethical,' but without any discussion of the grounds."[157] As noted before, that was sufficient to refute the Marxian claim that labor alone produced value, and hence labor alone was entitled to its rewards.[158] But it did not itself justify the distributive effects of the market. In the absence of any theory of costs, those effects could not be defended on strict Lockean grounds. If Clark intended some other grounds, he never stated them. As a result, Hale argued, Clark's claim that the market was just reduced to the tautological assertion that people are entitled to the market value of what they produced because that is what it fetched. Veblen had dismissed that same tautology, stating that it answers no pertinent question of equity to say "that the wages of labor are just and fair because they are all that is paid to labor as wages."[159] Davenport, making substantially the same point, noted that "[o]ne might concur in Clark's [descriptive] thesis and be yet the most radical of socialists. That rent is paid as the precise correlative of the productive efficiency of land has nothing to say as to the right of private ownership in land."[160]

But if most neoclassical economists themselves declined to infer from marginal analysis anything about the distributive justice of the market (or, in Clark's case, purported to but failed), by generalizing Ricardian rent theory to all factors of production, they provided the tools for others to do the job. Marginalism disproved the classical assumption that in competitive markets, prices would coincide with costs. More precisely, it showed that assumption held true only where inputs were reproducible at constant costs—in other words, where supply was completely elastic.[161] In all other cases, the owners of scarce resources would receive "economic rents" in excess of costs.

Although marginal analysis gave an analytical structure for generalizing Ricardian rent theory to all factors of production, it said nothing about the actual incidence of rents—that is, the extent of producer's surplus accruing to a given factor. For that, one needed two things: a normative theory of what ought to count as a cost, and an empirical guess about the shape of the cost curve. Despite the prominence of rent-theory arguments for redistribution at the turn of the century, the former question received surprisingly little attention. Most commentators simply assumed without discussion that "costs" for these purposes ought to be equated with incentive-based costs. That is to say, costs should be measured by the minimal price (the so-called "reservation price") that a would-be worker or saver would demand for forgoing leisure or present consumption. As to the latter question, while the first generation of marginalists had little interest in what determined supply of factors, Marshall and his successors supplied a partial answer, with some prodding from the rent-theory progressives.

In his piece on "Economic Theory and the Statesman," Hale provided an admirably lucid overview of the state of the supply-side portion of economic theory as of 1924. The summary that follows tracks in broad outline Hale's argument, with points overlooked by Hale and most other progressives liberally interpolated.

Wages. With the demise of Malthus's Iron Law of Wages, economists abandoned any notion that the relevant cost of labor was the physical cost of keeping workers alive and of reproducing the next generation of workers. In its place, most economists focused instead on the psychic disutility of work.[162] Unless one assumes that work is altogether a pleasure, said Hale, reflecting the common view, there is clearly some sacrifice involved in obtaining wages.[163] The assumption (implicit in Hale's statement) that the disutility of work entitles the worker to its product seems at first glance the most Lockean of all Lockean premises. But a number of peculiarities, both conceptual and moral, arise in defining the "costs" of labor for Lockean purposes, and in equating such costs loosely with the reservation price of workers—that is, with the minimum payment necessary to induce them to forgo leisure.

The first peculiarity was raised, virtually alone among progressives, by Herbert Davenport. The price that a worker demands for forgoing a marginal hour of leisure, Davenport argued, measures only the relative preferences such worker has for leisure and money (what modern economists would describe as the "marginal rate of substitution" between the two goods). It says nothing about the absolute pleasure or pain associated with either choice. For the artist who "may have enjoyed every hour of his productive activity, and may leave it . . . [only] at the call of some greater alternative pleasure awaiting him," the choice may be "between pleasant productive activity, on the one hand, and pleasant leisure on the other; [so that] even at the margin . . . there is no necessity of pain cost."[164] Moreover, for those workers for whom work may be unpleasant, one cannot deduce the degree of unpleasantness from the price that they demand for enduring it, as that price reflects only the *relative* values that they place on avoiding work and obtaining money. For Davenport at least, the latter point had important political implications. Accepting the general (post-Edgeworthian) view that the utility of money declines with increasing wealth, Davenport argued that the relative reservation prices placed on work were therefore likely systematically to understate the relative pain that work entailed for the poor as compared with the rich.[165]

Second, as Marshall noted, "[a] great part of a worker's earnings are of the nature of a deferred return to the trouble and expense of preparing him for his work," in the form of education and other training.[166] Assuming that those expenses should be included as part of a worker's costs, Marshall argued, it is no easy matter to calculate them. Because costs of education and rearing are already sunk costs for most of the existing workforce, they will not be reflected in the price actually demanded at any time for forgoing leisure (that is, in the short-run supply curve).[167] Moreover, as the worker's parents rather than the worker incurred many of those costs, compensation for them will constitute a surplus to the worker *unless* one treats the (intergenerational) family as one unit for these purposes.[168]

Finally, the notion that people are entitled to what they earn by the sacrifice entailed in their labor rests on the premise that people "own" the right not to work at all. One need not go so far as to advocate slavery to question that premise. One could, for example, believe that there exists a *moral* obligation on every citizen to contribute some amount of labor to society in accordance with her ability, in exchange for support from the state determined solely by her needs. In such a world, the state might well opt not to compel labor from those who are unwilling to give it; but it would regard the fruits of such labor as was voluntarily given as rightfully owned by all. Whether the resulting scheme of entitlements should be considered a collectivist variant of Lockeanism or a repudiation of it entirely is another matter.

Notwithstanding the preceding critiques, most progressive economists, including Hale, generally accepted that the minimum price that workers demanded for forgoing leisure should be equated with their relevant sacrifice for moral (Lockean) purposes. The fight was over whether the market actually set wages at that level. As Mill had long ago noted, casual empiricism cast serious doubt on the Smithian hypothesis that in a static economy, the labor supply would automatically adjust to equate wages with workers' sacrifices (with differences in wages explicable by differences in sacrifices). Contrary to Smith's assumption, Mill asserted, wages tended to vary inversely, not directly, with the disagreeableness of an occupation.[169] Later theorists, expanding on suggestions that Mill himself had offered, argued that the observed disparity between wages and sacrifice was explainable by several factors.

The first was the fact that natural scarcity of talent would always create (in Marshall's words) a "rent of rare natural abilities."[170] As Mill argued, however expedient it might be to remunerate people for such abilities in accordance with their scarcity value, the resulting distribution did not compensate for costs incurred in exercising those abilities: "[I]t is giving to those who have; assigning most to those who are already most favoured by nature."[171] Hale, quoting the foregoing passage with approval, noted that the remuneration commanded by scarce talents was no more deserved than that extracted by the passerby saving the drowning millionaire. If exploitation of the latter transitory monopoly position was clearly unjust, why was exploitation of a permanent monopoly position, created by fortuities of nature, any more just?[172]

Second, Smith had assumed that any remaining disparities between wage and sacrifice would be smoothed out by drawing labor from the less to the more favorable occupations. That process required, however, that labor be relatively mobile, an assumption that was refuted by the long lag time (often a whole generation) required to train workers for a new occupation,[173] and what Cairnes had long ago observed to be the effectively "non-competing" nature of labor groups in industrial society.[174] Frank Taussig, elaborating on Cairnes's theory, noted that at least some of the barriers between large groups that interfered with intergroup mobility—notably social stratification and the expense of education—tended to keep children in the range of occupations to which their parents belonged.[175] Furthermore, argued Hale, reflecting the general disrepute into which Malthusian population theory had fallen, there was no reason to believe that "the supply of labor [will] increase from within the group by a Malthusian response to the favorable condition therein." As a result, Hale argued, while conceivable that within the very lowest paid group, wages tend toward the minimum level that is necessary to support the cost of living, with laborers drifting in and out of the reservoir of the unemployed with any appreciable change in demand, for all groups above that, wages are from the laborer's point of view "an opportunity cost, not a sacrifice cost or an incentive cost."[176] In short, wages may reflect scarcity rents even to the marginal worker.

Third, assuming that the price demanded by most workers for an additional hour of labor increased with the quantity supplied (an assumption subscribed to by most post-Marshallian neoclassical economists), wage rates would generate an inframarginal surplus for most workers even in those occupations in which supply was relatively elastic, and hence in which each worker was paid for her marginal hour of labor only enough to compensate for her sacrifice.[177]

Capital. Early marginalists, following J. B. Clark's usage, conventionally divided payments to capital into interest paid on pure capital (money) and rent paid on all fixed capital, including land and equipment (durable capital goods).[178]

As to interest, as Hale noted, as long as opportunities exist to earn interest in some industries, such payments compensate for opportunity costs "from the viewpoint of industry as a whole."[179] The relevant question from the vantage point of rent theory was whether such payments compensate for real costs to individual investors.

Most commentators of the period (progressives and conservatives alike) accepted the Seniorian premise that the relevant "cost" for these purposes was the psychological irksomeness of abstaining from current consumption, measured by the minimum price a would-be saver demanded for enduring it.[180] That assumption—in effect equating "sacrifice" with reservation price—was vulnerable to attack on a couple of grounds, paralleling critiques suggested previously with regard to wages. First, as with a right to wages demanded for forgoing leisure, it presupposes a right to current consumption. That is to say, it presupposes that a would-be saver owns the capital to begin with. In a regime of severely curtailed inheritance or other property rights, where most capital escheats to the state, the community as a whole and not individual investors would be entitled to whatever payment was extracted in return for deferring consumption. One need not go as far as abolishing private property to reach that result. As G. A. Kleene noted, it is reached in a capitalist economy whenever the government invests the proceeds of an income or wealth tax in productive apparatus. The government thereby deprives the taxpayer of the right to spend *or* save a portion of his property, paying the taxpayer "no distinguishable personal return from the government's investment of tax funds."[181] Hale, in an early, unpublished review of H. G. Brown's *The Theory of Earned and Unearned Incomes*, suggested a subtler variant of the same argument to undercut an individual's claim even to interest earned on property left nominally in his hands:

> If a man is fairly in possession of a capital sum, which he is at liberty to spend, does it not follow that he is entitled morally to all he can get by investing it? Not necessarily. It may be good social policy to give him a large spending power—presumably as an incentive to service rendered in the past. It may none the less be consistent with that policy to limit the manner in which he may exercise that spending power—for instance by forbidding him to buy liquor or votes. If his power to spend his income in the formation of capital is made conditional on his sharing with the public some part of the interest—why not? provided only he be not thereby deterred from choosing to invest.[182]

In short, if all "rights" of ownership are merely conditional privileges held at the sufferance of the state, and the privilege of spending what one "owns" on current consumption has already been burdened with conditions, why should we think it unjust to burden as well the privilege of saving it for future consumption?[183]

Second, even granting a strong private property regime that bestows on owners the choice to save their wealth or to spend it currently more or less as they see fit, it was not self-evident why, as Senior and his followers had asserted, the irksomeness of abstinence for those who opt to save is the sort of sacrifice for which one has a right to compensation (or more precisely, the sort of sacrifice that gives one a Lockean entitlement to the minimal compensation that one demands for enduring it). As suggested before, Senior had self-consciously offered up "abstinence" as a counterpart to the exertions of labor, suggesting that both represented the underlying "real cost" to suppliers for which profit and wages, respectively, were fair recompense. The specter of all savers—the Rothschilds of the world included— suffering under the enormous weight of self-denial provoked (not surprisingly) a contemptuous response from the early socialist camp, of which Lassalle's diatribe against Senior is probably the most famous example: "The profit of capital is the 'wage of abstinence.' Happy, even priceless expression!

The ascetic millionaires of Europe! Like Indian penitents or pillar saints they stand: on one leg, each on his column, with straining arm and pendulous body and pallid looks, holding a plate towards the people to collect the wages of their Abstinence. In their midst, towering above all his fellows, as head penitent and ascetic, the Baron Rothschild! This is the condition of society! How could I ever so much misunderstand it!"[184]

It is conceivable that attacks like Lassalle's were meant to suggest (in inchoate premarginalist form) that a significant amount of savings particularly among the wealthy was inframarginal. The implications of that possibility are explored later. But as Davenport argued, translating Lassalle's skepticism into marginalist terms, there is reason to doubt the absolute sacrifice entailed in deferring consumption for the marginal saver as well. Applying the same analysis to savings that he had applied to labor, Davenport argued that if the "pain of abstinence" is taken merely to denote the fact that interest must embody attractions sufficient at the margin to displace the attractions of present consumption, the pain axiomatically exists for all savers. In that limited sense of an opportunity cost, equal to the margin of displacement between present and future uses of wealth, abstinence reflects a cost as much for a Rothschild as for a pauper. But the existence of such a margin of displacement says nothing at all about the absolute measure of pain undergone or the resistance overcome: "The marginal postponement of consumption, like any other case of margins, is a ratio relation; any particular item of saving is marginal, not because of the high significance of the abstinence protest, but merely because the forces making for present consumption, representative, it may be, of very great or of very limited present need, are at an approximate equilibrium against the estimates of the advantages promised by postponement."[185] As with wages, Davenport argued, by erroneously treating the absolute price demanded for saving as a measure of its absolute pain, we are likely systematically to understate the real sacrifice of the poor and overstate that of the rich.[186]

Indeed, Davenport argued, with deferred consumption even more than with labor, there is reason to doubt that forgoing one option (present consumption) for another (future consumption) inflicts pain at all, in a normal hedonic calculus. The choice between present and future consumption is merely a choice between "positive gratifications." If so, "it would be a waste of sympathy to grieve with one who has to choose between two pleasures, and to call either pleasure a pain because it is conditioned on going without the other pleasure."[187] If there is any pain involved in saving, Davenport concluded, it lies in the fact that a present pressing want remains unappeased, *not* in the fact that a saver possessed income that he could have used to alleviate it, had he not concluded that his future wants were even more pressing:

> [W]here the individual is in possession of sufficient money to buy him a meal, but decides to save his money and to lend it, . . . the *abstinence* [is not] a pain. It is only the *hunger* that is a pain. A man having the hunger but no money has unquestionably one pain and no more, that of hunger. So much is clear. If now we take this man to have both the hunger and the money, he has not now two pains, one of hunger and one of abstinence, but only the one original pain of hunger. His is, indeed, the fortunate case of one who need have no pain at all if only he would let go of his money. Perhaps to lose his money would be painful, but only in the sense that it would involve the continuance of the pain of hunger. But to lend the money is not a pain, and the only pain in the case is that gnawing at his vitals that he has declined to still . . . Were this not the truth, the case of one having both the hunger and the money would be the especially grievous case . . . the rich who could spend, but do not, would be the unfortunates of the world . . . There is nothing especially touching, then, in the fact that [a man] has the dollar, and that, in spending it now or later, he has to forego an alternative spending. It appears, then, that not only the necessity of a choice between pleasures is not a pain, but also, and with equal certainty, that the necessity of a choice between pains is not a pain."[188]

For Davenport, the normative implications of his analysis were clear. Senior's defense of interest as "the wages of Abstinence" presumes that interest is compensation for (as Davenport put it) the "grief and groan of saving."[189] But if "there is no relation between the income from property and the amount of pain or of deserving involved either in the getting of property or in the keeping of it," Davenport concluded, "nothing remains of the notion of abstinence as an ethical justification of interest."[190] However, Davenport's view garnered surprisingly weak support among ardent progressive rent theorists, who for the most part acquiesced without comment in the view that the pain of abstinence generated an entitlement to whatever minimal price was demanded in recompense.[191] The omission of any serious discussion on this point seems particularly surprising, given that it comes in the face of the persistent Marxian assertion, arguably equally undefended but politically potent nonetheless, that "the service performed by capital is a 'free' good, rendered without sacrifice."[192] For most progressives, the omission may simply reflect their twin allegiances to utilitarian and Lockean concerns. As most progressives (including Hale) accepted the necessity both of leaving a significant portion of capital in private hands and of inducing owners to invest some portion of it in productive capacity,[193] they were prepared to protect the marginal supply price for interest on purely utilitarian grounds. Under the circumstances, it is perhaps understandable that they failed to inquire deeply whether they should have reached the same conclusion on grounds of moral entitlement. Indeed, in many of their discussions of interest—and Hale's summary treatment of interest in "Economic Theory and the Statesman" is no exception—one often cannot tell on which of the two grounds the argument is proceeding at any given moment.

Be that as it may, if, as virtually all commentators including Hale seemed to agree, the irksomeness of forbearance ought to be treated as a real cost, the empirical question facing rent theorists was the extent to which interest payments in fact reflected compensation for that cost. In the case of marginal savers, the answer turned on whether supply was relatively inelastic at the point at which supply and demand intersected (that is to say, on whether the same quantity of loanable funds would be forthcoming even at a somewhat lower interest rate). If it was relatively inelastic, then price would be determined solely by demand, and some portion of the return even to marginal savers would constitute rents. If not, then the entire return to marginal savers would just compensate for the costs of forbearance.[194] Hale, inclining toward the latter view, accepted with it the utilitarian necessity (if not the justice) of protecting the return to the marginal investors.[195]

That situation would still leave a surplus for the inframarginal investor—yet another symptom, said Hale, of the "absence of perfect competition," in which "the marginal investors [are] competing with the intramarginal [sic] at a greater cost in terms of sacrifice."[196] Given the commonly shared view that wealthy savers were disproportionately inframarginal savers, this particular symptom had great political salience. But, concluded Hale, any plan to reduce that surplus (for example, by taxation) without reducing supply "depends for its success on the doubtful possibility of singling out those investors who are wholly 'intramarginal.'"[197]

With respect to fixed capital (durable capital goods, both land and equipment), the conventional definition of "surplus" was clearer: in a competitive industry it was simply the excess earnings obtained by low-cost firms over the earnings of the marginal firm.[198] Most economists followed J. B. Clark and Marshall in anticipating that the costs of marginal and inframarginal producers would diverge significantly, at least in the Marshallian short period, because land and capital equipment are subject to the law of diminishing returns and because the supply of most fixed capital goods is "fixed (or at any rate . . . not responsive to changes in the prices obtainable for their use)."[199] As a result, rents should accrue to those producers with a short-run cost advantage over marginal producers because they possess superior factors of production (a favorable site that reduces freight charges, superior equipment, technological know-how, patents, superior management, and so on). Marshall, reserving the word "rent" for the "free gifts of nature" in land, termed these excess returns to inframarginal producers "quasi-rents."[200] Such quasi-rents, Marshall believed, were only a short-run phenomenon, the result of temporary immobility of human or other capital.[201] In the long run, in competitive industries, those advantages that are not eliminated by innovation, education, and so on will be competed for by other firms, thus driving up the costs to the individual entrepreneur of acquiring them to an amount equal to their surplus value.[202] At that point, "the cost ladder must straighten out, and when all adjustments are completed in the long run, each firm will produce long run identical cost curves that include 'rents' as imputed or explicit costs."[203] The result, however, will not be to eliminate such surplus value entirely, but merely to transfer it to the ultimate owner of the superior resource (landlord, worker) in the form of higher rent or wages.

Thus, even in a competitive market the costs of providing capital (with cost defined liberally to mean the reservation price demanded for relinquishing it), like the costs of providing labor and land, would equal market price only for a small portion of supply. If private ownership of wealth was morally justified only on the Lockean basis that it rewarded its owners for the sacrifice involved in producing it, that fact meant that incomes from competitive markets were no more self-evidently justified than those from monopolies. Hale summarized the progressive argument in this way: "If orthodox economic reasoning would allow values of capital goods to equal their reproduction cost (less depreciation) even when that exceeds the actual cost of producing them, and would allow land (which cost nothing to produce) to have a value, what becomes of the theory that 'perfect competition' brings about values equal to costs? There seems to be a rift in the economic lute. I believe it is the same rift, at bottom, as that which led Ricardo to the view that the value of goods produced under conditions of increasing cost tended to conform, not to the average cost of all the products, but to the marginal cost." The truth, said Hale, is that " 'perfect competition' does not step in the moment 'perfect monopoly' is eliminated. The excess of reproduction over production cost of an artificial capital good, and the value of land (itself the result of Ricardo's 'rent'), are symptoms, I believe of the *imperfectness* of competition . . . [where] the owners of superior resources are subject to some competition, but to competition of others who lack the same opportunities."[204]

A Rent-Theory World

Given that orthodox neoclassical economic theory itself predicted the emergence of rents in competitive markets in precisely the circumstances that Hale outlined, it seems odd, one otherwise sympathetic ally suggested to Hale, to describe the existence of such rents as demonstrating the "failure of competition in the orthodox sense," rather than simply a condition of competition as orthodoxy defined it.[205] Hale, writing in response, agreed that the emergence of economic rents could as easily be described as a condition of perfect competition under one definition of competition as the result of imperfect competition under another, and conceded that the former definition was the conventional one. But putting the matter the latter way, he suggested, had this advantage: it forced people to recognize that rents were as much a deviation from perfect competition as monopoly profits, at least if the "thing of significance" about competition is its ability to "keep prices at cost."[206]

Hale was hardly the only progressive to note the analogy between rents and monopoly profits, and to recognize the political capital to be gotten by exploiting it.[207] But he was one of the few (if not the only one) to draw the analogy with economic precision, as in the following example he put to Henry Rottschaefer. Suppose that the best iron mine in the community is owned by person A ("best" for these purposes meaning that a given quantity of iron ore can be extracted at lower costs than from any other mine), and that the marginal cost to A of extracting the ore increases with quantity, to a maximum of $5/ton. At the next best mine, owned by B, the lowest marginal cost at which iron can be extracted is $7/ton. Assume the following four cases, said Hale: (1) A produces up to his intensive margin, where the equilibrium price is $5/ton. (That is to say, he produces until the marginal cost of producing the last ton equals the equilibrium price at that quantity of output ($5/ton).) Since marginal cost is increasing, however, the inframarginal tons A sold cost him less than $5 to produce. Since B can produce only at a marginal cost of $7/ton, B doesn't produce at all. (2) A produces up to full capacity (that is, it is absolutely impossible for him to extract any more tons at any cost), at a marginal cost of $5/ton. However, the quantity produced is insufficient to meet demand at $5/ton, and A gets $6/ton. B still produces nothing. (3) A could produce enough to meet demand at $5/ton, but deliberately restricts output, to force the equilibrium price to $6 a ton. Again, B produces nothing. (4) Demand increases sufficiently to call B's mine into production, and the equilibrium price settles at $7/ton.

In all four cases, A receives a price above his average cost per ton of coal produced. In all but the first case, the price is also in excess of marginal cost to A. Yet, noted Hale, classical economists, at least in the context of rate regulation of utilities, would describe the entire excess above cost as monopoly profits in the first three cases, but conclude that in the fourth case, A "is no longer getting monopoly profits, but rent," simply because A is no longer the sole supplier. But, Hale concluded, if what is significant in regulating monopolies is "the absence of sufficient competition to keep prices at cost, and costs equal," there is no basis for distinguishing among the four examples. In all four cases, A realizes a surplus not because there are no other suppliers in the market, but because there are no other suppliers *at A's lowest cost.* Indeed, case (2) and case (4) are (from A's point of view) structurally indistinguishable: A's surplus in both cases is attributable in part to the inframarginal surplus to A from production under diminishing returns, in part to the natural scarcity of iron ore relative to demand. The increase in price from (2) to (4) is attributable solely to the shift in the demand curve, and has nothing to do with B's entering the market. If, as was the general view, A's entire excess profits (including profits on inframarginal sales) "may be taken away legitimately by rate regulation . . . consistent with general classical doctrines" in the first three cases, why should the answer be any different in the fourth just because another seller has entered the market at a price well above A's highest marginal cost?[208]

As Hale acknowledged to Rottschaefer, there are two other possible definitions of "monopoly profits" that might explain not regulating A's profit in case (4). Both definitions, however, presented other difficulties. First, some economists argued that the distinctive sin of monopoly producers is their artificially restricting supply. If so, that circumstance would explain not regulating A in case (4). But it would likewise require one not to regulate A in cases (1) and (2), and in case (3) to limit "monopoly profits" subject to regulation to those "profits which accrue by virtue of the owner deliberately restricting supply." As Hale noted, whether or not A was in a position to restrict supply may have "a bearing on whether the process of transferring [excess profits] to the public should be [by] the process of price reduction or . . . taxation—the former being appropriate to monopoly profits the latter to rent." But why should it have any bearing on whether the transfer is an illegitimate taking of the owner's property?

Alternatively, one could take the view that "monopoly profits" are limited to that portion of profits that exceeds whatever return (including rent) the same producer would get "without regulation under hypothetical competition." But how do we decide what that hypothetical competition would be? If we assume a supplier with marginal costs of $7/ton (our actual B), then the results in cases (1), (2), and (3) are unchanged. That is, all of A's profits are "rents," not monopoly profits, since all would have been (indeed were) realized under hypothetical competition. If we assume a supplier with marginal costs of $5/ton whose entrance into the market drives the price down to $5/ton, we treat the difference between the $5 price and A's lower costs on inframarginal units as "rent," and any excess profits resulting from an actual price above $5 as monopoly profits. However, if we are willing to make that assumption in cases (1), (2), and (3), why not in (4) as well? Why give A the benefit of the higher equilibrium price just because an actual other seller has been induced into the market by the $7/ton price?

Although economists persisted for descriptive purposes in distinguishing among different forms of economic "rents" and in differentiating all such rents from monopoly profits, Hale's view that the distinctions were meaningless in justifying the (Lockean) right to market-generated incomes reflected the conventional wisdom of most socialist and progressive critics (economists and noneconomists alike) at the turn of the century.[209] Sweeping all such deviations from cost into the broad category of "rent," such critics found in the newly constituted "rent theory" the natural replacement for the largely discredited Marxian critiques of the distributive effects of unregulated capitalism.

The Development of Rent Theory

The Fabians were the first and the most significant proponents of an expansive view of rents.[210] In the winter of 1884 to 1885, a small discussion group that included Graham Wallas, Sidney Webb, and George Bernard Shaw—core members of the Fabian Society—and, at their invitation, the economists Wicksteed and Edgeworth, met biweekly at Hampstead. The meetings were convened to master the technical aspects of Marxian economics, in order to bolster the case for its political conclusions. By the end, however, the entire group had been converted under Wicksteed's and Edgeworth's tutelage to Jevonian marginalists.[211] Wallas, recounting the significance of that conversion years later, said, "[U]nder Webb's leadership, we worked out the Jevonian anti-Marx value theory as the basis of our socialism."[212] Accepting the marginalists' descriptive claim that all factors command a price based on their relative scarcity, not on their natural productivity, the Fabians drew from the claim the Ricardian moral about land rents, but extended it to all factors of production (land, labor, and capital). In an 1888 article that became the cornerstone of Fabian economics and political theory, Sidney Webb set forth his "law of three rents": just as superior land commanded its greater marginal product in the form of land rents, so also workers endowed with native talent and the social opportunities necessary to develop it commanded theirs in the form of "rents of ability" in excess of "economic wages" (Webb's term for Malthusian subsistence level wages); and capital employed in more favorable situations—as a result of luck, timing, monopoly, and other adventitious advantages—commanded a "rent of opportunity" in excess of the normal rate of interest.[213] In short, as one Fabian tract put it, "[Rent] is a genus of which [Ricardian] land rent is only one species."[214] While reserving special fire for unearned increments in value to land, they recognized that *any* factor that is in short supply will command a payment, the magnitude of which bears no necessary or reasonable relationship to the recipient's work or sacrifice to obtain it.[215] As a result, as Mill had remarked with reference to land, "it would be no violation of the principles on which private property is grounded,"—assuming those grounds to be Lockean—"if the state should appropriate this increase of wealth, or part of it, as it arises."[216]

In England, the Fabians' conversion from Marxian to "rent theory" socialism marked the course of radical critiques of income distribution for the next forty years. Most economists and political theorists on the left (that is, those sympathetic to some version of state-enforced equalization of wealth) abandoned the labor theory of value in favor of marginal productivity.[217] With that change in the purely descriptive account of distribution, they shifted their normative attack, from the Marxian claim that income paid to capital was a theft of labor's product, to the claim that "unearned incomes" accruing to any factor of society were unjustified. The Fabian influence was most evident in the work of Leonard Hobhouse and John Hobson, who were key figures in the emerging New Liberal consensus in the first two decades of the twentieth century.[218] Both men identified the existence of rents, variously referred to as the "unproductive surplus," "improperty," or the "Unearned Increment," as the central moral failure of market distribution, and argued (closely following the Fabians) that the key to any reform program lay in "communizing" the surplus by means of a steeply progressive income tax, higher death duties, and ("if we do not deal more drastically with [it]") taxation of ground rent.[219] Hobhouse described the claim in this way in his 1911 book, *Liberalism*, which became the manifesto of the New Liberalism: "The central point of Liberal economics, then, is the equation of social service and reward. This is the principle that every function of social value requires such remuneration as serves to stimulate and maintain its effective performance; that every one who performs such a function has the right, in the strict ethical sense of that term, to such remuneration and to no more; that the residue of existing wealth should be at the disposal of the community for social purposes."

When combined with the strong residue of Georgian hostility to unearned increments in land values, rent theory in both the Fabian and the New Liberal versions crystallized public opinion against "unearned income" in any form.[220] That opposition dominated political rhetoric and political reform in Britain in the first two decades of the twentieth century, and exerted an indirect but powerful influence long after. Lloyd George's Liberal Party Budget of 1909 was widely perceived by proponents and opponents alike as a triumph of Hobsonian economics and politics.[221] The British weekly *The Nation* (the New Liberals' chief organ), surveying the terms of the Budget with understandable glee, declared, "Under it no man can lose any fruit of labour or organisation; the State will merely aim at detecting and applying forms of wealth which cannot be traced to individual efforts at all."[222] The Fabian version of rent theory became the basis of Labour Party doctrine when Sidney Webb drafted its 1918 party platform. Its legacy is detectable in a more general way in the program of social welfare legislation championed by the Labour party in the decades after.[223]

In the United States, rent theory—except in its narrower Georgian incarnation—never achieved the political prominence that it had in England. Hostility to unearned incomes fueled support in the United States for antimonopoly legislation and inheritance taxes, although in both cases numerous other factors contributed as well. However, unlike in England, differentiation between earned and unearned incomes had little influence on the overall direction of income tax policy.[224] Among American political philosophers and economists, no identifiable group with political influence comparable to that of the Fabians or New Liberals in England seized on rent theory as the key to a just scheme of income distribution. The social gospeler Walter Rauschenbusch warmly embraced rent theory, arguing that eradication of "unearned profits" in all forms was the center of a "Christianized" (i.e., moral) social order, and strongly endorsed the Labour party's 1909 Budget as a means of implementing it.[225] In their early works, Walter Lippmann and Herbert Croly, in some respects the closest American counterparts to the New Liberals, targeted "unearned incomes" to fund the progressive social agenda.[226] So also did a number of progressive economists, including Henry Carter Adams, Simon Patten, Rexford Tugwell, and E. R. A. Seligman.[227] But none ever developed the argument into a coherent fiscal policy. Seligman's *Progressive Taxation in Theory and Practice,* the most prominent presentation of arguments for and against progressive taxation in the early part of the twentieth century, did not even consider rent-theory arguments for progressivity. Although Richard Ely incorporated classical (Ricardian) rent theory in his early work, he never developed it into a systematic theory of taxation, and indeed in his later work repudiated the notion that economic rent should be taxed at all.[228] Commons came somewhat closer to espousing rent theory. Although not a tax theorist, Commons supported a variety of land tax measures, including one that he drafted for the Wisconsin legislature, as well as preferential treatment of earned incomes under the income tax.[229] In addition, like many other progressives, he supported strong labor unions as a way to dislodge what he saw as permanent rents accruing to the capitalist classes.[230] In his first major work, *Distribution of Wealth*, he pinpointed the "owners of opportunities" as the residual claimants of the social product, akin to Ricardo's rentiers.[231] His structural analysis of a bargain, highlighting the surplus generated by the spread between buyers' and sellers' reservation prices, provided the analytical framework for a general rent-theory critique of market-based incomes.[232] But like most other American progressives, Commons never developed that critique. The one notable exception was H. G. Brown's *Theory of Earned and Unearned Incomes* (1918), which (as the title suggests) anchors its scheme of just taxation in the distinction between earned and unearned incomes. In its specifics, however, Brown's scheme is really more a modified single-tax scheme (including inheritance taxes along with a land tax) than one based on a broad rent theory.

But a rent-based theory of just distribution had a powerful influence on Hale, linking his technical writings on rate regulation to his more philosophical pieces on property, and (in a less developed fashion) tying both to his writings on coercion. Strongly embracing rent theory at the start of his career in 1913, Hale wrote as follows: "The solution of the whole industrial problem would seem to lie somewhere in the direction of ascertaining precisely where a man is enabled to enjoy tribute collected from the rest of the community for things other than services rendered; and then preventing him from enjoying this product of other men's labor, in some cases by directly prohibiting certain unfair methods of suppressing competition; in others by making him charge lower prices; and in still others by making him pay to the community the tribute he has collected, in order that it may be used for services which in their nature must be communistic" (that is, what economists term public goods).[233] While he became less optimistic in time about what a rent-theory-based scheme of redistribution could accomplish, Hale remained committed to the principle throughout his career. That commitment was clearest in his proposals for cost-based rate regulation of public utilities. As Hale recognized in his earliest writings on public utilities, courts, in their confused attempts to limit profits to a fair return on cost, were fumbling toward the strict Lockean version of property rights underlying rent theory. Once surfaced, Hale believed, the arguments for public ownership of any returns in excess of cost in the case of public utilities would point the way towards collectivization of all unearned incomes. In the area of coercion, Hale argued, if there was any moral ground on which to differentiate between market exchanges, all of which he had shown to be structurally coercive, it was in the degree to which a party's power to coerce terms favorable to itself enabled it to extract a reward in excess of sacrifice—that is, to collect economic rents. The greater the excess, the more readily a legislature should intervene to alter the terms of exchange through price controls, taxation, and the like.

The Politics of Rent Theory

Marxian critics, believing all surplus value to be produced by labor, had no difficulty ascribing moral ownership of it to labor.[234] Rent theorists, believing surplus value to be the product solely of the structure of market relations (that is, of the fortuity that demand exceeded available supply at a constant cost), concluded that it belonged to no factor at all, but to society at large. As Mill had put it many years before the Fabians and New Liberals had taken up the cause, in the passage quoted at the outset of this chapter, for the state to appropriate wealth produced "without any exertion or sacrifice on the part of the owners . . . whom the natural course of things progressively enriches [would be] no violation of the principles on which private property is founded . . . This would not properly be taking anything from anybody; it would merely be applying an accession of wealth, created by circumstances, to the benefit of society."[235]

That difference had significant political and practical implications for rent theory. First, unlike Marxian exploitation theory or Georgian rent theory, Fabian rent theory offered at least the possibility of avoiding the polarization of self-interest along strict class lines, a possibility eagerly (if somewhat disingenuously) seized on by its proponents in drumming up public support. While the Fabians and subsequent rent theorists tended to focus criticism on those "persons who deliberately live by owning instead of working,"[236] the Fabians' "law of three rents" (unlike Marxian exploitation theory) made no analytical distinction between labor and capital, and (unlike Georgian rent theory) made no analytical distinction between labor and pure capital on the one hand, and landowners on the other.[237] As a result, at least as a theoretical matter, the political conflict that rent theory posed was not between factors of production (labor, pure capital, and landowners). Rather, it was between the class of rentiers supplying each factor, and of nonrentiers whose sacrifices supported them.[238] That shift in focus is evident in Hale's insistence that his own cost-based theory of distribution did not exempt from scrutiny returns to labor that seemed disproportionate to effort.[239] To the considerable extent that the Marxian preoccupation with injustices to labor persisted in most progressive rent-theory critiques of market distribution, that preoccupation was grounded not on the (Marxian) analytical claim that labor was uniquely entitled to surplus value, but on the purely empirical claim that disparities in bargaining power caused the bulk of unearned surplus to go to capital rather than to labor.

At the same time, it was less obvious than with Marxian economics or Georgian rent theory how to translate the Fabian argument into a workable program. *The Nation,* commenting on Asquith's budget of 1907, optimistically declared, "Once [you] identify 'unearned' income with publicly created income, the fiscal policy of a progressive State becomes clear."[240] In fact though, it was far from self-evident how a government so inclined would isolate that portion of income that was "unearned." Shaw sidestepped the problem entirely, advocating absolute equality of incomes across the whole population, irrespective of effort.[241] While he rested the case for equality, at least in part, on the existence of rents, the cure fit the disease only loosely at best. Absent some argument that all sacrifices are equal—an argument that, at least with respect to labor, Shaw believed impossible to sustain[242]—the two were connected at most by the general assertion that because many incomes were unjustified, drastic remedies were in order. In fact, Shaw's support for equalization of incomes ultimately had little to do with his careful critique of rents. He supported it because he believed that for purely consequentialist reasons, eliminating poverty and equalizing wealth was the only decent thing to do. He was largely indifferent to whether such a policy could be reconciled with either individual merit or the need to create an incentive to work.[243] But Shaw's view was, characteristically, an eccentric one. Most rent theorists felt impelled at least to try to fashion a fiscal policy that was responsive to their critique of unearned incomes.

Of the various means available for appropriating unearned incomes,[244] the most obvious one was to alter the exchange value of goods and services to eliminate the surplus value. That goal could be accomplished either by altering the background conditions to exchange in order to equalize the bargaining positions of the parties, or by setting the exchange price to mimic what the market price would have been had the parties faced each other with equal bargaining power. Both alternatives appealed to bargain theorists of various stripes, who tended to locate the origin of surplus value, in Hobson's terms, in "the various hindrances to perfect equality of bargaining power" that allowed the stronger parties to obtain "forced gains."[245] It is not surprising that given Hale's writings on coercion, these alternatives had strong appeal to him as well. He embraced them in, among other places, his support of rate regulation of public utilities and de facto monopolies, as well as in minimum wage laws and the rights of workers to unionize and strike.

But most progressive economists, including Hale, viewed direct price intervention as of limited use in tackling the problem of surplus value. First, most of them accepted the proposition, embodied in the equimarginal principle, that at least in competitive markets, unregulated exchange was the most efficient mechanism for allocating resources. The Fabians, persuaded by the argument, rejected price controls out of hand.[246] As noted before, Hale had his doubts, in part because he believed that the equimarginal principle failed to account for changes in inframarginal surplus. But while Hale intermittently flirted with the possibility of extending price controls to normal market transactions, in the end he limited serious consideration in his own work to those noncompetitive markets (unilateral or bilateral monopolies and monopsonies) in which altering the price would merely reallocate joint producers'/consumers' surplus at the margin, with minimal effects on the quantity of goods or services provided. Even in such markets, where reducing rates would result in demand's outstripping available supply, as Hale noted, the effect would be to bestow a windfall only on those consumers who were able to secure the limited goods or services, a result hard to justify on fairness grounds.[247]

Indirect measures to alter the background conditions of exchange presented fewer of these problems. Many such proposals, including measures to eliminate artificial restraints on industrial competition and educate low-paid workers to compete in higher-wage groups, received at least notional support from a broad spectrum of economists.[248] But most progressives believed that the intractability of social groups, economies of scale in production, and the existence of natural scarcities not correctable (at least in the short run) by government intervention meant that there were severe limits to what such indirect measures could accomplish.

Second, as Hale noted, by altering the exchange value of goods or services, the government did not expropriate surplus value; it merely transferred it from one side of the transaction to the other.[249] If, as rent theorists argued, value in excess of cost was a social and not an individual product, why should the government intervene merely to reallocate the surplus from one undeserving party to another, rather than to appropriate it for public use?[250] Where (as in public utilities rate regulation) the beneficiaries were consumers at large, the transfer might be defended as reasonably approximating the results that would be obtained by the more cumbersome route of taxing the utilities' gain and then redistributing the proceeds to the community. But with programs designed to increase wages to the lowest-paid laborers in society, that defense was not available. Some progressives seized instead on Marshall's argument that the monopsony power of employers enabled them to pay wages far below what labor was worth to them. But if that was the case, why wasn't the appropriate remedy—as Shaw had asked of Marxian economics—simply to expropriate the employers' surplus through taxation for the benefit of the public? Why should it go to labor? To the extent that the community would have redistributed the proceeds of taxation to the neediest members of society, in which group the lowest-paid laborers were disproportionately represented, Hale suggested, one could defend the result as approximating what a system of pure rent-theory taxation, followed by social welfarist redistributive transfers, would have accomplished.[251] But for many exponents of wage regulation, the motivation was more likely to be found in residual Marxian sentiment that the surplus value was labor's product. In that case, redistributing the surplus value to labor through direct price controls (minimum wage laws) or indirect measures to bolster labor's bargaining power (pro-union laws) was not a shortcut to an ultimate social welfarist end, but merely what the Marxian version of Lockean justice demanded.

Instead, rent theorists turned to various forms of differential and progressive taxation, often in conjunction with education and other reforms to equalize opportunities over time. The marriage of rent theory and progressive tax reform offered something to both causes. Taxation offered rent theorists a practical mechanism for reaching unearned incomes on a broad scale, provided that there was some way to isolate those incomes. At the same time, rent theory appeared to offer advocates of progressive taxation what they had been sorely lacking: a plausible justification for a radically redistributive tax scheme that was reconcilable with private property entitlements.

Progressive taxation schemes of various sorts had strong support in both England and the United States from 1885 on.[252] But from the start, justifying progressivity proved to be something of an embarrassment.[253] The most obvious justification—that redistributing wealth in the direction of greater equality was a desirable end in itself—had its strong champions in the second half of the nineteenth century. Marx had famously proclaimed his support of "[a] heavy progressive or graduated income tax" as one means of "wrest[ing], by degrees, all capital from the bourgeoisie."[254] The view that the tax system ought to be used to promote equality found support in less radical quarters as well, notably in the work of Adolph Wagner.[255] Three things, however, limited the political appeal of a frankly egalitarian justification.

First, the argument had no apparent limit, short of absolute equality. Egalitarianism suggested that rates should be set at 100 percent on the highest income levels, and then the next highest, and so on down, until the government had raised all necessary revenue. If "necessary" included funds needed not only for direct government operations but also for in-kind and cash transfers to the relatively less well off, the rationale seemed to push the aggregate tax and transfer system to absolute equality of incomes. That result was understandably not disturbing to most socialists. However, it gave pause to most others, who, while prepared to support some lessening of economic inequalities, were inclined (in part for incentive reasons, in part for reasons left unexplained) to stop short of such a radical redistribution of wealth.[256]

Second, and of more importance, an egalitarian justification for a redistributive tax scheme was difficult to reconcile with private entitlements to the underlying property on which the tax was levied. In the case of taxes on inheritances and land rents, that objection posed no problem for those (like Mill) who maintained that no one was entitled to the underlying wealth to begin with.[257] But for wealth produced by the exertions of its owner, progressive taxation for the purpose of redistribution amounted to, critics insisted with varying degrees of heat, a form of theft.[258] Third, an egalitarian justification for redistribution took no account of the need, for incentive purposes, to protect higher incomes derived from greater exertion.

Eschewing frankly redistributive justifications for taxation, most commentators defended taxation instead as merely a necessary evil burdening an otherwise just distribution of wealth. Two theories prevailed throughout the nineteenth century about how that burden ought to be allocated. The first, the "benefit" theory, argued that taxes should be levied in proportion to the benefits conferred by the governmental services that they financed. The second, the "equal sacrifice" theory championed by Mill and Sidgwick, argued that taxes should be levied so as to equalize the sacrifices that payment of the tax entailed.[259] Neither theory, however, seemed to lead comfortably to progressivity.

Since it was impracticable to trace most government benefits to individual recipients, the precise tax scheme dictated by a "benefit" theory depended largely on the unverifiable assumptions that one made about the distribution of benefits. The assumption that most benefits were evenly distributed throughout the population would obviously yield a "head tax"—that is, an annual per capita fee, the amount of which was invariant with income, and hence steeply regressive. The assumption that most benefits varied in proportion to income would obviously yield a proportionate tax.[260] But the only assumption under which the benefit theory would yield a progressive tax—that the benefits conferred by government not only increased with income but also increased at a rate faster than the income itself—was sufficiently implausible to find few adherents.

By the end of the nineteenth century, through Mill's considerable influence, the "benefit" theory had been largely supplanted by the "equal sacrifice" principle. The latter held more promise for justifying progressivity, in part because it left ambiguous what was to be equalized: absolute sacrifice, proportional sacrifice, or marginal sacrifice. The most obvious choice, and the one made by Sidgwick and (somewhat more ambiguously) by Mill, was to require equality in the total sacrifice demanded from each person ("absolute sacrifice").[261] What rate structure that implied depended, among other things, on how one measured sacrifice. If, as was generally assumed, sacrifice should be measured by the utility to the taxpayer of the money relinquished,[262] one could arrive at a progressive rate schedule, but only by hypothesizing an extremely steep decline in the marginal utility of money for all taxpayers.[263] But for reasons largely unexplained, by the turn of the century, "equal sacrifice" was increasingly construed to require instead the sacrifice of an equal *percentage* of the total utility that each person derived from his or her income ("proportionate sacrifice").[264] In that case, almost any plausible declining marginal utility curve for money would yield some form of progressivity.[265] Nonetheless, as with "absolute sacrifice," the precise rate structure mandated would depend upon the precise configuration of the curve, a fact that (as critics and supporters of progressivity alike acknowledged) was fatally indeterminate.[266]

The principle of "minimum" or "equimarginal" sacrifice first enunciated by Thomas Carver in 1895 and elaborated by Francis Edgeworth two years later seemed to offer a way out, at least of the indeterminacy problem.[267] Assuming a declining marginal utility of money, they argued, the aggregate disutility imposed by taxation would be minimized by setting rates to equalize the *marginal* disutility to each taxpayer from the last tax dollar paid. Given any monotonically declining utility curve (that is to say, one declining over its whole range), equimarginal sacrifice not only would always result in progressivity. It also would result in the same progressive rate structure irrespective of the slope of the curve: taxes would be levied at 100 percent on the highest income until it was leveled down to the next highest, and so forth, until all necessary tax revenues were raised.[268] In short, minimum sacrifice pointed to the same end as egalitarianism, but by a different route. Moreover, like egalitarianism, the logic that supported minimum sacrifice theory—that money should be left in the hands of those to whom its marginal utility was the highest—had no apparent limit short of absolute equality. As Hale stated, taking Carver to task for failing to see that complete equality of incomes was the logical outcome of "minimum sacrifice" theory, "[N]ot only, according to this logic, would each dollar taken from the rich cause less sacrifice than a dollar taken from the poorer, but each dollar taken from the rich would cause less sacrifice than that which would be relieved in the poorer by adding a dollar to *his* income—until equalization resulted."[269] The implications of that fact were hardly lost on the friends or foes of "minimum sacrifice" theory. As Edgeworth (a sometime friend) declared, "The *acme* of socialism is thus for a moment sighted."[270]

Virtually all supporters of equimarginal (minimum) sacrifice theory agreed that the disincentives created by a confiscatory tax would require stopping considerably short of that acme.[271] However, that compromise was dictated by purely utilitarian considerations, not solicitude for private rights. Edgeworth and Pigou both tried in passing to defend equimarginalism as consistent with the individualist impulse behind "absolute" and "proportionate" sacrifice. That cause was covertly aided by the possibility of describing all three (equimarginal, absolute, and proportional sacrifice), by rhetorical sleight of hand, as variants on the same broad principle of "equal sacrifice."[272] But as Carver, Edgeworth, and Pigou all elsewhere frankly acknowledged, equimarginalism was ultimately rooted in the premises of utilitarianism, not individualism.[273] Those willing to embrace it on utilitarian grounds would shortly find the empirical assumptions on which equimarginalism rested under serious and (in Robbins's assault on interpersonal utility comparisons) ultimately politically fatal attack.[274] But many others were reluctant to throw their lot in with utilitarianism to begin with.

Thus, advocates of progressivity in the early part of the twentieth century found themselves in a difficult position. Egalitarianism and minimum sacrifice, the theories of distributive justice that led most naturally to progressivity, were impossible to reconcile with individualist premises. Those theories that could be reconciled—absolute and (arguably) proportionate sacrifice—did not lead with any certainty to progressivity.

By defining the portion of wealth appropriable by the state as that portion that reflected surplus value, rent theory bolstered the case for progressive taxation in two significant respects. First, to the extent that "costs" for purposes of rent theory were identical to suppliers' reservation prices for providing goods or services, rent theory answered utilitarian concerns that a progressive tax would discourage productivity, since (on a rent-theory model) such a tax would be levied only on that portion of income that reflected a surplus above the minimum demanded for one's efforts.[275] Second, by targeting only that wealth to which one could argue that individuals had no just Lockean claim at all, rent theory provided what the egalitarian and utilitarian (minimum sacrifice) justifications for progressivity clearly lacked: a theory for differentially taxing the wealthy that appeared to honor entitlements to that portion of private wealth that was justly acquired. As Hobhouse stated, "The true function of taxation is to secure to society the element in wealth that is of social origin, or, more broadly, all that does not owe its origin to the efforts of living individuals."[276]

The problem was to design a tax system that could separate individual from social factors in the production of wealth. In the case of inheritance and appreciation in land values, many followed Mill's lead in simply treating the entirety as "unearned."[277] Indeed, the ease with which one could isolate the "social" component of land values probably accounted for the continued popularity of site value taxation in England, as much as did any atavistic attachment to land as a unique resource. But the solution was harder to come by with interest, profits, and wages. Numerous voices supported in principle the differential taxation of "savers' rent" paid to inframarginal savers.[278] The problem was how to isolate it in practice. In the case of interest, the 1907 Asquith budget resolved the problem by treating the entirety as "unearned." But one could not reconcile that solution with the fact that most progressives treated abstinence as a legitimate sacrifice, except by assuming that for most savings, the cost of abstinence was so low as to justify ignoring it entirely.[279]

Wages were the most resistant to differentiation, at least for wage levels that exceeded the minimum cost of staying alive. Assuming that the portion of wages that compensated for the psychic cost of working—that is, a worker's reservation price for giving up leisure—ought to be treated as "earned" income, the question, obviously, was how to isolate it. Hobhouse had gamely suggested that "time and piece-work," although rough, might be serviceable measures of exertion, a suggestion that Shaw dismissed contemptuously as "the notion of a bricklayer."[280] As with interest, the 1907 Asquith budget resolved the problem categorically, this time classifying the entirety of labor income as "earned," and taxing it (on incomes below £2,000 a year) at a preferential rate.[281]

In the face of these difficulties, most rent theorists gradually came to the view that the only practical solution was to reach the "unearned" portion of wealth indirectly, through a progressive tax levied on incomes across the board (in most instances supplemented by steep taxes on inheritance and site value), a shift that was reflected in Liberal Party policy under the direction of Lloyd George.[282] Progressivity posed none of the practical difficulties of differentiation; at the same time, it less obviously addressed the ethical concerns raised by rent theory. As Hobson conceded, the case for progressivity as a cure for rents must rest necessarily on "the supposition that the proportion of unearned . . . income varies directly with the size of incomes."[283] Its proponents offered little support for that supposition, beyond the intuition that "when we come to an income of some £5,000 a year we approach the limit" both of what an individual would demand as the minimum price for his services and what he is worth.[284] The supposition came under attack from the socialist left as well as from the individualist right, in both cases on the grounds that, without any empirical support, it was merely a device for socialism to fly under the false colors of individualism.[285]

As Hale noted, the attack was unfair in one respect. Even assuming that a tax overestimates the portion of exchange value that reflects "unearned" income *when enacted*, with respect to services rendered *after* enactment, the tax cannot appropriate anything but surplus value to the producers. If the expected net revenue after the change is not sufficient to compensate for the hardships that producers expect to incur, they will not produce.[286] The argument, which is structurally identical to Hale's observations that all that is at stake under a minimum wage law is distribution of joint producer/consumer surplus, implies that a progressive tax will at worst understate the rent component of incomes. That result was unlikely to satisfy most individualist critics, however, who would presumably respond that unless the tax proportionally understates the unearned component of all taxed incomes, it remains unjust.

Hale's qualification aside, the attack on a rent theory defense of progressivity seems just. One could ascribe it to mere coincidence that, in the absence of any hard data, the New Liberals' intuitions about the distribution of unearned incomes pushed them to the same conclusion that egalitarianism or (Edgeworthian) utilitarianism taken alone would have mandated. But the more plausible explanation is surely that egalitarianism and utilitarianism together exerted an independent pull on the New Liberals that would have led them (like most other progressives) to embrace a redistributive tax scheme with or without a boost from rent theory. In the end, the rent theory justification for progressivity seems unlikely to have persuaded anyone not already inclined to support it on other grounds. Hale was probably typical in this regard. While early on he championed proposals to "discriminate . . . between 'earned' and 'unearned' incomes, and . . . eliminate the latter altogether . . . [as] the only fruitful approach to the subject of taxation,"[287] he was equally hospitable to egalitarian and utilitarian arguments for progressive taxation.[288] In the end, he abandoned any serious attempt to work out a general income tax policy along rent-theory lines.

It was in his writings on public utilities that Hale tried in earnest to put rent theory into practice. In two respects at least, public utilities regulation appeared to offer a uniquely promising vehicle for that endeavor. First, it was one of the few areas in which public opinion universally supported some form of government controls on the income that could be derived from private property. That fact itself, as Hale repeatedly noted, abandoned the classical laissez-faire "assumption . . . that whatever one can get for the use of his property is legitimate," and threw open for general debate "the question how much the owner really should be allowed to get."[289] By the time that Hale began his work on public utilities in the 1910s, the courts had been engaged for some twenty years in a vain quest for a formula that could simultaneously limit the earnings of public utilities without "taking" any of the value of the underlying property. Beginning with *Valuation and Rate Making,* and continuing in some twenty articles written over the next three decades, Hale tried to persuade the courts of the futility of that search. Given the economic truism that the value of income-producing property at any time was simply the capitalized value (that is, present value) of its expected future earnings stream, any reduction in future earnings would necessarily deprive its owners of some portion of the present value of the property. Once the courts were forced to recognize that elementary fact, Hale argued, they could turn their attention to the only meaningful question posed by government regulation: what portion of the value of their property *ought* public utilities, as a matter of policy, to be deprived of? For Hale, at least, the answer was to be found in rent-theory principles. Any unearned increment in the value of a public utility's property above the amount that investors had actually committed to the enterprise was merely the "capitalize[d] [value of] the right to prevent the community from being served by someone else."[290] As the public had bestowed that right to begin with, it was entitled to reclaim any portion of the unearned value that it wished. How the public might best do that—by reallocating that portion to consumers via rate regulation or to the public at large by a tax levied on surplus profits—and whether it should stop short of confiscating the full unearned increment to preserve incentives to invest or to protect the vested rights of investors, presented difficult questions to which Hale devoted considerable attention over his career. But they were, Hale insisted, questions of policy for the legislatures to resolve in their own best judgment, not matters of (constitutional) right addressed to the courts.

Second, the unrecovered capital that investors had committed to an enterprise at any given time could be fixed with relative certainty. Thus, unlike a rent-theory-based general income tax, which foundered on the difficulty of separating the earned from unearned portions of income, Hale believed that it would be relatively easy to devise a scheme for regulating public utilities along strict rent-theory lines.

From the start, Hale thus saw his relatively technical work on public utilities regulation as serving a larger purpose: to provide a test case for revising all property rights in accordance with rent-theory principles. "Such regulation has tremendous possibilities," Hale wrote at the start of his career, "not simply in the direction of giving us cheaper and better railroad, telephone and lighting service, nor merely in the direction of eliminating certain sources of corruption from politics, but by way of furnishing a laboratory wherein can be worked out a method for dealing with our entire system of property rights."[291] It is to the doings in that laboratory that we now turn.

5

PROPERTY THEORY IN PRACTICE: RATE REGULATION OF PUBLIC UTILITIES

Under a system of rate regulation, certain kinds of potage can no longer be withheld for as much as a birthright; they must be furnished provided a "reasonable" price is offered. The very essence of the right of property—the right to keep others from using it unless they comply with one's own terms—is thus denied. The assumption is abandoned that whatever one can get for the use of his property is legitimate, and the question how much the owner really should be allowed to get, is thrown open.

—R. Hale, Untitled typescript on rate regulation of public utilities (circa 1916)

I deny the power of any legislature under our government to fix the price which one shall receive for his property of any kind. If the power can be exercised as to one article, it may as to all articles, and the prices of every thing, from a calico gown to a city mansion, may be the subject of legislative direction.

—Munn v. Illinois, 94 U.S. 113, 152 (1877) (Field, J., dissenting)

In the early 1870s, four Midwestern states passed a series of laws (the so-called Granger laws) regulating the rates that railroads and grain elevators operating within their jurisdiction could charge. Over the next twenty years, a number of other states followed suit, some controlling rates through direct legislation and others (increasingly) by delegating rate-setting power to state railroad commissions. By 1887, twenty-four states had established railroad commissions, endowed with varying authority over rates. But local solutions to regulating what was essentially a national railroad system were widely regarded as unsatisfactory. Increasing pressure to have the federal government take over the job ultimately led to the establishment of the Interstate Commerce Commission (ICC) in 1887. It was not until 1906, however, that the ICC was finally invested with authority to set railroad rates.[1]

In the area of public utilities (gas, electric, and water), government regulation of rates came somewhat later, but established itself quickly. The first state public utilities commissions were created in Wisconsin and New York in 1907. By 1914, all but three states (Delaware, Utah, and Wyoming) had established similar commissions, virtually all with broad authority to prescribe reasonable rates.[2] For the next thirty years, the problems of public utility rate regulation attracted the attention of an impressive array of progressive economists and lawyers, including (in addition to Robert Hale) John Bauer, James Bonbright, Louis Brandeis, J. M. Clark, John Commons, Henry Edgerton, Richard Ely, Felix Frankfurter, Edwin Goddard, Walton Hamilton, Gerard Henderson, Thomas Reed Powell, Donald Richberg, and Frank Taussig. Hale wrote his doctoral dissertation on public utilities rate regulation, taught a public utilities course for many years at Columbia, and edited one of the leading casebooks in the field. Over half of Hale's scholarly writing dealt with some aspect of public utilities rate regulation.

To the contemporary eye, wont to view the field as the province of bureaucrats and technically-minded economists, the progressive romance with public utilities rate regulation may be hard to fathom. In part, it reflected what was perceived to be the economic significance of public utilities, measured both by the critical role that they played in industrial development and by the absolute wealth that they embodied. More importantly, however, it reflected the philosophical and political significance of public utilities in establishing the limits of government control of business. Rate regulation of railroads and public utilities represented the first wide-scale effort by modern legislatures to set prices in private market exchanges.[3] As a result, it simultaneously provoked a confrontation over the government's right to set prices, and provided the chief battleground from the 1880s to the 1940s for resolving it.[4] Frankfurter, writing in 1930, reflected the general sentiment of his contemporaries in describing the movement to regulate public utilities and railroads as "perhaps the most significant political tendency at the turn of the century."[5]

For most of those sixty years, legal dispute centered around two doctrines, both of which originated in the context of railroad regulation and were subsequently extended to public utilities. The first doctrine—what Hale termed "horizontal" constraints—purported to limit the government's right to regulate prices at all to those businesses that were deemed to be "affected with a public interest." That that category included public utilities themselves was never in doubt. The fight concerned how far beyond public utilities it would reach. The second doctrine—what Hale termed "vertical" constraints—mandated that where the government *could* regulate prices (that is, for businesses "affected with a public interest"), prices must be set so as to guarantee such businesses at least a "fair return on the fair value" of their investment.[6] Hale devoted a significant portion of his work over the course of his career to showing the internal incoherence of both limitations, in particular the second.

Hale was spurred on in that endeavor in part by an intellectual distaste for the inept flounderings of the courts. His unpublished writings are replete with exasperated remarks on the Supreme Court's technical incompetence in economic matters. He wrote to one colleague, "It seems to me that no progress will be made in the discussion of valuation until we rid our minds of all illusions as to the wisdom or even the capacity for logical reasoning on the part of the justices of the Supreme Court."[7] Echoing that sentiment in a letter to Brandeis—whom, along with Stone and Holmes, he excepted from his criticism—Hale lamented that a sensible view of rate regulation "would involve a little judicial thinking along economic lines as to the whole function of the law of property; and most judges, I know, are too proud to think along economic lines."[8] Although generally more tactful in print, even there Hale did not always bother to obscure his low opinion of the Court's competence in economic affairs, provoking outrage among establishment types in his audience.[9]

But Hale's ultimate motivation for discrediting both court-imposed constraints was not academic but political. He regarded public utilities as a type for all private property, and the fledgling attempts by the state to control them as a prototype for a more thoroughgoing revision of property rights. As he wrote in an early article, "Rate Making and the Revision of the Property Concept",

The truth which most rate bodies lack the courage to face is, that in regulating the rates of utilities the law is trying the experiment in one limited field of turning its back on the principles which it follows elsewhere. The experiment may perhaps be extended to other fields if successful. We are experimenting with a legal curb on the power of property owners. In applying that curb, we have to work out principles or working rules—in short a new body of law. Those principles will necessarily differ from the ones upon which the law acts in other fields—for in other fields it acts on the assumption that whatever income a property owner can get without fraud by virtue of his ownership is legitimately his. In the utility field, standards of what it is proper for an owner to get out of his ownership have to be worked out de novo . . . The revision of property rights worked out within the utility field may very well serve as a model, wherever applicable, for the revision of other property rights.[10]

"The fact remains," Hale elsewhere wrote, "that in curbing the working power of regulated companies [in cases like *Munn*], the government is revising the power of ownership itself, not merely of formal grants of monopoly."[11]

Once freed of both sets of court-imposed constraints, Hale believed, the state legislatures and Congress could proceed unhampered in devising standards to meet their notion of the public good. Hale's primary articulated goal, and the one that accounted for the bulk of his writing in the public utilities field, was thus a negative one: to get the courts out of the rate regulation business entirely, by forcing them to recognize that the property interests at stake were not constitutionally protected. Writing to Brandeis upon the latter's confirmation to the Court, Hale urged such deference upon him. The only radicalism that the Court could undertake, Hale argued, was "to sustain legislatures and commissions whenever they become enlightened enough to tackle the law of property through rate regulation or through taxation."[12]

But as Hale acknowledged, the problem of rate regulation was not resolved simply by moving discretion from the courts to legislatures or administrative bodies. The ultimate question was how such discretion ought to be exercised, wherever lodged.[13] For Hale, the answer lay in progressive rent theory. As applied to public utilities, Hale believed, the principle that people should be rewarded in accordance with their sacrifice dictated that utilities' investors be allowed to earn a market rate of return on the capital actually committed to the enterprise, but no more. Any return in excess of that amount, which utilities could claim only by virtue of the scarce resources over which they had control, should be remitted either to consumers through rate regulation, or the public at large through an excess profits tax. That excess included monopoly profits that utilities could extract by artificially constraining supply—the traditional target of monopoly regulation. But it also included, Hale argued, any unearned increments in other assets (land, capital equipment) used in the production process, that accrued as a result of the temporary or permanent scarcity of resources. Once it was acknowledged that *utilities* had no entitlement to the unearned increment in their property, Hale urged, it "would suggest a question as to why the familiar privately enjoyed increments [in competitive markets] should be permitted."[14] If that question were faced squarely, Hale concluded, "The result might be radical; if so it would be because on a piecemeal and candid review, many of the incidents of property would prove themselves to be without justification."[15]

Hale's view that the fight over public utilities regulation was a fight over the soul of property was widely shared among his contemporaries. Conservatives generally conceded the need for government control of public utilities

and other monopolies as "piecemeal rectification" of an otherwise individualistic, laissez-faire private property regime. But they regarded with abhorrence
the prospect that such regulation would be used as precedent for a more
thoroughgoing revision of property rights. That possibility, in the politically
explosive climate of the 1870s to the 1920s, inevitably raised for many conservatives the hated specter of socialism. The Granger laws had been widely
denounced at the time of their passage as "rank communism," a characterization that was liberally invoked by counsel seeking to have such laws overturned in *Munn.*[16] The Court's failure to do so was itself denounced as an
"advanced guard of a sort of enlightened socialism,"[17] opening up the way
for "yet more communistic and destructive legislation."[18] As one commentator put it somewhat more cagily, "[C]arried to its logical conclusion, this
method of control of the return on public utility investments can lead in
only one direction—to the *socialistic state.* Whether or not that would be a
desirable outcome is another question."[19]

Moderates and progressives, on the other side, welcomed the prospect
that public utilities regulation could serve as a model for more extensive
government control over property rights. Most progressives had no desire
to see those revisions end up in state ownership. Beginning with H. C.
Adams's influential 1886 essay, "The Relation of the State to Industrial Action,"[20] progressives conventionally called for state regulation rather than
state ownership of public utilities. Richard Ely, one of the few American
progressives strongly to advocate public ownership of utilities ("gas and
water socialism") in his early career, recanted in later years in favor of
government regulation of privately held corporations.[21] But, unlike conservatives, they saw no reason why such revisions necessarily *would* lead to state
ownership. Although public ownership of public utilities was widespread
in Europe by the turn of century, state legislatures in the United States had
by and large rejected it, in favor of private ownership subject to extensive
government regulation.[22] As a result, progressives argued, the threat such
regulation posed was not to capitalism per se, but to unregulated (that is,
laissez-faire) capitalism. In the view of most progressives, that threat was
long overdue. As Teddy Roosevelt stated in 1911, "we must abandon defi-
nitely the *laissez-faire* theory of political economy [as obsolete], and fearlessly
champion a system of increased Governmental control, paying no heed to
the cries of the worthy people who denounce this as Socialistic."[23] Indeed,
progressive commentators routinely suggested, regulation might be the best
friend capitalism had, given that public regulation of private property was
the only remaining viable alternative to outright public ownership.[24] Putting
that suggestion in more ominous terms, Hale warned, "If property is not

revised methodically by its friends, it is likely to be revised unmethodically by its enemies, with disastrous results."[25]

Championing the public utilities model of regulation on the legislative front, Teddy Roosevelt fought unsuccessfully for comprehensive federal regulation of all businesses under an ICC-like agency, first in the 1908 Hepburn Bill and later in early drafts of what eventually became the Federal Trade Commission Act.[26] Championing it on the judicial and legislative fronts, Hale and other progressives argued for courts to get out of the business of policing state regulation of businesses entirely, and for state legislatures (once left to their own devices) to apply the lessons learned in public utilities regulation to all property rights.

The Supreme Court, which got into the rate regulation business in 1877 with its decision in Munn v. Illinois, did not get out of it until its decision in *Hope Natural Gas* in 1944.[27] As a consequence, during virtually his entire career, Hale, like many of his contemporaries, remained preoccupied with the doctrinal disputes that engaged the Court. His most significant contribution to public utilities rate regulation was in that area. The first half of this chapter accordingly is devoted to the progressive assault on the "affectation with a public interest" requirement of *Munn* and the "fair return on fair value" rule of Smyth v. Ames.[28] Although most of his writing spearheaded this negative assault on the Court, Hale's affirmative proposal for revising rate regulation along rent-theory lines was incorporated in the "actual prudent cost" rate base championed by Brandeis, Bauer, Bonbright, and other leading progressive economists and lawyers working in the public utilities area. "Actual prudent costs" became the standard rate base used by state utilities commissions once the Supreme Court retired from the field. The second half of the chapter examines the "fair return on actual, prudent costs" standard as a form of applied rent theory, and suggests its serious limitations in theory and in practice. It concludes with the general lessons to be drawn for rent theory in practice from the public utilities experience.

Horizontal Constraints: Businesses "Affected with a Public Interest"

Years ago the Supreme Court of the United States introduced the slavery struggle with the Dred Scott decision. To-day, it may be that it has introduced the property struggle with the decision of Munn v. Illinois.[29]

In 1877, in the celebrated case of Munn v. Illinois,[30] the Supreme Court reviewed a constitutional challenge to an Illinois statute regulating rates charged by a de facto cartel of Chicago grain storage facilities. On the same day, the Court decided seven other cases, consolidated on appeal with *Munn*, challenging various other Granger laws regulating the rates that railroads charged for transporting grain and other produce. Plaintiffs in all eight cases argued that such price regulation deprived owners of their property without due process of law, in violation of the Fifth and Fourteenth Amendments. Consistent with its past decisions giving the state broad authority under the police power doctrine to regulate the use of private property, the Court upheld each statute. Writing for the Court in *Munn*, Justice Waite, in a soon-to-be-famous passage, purported to ground that authority on the fact that the property in question was "affected with a public interest":

> This brings us to inquire as to the principles upon which this power of regulation rests, in order that we may determine what is within and what without its operative effect. Looking, then, to the common law, from whence came the right which the Constitution protects, we find that when private property is "affected with a public interest, it ceases to be *juris privati* only." This was said by Lord Chief Justice Hale more than two hundred years ago, in his treatise *De Portibus Maris*, . . . and has been accepted without objection as an essential element in the law of property ever since. Property does become clothed with a public interest when used in a manner to make it of public consequence, and affect the community at large.[31]

Waite most likely invoked Lord Hale's remarks merely to restate in more elegant terms the standard harm-based defense for the state's police power: private things become subject to public regulation when they impinge on the welfare of others (that is, affect the public interest).[32] But subsequent courts hardened and transformed the phrase into an independent test *limiting* the state's police power. State regulation of economic interests not only had to be within the traditional scope of the state's police power—that is to say, designed to prevent injury to public health, safety, or welfare. It also was restricted to businesses that were "affected with a public interest," however that term was defined.

It is unclear what the "affectation" requirement accomplished that could not have been achieved simply by narrowing the definition of police power itself. Indeed, in the area of wage contracts, courts frequently struck down price controls without any reference to the "affectation" doctrine at all.[33] Be that as it may, the two doctrines together were at the center of the struggle over laissez-faire constitutionalism in the years from 1880 to 1940, with progressives predictably supporting an expansive view, and conservatives a constricted one, of legitimate police power and businesses that were "affected with a public interest." Although *Munn* itself did not distinguish among various forms of regulation, in subsequent cases the Court applied the "affectation" requirement principally to price regulations (not including wages).[34] Even within that narrow confine, it was not uncommon for state and lower federal courts to resolve the validity of legislation without reference to the doctrine at all.[35]

Notwithstanding the skepticism with which commentators greeted the "affectation" requirement from the start, it was routinely invoked in price regulation cases for the next sixty years, until finally repudiated by the Court in 1934 in Nebbia v. New York.[36] It is difficult to extract any consistent definition of "affectation with a public interest" from the numerous decisions construing it during those six decades. In the 1923 decision in Wolff Packing Co. v. Court of Industrial Relations, Chief Justice Taft, hazarding one of the few comprehensive lists, argued that the businesses that the Court had concluded were "affected with a public interest" fell into one of three classes: (1) those carried on under the authority of a public grant of exclusive privileges; (2) certain businesses (such as innkeepers, common carriers, and gristmills) historically singled out in England and the United States for state regulation; and (3) businesses in which "the owner by devoting his business to the public use, in effect grants the public an interest in that use and subjects himself to public regulation to the extent of that interest although the property continues to belong to its private owner and to be entitled to protection accordingly."[37]

Few disagreed with inclusion of the first category. Justice Peckham, for example, who had sharply criticized *Munn* while still on the New York Court of Appeals, simultaneously conceded the legitimacy of rate regulation in the case of special grants of monopoly.[38] Even the conservative constitutional commentators Thomas Cooley and Christopher Tiedeman excepted formal monopolies from their otherwise strong opposition to price regulation.[39] That position was hardly surprising, given the widely held view among conservatives that the formal grant of monopoly privileges was itself a violation of laissez-faire individualism, the "spoliation of private rights by public authority."[40]

The second category was more difficult to rationalize. Courts occasionally tried to articulate some "exceptional" character that tied together the disparate businesses (bakers, millers, ferrymen, innkeepers, common carriers, etc.)

that they identified as historically subject to regulation.[41] The Court in *Munn*, for example, offering metaphor in place of explanation, had suggested that all stood "in the very 'gateway of commerce.' "[42] But in the view of most commentators, the list shared nothing more than "barren historicity," as one critic expressed it.[43] A number of progressives, taking a bolder tack, argued that it did not even share that. Attacking the Court's history as flawed, they argued that prior to the eighteenth century, *all* businesses were considered fit subjects for regulation by the state, and that the ragtag list assembled by the Court merely exemplified that more general principle.[44] Whatever logical or historical difficulties the category entailed, as a practical matter, conservative forces were willing to tolerate it as a "relic[ ] . . . of a former system,"[45] provided that the class was treated as effectively "sealed by time."[46]

The first two categories together were sufficient to cover those businesses (railroads and public utilities) that accounted for the bulk of state price regulation. Regulation of railroads and public utilities would have been justifiable under the first category, since the government granted special privileges to virtually all such businesses, in the form of exclusive licenses, land grants, or easements over public property, and/or powers of eminent domain. In addition, railroads (as common carriers) would have been covered by the second. Had the Court limited the "affected" test to those two, it could have confined price regulation to a relatively few businesses—assuming, at least, that one rejected Hale's expansive view of *all* property rights as public grants of privilege.[47] But as Hale and others saw, the third category—those businesses, as Sutherland put it somewhat more grudgingly than Taft, that "bore such a substantial and definite relation to the public interest as to justify an indulgence of the legal fiction of a grant by the owner to the public of an interest in the use"[48]—was an ultimately uncontainable concession to the government's power to regulate all private industry in the interests of what it took to be the public good. Dissenting in *Munn*, Justice Field had forewarned as much, arguing that "there is hardly an enterprise or business engaging the attention and labor of any considerable portion of the community, in which the public has not an interest in the sense in which that term is used by the court in its opinion."[49] Justice Brewer, dissenting in another case fifteen years after *Munn*, issued a similar warning, with a clearer socialist-baiting tinge:

> There is scarcely any property in whose use the public has no interest. No man liveth unto himself alone, and no man's property is beyond the touch of another's welfare . . . If [the government] may regulate the price of one service, which is not a public service, or the compensation

for the use of one kind of property which is not devoted to a public use, why may it not with equal reason regulate the price of all service, and the compensation to be paid for the use of all property? And, if so, "Looking Backward" is nearer than a dream.[50]

Time proved those prophesies correct. Justice Waite in *Munn* held the grain elevators in question to be "affected with a public interest" in part because they formed a "virtual monopoly," in part because the business stood "in the very 'gateway of commerce.' "[51] But subsequent Court decisions adhered to neither rationale strictly. Over the next fifty years, the Court invoked a dizzying array of tests to determine whether a business was affected with a public interest, including what the importance was to the public welfare of the services provided;[52] whether the company acts as a substitute for the state;[53] whether the industry was monopolistic;[54] whether either side was in a position to administer prices, thereby extracting exorbitant profits;[55] what effect the industry had on commerce;[56] whether the owner "holds himself out" to serve the public, thereby subjecting his business to the public interest;[57] and whether the public has a legal right to demand and receive the good or service in question.[58]

By the 1920s, the Court's waffling on what constituted "affectation with a public interest" provoked Justice Stone, dissenting in Tyson v. Banton, to argue that the term was nothing more than a conclusory label for the Court's determination in a given case that it would be in the public interest to regulate prices.[59] Holmes, writing in a separate dissent, was characteristically more blunt: "[T]he notion that a business is clothed with a public interest and has been devoted to the public use is little more than a fiction intended to beautify what is disagreeable to the sufferers. The truth seems to me to be that, subject to compensation when compensation is due, the legislature may forbid or restrict any business when it has a sufficient force of public opinion behind it."[60] Or as one contemporary commentator declared, the whole notion of "affectation with a public interest" was nothing more than "legal phlogiston."[61]

During the five decades following *Munn*, while the Court fumbled around for some logical limit to the doctrine, commentators argued from the sidelines about the precise content that should be given the doctrine. The status of public utility regulation itself under the "affectation" test was never in dispute. Virtually all sides regarded railroads and public utilities as the archetypal property justly subject to regulation. The fight was over how far, and in what direction, the example of public utilities should be pushed by analogy.

For conservative commentators, the salient attribute of public utilities was their monopoly status, which bestowed immunity from the normal rigors of the competitive market. Some, like Cooley, insisted that only formal monopoly status could confer such immunity.[62] But most were willing to include virtual (de facto) monopolies as well. The defense of price regulation to correct market failures fit comfortably within an individualistic tradition. As one commentator stated, construing the decision in *Munn* as limited to monopolies, legal or de facto,

> In view of these facts, is it so certain that the principles of the doctrine of Munn v. Illinois are socialistic? May it not be that the upholders of individualism against socialism, alarmed at the tendency of combination to destroy the individualism of industry, have abandoned their old doctrine of *laissez faire,* and invoked the aid of the State to crush these forces which threaten the existence of their cherished belief? . . . [T]he doctrine of Munn v. Illinois may be regarded rather as an effort of individualism to stem the rising tide of combination, than as socialistic; a stand made by the individual rather than a move forward of socialism.[63]

Fighting for the rhetorical middle, many moderates and progressives embraced the conservative, ameliorist premise that price regulation was justified only as a piecemeal corrective for market failure. But they took a somewhat broader view of the appropriate occasions for correction, arguing that *any* business not adequately controlled by normal market forces was "affected with a public interest." Although the monopolistic structure of an industry was sufficient to ensure market failure, they argued, it was not necessary. Rexford Tugwell, in a well-known 1922 monograph, suggested that the government ought to control service and rates in a given market whenever "consumers' disadvantage" in the market made them dependent on sellers.[64] As J. M. Clark noted a few years later, if the Tugwellian suggestion were broadened to include sellers as well as buyers, it would support intervention whenever "the nature of the business is such that competition, for one reason or another, does not afford the protection to buyers and sellers which it is supposed to afford when working freely . . ."—that is, in any market that was less than perfectly competitive. With that correction, Clark argued, the theory described the universe of past decisions tolerably well—a view echoed the following year by Justice Stone in Tyson v. Banton[65]—and more importantly, prescribed the universe of desirable decisions perfectly.[66] Walton Hamilton echoed the call for a "newer and more realistic conception of competition," which would recognize that many apparently competitive markets were not self-regulating. He suggested that regulation should be governed by "three presumptions, which are to be taken in order: price is to be left to free enterprise; the antitrust laws are to be used, if need be, to keep enterprise free; and, if free enterprise cannot be made to work, resort is to be had to formal price-fixing."[67]

Numerous others at least at times rejected the rhetoric of individual rights entirely, in favor of the more radical view that *all* private property was ultimately public in nature. Harleigh Hartman, for example, called on others to abandon the notion that the monopolistic nature of public utilities is the basis of distinction between public and private service, and the "equally superficial conclusion that regulation is but a substitute for competition." In place of that "individualistic idea of private property," Hartman argued, all should embrace "the social concept which recognizes an extensive public interest in property."[68] Commons, making the same point more succinctly, stated merely that "the term 'private business' is a 'contradiction in terms.'"[69]

That view was grounded in part on what was perceived to be the public origins of private property, in part on its public consequences. Hale put the former justification most starkly in insisting that all private property was merely the delegation of public authority to exclude all others from its use, a view echoed by Commons in declaring every person a "public utility" to the extent that "public powers are employed in his behalf against others."[70] Making the same point elsewhere in more general terms, Hale argued that "[t]he advantages which various businesses possess cannot be classified into those peculiar to utility companies on the one hand, and those common to everyone else on the other. There is scarcely a single advantage possessed by a business affected with a public use which cannot be matched in the case of some unregulated concern."[71] Indeed, Walton Hamilton implied, progressives unnecessarily conceded a rhetorical advantage to the other side in even allowing the question to be framed as "whether property should be taken for the public use." Property, said Hamilton, was not "taken" and "put to a public use" "except by benefit of a figure of speech."[72]

The latter justification—what E. R. A. Seligman termed the "social utility" theory of private property—found the rationale for property rights instead "in the idea of the group that by permitting [such rights] the welfare of the group is enhanced."[73] Defined in this way, the "affectation" test, invoked as a limit on police power, simply converged with the broadest definition of that power. The argument was a staple in progressive thought going back at least to Mill. It gained currency in the late nineteenth century in the arguments of T. H. Green, Lester Ward, and others for the interdependence of all human action.[74] Mill, abandoning the ameliorist justification for state regulation offered in *Principles,* had argued in *On Liberty* that, unlike the realms of thought and expression, where one could distinguish between self-regarding acts and acts that affected others, all trade activities affected others. As a consequence, Mill concluded, the state must be free to regulate trade to whatever extent it wished.[75] J. M. Clark stopped just short of that point, arguing that the category of property "affected with a public interest" should include all businesses, but be limited to those "relations or functions" of each business in which the welfare of other sectors in the economy was implicated. Those, Clark suggested, would include the provision of inadequate information to consumers, misleading advertising, excessive prices, and inadequate working conditions for laborers.[76] As Clark noted, the definition closely paralleled one that Hale had offered in his Public Utilities casebook.[77] For the most part, however, Hale (at least in his welfarist mode) eschewed such nice distinctions, in favor of the more sweeping claim that since all property has public consequences, all may be deemed "affected with a public interest."

As suggested in Chapter 3, either justification for the publicness of private property could have been couched in the individualist premises of a Lockean property scheme. As to its public origins, to the extent that property owed its legal existence to public favors, one could argue that the public, as a sort of coinvestor, had a rightful claim to its profits—an argument that was universally invoked to justify price regulation of formal monopolies. As Harleigh Hartman put it, utilities "hold[] but the naked title of a trustee" with respect to land and other privileges granted by the state, so that "the return reverts to the public as *cestui que trust.* Denial of a return on such property is restrictive action under the police power in protection of the public's interest, not taking of private interest."[78] Hale and others argued that many of the state-created advantages enjoyed by utilities were also enjoyed by businesses in so-called competitive industries, entitling the state to claim a share of the profits there as well. Hale's insistence that all property rights amounted to the public grant of a privilege to exclude all nonowners merely carried that argument to its logical extreme: the state, as the necessary co-creator of all property, retained the (Lockean) prerogative to limit that grant as it saw fit. One could push the argument quite far in another direction as well. If, as neoclassical economists had insisted, the value of property was driven by demand, one could argue that the public, in desiring a given piece of property, was an indispensable co-creator of its value.[79]

Similarly, to the extent that private property had public consequences, one could justify its regulation under the state's police power on individualist grounds. The Court in *Munn* had relied on that argument, in defending the

Granger laws as merely implementing the harm-based exception built into even the strongest property rights regime.[80] Picking up on that suggestion, some commentators read *Munn* and succeeding cases to justify price regulation of monopolies on the ground that monopolies' artificial pricing policies injured the community.[81] Holmes, defending the Granger decisions in 1878, suggested that the same principle could be extended to justify *all* price regulation, at least where the purchasers of a good or service were dependent on the supplier:

> A hundred years ago, one could hardly use his land so as to injure another except by creating a nuisance. But things have grown more complex. The relations between property owners are not only those of mere contiguity: they are organic. Cities have grown up whose existence depends upon the railroad, and the products of millions of acres have to pass through the elevators of Chicago. If you cut the motor nerve, you paralyze the hand. If the railroads and elevators have a constitutional right to charge what they please, it is just as truly a right to destroy the property of others as a right to make noxious vapors would be.[82]

But it seems clear that either justification for state regulation, pushed to extremes, stretches the definition of individualism to the breaking point. Hale's argument that the public retained rights over private property because the public created it had no logical stopping point. The same was true of Holmes's defense of price regulation as merely policing economic harm. Stripped of its rhetorical flourishes, Holmes's argument simply states in other terms Hale's and Commons's observation about the reciprocal nature of gains from trade in any market exchange. Any price exacted by a seller represents an injury to the buyer, in the sense that it deprives the buyer of a portion of his wealth that he could have retained in the trade had a lesser price been charged.[83] But as Holmes noted when he confronted the same problem with more analytic care in "Privilege, Malice, and Intent,"[84] whether that factual injury constitutes a legal injury depends on what we take to be the parties' legal rights. Charging what the market will bear is an affirmative harm to the public, rather than merely a failure to bestow a larger benefit on it from trade, only if the public has a preexisting right to purchase such property at a lesser price.[85] The decision in *Munn* and elsewhere implicitly concluded that the public had a right *not* to pay that portion of the price that reflected excess profits attributable to monopoly status. Holmes perhaps intended the preceding remarks merely to extend the implicit right recognized by *Munn* to any less than perfectly competitive market. Yet neither of those limits, nor indeed any other, inhered in the notion of "police power" itself. Nothing in Holmes's argument prevented a state from concluding that the public has a right to acquire all goods for free, and hence treating any charge at all as an affirmative injury to the public regulable under the state's police power. One could defend the resulting regulatory scheme— preventing all market exchanges—as consistent with the individualistic premise behind the maxim, "sic utere tuo ut alienum non laedas." But one could as easily (indeed, more easily) ascribe it, along with lesser restrictions on the power of exchange, to a collectivist view of property rights, which finds them defensible only insofar as they promote the general good.

As with the progressive agenda more generally, little turned in practice on whether regulation was defended as individualist or collectivist. Either rationale—expanding government powers in the name of classic individualism or repudiating individualism entirely in favor of a collectivist view of property rights—led to the same practical result in progressives' hands. Given the growing conviction that all businesses in an economy increasingly dominated by large corporations were tending toward monopoly, or at least lay somewhere between perfect competition and perfect monopoly, the need for piecemeal rectification of market failures could justify virtually any regulatory effort that the states were likely to undertake.[86] On the other side, for purely utilitarian reasons, most progressives would have chosen to leave price-setting to the market in fully competitive industries. Thus, there were few, if any, regulatory ventures that the states were likely to *want* to undertake that they could not justify under either rationale.

By the early 1930s, with the appointments of Hughes and Roberts to the Court, the former progressive minority that had opposed the "affectation with a public interest" requirement (Stone, Brandeis, and Holmes, now replaced by Cardozo) became for the first time a clear majority. In 1934, in Nebbia v. New York,[87] the new majority seized the opportunity to repudiate the doctrine entirely. Justice Roberts, writing for the Court, made two points that had been recurring themes of progressive commentaries and dissents for some thirty years. First, Roberts argued, the long-standing notion that there was something "peculiarly sacrosanct" about the price one may charge for goods or services had no basis in constitutional language or in logic. Whatever constitutional constraints existed on the government's right to regulate other attributes of ownership should apply to prices as well.[88] Second, Roberts argued, the particular constraint imposed on price regulation—limiting the right to regulate prices at all to those industries "affected with a public interest"—was merely conclusory. "The phrase 'affected with a public interest' can, in the nature of things, mean no more than that an industry, for adequate reason, is subject to control for the public good." It is in short just the "equivalent of 'subject to the exercise of the police power.'"[89] As long as the reason *is* adequate, Roberts argued—as long, that is, as the regulation is a valid exercise of police power—it meets the constitutional requirement of due process.

Hale, writing to Roberts to compliment him on the decision, stated simply that "Your opinion in that case is such a masterpiece that it seems superfluous to comment on it."[90] Commenting nonetheless in an article on the significance of *Nebbia*, Hale concluded that "[a]s a result of the *Nebbia* case, the horizontal limit [on the government's power to regulate prices] has been removed."[91] By eliminating any categorical distinctions between public utilities and other businesses, the Court in *Nebbia* opened the way for state legislatures and Congress to regulate any enterprise, provided only that the legislation had some minimal rational basis. In fact, that invitation had already been accepted a year earlier by Congress, when it passed the National Industrial Recovery Act, authorizing industry-wide codes of "fair competition."[92] After *Nebbia*, the Court never again interfered with a legislature's decision about *which* enterprises were regulable.

Vertical Constraints: Fair Return on Fair Value

The whole doctrine of Smyth v. Ames *rests upon a gigantic illusion. The fact which for twenty years the court has been vainly trying to find does not exist. "Fair value" must be shelved among the great juristic myths of history, with the Law of Nature and the Social Contract. As a practical concept, from which practical conclusions can be drawn, it is valueless.*[93]

The Tyranny of Smyth v. Ames

The Court in *Munn*, in setting forth the "affectation" test, laid the groundwork for later courts to limit the categories of businesses that could be subject to price regulation at all. But for those businesses that were regulable, the Court unambiguously took a liberal view of the extent of regulation permissible. Refusing to inquire into the reasonableness of the rates at issue in *Munn*, Justice Waite wrote simply this: "We know that this is a power which may be abused; but that is no argument against its existence. For protection against abuses by legislatures the people must resort to the polls, not to the courts."[94]

That portion of *Munn*—its main holding—was regarded as an unambiguous defeat for the railroads and other industries that were the object of state rate regulation. Trying unsuccessfully to persuade the Court to review the reasonableness of the statute at issue in the case, counsel for one of the railroads in the Wisconsin Granger case argued as follows: "The average politician and Granger within [Wisconsin's] borders are now jubilant over the prospect open to their view of enjoying other people's property without compensation, or if any is to be paid, then only such as they may choose to dictate, and the grave question comes before this Court to determine whether such claims are to be recognized as law—whether, in fact, we are gravitating toward barbarism, or whether our course is still onward in the march of civilization and progress."[95]

In the years following *Munn*, the railroads and utilities, while trying to put teeth into the "affectation with a public interest" requirement, also argued strenuously for some limit on the *extent* of regulation permissible. A series of decisions in the late 1880s raised doubts whether (as *Munn* had suggested) the content of rate regulations was effectively unreviewable by the courts. In 1890, the Court resolved those doubts in favor of judicial review.[96] It was, however, silent about the criteria by which the constitutionality of rates should be determined. That question was resolved eight years later in the infamous case of Smyth v. Ames.[97] Picking up on suggestions in an earlier decision that a rate that was "confiscatory" might be unconstitutional,[98] the Court held that rates must not be "so unreasonably low as to deprive the carrier of its property without such compensation as the Constitution secures, and therefore without due process of law."[99] In a soon-to-be-famous phrase, the Court stated that that standard would be met only if rates were set high enough to allow a "fair return" on the "fair value of the property being used by [the company] for the convenience of the public."[100]

For the next forty-five years, all rate regulation of public utilities was at least putatively governed by the "fair return on fair value" rule in Smyth v. Ames. Under the Valuation Act of 1913 and the Transportation Act of 1920, Congress extended the rule to the ICC's rate regulation of railroads, telegraph companies, and telephone companies.[101] Few Supreme Court decisions of the period engendered as much criticism as *Smyth*. As with the "affectation" test in *Munn*, criticism of the fair value rule in *Smyth* cut across political lines, but it was strongest among progressives.[102] Hale, along with John Bauer, James Bonbright, and Gerard Henderson, was one of its most prominent and persistent critics. His dissertation, *Valuation and Rate-Making*, offered an early and influential attack on the logical coherence of the rule.[103] Over the next three decades, Hale refined the argument in some twenty-five books and articles.[104] His campaign against *Smyth* was directed to state regulatory commissions, state and lower federal courts, and Congress, but most of all to the Supreme Court. In private correspondence, he pressed the case against *Smyth* with individual justices of the Court, finding a receptive audience with Brandeis, Stone, Cardozo, and Douglas.

The fair value rule in *Smyth*, Hale argued, rested on two erroneous assumptions. The first was that there was such a thing as the "fair value" of a business that could be ascertained by scientific fact-finding. In fact, Hale argued, the word "value" was used in varying and inconsistent ways, depending upon the purpose for which a valuation was being done. As a result, in choosing a measure of value for rate-making purposes, courts and rate-setting commissions were necessarily setting policy, not ascertaining a fact.[105] The second assumption was that, however "fair value" was defined, there existed *some* rate of return on that value that could simultaneously reduce the net earnings of a company, while leaving the value of the company intact. That belief reflected a fundamental confusion about value. It was an economic truism that the value of income-producing property was merely the capitalized value of its future expected income. Thus, in reducing a utility company's expected earnings at all below the anticipated preregulatory level, commissions were necessarily reducing the value of the company as well. As Hale declared, "the determination of what is a 'fair value' is a determination of *how much* confiscation is proper (in the opinion of the court)."[106] As Hale wrote Brandeis upon his confirmation to the Court, once inquiry was freed of the "metaphysics" that one could reduce rates while avoiding taking property value, and assumed a "more serious realistic nature," it could center on the only question of interest: whether as a matter of policy "*too much* of the value" is taken.[107] The answer to that question was not scientific but political. As a consequence, Hale and other progressives insisted in their repeated refrain, it was the legislatures' and not the courts' to give.

The Court's confusion on both points produced what Hale termed "one of the most unreal fields of speculation in which the minds of metaphysicians have disported themselves since the days of the medieval schoolmen."[108] James Bonbright, putting the point more hyperbolically, described the fair value rule in *Smyth* as "one of the major tragedies of modern American jurisprudence."[109] For Hale, like most other progressives, the ultimate tragedy of *Smyth* was not intellectual but political. The morass created by *Smyth's* incoherent requirements delayed any serious consideration of what direction public utility regulation ought, as a matter of sound policy, to take.

The Search for an Objective Measure of "Fair Value."   The Court in *Smyth* had suggested that reasonable rates would meet two conditions: "What the company is entitled to ask is a fair return upon the value of that which it employs for the public convenience. On the other hand, what the public is entitled to demand is that no more be exacted from it for the use of a public highway than the services rendered by it are reasonably worth."[110]

As Hale argued at length, the second condition had no operational meaning. If by "reasonably worth" the Court meant the subjective value to consumers (what economists would term the utility of the service), it was simply a paraphrase of the "just equivalence" principle invoked in wage regulation and was subject to the same devastating critique. Whatever price was charged, it would by definition always be less than the value to those who bought, provided that would-be buyers had adequate information concerning their own needs. If instead the phrase meant "what the service is worth on the market," that criterion would automatically be met (whatever the exchange price) as long as there was some market. By definition, Hale argued, "[a]part from forced purchases, the most exorbitant rate could exceed market value only if it were so high that nobody at all would buy at that rate. And the most inadequate rate could fall short of market value only if the company were unable to serve all who offered to pay the rate, and forced them to buy elsewhere at a higher price or go without the service."[111]

Thus, concluded Hale, "[u]nder any possible definite meaning that can be given to the phrase, it is idle to forbid rates higher than the services are worth."[112] Whatever rates are charged, they will automatically meet that criterion, however defined. What was really at stake in the regulation of monopolies was not whether customers would be forced to pay more than the services are worth. It was, rather, that by altering prices, the government altered the distribution of consumer/producer surplus from the trade—the margin (on the consumer's side) between the subjective benefits that she derives from the service and its market value, and (on the producer's side) between the cost of producing it and its market value.[113]

In cases following *Smyth,* the Court intermittently reiterated the significance of the "worth to the consumer" in measuring the reasonableness of rates. But not surprisingly, it put no weight on the test in practice.[114] Instead, the Court's search for "reasonable" rates focused on the first criterion: whether the rates in question permitted a "fair return on the fair value" of the company's property. The central question was, What constituted "fair value"?

For economists, the term "fair value" referred to market value—that is, what the property would trade for on the market between a willing buyer and a willing seller. With some refinements, that was the meaning given when valuing property for eminent domain and tax purposes.[115] But, as economists universally acknowledged, it was the one meaning that couldn't apply in the case of rate regulation.[116] The exchange value of income-producing property was equal to the capitalized value (that is, present value) of the anticipated stream of future earnings that such property would generate. As a result, setting rates to provide a fair return on market value inevitably engaged the courts in a circular enterprise. As Justice Hughes remarked, in one of the few clear acknowledgments of that circularity in a rate regulation case, "when rates themselves are in dispute, earnings produced by rates do not afford a standard for decision."[117]

Justice Harlan, writing for the Court in *Smyth*, had stated that the "fair value" of the company's property was instead a composite value to be "ascertain[ed]" from a variety of factors, including (but not limited to) the original cost of constructing the company's property, the amount expended in permanent improvements on that property, the par value and market value of the company's stocks and bonds, and the present cost of replacing the company's property (generally referred to as replacement or reproduction cost).[118] In practice, commissions and courts largely ignored the par value and market value of the company's stocks and bonds, focusing instead on the remaining factors.[119]

As Hale and others argued, the search for "fair value" mandated by *Smyth* was logically doomed from the start. First, although any one of the factors listed in *Smyth* taken alone could have yielded a coherent (if pointless) measure of "fair value," together they produced only a hodgepodge of irreconcilable standards. Writing in 1914, Hale remarked, "Why anyone capable of uttering those much-quoted remarks of Justice Harlan's in Smyth v. Ames about the matters to be 'considered' in arriving at fair value should be presumed to have any clear idea of what he did mean by 'value,' I cannot see."[120] Elaborating on that criticism a few years later, Hale said, "Some figure can be found, it is true, after considering all those items, but what will it represent? A figure can be derived from a consideration of (a) the number of soldiers who fought in France, (b) the aggregate railroad mileage in the United States and (c) the tonnage of the Japanese navy; but no such figure indicates the magnitude of any conceivable reality."[121] The criticism was widely echoed among other critics of *Smyth*. Charles Prouty, who had resigned as ICC Commissioner to head up the new project (mandated by the Valuation Act of 1913) to value all railroad properties under the criteria of *Smyth*, stated that he would rather undertake to recite the Chinese alphabet backwards than to read the Valuation Act, because it does not mean anything after you have read it.[122] "Here," Walton Hamilton lamented, "is a great democracy of standards, all equal before the law."[123] Thomas Reed Powell derided "fair value" as a "compound of contradictory considerations concocted by the alchemy of uncontrolled and changeful compromise," and concluded, "How any sane men can be willing to continue with the existing amorphosity is more than one sufferer therefrom can comprehend."[124]

Second, and more fundamentally, Hale argued, the search for a "fair value" confused "two quite distinct concepts—what the value of the physical property *is*, and what the value of the entire business *ought* to be."[125] Everything about the process by which "fair value" was determined—the rhetoric of the courts and counsel; *Smyth*'s list of factors to be considered, which (as one commentator noted) had the reassuring ring of instructions from the court to the jury in an eminent domain proceeding; the ritual obeisance commissioners paid to that list in rate determinations—conspired to create the illusion that commissions were on an evidentiary search for a "fact."[126] As Walton Hamilton described the resulting process (only slightly parodically), "[T]he rhetoric of impartiality is consciously employed; and from Olympian heights the court solemnly takes presumption, burden of proof, and inconclusive evidence—and gives the commission a little the better of it or remands cases to begin all over again their leisurely litigious journeys."[127]

The problem, critics argued, was that there was no such thing as "fair value." The word "valuation" had different meanings in different contexts. What meaning it should be given in any particular context depended on the purpose for which the valuation was done. Seeking to drive home that quintessentially Realist moral by example, in the early 1920s James Bonbright and John Bauer, with numerous participants (including Hale), undertook a massive Valuation Project under the auspices of Columbia. The resulting two-volume treatise on "Valuation of Property" covered such disparate areas as capitalization, consolidation, rate-making, and recapture. From a contemporary vantage, yoking together such unrelated questions seems a peculiar enterprise. But understood as an implicit rejoinder to *Smyth*, it makes sense. The authors' aim was precisely to show what disparate enterprises were housed under a common name, in order to free "valuation" for rate-making purposes from its erroneous moorings to value as a commercial term, and free the Court more generally from the illusion that it could find some preexisting thing called "fair value."[128] Once freed, they hoped, the Court would be forced to recognize that "value for rate-making purposes" was merely (as one participant described it) "that sum upon which under all the circumstances and upon a fair consideration of all the facts and elements to be taken into account a fair return should be permitted."[129]

The Hopeless Search for a Nonconfiscatory Rate. However it arrived at "fair value," Hale argued, the Court in *Smyth* appeared to believe that there existed some "fair" rate of return on that value that would simultaneously allow the state (pursuant to its police power) to reduce the net earnings of public utilities, while (consistent with eminent domain principles) leaving the value of the utilities' property intact.[130] As the Court in *Smyth* had described those two objectives, "[T]he government . . . may by legislation protect the people against unreasonable charges for the services rendered by it," but "[t]he corporation may not be required to use its property for the benefit of the public without receiving just compensation for the services rendered by it."[131]

There is some doubt how literally the Court in *Smyth* meant to apply eminent domain principles to rate regulation. In subsequent cases, there was none. As Justice Roberts wrote in West v. Chesapeake & Potomac Telephone Co.,

> The established principle is that as the due process clauses . . . safeguard private property against a taking for public use without just compensation, neither Nation nor State may require the use of privately owned property without just compensation. When the property itself is taken by the exertion of the power of eminent domain, just compensation is its value at the time of the taking. So, where by legislation prescribing rates or charges the use of the property is taken, just compensation assured by these constitutional provisions is a reasonable rate of return upon that value.[132]

In short, when the state physically took property, the "just compensation" clause required it to make the owner whole by paying the value of the property. When the state took some portion of the value of the property by reducing rates that could be charged for its use, the same clause required the state to make the owner whole by guaranteeing rates that preserved the property's "fair value."

The analogy to eminent domain proceedings, Hale argued, betrayed a fundamental confusion about the meaning of value. In eminent domain proceedings, to preserve the value of the owner's property holdings, the state was required to pay an amount equal to the market value of what it had taken. The application of eminent domain principles to rate regulation cases would seem to require the state to permit railroads and utilities to exact "just compensation" from customers, in the form of rates that preserved the market value of what railroads and utilities possessed.[133] But, given that the market value of that property at any time was simply the capitalized value of its expected future earnings stream, that requirement led to one of two circular, and equally preposterous, results.

If by "market value" the Court meant the exchange value of property *after* rates were reduced, *any* rate reduction would by definition generate a "fair return" on that value, since the market value would automatically adjust to equal the capitalized earnings under the new rates.[134] Hammering the point home, Hale noted, "Since the value of the property as a going concern depends upon the earnings to be anticipated . . . the anticipated earnings could never amount to more than a fair return on that value—any more than the circumference of a circle could ever amount to more than 3.1416 times its diameter."[135]

If by "market value" the Court meant instead the exchange value of the company prior to rate regulation, as the analogy to eminent domain proceedings would suggest, then by definition *no* reduction would be permitted, at least with respect to existing investments.[136] Since the value of the company prior to regulation was simply the capitalized value of anticipated future earnings in the absence of regulation, any reduction in anticipated earnings would necessarily reduce the value of the property. The Court's insistence that commissions reduce rates without reducing value thus amounted, Hale argued, to the injunction that "[y]ou may cut out the man's heart provided you draw no blood."[137] That conclusion was hardly disturbing to those, like counsel for the railroads and utilities, who opposed any rate reductions.[138] But it could not be supposed to be what the Court itself had in mind in *Smyth*, given that, in many of the cases in which it loosely invoked the rhetoric of eminent domain, the Court proceeded to affirm a reduction in rates.

Of more importance, perhaps, the Court's willingness to subject what was in essence an exercise of police power to the requirements of eminent domain betrayed a fundamental confusion about the purpose of rate regulation. In eminent domain proceedings, the government took property not to deprive the owner of any economic advantage of ownership. It took it because the property had a unique use value to the public—for example, as the site of a highway or a public beach—as a result of its location or physical attributes. Thus, the government could obtain use of the property for the public while making the owner whole in monetary terms, by paying the owner the market value of the property as determined in a condemnation proceeding. But in rate regulation cases, the government deprived utilities of some portion of the value of their property, by reducing the rates that they could charge for its use, for the very purpose of transferring wealth from utilities to consumers, in the form of lower rates. Demanding that the government simultaneously make the utilities whole for the deprivation, Hale argued, was thus "a palpable absurdity," tantamount to saying that "prices may be regulated to remedy an economic maladjustment, but that in the process the economic maladjustment must not be remedied."[139] Thus, Hale argued, it should have been obvious from the start that the "just compensation" principle operating in eminent domain proceedings had no place in rate regulation: "To adjudge that a man's farm is essential for some public purpose [and hence should be taken by eminent domain] is not to adjudge that that man is in an economic position which needs correction. . . Since the function of regulation [unlike the payment of just compensation in eminent domain takings] is to alter the relative economic positions which would result from unregulated property rights, regulation must of necessity require a reappraisal of the economic incidents of ownership."[140]

In practice, the Court evaded the vicious circle to which an eminent domain analysis conscripted it by (as Hale put it) "the simple expedient of taking care to measure value by methods which did not really measure it at all."[141] The consequence in all cases was to adopt *sub silentio* a definition of "fair value" that permitted some reduction in rates, but only by confiscating some portion of the preregulatory value of the company. The numerous permutations that were tried out over the course of *Smyth*'s fifty-year reign can be grouped in two categories: cost-based measures of value; and market-based measures of value, but of less than the entire enterprise.

Value as Cost. Two of the factors included by the *Smyth* Court were "the original cost of construction [and] the amount expended in permanent improvements."[142] Together, these equaled the total historical cost of the company's assets. Unlike the market value of the company, the actual cost of the company's assets provided a measure of value independent of earnings. At least where the present value of the company (based on earnings) exceeded historic cost, it also would permit a reduction in rates. But precisely because the cost of the company's assets had no logical relationship to the current market value of those assets, let alone the market value of the company as a whole, a cost-based measure of value was irreconcilable with the Court's professed goal in *Smyth* to protect the preregulatory value of the company's property. As Justice Butler declared bluntly, "[i]t is elementary that cost is not the measure of value."[143]

Value as Market Value of Less than the Whole Company. Alternatively, courts and commissions had argued that "fair value" should be measured by market value rather than cost, but the market value of less than the entire company. The most frequent variant used was the market value of the company's *physical* assets, including land and all other tangible assets, measured by the cost of replacing those assets.[144] For at least half of *Smyth*'s reign, it was the closest thing to a de facto standard of "fair value" provided by the Court.[145] Like actual costs, this measure of fair value—generally referred to as the "reproduction" or "replacement" cost standard—would allow a reduction in rates to the extent that the capitalized value of a company's anticipated earnings under existing rates exceeded the replacement costs of its physical assets alone.[146] But also like the cost standard, to the extent that it permitted a reduction in rates, a reproduction cost standard would necessarily impair the market value of the company. As Hale noted, the effect of the reproduction cost standard was to eliminate that portion of earnings that represented a return on the "intangible" assets of the company, (franchise or natural monopoly status, going concern value, and the like).[147] Since the value of those assets was nothing more than the capitalized value of anticipated earnings in excess of the normal return on investment in tangible assets, destroying that portion of the company's earnings would necessarily destroy the value of the intangible assets themselves. As land was the primary tangible asset possessed by utilities that appreciated in value, the result of protecting tangible but not intangible assets, ironically, was to embrace Georgian rent theory for everything *but* land—the very thing for which Henry George had argued that it was impossible to justify private ownership.

In an effort to address the complaint that a reproduction cost base confiscated the value of the company's intangible assets, courts and commissions intermittently proposed expanding the rate base to include some intangible assets. Those most frequently proposed for inclusion were franchise value and going concern value.[148] Franchise value was the value of the exclusive license to serve the community. "Going concern" value, although more ambiguous, generally referred to the additional value to a company, over and above the replacement costs of physical assets, of having those assets up and running as part of a going business.[149] That value, unlike a franchise value, existed even in competitive businesses.

As Hale noted, the effect of even partially including intangible values was to push "fair value" in the direction of the full (unregulated) value of the company. At the extreme, the expanded "fair value" standard put the rate commission through the self-canceling exercise of subtracting the intangible value of the company from its total value as a "going concern" to yield the value of physical assets alone, merely to add it back in to produce its total going-concern value.[150] The resulting measure of "fair value" would meet the requirement that rate regulation not confiscate value, but it would do so (familiarly) by precluding any reduction in rates at all. In the first case to confront the problem squarely, the Court tried to have it both ways, by holding that a company was entitled to include the franchise in its "fair value," but valuing the franchise in light of the company's lower earning expectations under rate regulation.[151] Three years later, in the *Cedar Rapids* case, Holmes acknowledged the difficulty, but suggested only that the fair solution was to split the difference, steering (as Holmes put it) between the Scylla of protecting a franchise fully, thereby holding "the power to regulate is null," and the Charybdis of concluding that the state's right to regulate is unfettered by the Fourteenth Amendment, thereby holding that "property is nought."[152] Most progressives would have steered closer to Holmes's Charybdis. As franchise value was really the value of the monopoly privilege granted by the public, progressives argued, it is "not justly subject to capitalization against the public."[153] Some legislatures took matters into their own hands, prospectively limiting by statute or contract the value that utilities could place on their franchises to what it cost utilities to obtain them.[154] By 1923, the Court appeared to settle the issue against inclusion,[155] although lower courts and commissions continued to smuggle some portion of franchise value in under a broad reading of "going concern" value. But wherever the line was drawn, one would necessarily compromise either the rights of property, the power to regulate, or both.

Fair Value of the Business Based on Rates that Are "Just and Reasonable." In a final effort to escape the central paradox of *Smyth*, Justice Butler, writing for the Court in the 1938 decision in Denver Union Stock Yard v. United States, stated that the "fair value" of the property should be measured by what the value would be under rates that are "just and reasonable as between the owner of and those served by the property."[156] The decision, Hale argued, was the final absurdity in the saga of Smyth v. Ames, reducing to its clearest form the tautology of all Supreme Court decisions going back to *Smyth* itself.[157] Once the Court fixed rates at what it deemed to be "a just and reasonable level," the property would automatically assume a fair value under the Court's definition. There was no need for a valuation at all. Moreover, the Court's belief that the resulting rates would not confiscate property depended either on the "astounding [factual] assumption that the profitableness attributable to so much of the rates as were in excess of those that would be 'just and reasonable' added nothing to the value of the going concern before regulation made it unlawful to charge such rates, no matter how clearly the continuance of such profitableness might have been anticipated";[158] or on the legal fiction that existing rates were rendered retroactively unlawful by the Court's or the commissions' decision to lower them.[159] "By this declaration," Hale argued, giving vent to twenty-five years of accumulated exasperation, "the Court, without repudiating the doctrine of Smyth v. Ames, reduced it to the utmost limits of absurdity."[160] "Absurd though this opinion is," Hale concluded, "it bears the official imprimatur of the United States Supreme Court."[161]

The Demise of Smyth

Louis Brandeis's appointment to the Court in 1916 gave the progressives their first clear hope for repudiating *Smyth*. (Holmes, who might normally have been counted on to oppose the sort of judicial intervention in economic affairs at work in *Smyth*, hated rate regulation cases and acquiesced in *Smyth* until Brandeis forced the issue in 1923 in *Southwestern Bell*.)[162] Brandeis, unlike Holmes, delighted in the sort of technical economic issues posed by *Smyth*, and he had worked on a number of utility and railroad rate regulation cases before his appointment to the Court. Although he had not taken on the rule in *Smyth* directly in the course of that work, Brandeis was known to be hostile to any strict interpretation of "fair value," arguing instead for a "just and reasonable" standard that would take into account both utilities' and consumers' interests. Thus, progressives were cautiously optimistic that Brandeis could be persuaded to spearhead the effort to overrule *Smyth*. Hale wrote to Brandeis on his confirmation to the Court to urge that task on him,[163] and continued to lobby Brandeis over the next few years, regularly sending reprints of his articles critiquing *Smyth*.

Hale's initial efforts were unsuccessful. Brandeis implicitly acquiesced in *Smyth* in the handful of rate cases that came before the Court from 1916 to 1923, most notably the *Galveston Electric* case, for which he dutifully went through the litany of *Smyth* factors to uphold the lower court decision.[164] Writing to Brandeis on April 3, 1922, Hale again urged Brandeis to present the fallacy of *Smyth* "squarely . . . in some dissenting opinion."[165] A year later, in Southwestern Bell v. Public Service Comm'n of Missouri, Brandeis finally gave Hale and the other progressive critics of *Smyth* what they wanted. In a strongly worded concurrence joined by Holmes, which echoed many of Hale's arguments, Brandeis declared, "The experience of the twenty-five years since [*Smyth*] was decided has demonstrated that the rule there enunciated is delusive." Summarizing the progressive case against *Smyth*, Brandeis argued first that "[v]alue is a word of many meanings."[166] The meaning to be given to the word in the rate regulation context was necessarily a matter of policy, not a question of fact. Construing it to mean exchange value, Brandeis argued, would lead to the "vicious circle" of deducing rates from a value that was itself determined by rates. Construing it instead to require that one balance all the factors enumerated in *Smyth* was equally untenable, since the factors "are very different; and must, when applied in a particular case, lead to widely different results."[167]

The time had come to end the doubts and uncertainties created by Smyth, Brandeis concluded, and to articulate a new standard for the rate base. The reproduction cost standard favored by utilities, Brandeis argued, was unadministrable, and rested on the dubious claim that "the constitutional protection against confiscation guarantees [utilities] a return . . . upon unearned increment."[168] In its place, Brandeis urged the Court to adopt an "actual prudent costs" standard—that is, a rule permitting utilities a fair return on the capital actually (and prudently) invested in the enterprise. That standard, Brandeis argued, would provide a stable rate base. Moreover, it would protect the legitimate interests of both the public and the investors, by protecting from confiscation only that which the investor had actually devoted to public use—the "capital embarked in the enterprise."[169]

Most progressive critics of Smyth would have rejected Brandeis's suggestion that an "actual prudent cost" standard was constitutionally mandated, rather than merely desirable as a policy matter. As Hale argued, legislatures should no more be hampered by that judicially created standard than by any other.[170] But with that exception, Brandeis's opinion was all that they could have hoped for, and it became a centerpiece of the progressive assault on Smyth for the next twenty years.[171]

With Stone's appointment to the Court in 1924, Brandeis and Holmes gained another ally in the fight against Smyth, his support secured in significant part through Hale's influence. A friend and colleague of Stone's from Columbia Law School, Hale corresponded with Stone throughout his time on the Court. The majority of the correspondence concerned rate regulation. Hale wrote Stone in early 1926, when the first rate case of Stone's tenure was pending before the Court, to urge him (in an act of "economic statesmanship") to repudiate Smyth.[172] In response, Stone requested reprints of Hale's articles on the fair value problem, which Hale sent, along with others by Gerard Henderson, James Bonbright, and J. M. Clark. Hale lobbied Stone hard over the next few years on the fair value fallacy of Smyth.[173] Stone was interested and sympathetic from the start. Responding to Hale's first letter, Stone stated, "I shall make good use of your material and hope to be able to contribute something to the working out of a more satisfactory doctrine than we have at present."[174] It was more than a decade after Southwestern Bell, however, before anyone on the Court took on Smyth directly again. In the ensuing years, the three—joined by Cardozo, when he replaced Holmes on the Court in 1932—conducted their assault on Smyth largely by covert means. Voting to uphold virtually all rate reductions that came before them for review, they nonetheless continued to pay lip service to *Smyth's* "fair value" rule, arguing only that the commission in question had given "due consideration" to the factors that *Smyth* enumerated.[175]

With the appointments of Charles Evans Hughes and Owen Roberts in 1930, the Court gained two more members generally deferential to commission rulings. By the late 1930s, the Court routinely upheld rate reductions as long as they appeared to leave the company financially solvent.[176] But it still stopped short of repudiating *Smyth* outright. Putting the best face on the matter in a letter to Brandeis in 1934, Hale purported to "express delight" at the Court's recent handling of two rate cases, stating, "As the Court is presumably not ready to repudiate the 'value' test outright, as a fallacious criterion of confiscation, your opinions seem to me to do the next best thing."[177] However, the Court's failure to inter *Smyth* obviously frustrated Hale and other progressive critics. As Hale recognized, his own efforts to persuade lower courts and commissions of the inherent fallacy of *Smyth* were unavailing until the Supreme Court itself repudiated it.[178]

Roosevelt's first four appointees to the Court—Hugo Black, Felix Frankfurter, William O. Douglas, and Frank Murphy—finally provided more than enough votes to overrule *Smyth*. In a blistering dissent in the 1938 decision in McCart v. Indianapolis Water Co., his first rate case on the Court, Black stopped just short of calling for the overrule of *Smyth*.[179] The following year, in his first decision on the Court, Frankfurter went further. Frankfurter, who shared Black's general hostility to judicial intervention in economic regulation, also came to the Court with a background in public utilities rate regulation, and committed to the progressive critique of *Smyth*.[180] Concurring in the majority's decision in Driscoll v. Edison Light & Power Co. to uphold a rate reduction as nonconfiscatory under *Smyth*, Frankfurter decried the majority opinion for "giv[ing] new vitality needlessly to the mischievous formula [of] *Smyth v. Ames*," which "reason, confirmed by events, has gradually been rendering . . . moribund by revealing it to be useless as a guide for adjudication."[181] Marshaling the list of experts that had rejected *Smyth*, Frankfurter implicitly invited the Court to join them.[182]

It was five more years before the Court accepted that invitation—and then, mysteriously, without Frankfurter's support. Douglas and Murphy, appointed in 1939 and 1940, got their first crack at *Smyth* in 1942 in Federal Power Commission v. Natural Gas Pipeline Co. In a concurring opinion, Douglas and Murphy, joined by Black, forcefully stated the case against *Smyth*, and argued strenuously that the time had come "to lay the ghost of *Smyth v. Ames*, . . . which has haunted utility regulation since 1898."[183] The opinion, even more than Brandeis's concurrence in *Southwestern*, was all that

Hale could have hoped for, and shows his clear imprint.[184] However, Stone and Frankfurter—who should have provided the other two votes needed to bury *Smyth*—inexplicably failed to join Black, Douglas and Murphy.[185] For Hale, Frankfurter's, and even more Stone's, inexplicable failure to deliver was the last, maddening twist in the endless saga of *Smyth*. Hale had sharp words for Frankfurter's apparent turnabout since *Driscoll*.[186] But Stone's reluctance to say what (so far as Hale knew) he continued to believe—that *Smyth* should be overruled—was even more exasperating. In an article published shortly after the decision was handed down, Hale invoked the trio of concurring Justices as a stand-in for himself, to coax Stone out into the open: "Justices Black, Douglas, and Murphy, being familiar with Mr. Chief Justice Stone's views from his dissenting opinions in other cases, and perhaps from contact in judicial conferences, may be warranted in thinking that he would not interpret his pronouncements [as affirming *Smyth*]."[187] Hale concluded as follows, with an implicit rebuke to Stone and Frankfurter: "Certainly a majority of the present Court must recognize that the argument [in the concurrence] is unanswerable. Had they felt free to make that recognition explicit, they would have taken a long step towards undoing the mischief for which the Court itself is responsible, and towards enabling regulatory bodies, in Mr. Justice Frankfurter's words, 'to escape the fog into which speculations based on *Smyth v. Ames* have enveloped the practical task of administering systems of utility regulation.' "[188]

Two years later in the *Hope Natural Gas* case, Douglas, Black, and Murphy, joined by Wiley Rutledge and (at last) Stone, finally laid *Smyth* to rest. In language closely tracking his concurring opinion in the *Pipeline* case, Douglas (writing for the Court) dismissed the "fair value" measure of *Smyth* as circular, and its mandate to reduce rates without reducing value as logically impossible.[189] Declining to propose any other formula or combination of formulas in its place, Douglas strongly implied that henceforth the Court would not subject rates to substantive review at all under a constitutional "due process" analysis. After *Hope*, the Court held to its implicit promise to retire from the field, never intervening again under a constitutional due process analysis in any public utility rate determinations of the traditional sort.

The Significance of Smyth v. Ames

It is hard to assess the practical effect that *Smyth* had on rate regulation for the forty-five years that it putatively governed all rate determinations. In the vast majority of cases, commissions and courts at least purported to consider themselves bound by *Smyth*. Some rate-setting commissions, in an honest (if vain) attempt to comply with the incoherent dictates of *Smyth*, simply averaged the numbers produced by its various measures of "fair value," a practice that one commentator justly termed "absurd and childish, not worthy even the experiment of rational men."[190] More often, however, commissions paid verbal obeisance to the rule in *Smyth*, as a prelude to resolving the rate case before them (necessarily) on other, unstated grounds.[191] As Bonbright put it, "[t]he courts still require the commissions to do the impossible, and of course the commissions do it. One suspects that, if the courts were to hold that the rate base must be measured by the number of redheaded men on the planet Mars, the commissions would come forward with figures precise to the last digit, with dissenting opinions from some of their members as to whether the count should include Martian women and minors. And, oddly enough, the resulting rate base would seem to justify the very rates of charge which the commission deems it expedient to enforce for unofficial reasons."[192]

Courts, which either looked the other way or failed to see the problem to begin with, rarely reversed rate determinations, unless provoked by a commission's explicit mutiny from *Smyth*.[193] But the very fact that rates were subject to judicial review at all during *Smyth*'s long reign of error imposed significant costs on all parties involved. The out-of-pocket costs alone in complying with *Smyth* were enormous. Utilities and municipalities were forced (as Brandeis noted) to "maintain[] an army of experts and of counsel" to develop and defend the futile valuations mandated by *Smyth*.[194] In the area of railroad rate regulation, the costs thereby incurred are easier to calculate. As noted earlier, under the Valuation Act of 1913 and the Transportation Act of 1920, the ICC was required to value all railroad assets subject to its jurisdiction, giving "due consideration to all factors used for rate making purposes," including original cost, cost of reproduction new, cost of reproduction less depreciation, and "other values and elements of value if there be any." Congress provided no further guidance as to how the valuations should be done, leaving the ICC (as one commentator put it) "to work out its own salvation."[195] By 1923, the ICC had spent about $100 million to value 250,000 miles of roads according to the amorphous requirements of the 1913 and 1920 Acts.[196] Most of those valuations were thrown out by the Court in the *O'Fallon* case for failure to consider reproduction costs.[197] The rest were rendered practically moot by the Depression. By the time that the Valuation Project was abandoned in 1933, its total costs ran into the hundreds of millions of dollars.[198] In the end, no use was made of the valuations at all, bearing out one commentator's prophesy that the entire exercise would prove futile because of Congress's failure to decide ahead of time how it *wished* to regulate railroads.[199]

But there were other costs as well. The good faith attempt by at least some commissions to comply with the incoherent dictates of *Smyth* produced rates that could not be rationalized on any sensible policy grounds. Even when commissions successfully evaded *Smyth*, the time lag between the initial rate determination and the end of the review process—often as much as ten or even twenty years—made determinations obsolete before they had ever been implemented.[200] Perhaps the most important loss from the progressives' point of view was that in forcing regulatory bodies to do their work in the shadow of *Smyth*, the courts "fail[ed] to give the regulatory experiment a fair trial as a substitute for government ownership and operation."[201]

The Supreme Court's dogged adherence to *Smyth*, in the face of such patent waste and error, seems to require some account. To some extent, such doctrines take on an institutional life of their own, long after the initial reasons for embracing them are lost sight of. But more than inertia seems to have been at work with *Smyth*. As one contemporary commentator re-marked, "So persistent is the theory [that one can reduce rates without changing values] that one suspects there must be some significance to it which mere logic fails to destroy. It must satisfy some objective which its proponents have at heart, and which the bare formula does not reveal."[202]

In part, the persistence of *Smyth* reflected the Court's inability to shake its primitive view of property as a physical 'thing,' with an inherent value unrelated to earnings. That view, which was closely tied to the classical economists' notion that objects have a "natural" value to which their ex-change price over the long run will equilibrate, persisted in legal circles long after neoclassical economists had abandoned it.[203] As Hale noted, the courts that had embraced *Smyth* could never have subscribed completely to the view that value was divorced from earnings. Otherwise, the entire premise of *Smyth* that there was some reduction in earnings so great that it would confiscate property made no sense.[204] But the lingering hold that a physicalist view of property had on the courts explained why some courts thought that by keeping the value of physical assets intact, they could reduce earnings to *some* extent, while (consistent with the dictates of eminent domain law) not confiscating property. Hale described that half-logic in a letter to Thomas Reed Powell in this way:

> You ask me if I think the court so simple as to think a reduction of earnings would not result in economic loss. They realized it would be an economic loss in *income*, but not in the value of the income-yielding

property . . . They were only concerned with protecting *property* (as distinct from annual income) from confiscation . . . [T]hey thought of the physical things as having a sort of inherent value; and they did not think that this would *necessarily* be lessened by any reduction in earnings. But they certainly did think that an *unreasonable* reduction would impair this value. Otherwise, how could they think of rate reduction as a confiscation at all? Their mistake was in thinking this exchange value . . . could be protected and yet some reduction in earnings permitted.[205]

Viewed in that light, the fight over *Smyth* was a fight between the old formalist (verbalist) and emerging Realist (functionalist) views of property.[206] The Realist observation that *any* rate reduction would reduce value, like Hale's observation that coercion was ubiquitous, was itself apolitical, and was endorsed across political lines. The Realists merely insisted that opponents shift debate from whether rate regulation was a deprivation of property—a factual truth beyond dispute—to whether the deprivation was justifiable. As in the debates over coercion, however, the answers given to the latter question tended to fracture along partisan lines. Conservatives, who believed that the Court had correctly characterized rate regulation as an exercise of eminent domain powers, concluded that *no* rate reductions were therefore constitutional. As Field said, dissenting in *Munn*, "[i]f the constitutional guaranty extends no further than to prevent a deprivation of title and possession, and allows a deprivation of use, and the fruits of that use, it does not merit the encomiums it has received."[207] Progressives, who believed that rate regulation fell within the police power of the state, concluded that any reductions were constitutional, provided only that they met some minimal test of rationality. As Henderson put it, "[t]he constitutional function of the courts should be merely to guard against a rule of compensation so outrageous as to shock the common sense of justice."[208]

But suggesting that the "fair value" rule in *Smyth* endured because the Court's formalist view of property endured just relocates the mystery. Why did that formalist view endure, in the face of repeated, irrefutable attacks from both inside and outside the Court? In large part, its endurance may reflect how urgently the political center on the Court desired to avoid the distributive conflicts inherent in rate regulation, by believing that it could do the impossible: redistribute wealth from utilities to consumers without confiscating any portion of the property of the utilities. As one commentator remarked, "[t]he conflicting desires which plagued the Supreme Court in the [rate] cases were reconciled by the unanimous adoption of a formula which conceded what the majority of the court desired, the power to regulate, and yet guarded against what the minority feared, confiscation."[209] Arthur Hadley, attributing somewhat more cunning to the Court, argued that it used the word "valuation" to describe what was in fact a taking of property without compensation precisely to obscure the confiscation that it thereby effected: "Calling what is offered a value," he concluded, "is simply adding insult to injury."[210] In its decision in *Hope,* the Court acknowledged at last that the two goals could not coexist, and that it had opted for government power over private rights. The larger significance of that concession was not lost on either the left or the right. If it was permissible to alter the distribution of wealth that results from normal market relations in this context, why not in all? The Court in *Nebbia* had taken the first step in that direction, in holding that there was "no closed class or category of businesses affected with a public interest."[211] In *Hope,* the Court took the next step, holding that there were no meaningful constitutional limits on what the state could do to further that public interest, short of taking title to the property for public use under a narrowly construed doctrine of eminent domain.

Rent Theory in Action

Rate valuation is distinctly different from all other valuation. In rate-making the value sought is that socialistic value based upon cost to the owner in the way of toil and sacrifice . . . It is in reality the cost, not the value, of the utility property that is considered.[212]

[I]f economists countenance the idea that cost measures value, they lead immigrants to think that Marx was right, and that economic justice is to be had through advanced Socialism.[213]

While progressives were preoccupied for most of *Smyth's* tenure with the negative task of getting courts out of the rate regulation business, their ultimate objective was an affirmative one: to figure out, once commissions were freed up to make "intelligent use of the regulatory power," how they ought to use that power.[214] Throughout that period two possibilities garnered significant support from economists and interested parties. The first was that utilities be permitted to earn a market rate of return on the present value of their tangible property, equal in most cases to the current cost of reproducing it, less any accumulated depreciation ("reproduction costs"). The second was that utilities be permitted to earn a market rate of return on the capital prudently invested in their property ("actual prudent costs").

For counsel representing utilities and state public commissions, allegiance to one standard or the other was purely instrumental, and shifted as their views shifted about which standard was likely to further their clients' interests. In the first two decades of rate regulation, from the 1870s to the 1890s, prices fell steadily, causing reproduction costs to fall below historic costs. In view of that fact, it was not surprising that the states rather than the utilities first championed a reproduction cost rate base. In *Smyth* itself, William Jennings Bryan, arguing on behalf of the state, strongly urged a reproduction cost base, while counsel for the railroads implicitly supported actual costs.[215] In the years following *Smyth*, prices rose, modestly at first and then sharply from 1913 through 1929, causing the two sides to reverse positions.[216] As Edwin Goddard remarked, writing in 1924, "it is a fair guess that if the attorneys in *Smyth v. Ames* had possessed a prophetic sight they would have swapped arguments."[217] Commissions, which had initially opposed an actual cost standard, came to support it, whereas counsel for utilities and the railroads championed reproduction costs.[218] Pierce Butler, in his capacity as counsel to the railroads prior to his appointment to the Court, took up Bryan's role as chief advocate for reproduction costs, at least as setting a floor on "fair value," and once on the Court, pushed for a reproduction cost interpretation of *Smyth*.[219]

Among academics, reproduction costs had the support of a number of reputable economists, chiefly on efficiency grounds.[220] Under a reproduction cost standard, all intangible values attributable to the monopoly position of utilities would be stripped out of the rate base, leaving only the hypothetical cost of reproducing the utility's service if entry into the industry were unrestricted—the maximum value that the business would have if subject to competition.[221] As a result, it was argued, a reproduction cost standard would replicate the investment and pricing decisions in a competitive market, thereby guaranteeing an optimal level of investment and use over the longrun.[222] Setting prices on any other basis, it was argued, would also cause prices for identical commodities to vary by geographical region solely because of variations in the average age of the plants used for production, rather than because of regional differences in the real, longrun cost of supplying the good. The result would be to distort locational choices, and create hard-to-defend price discrimination in favor of those users who migrated to low-cost areas.[223]

Most progressive or institutional economists, however, ended up supporting an actual prudent investment rate base.[224] Hale was typical in this regard. He believed that rate regulation ought to balance efficiency and equity concerns, and respected many of the efficiency arguments for a reproduction cost rate base.[225] In his earliest writings, Hale had suggested that one could devise a workable rate base by using the value of physical assets.[226] But by 1921, he concluded that the entire premise had to be scrapped in favor of a non–value based measure.[227] His change of heart partly reflected practical problems with a reproduction cost standard. To achieve efficiency objectives, reproduction costs should be measured by the cost of building the most efficient hypothetical replacement, given current technology—that is, the cost that a new entrant in a competitive market would actually incur. Because that figure was extremely speculative, commissions and courts instead generally used the cost of replicating the existing facilities.[228] Such a measure, it was argued, had nothing to recommend it from an efficiency perspective. It also posed serious administrative problems of its own, as it was based on debatable cost estimates that were highly politicized and unreliable.[229] Moreover, the cost estimates by their nature had only transitory validity, as they fluctuated with changes in price levels. In contrast, many believed that an actual cost rate base would pose few of these administrative problems, at least once utilities had begun keeping adequate financial records after World War I.[230]

But a cost rate base appealed to Hale, as it did to many other progressive economists, primarily for reasons of distributive justice. From the start, Hale argued, rate-setting commissions were unclear as to whether they were trying to mimic the competitive market or instead to work out a notion of fairness from first principles.[231] A reproduction cost standard eliminated franchise and other intangible values attributable to the monopoly status of utilities. However, it left intact any appreciation in the value of physical assets, in particular land, resulting from the relative scarcity of such assets.[232] The effect was to deprive utilities of the advantages of monopoly status, but not those that came from being an inframarginal (that is, low-cost) producer in a competitive market. Recapitulating his general attack on the fairness of incomes in a competitive market, Hale argued that result was hard to defend under prevailing (Lockean) notions of distributive justice. Both forms of surplus were an unearned windfall bestowed by social or natural circumstance, owing nothing to individual effort. If, as was universally agreed, that fact defeated any moral claim to monopoly profits, it should be equally fatal in the case of inframarginal rents.[233]

Followed to its logical conclusion, Hale argued, the attack on monopoly profits suggested that utilities were entitled only to payment for the "sacrifices made [i.e., cost incurred] in rendering that service."[234] The most obvious means to that end appeared to be a cost rate base, which would limit utilities' income in the first instance to a market rate of return on actual capital invested. Although one of the chief proponents of a cost rate base, Hale believed its usefulness was limited to utilities that were true monopolies and could meet all demand at the cost-based price. In all other cases, cost-based charges would result in misallocation of resources, price discrimination among different groups of consumers based on the differential costs of their suppliers, and/or arbitrage by middlemen who would profit from reselling low-cost water or power at high cost-based prices. In such cases, Hale argued, the optimal solution instead was to set uniform prices based on the costs to the high-cost producers (approximating the unregulated equilibrium market price), and to expropriate the surplus paid to low-cost producers by an excess profits tax.[235] The latter solution was adopted for railroads in the "recapture" provision in Transportation Act of 1920. Although the provision proved a total failure in practice, it achieved celebrity status among progressives as a model for fair compensation.[236]

Either solution—a cost rate base or an excess profits tax on any returns above cost—would limit the utilities roughly to a fair return on their actual investment. But the two solutions had quite different distributive implications. A cost rate base transferred any surplus value generated by the exchange to consumers, in the form of lower rates; an excess profits tax transferred it to the government. That most progressives, including Hale, saw the two solutions as morally interchangeable underscores their belief that the core injustice to be corrected by regulation was not exorbitant charges but exorbitant profits.[237] Hale, defending that position explicitly, argued that the government could justly appropriate through taxation the excess that a seller receives above its cost, "since the appropriation would take away 'nothing which equitably belongs either' to the buyer or the seller."[238] The Court appeared to embrace that view when it upheld the railroad recapture provision in 1924 on precisely those grounds.[239]

The roots of that conception of distributive justice clearly lay in Lockean rent theory. Both the railroad recapture provision and a cost rate base were widely viewed by proponents and opponents alike as derived from Georgian rent theory, or its broader Fabian version.[240] Where proponents did not make that connection expressly, they often implied it, in describing the profits to which utilities were *not* entitled in the telltale Georgian phrase, "unearned increment," and those to which they *were* entitled as payments for investors' "sacrifices."[241] Thus, the young Hale wrote to Frank Stevens, counsel for the New York Central Railroad, in response to Stevens's argument that *Smyth* protected the value of the entire business as a going concern, "It strikes me that it might be well for you railroads to stop trying to grab all future increments of value which you have done nothing to earn, or you may some time find yourselves deprived of what you *have* actually and honestly invested."[242] Writing to Learned Hand a few years later, Hale made the same point in more conciliatory rhetoric. His aim in *Valuation and Rate-Making,* he told Hand, was to "work out a method for revising property rights, by keeping the value from increasing in the future beyond such increases as are needed to induce investment and efficiency." The same methods, concluded Hale, "if applicable at all, would apply as well to the taxation of surplus profits as to rate regulation."[243]

In either form—a cost rate base or an excess profits tax—Hale's contemporaries anticipated a number of practical and conceptual difficulties in putting rent theory into practice.[244] The first difficulty was how to account for temporary shortfalls or surpluses, when actual expenses and revenues deviated from those anticipated when rates were set. The solution, all agreed, was to add temporary shortfalls to, and subtract surpluses from, the accumulated cost base. Precisely what form those adjustments should take, however, was a matter of much dispute.[245]

The second difficulty was that a straight cost rate base automatically passed through all costs to consumers and denied any premium to companies that kept costs below normal. As a result, utilities had no incentive to manage efficiently, at least if their business faced no competition. To counteract that problem, proponents suggested limiting includable costs to those that were "prudently" incurred, a modification that came to be known, following Brandeis's usage in *Southwestern Bell*, as the "actual prudent costs" standard. Since everyone acknowledged the need to resolve doubtful expenditures in management's favor, the standard only partially solved the incentive problem, and at the cost of reintroducing many of the administrative complexities that people hoped could be avoided by moving from a reproduction cost to an actual cost rate base.[246] Hale's proposed solution was to treat a small margin (say, 2 percent) above and below costs as a risk borne by the utility company. Thus, if the market rate of return were 8 percent and the company earned 10 percent, the company could keep the 2 percent excess. If it earned 6 percent, it would be prohibited from adding the deficiency to the rate base. Only returns greater than 10 percent or less than 6 percent would be subtracted from or added to, respectively, the rate base. The effect, Hale argued, would be to give the company an incentive to conserve costs, by allowing it to retain some of the advantages of its efficiency, or feel some of the adverse consequences of its profligacy.[247]

A third difficulty was that one had to decide what to do with a utility's existing investors at the time that a cost rate base was adopted, those investors having purchased stock at a price that reflected the possibility of supernormal profits. The same problem had been raised by the Georgian land tax, which, if applied to all land values at the time enacted, would have expropriated value for which at least some owners had paid full price. In both contexts,

Hale was sympathetic to protecting the "vested rights" of existing owners.[248] In the case of public utilities, he supported some compromise rate base along the lines proposed by John Bauer and James Bonbright. Under the Bauer-Bonbright plan, a pure cost rate base would be applied only prospectively, to investments made by utilities after the rate base was in effect. Existing investments would be permitted to earn a return on a compromise rate base, initially using market value at the time of regulation, and then phasing it out gradually in favor of a cost base.[249]

But Hale's contemporaries objected to a cost rate base, not principally because of administrative difficulties or efficiency costs but because of what it implied about property rights. Some attacked the application of rent theory to public utilities regulation on the narrow ground that it disadvantaged utilities as compared with producers in competitive markets. Two leading authorities on railroad regulation, for example, dismissed the recapture provision in the 1920 Transportation Act as an unfairly discriminatory application of the doctrine of Henry George: "It means, after all, a taking of an unearned increment from one class of property owners in the community while permitting others to receive it."[250] Responding with his standard, functionalist critique of rights, Hale pointed out that producers in competitive industries were not themselves on an equal footing with one another with respect to the right to an "unearned increment," at least if one measured rights by results. "[S]ome men get 'intangible' values, some get large increments, some small increments, and some no increments at all."[251] Defending the recapture provision in particular against the charge that it discriminated against railroads, Hale argued as follows: "[T]he whole body of the law, in the absence of the recapture clause, discriminates in favor of the owners of unregulated appreciating land *and* some railroad owners, against the rest of the world. *With* the recapture clause and the actual cost rate-base, the law would be no more discriminatory, only the railroad owners would join the majority class against whom the discrimination works."[252] "Since equality among all is out of the question," Hale concluded, "there is no force in the contention that the utility must be given an increment in value for the purpose of giving it the same share in the community's prosperity that other men enjoy."[253] "The most we can do is to consider each case of special advantage on its merits."[254]

Moreover, even if the recapture provision did treat railroads more harshly than other businesses, Hale argued, that was not itself grounds to condemn the provision. That some businesses earn incomes to which they may not be entitled cannot justify treating others as generously: "[I]t would be as absurd to justify any particular utility values on the ground that their legitimacy is generally recognized" with respect to unregulated, competitive businesses "as it would be for a municipal administration to justify a salary of a sinecure on the ground that some other administration of some other city still pays that sort of salary. Any value which is still to be allowed to a utility company must be justified on some independent ground of policy."[255] In short, "In the utility field, standards of what it is proper for an owner to get out of his ownership have to be worked out *de novo*."[256]

Others attacked a cost rate base more directly, as a form of socialism. Arthur Hadley offered that observation in a purely descriptive vein, noting that theories of value fall under two main heads: "[T]he commercial or competitive theory, which bases value upon what the buyer is willing and able to offer for an article; and the socialistic theory, which bases it upon what the article has cost the seller in the way of toil and sacrifice."[257] Elsewhere, however, Hadley sounded a less impartial note:

> One of the lessons of history is that a democratic form of government in a complex state cannot last very long unless it protects property rights. . . This is not a fanciful danger, it is a real danger. A great deal of our immigration comes from countries where people have had little experience in property holding and where they cherish impracticable ideals of what democracy can accomplish in the way of equality. Such men generally have a passion for justice. But it is an unintelligent passion; and if economists countenance the idea that cost measures value, they lead immigrants to think that Marx was right, and that economic justice is to be had through advanced Socialism.[258]

Hale and other progressives did not dispute the characterization of a cost rate base as "socialistic," a somewhat surprising fact given their care in avoiding the label in other contexts.[259] But they emphatically disputed the implication that it was therefore equivalent to a theft of utilities' rightful property. That would be true only if utilities, and by extension all property owners, had a moral or legal right to whatever exchange value their property would have had under some other regulatory regime, or in the absence of price regulation at all. In Hale's view, he had spent his career proving that no such right could exist.

The Legacy of Public Utilities Rate Regulation

Hale and his progressive colleagues ultimately prevailed in their narrow aim to make actual, prudent costs the standard rate base in public utilities regulation.[260] They succeeded as well in persuading commissions and legislatures that a prime motive for cost-based pricing was to eliminate unearned scarcity rents from land and other nonreproducible factors of production.[261] But their hope that public utilities regulation would serve as a model for a wholesale revision of property rights along rent-theory lines was almost entirely disappointed. At least two factors account for that failure.

The first was the at-best mixed experience with rate regulation in the case of public utilities and railroads. The enormous out-of-pocket costs and delays, some intrinsic to the regulatory process and some produced by the incoherent regime imposed by *Smyth*, have already been alluded to. But even ignoring the costs of regulation and looking only to effects on price, the results were not encouraging. One of the recurring ironies in railroad regulation was that the legislature's right to reduce prices was vindicated just as the right was rendered useless, because market forces made it economically impossible to extract rates even close to those set by law. The Granger laws, enacted in the early 1870s to control railroads' exploitation of consumers, by the mid-1870s were (because of economic changes in the industry) protecting the industry from economic collapse. The railroad recapture clause in the Transportation Act of 1920, heralded by progressives as a model for rent-theory distribution, was mooted by economic forces by the time that it was enacted. While regulation in the area of electric power and natural gas was not a similarly spectacular failure, its record at keeping down rates was ambiguous at best.[262] That experience made many reluctant to extend the experiment beyond those narrow spheres, and dubious as to its value even there. Indeed, dissatisfaction with rate regulation in the 1930s and 1940s, in conjunction with the economic dislocation caused by the Depression, spurred a renewed interest in public ownership and management as an alternative to public regulation, most notably in the area of electric power.[263]

The second factor that tended to confine the public utilities experiment to its narrow field was that succeeding generations of economists strongly resisted using rate regulation to achieve any distributive objectives. Most of Hale's contemporaries would have agreed that distributive fairness ought to be weighed along with economic efficiency in setting utility prices. Many would have gone even further, arguing that the main problem with monopoly pricing was its distributional inequities. That view has simply perplexed later generations of economists, who have almost universally concurred that efficiency concerns alone should dictate pricing policy, with distributional concerns addressed through the tax system and income transfer programs.[264]

Judged by efficiency criteria, cost-based pricing has proved an acceptable, if not theoretically ideal, solution to the pricing inefficiencies of natural monopolies like public utilities, arising from the fact that monopolies will maximize their own profits by setting prices above the optimal level for social welfare purposes.[265] But virtually all economists agree that in competitive industries, the unregulated market will do a better job at efficient pricing than will regulation in any form, at least once the costs of regulation are taken into account.[266] Thus, so far as succeeding generations of economists have been concerned, there is no justification for expanding the lessons of public utility regulation beyond public utilities and other formal or natural monopolies. As suggested previously, economists' conviction that efficiency objectives alone should determine regulatory policy has not permeated regulatory practice of public utilities commissions. But it has no doubt undercut any legislative efforts to expand the example of cost-based price regulation beyond public utilities.

The two preceding factors suggest why, as a historical matter, the experiment with cost-based rate regulation of public utilities might not have been extended beyond monopolies, to attack inframarginal rents in all market exchanges. But there is also reason to doubt how successful such an extension *could* have been in achieving the redistributive goals that Hale and other progressive rent theorists had in mind. A number of things make rent-theory-based regulation a relatively unpromising mechanism for broad income redistribution.

First, at least with respect to future investments, it was futile to attempt to eliminate inframarginal returns to capital in selected industries only. Most investors regard (equally risky) investments of financial capital as fungible.[267] Thus, the cost of capital in any particular industry is always equal at a minimum to the opportunity cost of forgoing investment in other (unregulated) industries. As long as capital can earn a higher expected return in unregulated industries, it will not gravitate to regulated ones.[268] That condition meant that any attempt to reduce the expected return to new capital beyond eliminating pure monopoly profits could not be localized to one industry; instead, it had to apply to all capital investments, through some more broad-based scheme of administered prices or (more likely) confiscatory taxes on excess profits. The same objection did not hold for schemes to confiscate excess returns to old capital already committed to a particular venture. But as noted before, at least in the public utilities context, Hale and others were reluctant to attack windfall gains to past investments, recognizing that investors may have purchased such investments at a price that reflected the possibility of inframarginal rents.

The second problem, already alluded to, is the costs of regulation itself. Any regulatory scheme to isolate rents inevitably requires extensive fact-finding and adherence to due process. In some cases, the difficulties of fact-finding are probably insuperable. One could feasibly isolate rents in the form of an explicit, supernormal return to financial or human capital. Windfall profits taxes, rate regulation for public utilities and other natural monopolies, and cost-based rent control, are all examples of real-world efforts to target such rents. But the problems of isolating that portion of rents that reflect inframarginal tastes for current consumption or leisure seem far more intractable. One is perhaps driven inevitably to the Hobsonian solution of assuming that such rents are proportional to total income, or some other measurable quantity. Given that fact, it is no surprise that Hale's one practical excursion into rent theory—public utilities rate regulation—like all contemporary applications, concentrated on the relatively easy case of supernormal market returns.

Third, progressive rent theory, at least as applied to financial investments, appeared to be largely an attack on returns to risk. Hale and other proponents of a historic cost rate base for public utilities took as given the investors' right to a return equal to the normal market rate of return on investments. Although never entirely clear on this point, Hale seemed to define "normal" as the expected return on relatively riskless investments. His attack, which was limited to returns in excess of that amount, thus amounted, in effect, to a scheme to confiscate the positive returns to risk, with the risk arising from the possibility that assets used in the utility's business could rise or fall in value over their historic cost.

This attack on returns to risk poses some peculiarities, or at the least raises unanswered questions. In attacking positive returns to risk only, Hale implicitly assumed that the entire *riskless* interest rate (at least to the marginal investor) was earned—a position consistent with the general progressive concession to Seniorian abstinence theory.[269] In proposing that returns to risk be confiscated, he also assumed that such returns were unearned—that is, that investors' willingness to bear risk should not be treated as a true sacrifice for (Lockean) rent theory purposes. Although both were plausible views, neither was indisputable.[270] In addition, it is curious that Hale, like other rent theorists, ignored the question of how a fair Lockean scheme would treat losses. If investors are entitled to no more than fair compensation for their sacrifice, are they also entitled to no less? If so, then the government should protect losers to the extent that assets fall in value from their historic cost, either by artificially keeping price levels high enough to generate a fair return on costs or by reimbursing their losses—a scheme that in effect shifts all private risk to the public sector.

More serious, however, was the disincentive effect that such a scheme would have on private investment. A wholesale effort to eliminate prospectively all positive returns to risk would almost certainly eliminate private risk-taking. The only obvious solution to that problem lay in a broad-based, *non*confiscatory tax on capital that expropriated a portion of surplus to infra-marginal investors without unduly discouraging investment. The inevitable cost of imposing a general tax on investment returns, however low the rates, would be to discourage some (marginal) investment.[271] But set at the right levels, the investment thereby lost might be relatively little, compared with inframarginal surplus captured. In short, the solution lay in what economists would now think of as an optimal tax on capital, where rates are set to fall, as far as possible, on the inelastic portion of the supply curve for savings. As noted in Chapter 4, a number of rent theorists in both England and the United States had embraced that solution in principle, in supporting a general, progressive income tax on labor and capital as an indirect way to appropriate rents.

In the end, some form of optimal tax scheme seems to offer the only avenue by which progressive rent theory could have any broad application to market transactions. That conclusion, ironically, brings progressive rent theory to the same solution that contemporary economists have reached on purely efficiency grounds. It also brings to the fore the last, and perhaps most troubling, problem with rent theory: whether "cost" or "sacrifice" can provide a morally satisfactory criterion for distributive justice, once one extends "cost" beyond the narrow meaning given it in the public utilities context (the opportunity cost of capital). The thrust of rent theory is to return workers and investors to the same place on their indifference curve after any transaction—that is, to eliminate the producers' surplus generated by any trade, with surplus defined as the excess return over reservation price. That solution abandons all independent, moral inquiry into what constitutes a real sacrifice for Lockean purposes, in favor of the rule that one is entitled to one's reservation price for deferring consumption, bearing risk, or forgoing leisure, whatever the reason for demanding the price. In short, the solution merges equity and efficiency concerns. The result is a definition of rents that fits uncomfortably at best with most intuitions of justice. The problems are perhaps best underscored by noting the parallels of rent theory to a so-called Ramsey (or optimal) tax.[272] In order to minimize the efficiency loss from tax-induced distortions in people's behavior, a Ramsey tax sets tax rates on different commodities inversely proportional to the elasticity of demand. That is to say, the less price-sensitive (or elastic) the demand for a good, the higher the rate at which it is taxed. The now-familiar efficiency justification for this scheme is apparent: the less price-sensitive one's desire is for a given good, the less likely one is to be deterred from purchasing it if the price is raised by a tax. Thus, ideally, the effect of the tax is to reduce consumer surplus from a given purchase, without deterring the purchase entirely. But as numerous economists have noted, such a tax scheme has some distasteful distributive implications. It suggests, among other things, that tax rates ought to be highest on the necessities of life like food and shelter, and lowest on discretionary luxury purchases like yachts. The relevance of the criticism becomes clear once one recognizes that a rent-theory tax is, in effect, a Ramsey tax placed on producer (worker's or saver's) surplus rather than on consumer surplus. Thus, as Herbert Davenport intuited, rent theory replicates the distributive embarrassments of Ramsey taxation, when (for example) it taxes the $1 surplus value accruing to the worker paid $3/hour, who (being destitute) would work for $2 if necessary, but leaves untouched the $1,000 an hour paid to a millionaire, who (little valuing additional money) would not work for a penny less.[273] It is one thing for such embarrassments to attach to a Ramsey tax scheme, which purports to care only about efficiency. It is quite another for them to attach to rent theory, which is motivated in the first instance by concerns of distributive justice. In view of these and other conceptual problems with rent-theory Lockeanism, it is hardly surprising that many who shared its general redistributive goals preferred to defend and pursue those goals on more conventional social welfarist (utilitarian) or communitarian premises.

In the end, the efforts of Hale and other progressive rent theorists to use public utilities rate regulation as a beachhead to colonize all of private property must be judged a failure. Nonetheless, one can see rent-theory impulses at work in contemporary American society, in regulatory schemes like rent control, minimum housing standards, windfall profits taxes, or developer exactions that target sectors in which large rents are believed to exist.[274] One can see it as well in proposals to tailor property rights de novo to limit private ownership of societally-generated surplus value.[275] The more important lesson of progressive rent theory, however, is almost certainly not an affirmative one but a negative one. Progressive rent theorists, by taking seriously the premises of Lockean liberalism, unsettled its conventional conclusions, leaving as a legacy a salutary skepticism about the distributive fairness of the (unregulated) market itself.

6

CONCLUSION

It is inconceivable that Hale's work would have taken the shape that it did, except as a response to a historical moment. Hale's choice to focus on coercion, property rights, and public utilities rate regulation reflected the central political preoccupations of the progressives: bolstering labor's relative bargaining position, and protecting the government's right to regulate the exchange value of property and services. His argument in all three areas is best read as an elaborated response to the particular version of laissez faire ascendant in turn-of-the century politics and briefly enshrined in constitutional law by the *Lochner*-era Court. At its core, Hale's argument changed little from his earliest writings in the 1910s through his latest in the 1950s. By the time that *Freedom Through Law* was published forty years after the start of Hale's career, its odd agglomeration of memorialized obsessions stood as a ghostly reminder of its ancient agonist, long since vanquished.

But it is a mistake to read Hale's work as solely of historical interest. Some of the particulars that preoccupied Hale, notably the squabbles over "affected with the public interest" and "fair value" in public utilities rate regulation, have long since receded from public debate. Nevertheless, the core philosophical issue that engaged him, the appropriate limits of individual rights in a modern, interdependent society, is unlikely ever to be put to rest. Hale's work retains surprising vitality today as a trenchant rejoinder across the decades to some of the more reductive contemporary attacks on the moral legitimacy of the expansive, social welfarist state. If his basic argument changed little over the forty years that he was writing, that fact at least partly reflects the stubborn resistance of mainstream legal and political thought to absorbing the lessons that he had to teach. Indeed, the last twenty years have seen a resurgence of libertarian arguments for a strong private property regime and freedom from governmental regulation in both academic and political arenas. That resurgence has triggered debate around a set of issues remarkably similar to those that engaged Hale and his contemporaries, including what the moral significance of "negative" freedom is; what the meaning of coercion is; whether it is possible to distinguish "good" from "bad" coercive pressure other than by reference to a baseline set of entitlements that are the positive creation of the state; whether state-imposed obligations present a unique moral instance of "bad" coercion; whether private property and the private market represent in any meaningful philosophical or legal sense a private, autonomous order; and whether the particular set of private ownership rights that make up our current legal landscape, which includes a private claim on socially created surplus value, can be justified by a Lockean labor theory of ownership, utilitarianism, or some combination of the two.[1] In the legal literature, there has been renewed interest as well in the problem of coercion as it arises in an arcane area of constitutional doctrine that Hale pioneered, with a less clear political valence: the problem of "unconstitutional conditions."[2] So also, the materialist tradition of positive liberty, to which Hale's work on coercion is closely allied, remains an important response to the persistent notion of negative liberty that underlies virtually all contemporary libertarian theories.[3] The "capability theory" developed by Amartya Sen, Martha Nussbaum, and others, which argues that egalitarian efforts should be directed at equalizing people's functional capacity to achieve a meaningful life, explores the same regions under a different rubric.[4]

At the same time, the historical occasion that motivated Hale's arguments predictably distorted them as well in certain respects. Hale's immediate political objective—to immunize economic legislation from judicial review, at least under the "glittering generalities" of substantive due process— undoubtedly contributed to what some may justly view as the extreme, reductive reach of Hale's own argument. In area after area, Hale's strategy was to sweep away middle (muddled) premises that appeared to constrain legislative powers: coercion, fair value, or harm-based limits to private power under either a narrowly drawn definition of police powers or the common law tort doctrine of *sic utere tuo ut alienum non laedas*. As suggested repeatedly throughout this book, the strategy had obvious political advantages to Hale and other progressives. If successful, it meant that one could distinguish among different coercive acts or different usurpations of property only by the sort of prudential line-drawing generally agreed to be legislative and not constitutional in nature. But the strategy had its problems, some political and some analytical.

Among its political dangers, the strategy put Hale in the unusual position of agreeing with his more extreme conservative opponents that the middle way hewn by the Supreme Court's version of constitutional laissez faire was analytically incoherent—agreeing, for example, that any rate regulation at all would "take" from owners a portion of their property's value. That observation was susceptible to two resolutions: that any state intervention was constitutionally permissible, or that none was. The progressives' political agenda depended on everyone's opting for the former, a choice, as recent developments underscore, that one could not always rely on others to make. A similar danger lurked in Hale's arguments about state action, for which (uniquely) Hale's agenda was to expand constitutional protections rather than constrict them. Hale hoped that by showing that *all* private action ultimately rested on state authority, he could persuade others to treat all private action as state action, at least for the purpose of interpreting the equal protection clause of the Fourteenth Amendment. But others who accepted Hale's descriptive point have drawn the opposite moral from it: if it is impossible to differentiate among forms of private action, those who are loathe to subject all private action to the constitutional rigors designed to contain the state are ill-advised to start down that road at all.[5] Such skepticism about whether an expansive state action doctrine can be contained is at least a professed motive for the Court's eviscerating the doctrine over the past twenty years.[6]

Second, Hale's and others' broad arguments for deconstitutionalizing private rights in the area of economic regulation would come to haunt a later generation of progressives in the post–Brown v. Board of Education era. It is a commonplace to note that *Lochner*-era progressives who lobbied for courts to defer to Congress became transmuted in the Warren Court era into champions of an activist judiciary. The shift coincides with, and is largely explained by, the shift in the Court's focus from economic regulation to regulation of civil rights, privacy, and other individual liberties. It has been a perennial problem for left liberal political theorists over the past forty years (as it was in more muted form for their progressive forebears) to explain why the Court is not merely engaged in that most dread of all pursuits, "*Lochnerizing*"—that is, substituting its own raw political preferences for the political majority's—when, for example, it overturns state antiabortion laws or mandates school desegregation. As suggested later, progressives of Hale's times and since have not been without answers. But the answers require a more nuanced reading of the Constitution, of rights, or of the shortcomings of the political process in protecting particular rights, than Hale's formal and often schematic antirights argument readily lends itself to.

In addition to its political dangers, Hale's broad argument for deconstitutionalizing private rights probably misstates his private views, or at least the views that he would have come to on second thought in different political times. In the area of coercion, for example, Hale's materialist view of liberty as a stand-in for economic wealth may have been appropriate in assessing whether state regulation of economic activity was a priori more coercive than so-called laissez faire. But it fit less well with other freedoms, in particular expressive freedoms. So, at least, Louis Brandeis, Zechariah Chafee, and other progressives concluded, in arguing that freedom of expression differed from economic freedom, philosophically and constitutionally, in ways that made government regulation suspect in the first case but not in the second.[7] More recent generations of left-liberal constitutional scholars have had their doubts about that dichotomy, arguing (sometimes with an explicit nod to Hale) that disparities in private economic power could be as corrosive in the marketplace of ideas as in the marketplace of goods and services. As a result, they have looked more kindly on government regulation of speech in a variety of areas, including campaign contributions, hate speech, and pornography, than their progressive forebears would have.[8] But that (Halean) skepticism about the value of the essentially negative freedom of expression protected by laissez faire was for another day. Hale was in this respect, as in many others, a child of his times. Had he been forced to address the question of expressive freedoms directly in his scholarly writing, he undoubt-edly would have sided with Brandeis and Chafee. Such apparently inconsis-tent positions on economic and expressive freedoms are not without defense, as Holmes, Brandeis, Chafee, and others showed. Yet the very act of defend-ing them might have been salutary for Hale, providing an occasion to justify in substantive and not just in formal terms his claim that direct economic coercion by the state posed no greater threat to freedom than the combined coercive effects of private property and contract.

So also, Hale's positivist view of property rights leaves a number of things unexplained. Among them is what meaning, if any, is to be given to the express prohibition in the federal and state constitutions on the state's "tak-ing" property by eminent domain without just compensation. Hale, like Holmes before him, correctly observed that regulating the return that an owner could get on her property "took" a portion of the economic value of that property, as surely as physical seizure or taxation. He made the argument to debunk the incoherent premise of Smyth v. Ames that one could subject the return on property to eminent domain protection, while simultaneously reducing that return through rate regulation. But that observation led to opposite conclusions at the extremes: that rate regulation (like taxation) does not fall under eminent domain protection at all, and hence is limited only by the limits of the state's police power; or that it does fall under eminent domain protection, and hence is impermissible in any form. Hale, like the

Court that finally vanquished *Smyth*, opted for the former view. Again, as recent expansive libertarian readings of the "takings" clause have shown, that view was not inevitable.[9] In addition, it leaves unanswered the much vexed question among academics and jurists in the last twenty years of precisely what does fall under eminent domain protection. Virtually everyone has agreed that the government's seizure or permanent physical occupation of the entire property is protected. However, there is little agreement on anything else, or on why, as a matter of policy (as opposed to interpretation), those two classes of government actions should be an easier case for compensation than any others.

It is interesting that Hale had little to say directly about the "takings" problem. Again, there is little doubt that he would have conceded that the takings clause in the federal constitution had some content that stopped short of pure positivism. Like heightened protections for expressive freedoms under the First Amendment, that concession would hardly have been fatal to Hale's generally positivist view of property, since he could have justified walling off core "takings" from all other government actions that may have identical economic effects, by arguing that (wisely or not) the explicit language of the takings clause mandates exceptional treatment for some class of cases. But again, had Hale addressed the problem of takings directly, it might have helped to clarify the extent of his positivism, as well as the view of state legitimacy that impelled it.

Finally, the difficulties with Hale's analytical extremism are evident as well in his radical interpretation of the state action doctrine. As noted earlier, Hale's broad reading of state action potentially turned all private discriminatory action into a constitutional wrong. Thus, a private citizen's refusal to sell his house to members of a protected racial minority, like his refusal to admit them to his own private club or home, potentially violated the equal protection clause of the Fourteenth Amendment. Hale, a staunch champion of racial equality long before such positions were popular, strongly advocated the first result. But he would not have gone as far as the second or third, thinking it prudent for the state to leave a loophole for the soul, even when it housed private hatred. Congress worked out a statutory compromise precisely along these lines in the public accommodations act and other civil rights legislation beginning in the 1960s. It is unclear, though, how Hale could have reached that compromise as a matter of constitutional law under his version of state action. If (as Hale argued) all private action is state action for purposes of the equal protection clause, courts would normally have no choice but to enforce the clause against private actors in all contexts to the same extent that they enforced it against the state. Hale tried to avoid that conclusion by suggesting that courts are constitutionally free not to enforce the Fourteenth Amendment against some acts of private discrimination, notwithstanding that those acts constitute state action, "provided that carrying out the owner's will does not involve some matter of high public importance."[10] The constitutional logic of that qualification is somewhat doubtful.[11] Be that as it may, the qualification puts Hale more in the post-*Shelley* mainstream liberal tradition than his categorical rhetoric on state action would suggest, differing with others perhaps only as to where the prudential line should be drawn.

All this underscores a point made in earlier chapters—that while Hale's argument was analytically radical, it did not lead necessarily to politically radical conclusions. Like Holmes before him and his fellow Realists, Hale sought to dismantle the formalist foundations of legal argument in the early years of the twentieth century, and to put it on a more solid, functionalist footing. Nothing logically followed from that change in Hale's view, beyond the all-important conclusion for Hale's contemporaries that most legal questions were questions of policy for the legislature, not matters of constitutional rights for the courts. How legislatures ought to resolve them was, of course, another matter, and one on which Hale's skeptical, deconstructive analysis offered little guidance. This omission will no doubt strike many modern readers of Hale's work as its most serious limitation. One can stand persuaded that the conventional distinctions between public and private actors, harmful and nonharmful uses of property, public and private coercion, regulations that "took" value of property and those that did not, are all incoherent or useless, without being any closer to a sensible government policy in any of these areas. Hale's one sustained effort to supply such a policy, his work in public utilities regulation, underscores how difficult it is to do so.

But the obvious limits of Hale's work should not obscure his considerable achievement. First, Hale perfected the Realists' methodological attack on legal formalism, an attack from which law (at least legal academic thought) has never recovered. As the saying goes, "Legal Realism is dead; we are all Realists now." What the saying has in mind, above all, is that we can never again unselfconsciously regard law as an autonomous set of principles or rights from which the "correct" result in a particular case can be deduced as a matter of logic.

In its place, Hale and a number of the other key Realists insisted on a functional approach: the law is what the law does, and what it does in any particular case is far more complex and politically contingent than the architectonics of legal formalism suggested. That methodological revolution has left its mark on a number of discrete areas of legal and philosophical thought. It has also paved the way for two very different strands of contemporary legal thought, united by their methodological hostility to formalism: the contemporary law and economics movement; and the deconstructive wing of Critical Legal Studies, which has (among other things) trained a skeptical eye on the functional pretensions of law and economics.[12] When Hale noted that eminent domain rules, duress cases, and conventional market transactions all constructed different versions of "exchange value," or that all regulation that restricts opportunities to exploit property "takes" a portion of its value, he was speaking a functionalist language that was revolutionary in his time but has (in part through his and other Realists' efforts) become commonplace in ours.

The Realist method had its greatest impact in the area of liberty and property rights. By training attention on what the law actually does, Hale and a number of other Realists showed that the constellation of liberty and property rights protected in the supposed heyday of laissez faire fell far short of the absolutism that its champions imagined. Of more importance, by developing the Hohfeldian insight that all rights are defined by the corresponding duties imposed on others, Hale showed that any alternative arrangement of rights would necessarily fall short of that ideal as well. As Holmes put it, my liberty to be free of unprovoked physical harm constrains your liberty to slap me for no reason but "the gratification of ill will."[13] If the law chooses my liberty over yours, it is only because of an underlying value judgment that my liberty is more deserving of protection than yours. That realization served the Realists' immediate agenda of putting such contestable political choices into the hands of the legislature. It also foreshadowed the Coasian revolution in law, in which (in the language of economics) all social "costs" are acknowledged to be the joint costs of competing desires in a world of scarcity.

Hale's functionalist method also recast the purely philosophical inquiry into the nature of coercion. When we characterize some pressures as bad (coercive threats) rather than good (offers), Hale showed, it is not because of any properties inherent in the pressure itself. It is because of a prior, often unarticulated, moral judgment that the "coerced" party has a right to be free of the pressure in question, and the "coercing party" has a duty not to impose it. Talk of coercion as a freestanding moral problem thus merely distracts attention from what is the real issue: what baseline entitlements and duties we wish to establish, as a moral or legal matter. That shift in focus does not render pointless all talk of "good" and "bad" threats. There remains a difference, after all, between pointing a gun at another's head and demanding "Your money or your life," and threatening to withhold bread from a starving person unless she consents to pay the market price. But it forces us to recognize that the difference derives not from the quality of the threat itself, but instead from a common understanding that we have a right not to have others shoot us but not necessarily a right to have them save us from starvation. Hale's insight—what is referred to in contemporary legal and philosophical circles as the "baseline" problem—has informed most contemporary inquiries into the problem of coercion. That it has done so only incompletely is testament to how nonobvious the insight is, and how tricky to sustain.

Finally, Hale's functionalist critique obliterated the distinction between "public" and "private" activity that had historically framed many discrete issues in law and that was logically indispensable to the notion of laissez faire. If, as Hale and other Realists argued, the government constructs the private market through property and contract law, as well as through innumerable public interventions in economic life (building infrastructure, regulating money supply, subsidizing education, and so on), it is nonsensical to imagine a state that could leave economic life alone. What proponents championed as laissez faire turned out on closer inspection to be merely a different form of public meddling with so-called private affairs. In addition to undercutting the legal and philosophical arguments for constitutional laissez faire, Hale's attack on the public/private distinction blurred the conventional lines drawn between public and private coercion, public and private discrimination, and (through the example of public utilities) public and private property. His arguments have fueled a continuing debate in legal academic circles about whether the distinction between public and private spheres has any explanatory power at all. They are relevant as well in responding to libertarian arguments against regulation and taxation that have regained political force in recent years. If the value of a parcel of land, for example, is determined in the first instance by an enormously complicated network of property, tort, and zoning laws that regulate permissible uses of that parcel and neighboring ones, along with numerous government policies that affect regional development and hence demand (highways, mass transit, tax-subsidized mortgage rates, government-regulated insurance, macroeconomic policies that affect employment, and the like), what is the prepolitical "baseline" property value against which we declare one additional environmental regulation or one additional tax to be a theft of private property? In this area, as all others, it would be a mistake to read Hale's critique of conventional liberal laissez-faire arguments as simply nihilistic. The critique was not meant to shut down discussion about the appropriate limits to state power. It was meant to open it up by showing that the answer could not be deduced mechanically from a prepolitical arrangement of rights, but instead had to grow out of some political consensus about the sort of society that we wish to live in.

With all of its limitations, Hale's affirmative effort to recast property rights along rent-theory lines retains contemporary interest as well. When it emerged, progressive rent theory was the latest in a long line of leftist attacks singling out private entitlement to surplus value (rents) as the soft underbelly of libertarian Lockeanism. The difficulty of justifying a right to surplus value continues to plague many contemporary libertarian theories. Robert Nozick's principle of "justice in transfer," for example, elaborated in *Anarchy, State, and Utopia*, assumes (and in turn purports to shore up) a private right to whatever exchange price the market will bear. But as Nozick himself concedes, that principle is not always easy to defend. It is also inconsistent with Nozick's own treatment of surplus value or rents elsewhere in *Anarchy, State, and Utopia*.[14] So also, much of Richard Epstein's *Takings*, the best-known recent attempt to translate libertarian principles to a legal regime, rests on the (undefended) assertion that individuals have a right to appropriate the surplus value created by society, in proportion to the value of assets that they bring into society from a hypothetical state of nature.[15]

In place of the conventional, libertarian defenses of unfettered exchange, progressive rent theorists read Lockean defenses of private property rights to imply a more exacting definition of individual desert: individuals are entitled to a portion of their social product, equal to a fair return on cost or sacrifice; but the surplus above that is rightly society's, to do with as it sees fit. That definition provides a theoretical alternative to Rawlsian liberalism for reconciling public obligations with private rights, starting (at least rhetorically) from individualistic premises. As suggested at length in Chapters 4 and 5, progressive rent theory poses a number of difficulties of its own, both conceptual and administrative. Among the more severe problems are how to define costs, or sacrifices, at the individual level, and whether a satisfactory moral account can simply equate them with reservation price; and whether ex post rents in fact represent a fair return to risk, or (fair or not) are a necessary incentive to socially useful activities. In the end, these and other problems probably doom rent-theory Lockeanism as a serious program for broad-based income redistribution. But it still stands as a trenchant critique of the more conventional (libertarian) Lockean defense of the justice of market-based distribution.

There is a perhaps irresistible temptation in writing on one person's work to exaggerate his singular contribution. Like a light shining on a polished surface, which creates the optical illusion that random scratches on the surface are arranged in concentric circles around it—George Eliot's arresting simile a century ago for the distortive effects of egoism—one is inevitably tempted to cast one's subject as the source of ideas that swirl around and through him. When the subject is an obscure one, the temptation is even stronger, since one is obliged to prove at least enough significance to justify plucking him from obscurity to begin with. As a partial corrective to the sins of perspective inevitably committed here, it is worth stressing again how much Hale owed to the intellectual traditions of which he was a part. His methodological attacks on formal, deductive reasoning in law were echoed in the work of all of the Legal Realists, and mirrored methodological and philosophical shifts more generally in the social sciences. His substantive attack on liberty and property rights, the core concepts of laissez faire, reflected a common agenda that united the Legal Realists and institutional economists, along with a wide array of left-leaning intellectuals in the United States and Great Britain from the 1880s through the 1930s. In the area of rent theory, he borrowed an idea already well developed by the Fabians and New Liberals in Great Britain, and applied it to the local problem of public utilities. At the same time, Hale's critical work endures as among the best examples of the Realist and institutionalist tradition, casting the nature of legal rights and private economic relations in a new and significantly different light.

NOTES

INDEX

NOTES

Preface

1. "The Economy as a System of Power and Its Legal Bases: The Legal Economics of Robert Lee Hale," 27 *University of Miami Law Review* 261 (1973).

2. Three recent articles have considered Hale's work in some depth. Neil Duxbury, "Robert Hale and the Economy of Legal Force," 53 *The Modern Law Review* 421–444 (1990); Pavlos Eleftheriadis, "Unfreedom in a Laissez-Faire State," 80 *Archives for Philosophy of Law and Social Philosophy* 168–190 (1994); Duncan Kennedy, "The Stakes of Law, or Hale and Foucault!" in *Sexy Dressing, Etc.* (1993). Briefer appreciations of Hale's significance include Robert W. Gordon, "Critical Legal Histories," 36 *Stanford Law Review* 104–105 (1984); Morton J. Horwitz, "Comments: The History of the Public/Private Distinction," 130 *University of Pennsylvania Law Review* 1426 (1982); Morton J. Horwitz, *The Transformation of American Law, 1870–1960*, 163–165, 169, 182, 195–198, 208, 307 n.119, 322 n.12 (1992) (hereinafter *Transformation II*); Mark Kelman, *A Guide to Critical Legal Studies*, 21, 103–104, 226, 321–322 n.60 (1987); Duncan Kennedy, "The Role of Law in Economic Thought: Essays on the Fetishism of Commodities," 34 *American University Law Review* 952 n.28 and passim (1985); Duncan Kennedy and Frank Michelman, "Are Property and Contract Efficient?" 8 *Hofstra Law Review* 732 n.25, 751 (1980); Gary Peller, "The Metaphysics of American Law," 73 *California Law Review* 1232–1240 (1985); Cass R. Sunstein, *The Partial Constitution*, 51–52 (1993).

3. See, e.g., "Coercion," in *Philosophy, Science, and Method: Essays in Honor of Ernest Nagel* (Sidney Morgenbesser, Patrick Suppes, and Morton White, eds., 1969).

4. See Sidney Fine, *Laissez Faire and the General-Welfare State* (1956); Mary O. Furner, "Knowing Capitalism: Public Investigation and the Labor Question in the Long Progressive Era," in *The State and Economic Knowledge: The American and British Experiences*, 245 (Mary O. Furner and Barry Supple, eds., 1990); Dorothy Ross, "Socialism and American Liberalism: Academic Social Thought in the 1880's," 11 *Perspectives in American History* 14 (1977–1978). Hale's own contemporaries variously termed the politics of the middle way "democratic liberalism," "partial state socialism," and "gas and water socialism." The latter two terms contemplated that the government might engage in business itself in monopolistic or quasi-monopolistic industries, as a substitute or disciplining mechanism for private industry, but would limit its control of the rest of private enterprise to extensive regulation, including public adjustment of labor disputes and a thoroughgoing system of social insurance. John M. Clark, *Social Control of Business*, 501 (1926).

5. *Uncertain Victory: Social Democracy and Progressivism in European and American Thought, 1870–1920,* 311 (1986). See also Horwitz, *Transformation II,* for use of the term "Legal Progressives" broadly to describe legal theorists sympathetic to aspects of the left-liberal political agenda.

6. For the argument that progressivism was not a coherent movement but was instead shifting coalitions around a set of issues preoccupying the period (constraints on monopolies, trusts and banks; regulation of railroad rates; women's suffrage; female and child labor laws; curbs on political and economic power of the privileged classes), see Peter G. Filene, "An Obituary for 'The Progressive Movement,'" 22 *American Quarterly* 20 (1970). For another version of the different progressive factions, see Kloppenberg, *Uncertain Victory,* 311, 362–363.

7. For the traditional view among historians that some variant of these goals was a major theme of progressivism, see Richard Hofstadter, *The Age of Reform: From Bryan to F. D. R.,* 5–6, 168, 227, 238, 240, 254, 257 (1955); Arthur S. Link, "What Happened to the Progressive Movement in the 1920s?" 64 *American Historical Review* 836–837 (1959); Arthur S. Link, *Woodrow Wilson and the Progressive Era, 1910–1917,* 1–2, 59 (1954); George E. Mowry, *The Era of Theodore Roosevelt and the Birth of Modern America, 1900–1912,* 41–42, 81–82 (1958); Benjamin Parke De Witt, *The Progressive Movement: A Non-partisan Comprehensive Discussion of Current Tendencies in American Politics,* 4–5 (1915), all cited in Filene, "An Obituary for 'The Progressive Movement,'" 21, 31–32.

1. Introduction

1. *A Treatise on the Limitations of Police Power in the United States* (Da Capo 1971).

2. Id. at vi. For a good summary of the social conflict out of which the treatise emerged, including agrarian revolts against railroads, grain elevators, and other large businesses servicing farmers; labor unrest, culminating in the 1885–1886 strikes by the Knights of Labor and the Haymarket riots in 1886; and the popularity of Henry George and the single-tax movement, see Arnold M. Paul, *Conservative Crisis and the Rule of Law,* 19–29 (1960); Dorothy Ross, *The Origins of American Social Science,* 98–101; Robert H. Weibe, *The Search for Order 1877–1920* (1967); Chester Destler, *American Radicalism 1865–1901* (1966 [1946]). Tiedeman was hardly subtle about the political motivation for the treatise, most notably in his much-cited Preface. Id. at vii–viii.

3. Id. at 10–11.

4. Id. at vii. For other of Tiedeman's frequent references to "sic utere" as the appropriate limits on police powers, see, e.g., id. at 1–5 and 196–197; *The Unwritten Constitution of the United States,* 76–82 (1890).

5. *Limitations of Police Power,* 198.

6. Id. at vi, 233, 239. The burden of Tiedeman's argument in *Limitations of Police Power* is repeated, sometimes verbatim, in *The Unwritten Constitution of the United States,* published four years later.

7. 6 *The New Englander and Yale Review* 533 (1886).

8. The early Clark's philosophical predilections, which had a decidedly Christian socialist cast, were evident as late as the spring of 1886, with the publication of *Philosophy of Wealth.* Dorothy Ross dates his conversion to the Haymarket riot in May 1886 and its intellectual aftermath. *Origins of American Social Science,* 115. Whatever the triggering event, it is clear that by the publication of "The Moral Outcome of Labor Troubles" later that year, he had crossed a significant divide. On Clark's early socialist sympathies and his conversion to

the cause of capitalism, see Ross, id. at 106–122; Dorothy Ross, "Socialism and American Liberalism," 11 *Perspectives in American History* 7, 35–79 (1977–1978); John F. Henry, "John Bates Clark and the Marginal Product: An Historical Inquiry into the Origins of Value-free Economic Theory," 15 *History of Political Economy* 375 (1983).

9. "The Law of Wages and Interest," 1 *The Annals of the American Academy of Political and Social Science* 43, 44 (1890).

10. Clark wrote in the 1886 article: "As [competition] came gradually into existence it demonstrated its capacity for dividing products with a certain approach to justice. It commended itself to men's sense of right, and was established . . . on a moral basis." "Moral Outcome of Labor Troubles," 553. As Henry notes, although the passage does not refer specifically to marginal productivity theory, it seems clear that theory is the "just" distribution of output that Clark has in mind. "John Bates Clark and the marginal product," 378. For the "mature" Clark's development of the politics of marginal productivity, see chap. 4.

11. On Tiedeman's influence, in conjunction with Thomas Cooley, the other great "publicist" for laissez faire, see Clyde E. Jacobs, *Law Writers and the Courts: The Influence of Thomas M. Cooley, Christopher G. Tiedeman, and John F. Dillon Upon American Constitutional Law* 58–85 (1954); Paul, *Conservative Crisis and the Rule of Law*, 16–87. A number of commentators (consistent with the general revisionist trend in historiography of the *Lochner* era) have suggested that Tiedeman's views were more complicated than the doctrinaire defense of laissez faire that at least Jacobs ascribes to him. See, e.g., Thomas Grey's Introduction to Tiedeman, *The Unwritten Constitution of the United States* [1890], iii–vii (reprinted W. S. Hein & Co., 1974); Louise A. Halper, "Christopher G. Tiedeman, 'Laissez-Faire Constitutionalism' and the Dilemmas of Small-scale Property in the Gilded Age," 51 *Ohio State Law Journal* 1349 (1990); David N. Mayer, "The Jurisprudence of Christopher G. Tiedeman: A Study in the Failure of Laissez-Faire Constitutionalism," 55 *Missouri Law Review* 93 (1990). Although that may well be a more judicious reading of Tiedeman, Jacob's more conventional reading probably more accurately captures how Tiedeman was read by his contemporaries and the uses to which his work was put.

12. See chap. 4.

13. See Hale's letter of June 22, 1950, to Ordway Tead, an editor at Harpers, describing the manuscript ultimately published as *Freedom Through Law*. Hale Papers, folder 84.

14. *Valuation and Rate-Making: The Conflicting Theories of the Wisconsin Railroad Commission, 1905–1917.*

15. "Coercion and Distribution in a Supposedly Non-Coercive State," 38 *Political Science Quarterly* 470 (1923); "Force and the State: A Comparison of 'Political' and 'Economic' Compulsion," 35 *Columbia Law Review* 149 (1935); "Bargaining, Duress, and Economic Liberty," 43 *Columbia Law Review* 603 (1943). Hale's argument on this point was developed in a number of other, less well-known articles, as well as in the Legal Factors materials.

16. Robert Lee Hale, "Economic Theory and the Statesman," in *The Trend of Economics* 191–225 (R. Tugwell, ed., 1923).

17. Edwin R. A. Seligman, "Continuity of Economic Thought," in *Science Economic Discussion*, 22 (1886). The *locus classicus* of that proposition for most progressives was John Stuart Mill's *Principles of Political Economy*.

18. For this persistent strain in progressive thought, see David E. Price, "Community and Control: Critical Democratic Theory in the Progressive Period," 68 *American Political Science Review* 1663, 1675 (1974).

19. "Law Making by Unofficial Minorities," 20 *Columbia Law Review* 451, 456 (1920). For an eloquent statement of that principle, see Edwin R. A. Seligman's manifesto for the

220

"new movement" of institutional economics, "Continuity of Economic Thought," in *Science Economic Discussion*, 22–23 (1886).

20. For an early and uncharacteristically forthcoming declaration of his utilitarian allegiance, see the opening of Hale's ms. dated 1914–15, entitled "Regulation of Public Service Companies" (which appears to be an early draft of *Valuation and Rate Making*): "I. General Principles of Distribution. Object of our whole legal system should be not the attainment of certain abstract principles, but the attainment of the utmost welfare of everyone." Hale papers, folder 49.

21. "Law Making by Unofficial Minorities," 456.

22. The growing literature on British New Liberalism includes Michael Freeden, *The New Liberalism: An Ideology of Social Reform* (1978); Stefan Collini, *Liberalism and Sociology* (1979); Peter Clarke, *Liberals and Social Democrats* (1978); Peter Weiler, *The New Liberalism: Liberal Social Theory in Great Britain 1889–1914* (1982). The movement in Britain, as Mary Furner has suggested, "took shape as a fairly unified body of theory and argumentation, culminating in Keynesianism." "Knowing Capitalism: Public Investigation and the Labor Question in the Long Progressive Era," in *The State and Economic Knowledge*, 241, 243 (Mary O. Furner and Barry Supple, eds., 1990). The movement also had considerable political clout in Britain during the first two decades of the twentieth century. Although the New Liberals had no clear counterpart in America, a number of progressives (including Hale) who belong in what Furner has identified as the "democratic collectivist" tradition were strongly influenced by New Liberal ideas. For further discussion of these intellectual ties, see chaps. 2 and 4.

23. For Hale's strong support of the Wagner Act, see Mark Barenberg, "The Political Economy of the Wagner Act: Power, Symbol, and Workplace Cooperation," 106 *Harvard Law Review* 1379, 1409 (1993); Kenneth M. Casebeer, "Holder of the Pen: An Interview with Leon Keyserling on Drafting the Wagner Act," 42 *University of Miami Law Review* 285, 304 (1987). Hale testified on behalf of the Act, presenting a version of his argument that coercion was ubiquitous in the marketplace. See *To Create a National Labor Board, 1934: Hearings on S. 2926 before the Committee on Education and Labor*, 73d Cong., 2d Sess., at 50–58, reprinted in 1 *Legislative History of the National Labor Relations Act, 1935*, 80–88 (1985). Barenberg suggests that Hale's rhetoric was picked up by Wagner himself in arguing for the bill. Id. at 1409 n.124. For an account of Hale's participation in drafting an influential prolabor amicus brief in Interborough Rapid Transit v. Green, 227 N.Y.S. 258 (1928), in conjunction with Robert Wagner, Herman Oliphant, and Simon Rifkind, see Barenberg, id. at 1409 n.125 and 1429 n.230.

24. The description is James T. Kloppenberg's, from *Uncertain Victory: Social Democracy and Progressivism in European and American Thought, 1870–1920*, 355 (1986).

25. For an excellent study of the socialist influences on American progressives, in particular Richard Ely, Henry Carter Adams, and (the early) John Bates Clark, see Ross, "Socialism and American Liberalism," 7. Ross persuasively refutes the generally accepted view (based in part on the political failures of socialism) that socialism had relatively limited significance among American intellectuals. See also J. A. Hobson, *Veblen*, chaps. 3 and 4 (1936) and Joseph Dorfman, *Thorstein Veblen and His America*, 76–77, 241–245, 285–286, and passim (1934), on Veblen's interest in socialism and the socialist influences on his own work; Willard Wolfe, *From Radicalism to Socialism*, 79–93, 240, 270–271 (1975); Kenneth McNaught, "American Progressives and the Great Society," 53 *Journal of American History* 504 (1966); Benjamin G. Rader, *The Academic Mind and Reform*, 96–105 (1966).

26. On the progressives' preference for the politics of the middle way, see Kloppenberg, *Uncertain Victory*. See also Peter Clarke, *Liberals and Social Democrats*, 163 (1978); H. V. Emy,

Liberals, Radicals and Social Politics 1892–1914 (1973); Daniel Ernst, "Common Laborers? Industrial Pluralists, Legal Realists, and the Law of Industrial Disputes, 1915–1943," 11 *Law and History Review* 59 (1993).

27. *The Promise of American Life* [1909] 209 (E. P. Dutton & Co., 1963).

28. Hale Papers, mss. folder and box 9, unnumbered folder on "Sacco and Vanzetti materials." See also Hale's correspondence with Wilson Powell, chairman of the Harvard Law School Fund, in June and July of 1927, concerning Hale's refusal to contribute to the Fund because of criticisms from Powell (among others) of Frankfurter's brief in the case. Hale Papers, box 9, id.

29. Hale's notes for the article are contained in box 9, unnumbered folder on "Sacco and Vanzetti materials." See also Hale's letter to Harlan Fiske Stone, June 29, 1929, on his participation in the symposium. Hale Papers, mss. folder; Stone Papers, Library of Congress.

30. See, e.g., Hale's exchange with the editors of the Supreme Court Law Review about the reverence owed judges, Hale papers, folder 34; his early correspondence defending the single taxers, id., folder 62; letters defending the free speech rights of radicals, id., folders 64 and 65; and various letters attacking antiunionism, id., folders 62, 64, 74, and 75.

31. For accounts of the American Legal Realist movement, see G. Edward White, "From Sociological Jurisprudence to Realism: Jurisprudence and Social Change in Early Twentieth-Century America," 58 *Virginia Law Review* 999 (1972); N. E. H. Hull, "Restatement and Reform: A New Perspective on the Origins of the American Law Institute," 8 *Law and History Review* 55 (1990); Laura Kalman, *Legal Realism at Yale, 1927–1960* (1986); Edward Purcell, *The Crisis of Democratic Theory*, 74–94 (1973); Morton J. Horwitz, *The Transformation of American Law 1870–1960*, 169–246 (1992) (hereinafter *Transformation II*); Daniel Ernst, "The Critical Tradition in the Writing of American Legal History," 102 *Yale Law Journal* 1019, 1062–1074 (1993); Joseph Singer, "Legal Realism Now," 76 *California Law Review* 465 (1988); Gary Peller, "The Metaphysics of American Law," 73 *California Law Review* 1151, 1219–1258.

For overviews of the first and second waves of institutionalism, see Benjamin B. Seligman, *Main Currents in Modern Economics*, 129–253 (1962); Joseph Dorfman, *The Economic Mind in American Civilization*, vol. 3, chaps. VII, XIX, and XX, and vol. 4, chap. XIII (1959); David Seckler, *Thorstein Veblen and the Institutionalists* (1975); Ross, *The Origins of American Social Science*, 372–386, 407–420. For a more detailed portrait of Veblen, see Dorfman, *Thorstein Veblen and His America*. None of the foregoing works on institutionalism discusses Hale, a fact that is not surprising in light of his obscurity until recently. Of more recent studies, Daniel Ernst's "Common Laborers?," at 70, appropriately locates Hale in the neo-Veblenite wing of institutionalism. Warren Samuels's extended study of Hale also notes the connections between Hale and leading institutionalists John R. Commons, Wesley Mitchell, and J. M. Clark. "The Economy as a System of Power and Its Legal Bases: The Legal Economics of Robert Lee Hale," 27 *University of Miami Law Review* 261, 265–267 (1973).

32. Course description for Economics 11: Legal Factors in Economics, Hale Papers, folder 83.

33. For Hale and Commons's correspondence, see Hale Papers, folders 10 and 28.

34. For Hale's telling praise of Clark's *Social Control* as "well reasoned and very realistic, in marked contrast with the work of his father (John Bates Clark)," see letter to Harlan Fiske Stone, Aug. 11, 1926 (Stone Papers, Library of Congress).

35. The description is Lionel Robbins's, in his foreword to Seckler, *Thorstein Veblen and the Institutionalists*.

36. "The Limitations of Marginal Utility," 17 *Journal of Political Economy* 620 (1909), reprinted in Thorstein Veblen, *The Place of Science in Modern Civilisation and Other Essays,*

231, 233 (1919). For further exploration of this critique of traditional neoclassical economics, see chap. 4.

37. Walton Hamilton, "Institution," in 8 *Encyclopaedia of the Social Sciences*, 84. Joseph Dorfman identifies as "[p]erhaps the first use of the term 'institutional economist'" Hamilton's 1916 essay on Robert F. Hoxie, "The Development of Hoxie's Economics," 24 *Journal of Political Economy* 855, 863 n.5 (1916). Dorfman, 4 *The Economic Mind in American Civilization*, 353. The use of the word "institution" itself in this context, however, predates that. Edwin Seligman used the word in 1886, in noting that the German Historical School "denies the existence of immutable natural laws in economics, calling attention to the interdependence of theories and institutions," and noting the "new movement" to which it is closely allied (what we would now call institutional economics) "maintains that the explanations of phenomena are inextricably interwoven with the institutions of the period. . ." "Continuity of Economic Thought," in *Science Economic Discussion*, 19, 20 (1886). Veblen used the word in his 1909 essay on "The Limitations of Marginal Utility," defining it as "settled habits of thought" and "principles of action . . . [by which] men order their lives . . . and, practically, entertain no question of their stability and finality." *Place of Science in Modern Civilization*, 239. John Commons defined an "institution" a bit more cryptically, although not inconsistently, as "Collective Action in Control of Individual Action," citing as examples everything from the family, the corporation, the trade union, up to the state itself. 1 *Institutional Economics*, 69 (1934). For other definitions of institutionalism advanced by its adherents, see Seckler, *Thorstein Veblen and the Institutionalists*, 3–5.

38. See, e.g., Commons, *The Economics of Collective Action*, 25–35 (1950); Robert F. Hoxie, *Trade Unionism in the United States* (1917).

39. See, e.g., Commons, 1 *Institutional Economics*, 390–457.

40. See, e.g., *A History of the Greenbacks* (1903); *The Backward Art of Spending Money* (1937).

41. Adolph A. Berle and Gardiner Means, *The Modern Corporation and Private Property* (1933).

42. See, e.g., John R. Commons, "Law and Economics," 34 *Yale Law Journal* 371, 376 (1925); Commons, *Legal Foundations of Capitalism*, 299–300 (1924). On the Sumnerian strains in Commons's writings, see Jeff E. Biddle, "Purpose and evolution in Commons's institutionalism," 22 *History of Political Economy* 19, 38–45 (1990).

43. An early, illuminating presentation of these core tenets of institutionalism can be found in the articles prepared for an 1886 conference on the "new movement" in economics (that is, institutionalism), reproduced later that year in *Science Economic Discussion* (The Science Company). One of Henry Carter Adams's two articles contributed to the volume, "Economics and Jurisprudence," succinctly summarizes the dispute between fatalistic and nonfatalistic views of society, resoundingly opting for the latter. Id., 85–86.

44. See Stephen Skowronek, *Building a New American State: The Expansion of National Administrative Capacities, 1877–1920*, 132–133 (1982) on Adams and the AEA. Two collections of essays by the main protagonists in the first and second waves of institutionalism provide a good feel for their preoccupations: the 1886 *Science Economic Discussion* and *The Trend of Economics* (Rexford Tugwell, ed., 1924).

45. Letter from Smith to Dean Harlan Fiske Stone, May 3, 1921, quoted in Alpheus Thomas Mason, *Harlan Fiske Stone*, 128 (1956). Smith is the source of the comment that Cook and Moore were trying to "annex" Hale. Id.

46. Hale cotaught Ec. 320, a seminar in Economics, Law and Politics, with Llewellyn, Clark, and others. Hale Papers, folders 68, 82. He also participated, along with Underhill

Moore and Llewellyn, in a seminar on business organizations cotaught in the fall of 1924 by Oliphant and Bonbright. John Henry Schlegel, *American Legal Realism and Empirical Social Science*, 16 (1995). Hale contributed to Bonbright's treatise on *Valuation of Property*, and his work on public utilities closely paralleled Bonbright's. For Frank's gratuitous and high praise for Hale, see Witmark & Sons v. Fred Fisher Music Co., 125 F.2d 949, 963 (1942)(dissenting).

47. The seminar cotaught by Bonbright and Oliphant on business organizations in 1924, in which Hale was a participant, was envisioned by Oliphant as part of the "functional" curriculum that lay at the heart of the reform movement. See Schlegel, *American Legal Realism and Empirical Social Science*, 16. On curricular reform, Hale said in a postscript of a letter to Harlan Fiske Stone, Mar. 28, 1927, that "I think we are on the verge of a very significant advance in legal education at Columbia." Stone Collection, Library of Congress.

48. Letter from Llewellyn to Pound, Apr. 6, 1931, HLS Library, Pound Papers, 24–26, quoted in N. E. H. Hull, "Some Realism about the Llewellyn-Pound Exchange over Realism: The Newly Uncovered Private Correspondence, 1927–1931," 1987 *Wisconsin Law Review* 921, 968.

49. For sensitive discussions of this school of Realist thought, see Horwitz, *Transformation II*; Peller, "Metaphysics of American Law," 1219–1240. Borrowing from Peter Novick, Horwitz terms it "cognitive relativism," and its members "Critical Realists." Id., 200, 209. Peller terms it the "deconstructive wing" of Realism, to distinguish it from the "constructive wing" most interested in reconstructing law along more functional lines. Peller puts Hale in the former camp, along with Morris Cohen, Felix Cohen, Dewey, and Pound, but Hale clearly belongs in both.

50. On Bentham's famous hostility to the common law as nonsense best left "to Mother Goose and Mother Blackstone," see generally Gerald J. Postema, *Bentham and the Common Law Tradition*, chaps. 5–9 (1986); David Lieberman, *The Province of Legislation Determined: Legal Theory in Eighteenth-Century Britain* (1989), chap. 11. Unlike at least some of the Realists, however, Bentham was not ultimately anticonceptualist. He believed that one could squeeze most of the discretion out of judicial decision-making by a properly scientific codification of principles (a view none of the Realists would have embraced), and he spent a good portion of his career pursuing that goal in the Pannomial Fragments. See Lieberman, id., 217–276. On the romanticized view of the common law embraced by Burke, Maine, and successive historicists, who championed its intuitive, experience-based reasoning over deductive reasoning from natural law premises, see Peter Stein, *Legal Evolution: The Story of an Idea*; J. G. A. Pocock, "Burke and the Ancient Constitution," 3 *Historical Journal* 125 (1960), reprinted in *Politics, Language and Time* (1971).

51. On Holmes's possible debt on this score to Rudolph von Jhering, himself a hero to the Realists, see Mathias W. Reimann, "Holmes's Common Law and German Legal Science," in *The Legacy of Oliver Wendell Holmes, Jr.*, 101–105 (Robert W. Gordon, ed., 1992).

52. *Lochner v. New York*, 198 U.S. at 76 (dissenting).

53. On Pound's "sociological jurisprudence," see Roscoe Pound, "The Scope and Purpose of Sociological Jurisprudence," 24 *Harvard Law Review* 591 (1911), 25 *Harvard Law Review* 140, 489 (1911, 1912). One should also note the proto-Realist Nicholas St. John Green, whose anticonceptualist writings helped bridge the argument from Holmes to the Realists. See Horwitz, *Transformation II*, 52–56. For a good summary of this aspect of the Realist critique, see Peller, "Metaphysics," 1223–1224; Horwitz, *Transformation II*, 200–202. Important examples include Felix Cohen, "The Ethical Basis of Legal Criticism," 41 *Yale Law Journal* 201 (1931); Felix Cohen, "Transcendental Nonsense and the Functional Approach," 35 *Columbia*

Law Review 809 (1935); L. L. Fuller and William R. Perdue, "The Reliance Interest in Contract Damages: 1," 46 *Yale Law Journal* 52 (1936).

54. Cohen, "Transcendental Nonsense," 827.

55. Cohen, "Transcendental Nonsense," 823.

56. See Singer, "Legal Realism Now," 475, 482–495, tracing a line of Realist attacks on the idea of the self-regulating market from Holmes's "Privilege, Malice, and Intent" (1894) through Dawson's "Economic Duress" (1947).

57. See Robert Gordon, "The Elusive Transformation," 6 *Yale Journal of Law and the Humanities* 159–160 (1994) (reviewing Horwitz, Transformation II).

58. See, e.g., Hale's correspondence with Parker T. Moon over the incensed reaction to his "Coercion and Distribution," Hale Papers, mss. folder; correspondence with N. T. Guernsey, the editor of the American Bar Association Journal (ABAJ), with regard to Hale's vituperative criticism of the Supreme Court's handling of rate regulation cases, id., folder 74; letter from Lawrence C. Brooks to Hale (Jan. 4, 1923), quoted in Gerald Fetner, "The Law Teacher as Legal Reformer: 1900–1945," 28 *Journal of Legal Education* 508, 528 (1977), attacking Hale for the "Bolshevistic" ideas he espoused in his ABAJ column.

59. "Transcendental Nonsense," 824. For an almost identical statement by Llewellyn, see "Some Realism about Realism—Responding to Dean Pound," 44 *Harvard Law Review* 1222, 1223 (1931).

60. On the empirical wing, see Schlegel, *American Legal Realism and Empirical Social Science*. On its connection to more general trends in the social sciences, formative and still illuminating accounts are given in White, *Social Thought in America: The Revolt Against Formalism* (1949); Purcell, *The Crisis of Democratic Theory*, chap. 10. See also Robert Weibe, *The Search for Order*, chap. 6, and Rodgers, *Contested Truths*, 187–193, on the cult of fact-mongering and social empiricism among progressive-minded social scientists in the first few decades of the twentieth century. On the empirical strain in institutional economics, which, like the empirical wing of Realism, talked more about the need for empirical work than it actually engaged in it, see Ross, *Origins of American Social Science*, chap. 10. Commons himself traced the attraction to empiricism back at least in part to Peircean pragmatism. 1 *Institutional Economics* 107.

The famous exchange between Pound and Llewellyn that started the controversy is contained in Pound, "The Call for a Realistic Jurisprudence," 44 *Harvard Law Review* 697 (1930) and Llewellyn, "Some Realism about Realism." Perhaps the most thoughtful and durable of the critiques of Realism on this score is Lon Fuller, "American Legal Realism," 82 *Pennsylvania Law Review* 429 (1934). The charge of nihilism took two forms: that the Realists' focus on the "is" to the exclusion of the "ought" invited moral nihilism; and that their particular version of "is"—that law is what judges do—was a form of "rule phobia" that amounted to cognitive nihilism. As their critics demonstrated, there was no shortage of Realist writings to cite to substantiate both charges, although the nihilistic strain represented at most a minor theme of Realist writings. At the same time, both charges seem somewhat harsh, as recent, more sympathetic commentators (along with the Realists themselves) have argued. See, e.g., Singer, "Legal Realism Now"; Peller, "Metaphysics of American Law"; Ernst, "Critical Tradition."

None of this is directly relevant in judging the worth of Hale's work, which no one would place in the empirical wing of Realism, except insofar as Hale's critical project of debunking traditional legal concepts has been tarred with the same brush of "cognitive nihilism" as the empirical wing of Realism. See, e.g., Peller, "Metaphysics of American

Law," 1232–1240. It is, however, helpful in situating Hale's work in the larger Realist movement, as it suggests (not surprisingly) that the different strains of Realism were more closely connected to each other, and more complicated in their aspirations, than any of the (understandably reductive) attempts at categorizing the Realists would suggest.

61. Peller, "Metaphysics of American Law," 1226.

62. "Economic Theory and the Statesman," 225.

63. See Hale's letter to Elliott Cheatham, Nov. 2, 1933, Hale Papers, folder 57.

64. Rodgers, *Contested Truths*, 144–156, provides a good overview of the rise of judicial constitutional activism in the 1880s to its final demise midway through the New Deal. See also Robert G. McCloskey, *American Conservatism in the Age of Enterprise: A Study of William Graham Sumner, Stephen J. Field and Andrew Carnegie* (1951); Paul, *Conservative Crisis and the Rule of Law;* Morton J. Horwitz, "The Rise of Legal Formalism," 19 *American Journal of Legal History* 251 (1975); John Semonche, *Charting the Future: The Supreme Court Responds to a Changing Society, 1890–1920* (1978). For efforts to discern some overarching logic to court decisions during the period, see Michael Les Benedict, "Laissez-Faire and Liberty: A Reevaluation of the Meaning and Origins of Laissez-Faire Constitutionalism," 3 *Law and History Review* 293–331 (1985), and Robert W. Gordon, "Legal Thought and Legal Practice in the Age of American Enterprise, 1870–1920," in *Professions and Professional Ideologies in America,* 70 (Gerald L. Geison, ed. 1983).

65. For a fuller account of the evolution of the doctrine, see chap. 2.

66. 300 U.S. 379.

67. Important examples of the recent revisionist historiography of the period include Charles McCurdy, "Justice Field and the Jurisprudence of Government-Business Relations: Some Parameters of Laissez-Faire Constitutionalism, 1863–1897," 61 *Journal of American History* 970 (1975); Janet S. Lindgren, "Beyond Cases: Reconsidering Judicial Review," 1983 *Wisconsin Law Review* 583; Gordon, "Legal Thought and Legal Practice," 92–93; Alan Jones, "Thomas M. Cooley and 'Laissez-Faire Constitutionalism': A Reconsideration," 53 *Journal of American History* 751 (1967); David N. Mayer, "The Jurisprudence of Christopher G. Tiedeman: A Study in the Failure of Laissez-Faire Constitutionalism," 55 *Missouri Law Review* 93 (1990); Robert E. Gamer, "Justice Brewer and Substantive Due Process: A Conservative Court Revisited," 18 *Vanderbilt Law Review* 615–645 (1965); Stephen A. Siegel, "Historism in Late Nineteenth-Century Constitutional Thought," 1990 *Wisconsin Law Review* 1431; Gordon, "Elusive Transformation," 152. For a revisionist account of state court decisions from that era, see Melvin I. Urofsky, "State Courts and Protective Legislation during the Progressive Era: A Reevaluation," 72 *Journal of American History* 63 (1985).

68. "Experiments in Government and the Essentials of the Constitution—I," 198 *North American Review* 1, 2 (1913).

69. Jeremy Waldron, *The Right to Private Property,* 3–4 (1988).

70. For a typical example, see Holmes's opinion in Portuguese-American Bank v. Welles, 242 U.S. 7, 11 (1916).

71. On this shift in perspective in the context of public utilities rate regulation, see chap. 5.

72. For further discussion of the state action doctrine, see chaps. 3 and 6.

73. "Bargaining, Duress, and Economic Liberty," 628.

74. See Morton Horwitz, *Transformation II,* 196, 199; Robert Gordon, "Legal Thought and Legal Practice," 94; Peller, "Metaphysics of American Law," 1225, 1240–1259. For Holmes as the original philosopher of degrees, arguing that most legal disputes turn on questions of degree, see Grey, "Molecular Motions: The Holmesian Judge in Theory and Practice," 37 *William and Mary Law Review* 19 (1995).

75. *The Promise of American Life*, 21. On Spencer's teleological view of history, see Sidney Fine, *Laissez Faire and the General-Welfare State*, 32–46. For an illuminating discussion of the teleological and nonteleological strains of historicism at war in the social sciences past the turn of the century, see Ross, *The Origins of American Social Science*, 85–97, 106–113, 153–156. For a discussion of the parallel strain in American legal thought, see Siegel, "Historism in Late Nineteenth-Century Constitutional Thought"; Ernst, "The Critical Tradition," 1042–1044, 1049–1057 (from whom I borrow the term "nonteleological historicism"). As noted earlier, the exceptions to nonteleological historicism among progressives included Commons, Llewellyn, and Corbin, all of whom embraced in at least a portion of their work a romanticized view of custom (as configured at any given time) as both inevitable and desirable. That view fit more comfortably with the political vision of Spencer, Sumner, et al. than with their own agenda of social reform.

76. Letter to Elliott Cheatham of Columbia Law School, Nov. 2, 1933, Hale Papers, folder 57.

77. *The Promise of American Life*, 190–191.

78. 1 *Dynamic Sociology*, 35 (1883). On the influentialness of Ward's calls for a "sociocracy," by which he meant conscious control of society by the positive state, see Fine, *Laissez Faire and the General-Welfare State*, 253–263; Henry Steele Commager, *The American Mind: An Interpretation of American Thought and Character since the 1880s*, 203–216 (1950).

79. On James's championing of "the active role of the mind in an unfinished universe," as a conscious reaction to Spencer's "monistic, deterministic conception of the world" as "one unbending unit of fact," see Fine, *Laissez Faire and the General-Welfare State*, 282–283. On Holmes's somewhat more pessimistic pragmatism, see generally Thomas Grey, "The Colin Raugh Thomas O'Fallon Memorial Lecture on Law and American Culture: Holmes, Pragmatism, and Democracy," 71 *Oregon Law Review* 521 (1992). As Grey notes, Holmes's classic statement that "[A]ll thought is social, is on its way to action" is "perhaps the best short summary of the pragmatist creed," reflecting both sides of the pragmatist duality: the social roots of individual thoughts and actions and the importance of shaping one's actions for instrumental ends. Id. at 2. A staunch pragmatist, Holmes was no progressive, at least when it came to optimism about what exactly would be forged in the laboratory of democracy. As Holmes declared, "I loathe the thickfingered clowns we call the people— especially as the beasts are represented at political centers—vulgar, selfish, and base." Quoted in Mark deWolfe Howe, 1 *Justice Oliver Wendell Holmes: The Shaping Years, 1841–1870*, 140 (1957).

80. On the development of Dewey's philosophy of instrumentalism, see Fine, *Laissez Faire and the General-Welfare State*, 284–288. Fine argues that Dewey's instrumentalism, "first explicitly proclaimed in 1903, supplied pragmatism with a social conscience and made it the philosophy of Progressivism." Id. at 280. On Dewey's significance to the institutional economists, see Seligman, 1 *Main Currents in Modern Economics*, 134, 137, 179–180, 194–195, 239.

81. L. T. Hobhouse, *The Labour Movement* 53–54 (2d ed. 1906).

82. "Law Making by Unofficial Minorities," 456. For strikingly similar rhetoric from Lippmann, see *Drift and Mastery*, 269 (1914): "This is what mastery means: the substitution of conscious intention for unconscious striving."

83. James Kloppenberg persuasively argues that experimentation in questions of social policy was an article of faith among the first generation of progressives (T. H. Green, Sidgwick, and others) "not because it was expedient but as a matter of principle, as the

political corollary of their radical empiricism." *Uncertain Victory*, 186. For similar statements about the later generation of the democratic process school of politics, of which Lippmann, Croly, and Dewey were the chief exponents, see id., 399–401. For a typical Deweyian expression of the conviction that political experimentation was the means to a better world, see Dewey, *Freedom and Culture*, 114–115 (1939). For other examples, see Brandeis's dissent in New State Ice Co. v. Liebmann, 285 U.S. 262, 311 (1932); Benjamin Andrews, "A Symposium on the Relation of the State to the Individual," 2 *The Dawn* 299–300 (1890); Barenberg, "The Political Economy of the Wagner Act," 1413–1415 (on Robert Wagner).

84. For comments to that effect, see Hale's Jan. 12, 1912, letter to his cousin, Robert S. Hale. Hale Papers, folder 62.

85. On the history of "aggressive natural rights radicalism" with respect to property in the first half of the nineteenth century, see Rodgers, *Contested Truths*, 72–75, 122–130. For its later manifestations, see chaps. 3 and 4.

86. For further development of this point, see chap. 2.

87. *Two Treatises of Government*, 288 (Peter Laslett ed., student ed. 1988) [3d ed. 1698].

88. For a good summary of the radical usurpation of Lockean natural rights theory by the early (Ricardian) socialists, see Maurice Dobb, *Theories of Value and Distribution since Adam Smith*, 137–141 (1973); Alexander Gray, *Socialist Tradition*, chap. 11 (1946); Anton Menger, *The Right to the Whole Produce of Labour* (1899). I deliberately sidestep the notoriously difficult and much debated question whether Marx's own labor theory of value is a natural rights theory. For the view that it is not, see Dobb, id., chap. 6.

89. *Distribution of Wealth*, 3, 9 (1899).

90. Alfred Kahn, 1 *The Politics of Regulation*, 9 n.30.

91. Edward Chamberlin, *The Theory of Monopolistic Competition: A Reorientation of the Theory of Value* (1933); Joan Robinson, *The Economics of Imperfect Competition* (1933). On Chamberlin and Robinson, see Mark Blaug, *Economic Theory in Retrospect*, 391–396 (4th ed. 1985); Seligman, 3 *Main Currents in Modern Economics*, 716–729. Other versions of the argument that imperfect competition was the dominant market structure, some predating Robinson's and Chamberlin's books and some following, are discussed in Seligman, id. at 713–715, 725–729.

92. Seligman, 3 *Main Currents in Modern Economics*, 716–725.

93. See Dobb, *Theories of Value and Distribution since Adam Smith*, 150–155. I sidestep here, as unnecessary to the point at hand, the much-vexed question of how Marx thought the prices of outputs were themselves set, and whether such price theory is reconcilable with his labor theory of value.

94. *Progress and Poverty*, 365 (Robert Schalkenbach Found., 1955).

95. For an acknowledgment that socialism in its most common forms, like his own brand of libertarianism, is a historical entitlement theory, see Nozick, *Anarchy, State and Utopia*, 155 (1974).

96. Thus, one could argue that in this one analytical respect many socialists had more in common with extreme proponents of laissez faire than with the progressive rent theorists who were their closer political allies. Socialists like Bellamy believed that because the social machinery contributes some value to all production, the entire fruits of society are transformed into common property. That view, one could argue, is merely the flip side of the traditional laissez-faire Lockean view that because labor is joined to the land and other natural resources to produce value, it is entitled to the entire resulting joint product. In contrast to both extreme positions, the progressive rent theorists tried to differentiate private from common contributions with what they believed to be greater precision.

228

2. The Empty Idea of Liberty

1. "The Evolution of Industrial Society" (1897 address to the Madison Literary Society), Ely Papers, quoted in Sidney Fine, *Laissez Faire and the General-Welfare State*, 210 (1956). For an almost identical version, see Richard Ely, *Studies in the Evolution of Industrial Society*, 98–99 (Macmillan, 1903).

2. For typical economistic (utilitarian) defenses of the free market, see Stephan Collini, *Liberalism and Sociology*, chap. 1 (1979); John Cairnes, *Essays in Political Economy*, 244–245 (Macmillan, 1873). For a typical incorporation in the judicial opinions of the day, see Coppage v. Kansas, 236 U.S. 1, 17 (1915).

3. For a sensitive summary of the linked history of the two arguments in late nineteenth-century England, see Collini, *Liberalism and Sociology*, chap. 1. For a discussion of the influence of both arguments in America, see David E. Price, "Community and Control: Critical Democratic Theory in the Progressive Period," 68 *The American Political Science Review* 1663 (1974).

4. Henry Carter Adams, "The Relation of the State to Industrial Action," in *Two Essays by Henry Carter Adams* 76 (Joseph Dorfman, ed., 1969).

5. Herbert Spencer, *The Man Versus the State* [1884], 10 (LibertyClassics, 1981).

6. Collini, *Liberalism and Sociology*, 16–19. For typical contemporary accounts that take this as its common meaning, see W. S. M'Kechnie, *The State and the Individual: An Introduction to Political Science, with special reference to Socialistic and Individualistic Theories*, 220 (1896); Henry Carter Adams's two essays, "Relation of the State to Industrial Action" (1887) and "Economics and Jurisprudence" (1896), both reprinted in *Two Essays by Henry Carter Adams*; letter from Robert Hale to Thomas Carver, Nov. 22, 1923, pp. 3–4, Hale Papers, folder 1.

7. Herbert Spencer, *Social Statics*, 341–444 (1865).

8. Hardcore Spencerians in England included Wordsworth Donisthorpe and Auberon Herbert, who, along with an odd assortment of other individualist radicals and old-style conservatives, in 1882 formed the Liberty and Property Defence League. See David Nicholls, "Positive Liberty, 1880–1914," *The American Political Science Review* 118–120 (1962); Taylor, *Men Versus the State*, 21–26, 32–35. Even among this small group, however, there was dissent from some of Spencer's categorical pronouncements in favor of the minimal state. See Taylor, id., 240. Among academically respectable American supporters, William Graham Sumner was probably the closest in views to Spencer, but even he parted company on a number of key points. Fine, *Laissez Faire and the General-Welfare State*, at 79–91. Once one moves beyond the inner circle of Spencerians, most proponents of laissez faire on both sides of the Atlantic tended to be far more moderate in their politics than Spencer. Taylor, id. at 220–230; John G. Sproat, *"The Best Men": Liberal Reformers in the Gilded Age*, 157–168 (1968); Fine, id., chap. 3.

9. Collini, *Liberalism and Sociology*, 19; Nicholls, "Positive Liberty," 120.

10. *The Common Law*, Lecture III, 96. For the earlier Mill quote, see Mill, 2 *Principles of Political Economy*, bk. 5, chap. XI, sec. 7 [1848] (1929). Formulations like Holmes's brilliantly opaque one verged dangerously close to being meaningless nostrums. It is hard to see how Holmes's meaning would be changed by reversing his statement, at least without more specificity as to the burden of proof. But the formulation that Holmes chose, with its verbal nod towards the virtues of minimal government, accurately reflected the political atmospherics in which he wrote.

11. See Spencer's "law of equal freedom," quoted later. For similar sentiments, see Frederic Bastiat, *Harmonies of Political Economy*, 263, defining competition as the absence of

constraint, and the absence of constraint as liberty: "To take away [this] liberty . . . is to annihilate intelligence, to annihilate thought, to annihilate man." To Bastiat's expostulation, Henry Carter Adams responded with contempt, "[H]e conceives all the complicated questions of society to have been asked and answered when he exclaims: 'Who so base as to be a slave!'" "The Relation of the State to Industrial Action," 68.

12. *Principles of National Economy,* 101 (1921). See also id. at 83–84. Collini, *Liberalism and Sociology,* 19, identifies freedom of contract as the heart of individualist objections to the Trade Union legislation of 1906 to 1914 in England. For similar sentiments from conservative lawyers and judges in the United States at the time, see Arnold Paul, *Conservative Crisis and the Rule of Law,* chap. 4 (1960).

13. The traditional view that laissez-faire philosophy dominated mid–nineteenth-century legislative politics in Britain is usually traced back to A. V. Dicey's enormously influential 1905 *Law and Public Opinion in England.* A good summary of the revisionist, anti-Diceyian historical account, beginning with David Roberts's *Victorian Origins of the British Welfare State* (1960), is given in Collini, *Liberalism and Sociology,* 13–14. See also Atiyah, *The Rise and Fall of Freedom of Contract,* 231–234 (1979); Harold Perkin, "Individualism versus Collectivism in Nineteenth-Century Britain: A False Antithesis," XVII *The Journal of British Studies,* reprinted in Perkin, *The Structured Crowd,* chap. 4 (1981). Most historians agree that whatever influence the more dogmatic versions of laissez-faire philosophy, and in particular freedom of contract, had had on British politics in earlier years, they were largely discredited by the turn of the century. See Atiyah, id. at 586–589. For the traditional view that laissez-faire philosophy dominated mid- and late-nineteenth-century America, see Fine, *Laissez Faire and the General-Welfare State;* Morton Horwitz, *The Transformation of American Law, 1780–1860,* (1977) (hereinafter *Transformation I);* Arnold Paul, *Conservative Crisis and the Rule of Law;* Clyde E. Jacobs, *Law Writers and the Courts: The Influence of Thomas M. Cooley, Christopher G. Tiedeman, and John F. Dillon Upon American Constitutional Law* (1954); Benjamin R. Twiss, *Lawyers and the Constitution: How Laissez Faire Came to the Supreme Court* (1942). For a good summary and exemplar of recent revisionist historiography, stressing that government regulation was widespread throughout the nineteenth century and that most of it was never challenged or was upheld by the courts, see Michael Les Benedict, "Laissez-faire and Liberty," 3 *Law and History Review* 297 nn.15,16, 301–303 and passim (1985).

14. For good overviews of the more sympathetic, revisionist explanations of judicial intervention, see Edward A. Purcell, Jr., *Litigation and Inequality,* 401 n.50 (1992); James L. Kainen, "The Historical Framework for Reviving Constitutional Protection for Property and Contract Rights," 79 *Cornell Law Review* 87, 91–102 (1993).

15. H. Scott Gordon, "The Ideology of Laissez-Faire," in *The Classical Economists and Economic Policy,* 180 (A. W. Coats, ed., 1971), notes a similar paradoxical tension in England. Perkin suggests that in English politics, the false dichotomy between "collectivism" and "individualism" cemented by Dicey was really a stand-in for the line that truly mattered, that between state ownership of the means of production and all more modest collectivist measures. "Individualism versus Collectivism," 68. Perkin's view probably sheds some light on the American experience as well, given the demonized specter of socialism that lies barely beneath the surface of many defenses of laissez-faire individualism.

16. For typical examples of Spencerianism enlisted against prolabor legislation, see Fine, *Laissez Faire and the General-Welfare State,* 44, 58–64. For a forceful argument that the rhetoric of liberty of contract shaped not only the strategy but also the ideology of organized labor, see William Forbath, *Law and the Shaping of the American Labor Movement,* chap. 5 (1991).

17. The classic texts here are Paul, *Conservative Crisis;* Jacobs, *Law Writers and the Courts;* Twiss, *Lawyers and the Constitution.* For the more recent, revisionist view, arguing that laissez-faire constitutionalism reflected a sincerely held (if misguided) autonomous system of beliefs, derived in some cases from a Jacksonian hostility to special privileges, in others from the judges' view of positive, constitutional law, see the later discussion.

18. 113 Pa. St. 431. "Freedom of contract" as a constitutional principle was first explicitly formulated in Jones v. People, 110 Ill. 590 (1884), and reiterated by the New York court the following year in In the Matter of *Jacobs,* 98 N.Y. 98. In 1886, Illinois became the first state court explicitly to rely on freedom of contract to strike down a state law, in this case a law requiring mine owners to install and use track scales to weigh coal for purposes of calculating miners' wages. Millett v. People, 117 Ill. 294 (1886). But it was *Godcharles* that made the doctrine famous, perhaps (as Jacobs suggests) because Pound and others mistakenly believed it and not *Millett* to be the first decision relying on the doctrine. For an excellent summary of the genesis and development of the liberty of contract doctrine in the courts, as well as the events leading up to it, see Jacobs, *Law Writers and the Courts,* chap. 2. For discussions of the impact of the *Godcharles* case and evolution of the freedom of contract doctrine in the two decades that followed, see Roscoe Pound, "Liberty of Contract," 18 *Yale Law Journal* 454, 471–478 (1909); Jacobs, id. at chap. 3; Paul, *Conservative Crisis,* 45–54.

19. For a compendium of cases in which courts struck down labor legislation, see Forbath, *Law and the Shaping of the American Labor Movement,* Appendix A. Arnold Paul estimated that in the six years following *Godcharles,* two-thirds of all challenges to legislative power under "freedom of contract" were sustained. *Conservative Crisis,* 45. As Lawrence Friedman notes, "[c]onstitutional madness was not distributed evenly across the country" during the 1880s and 1890s, with some state courts (notably Illinois) hewing to a far more conservative line. *History of American Law,* 361 (2d ed. 1985).

Historians have offered a number of explanations for the fact that courts invoked the doctrine almost exclusively to attack regulation of *employment* contracts. The least uplifting is offered by Lawrence Friedman, who argues that the other commercial relationships (debtor / creditor, consumer / producer) that were heavily regulated during that period *without* judicial objection were relationships in which the middle class was the prime beneficiary of government regulation. In contrast, the prolabor legislation under judicial attack benefited primarily the working classes. Id. at 362, 542. A less materialistic explanation is offered by William Nelson, who suggests that the strong tradition of free labor growing out of the antislavery movement led even progressives to think that the labor contract was different from, and more sacrosanct than, than other commercial relationships. *The Roots of American Bureaucracy,* 136–139 (1983). For a sympathetic overview and discussion of these and other theories, see Charles McCurdy, "The Roots of Liberty of Contract Reconsidered: Major Premises in the Law of Employment, 1867–1937," in *Yearbook 1984: Supreme Court Historical Society,* 20. Whatever the explanation, the political explosiveness of the "labor question" is poignantly demonstrated by Henry Carter Adams's insistence in 1887 (under imminent threat of losing his teaching position at Michigan because of his "socialist" leanings) on *excepting* labor contracts from his otherwise broad-based attack on any simple-minded notion of "liberty of contract." See "Relation of the State to Industrial Action," 129–133.

20. The literature on the constitutional and political fight over labor legislation is immense. The classic work on labor injunctions is Felix Frankfurter and Nathan Greene, *The Labor Injunction* (1930). Recent historical treatments include McCurdy, "The Roots of 'Liberty of Contract' Reconsidered"; William E. Forbath, *Law and the Shaping of the American Labor Movement.*

231

21. 198 U.S. 45 (1905).

22. 198 U.S. at 57, 64.

23. 208 U.S. 161 (1908).

24. 208 U.S. at 172–173. The Court also held that the statute was an unconstitutional invasion of the right of property guaranteed by the Fifth Amendment. It is unclear what property interest it had in mind. Reading *Coppage* back into *Adair*, it perhaps had in mind the "right to make contracts for the acquisition of property"—here, property in the form of wages to be paid for work. Coppage v. Kansas, 236 U.S. at 14. Alternatively, it might have had in mind the contract itself, which (being at-will) the Court construed to give the employer the right to fire without cause, or with any cause at all. The more straightforward invocation of property rights as a side constraint on social legislation, particularly legislation controlling the price at which property could be sold, is explored at length in Chapters 3, 4, and 5.

25. 236 U.S. at 20.

26. 245 U.S. 229 (1917). The only remedy a yellow-dog contract was thought to give employers prior to *Hitchman* was the right to sue individual employees who joined the union for breach of contract. Given the costs of litigating such suits case by case and the difficulty of collecting damages, the right was valuable to employers only for its *in terrorem* effect in discouraging employees from joining unions to begin with. Partly as a consequence, yellow-dog contracts were rarely used prior to *Hitchman*. In contrast, the injunctions against union-organizing activities authorized by *Hitchman* gave employers an enormously powerful tool to fight unionization. For a discussion of the development of yellow-dog contracts and their ascendency following *Hitchman*, see Edwin Witte, "'Yellow-dog' Contracts," 6 *Wisconsin Law Review* 21 (1930); Daniel Ernst, "The Yellow-Dog Contract and Liberal Reform, 1917–1932," 30 *Labor History* 251 (1989).

27. For typical examples of the extensive progressive literature on the three cases, see John Commons, *Legal Foundations of Capitalism*, 288–298 (1924); Walter Wheeler Cook, "The Privileges of Labor Unions in the Struggle for Life," 27 *Yale Law Journal* 779 (1918); John Dewey and James H. Tufts, *Ethics*, 441–448 (rev. ed., 1932); Pound, "Liberty of Contract." Hale began his course materials for Legal Factors with a quote from Coppage v. Kansas, and the materials are structured as an elaborate and extended response to the logic of the three Court decisions. In conjunction with Robert Wagner, Herman Oliphant, and Simon Rifkind, Hale also drafted an important amicus brief in Interborough Rapid Transit v. Green, 227 N.Y.S. 258 (1928), a landmark case among the second generation of legal challenges to yellow-dog contracts. See Mark Barenberg, "The Political Economy of the Wagner Act: Power, Symbol, and Workplace Cooperation," 106 *Harvard Law Review* 1381, 1409 n.25 and 1429 n.230 (1993).

28. Collini, *Liberalism and Sociology*, 77. For the earlier, less cynical views of the Fabians, see Bernard Shaw, "The Impossibilities of Anarchism," *Fabian Tract No. 45* 17 (1891), and Nicholls, "Positive Liberty, 1880–1914," 125.

29. *Liberalism* [1911], reprinted in L. T. Hobhouse, *Liberalism and Other Writings*, 81–83 (J. Meadowcroft, ed., 1994). The term "socialism," like the allied but distinct term "collectivism," had a number of meanings to contemporaries. A good summary of the different usages is given in Collini, *Liberalism and Sociology*, 34–35. For a catalog of the different meanings of "collectivism," see Perkin, "Individualism versus Collectivism," 65–67. For present purposes, I mean by "official Socialism" to denote the collectivization of significant property rights, in particular the means of production, coupled with programs for the radical redistribution of residual private wealth through some form of taxation and transfer system.

30. For typical expressions of that view, see Benjamin Andrews, "A Symposium on the Relation of the State to the Individual," *Dawn*, *II*, 299 (November, 1890); Hobhouse, *Liberalism*, 68; J. A. Hobson, *The Crisis of Liberalism*, 134 (1909); Ely, *Studies in the Evolution of Industrial Society*, 421–422; Edwin R. A. Seligman, "Continuity of Economic Thought," *Science Economic Discussion* 23 (The Science Company, 1886); T. S. Adams and Helen Sumner, *Labor Problems*, 15 (1905); Herbert Croly, *The Promise of American Life* [1909], 209 (Dutton & Co., 1963). On the history of "social control" as a term of art, see Dorothy Ross, *The Origins of American Social Science*, chap. 7 (1991). Ross traces the term at least back to John Stuart Mill's *On Liberty*. The term was popularized by the sociologist Edward A. Ross, who (as Richard L. McCormick noted) made " 'social control' bywords in the Progressive era." *The Party Period and Public Policy*, 282–283 (1986). Edward Ross used the term, much as Mill had done, to denote the formally and informally constituted processes by which society modified individual behavior to conform to the needs of society. However, most progressive social scientists ascribed to it a somewhat narrower and decidedly more prescriptive meaning, denoting "public control of the private capitalist economy." Dorothy Ross, id. at 230, 235.

31. Ludwig von Mises, "Freedom Is Slavery," *The Freeman*, 410 (Mar. 9, 1953).

32. On the centrality of the concept of liberty in political debate in the late nineteenth and early twentieth centuries in England, see Collini, *Liberalism and Sociology*, 13–50, 122–123. As Collini notes, "the status of liberty-citations in the hierarchy of evaluative language was such that it was nearly always necessary to adopt some strategy for undermining the objection." Id. at 122. For the astute suggestion that this might have been even more true in America than in England, see Daniel T. Rodgers, *Contested Truths*, 30–44 (1987). Even though American politics and the American soul were resolutely more utilitarian than the British version, political rhetoric in America far more than in England, as Rodgers notes, was saturated with appeals to abstractions like liberty, rights, and natural law. That taste for grand words, Rodgers suggests, explains the somewhat surprising unpopularity of Benthamite utilitarianism in America. Although in substance Bentham's program should have found a natural home in the America of Ben Franklin and a host of other pragmatic tinkerers, Bentham's unvarnished consequentialist rhetoric did him in. It also explains more generally, Rodgers suggests, why natural rights talk survived in America long after it gave out in England. Id. at 44.

33. Collini, *Liberalism and Sociology*, 35–36, citing to L. T. Hobhouse, "The Ethical Basis of Collectivism," 8 *International Journal of Ethics* 139 (1897–1898). Collini, id. at 32–39, supplies a useful summary of how the public in England received socialism and its closely allied collectivism during the latter half of the nineteenth century, and he argues persuasively that the growing hostility to programmatic forms of socialism makes it difficult to figure out whether most progressives were motivated by prudence or conviction in distancing themselves from anything to which the label "socialist" was likely to be attached.

34. On the prudential reasons for Ely, Adams, Rauschenbusch, and other left-leaning social reformers to distance themselves from socialism, see James Kloppenberg, *Uncertain Victory*, 264–266 (1986); Ross, *The Origins of American Social Science*, 113–118; Dorothy Ross, "Socialism and American Liberalism: Academic Social Thought in the 1880's," 11 *Perspectives in American History* 5, 45–79 (1977–1978); Mary O. Furner, *Advocacy and Objectivity: A Crisis in the Professionalization of American Social Science, 1865–1905*, chaps. 4 and 5 (1975). Ely almost lost his job at the University of Wisconsin when he was alleged to be a socialist, and he spent the balance of his life fighting off the vanquished specter. For a brief account of Henry Carter Adams's similar problems at Cornell and Michigan, see Introduction, *Two*

Essays by Henry Carter Adams, 36–42. Adams himself anticipated those problems, hesitating to publish his first article on socialism, for fear that it would jeopardize a possible appointment at Johns Hopkins. Ross, *Origins*, at 109 n.19. For Hale's attempt to parry Carver's charges that he was a socialist, see letter to Thomas Carver, Nov. 22, 1923, p.3, arguing that "the only sense of the word in which I am conscious of being a 'socialist' is in the sense of not being an 'individualist.'" Hale Papers, folder 1.

35. In *Uncertain Victory*, his splendid study of Hobhouse, Dewey, Lippmann, and other key adherents to some form of New Liberalism or social democracy, James Kloppenberg argues persuasively that the central concern unifying all the disparate figures was a quest for a middle way between the new socialism and the old liberalism—one that would eschew the statism of Hegelian idealism or official socialism on the one hand and the excesses of unchecked individualism on the other, while honoring their respective aspirations toward equality and liberty. For similar comments, see Fine, *Laissez Faire and the General-Welfare State*, 211; Price, "Community and Control," 1663. For typical expression of that view from progressives, see John Commons, "Progressive Individualism," VI *The American Magazine of Civics* 561–565 (June, 1895); Adams, "The Relation of the State to Industrial Action," 125, 128–129; Andrews, "A Symposium on the Relation of the State to the Individual"; Edwin R. A. Seligman, "Continuity of Economic Thought," 23; Hobson, *The Crisis of Liberalism*, 91–95; Hobhouse, "The Ethical Basis of Collectivism," 138–143. In addition, Lester Ward's "scientific utilitarianism," outlined in his 1883 *Dynamic Sociology*, provided a formative critique of traditional laissez-faire politics in the name of a utilitarian individualism.

36. Letter to President Angell of the University of Michigan, Mar. 15, 1887, quoted in *Two Essays of Henry Carter Adams*, 39.

37. As James Kloppenberg has said, "When the author of *On Liberty* endorsed in principle the ideal of socialism, he signaled as no other individual could have done the convergence of the values of individualism and community." *Uncertain Victory*, 159. For Mill's formative influence on later progressives in this regard, see id. at 159–160; Nicholls, "Positive Liberty, 1880–1914," 118 n.26.

38. *Liberalism*, 83–84.

39. "The Ethical Basis of Collectivism," 142. A full account of the evolution of Hobhouse's views from socialism to New Liberalism is given in Collini, *Liberalism and Sociology*, 51–146.

40. *Crisis of Liberalism* [1909] xii, 134 (reprinted 1974).

41. David Seckler, *Thorstein Veblen and the Institutionalists* (1975), argues persuasively that there were two Veblens: Veblen the determinist, who viewed human desires as a product of historical processes over which individuals have little control, and Veblen the humanist, who viewed all significant human behavior as the result of individual, purposive choice. Seckler suggested that the latter Veblen, along with Wesley Mitchell and John Commons, the two other significant figures in the humanist wing of institutional economics, was on a path of convergence with the radical individualist school of Menger, Hayek, von Mises, Robbins, Knight, and Popper.

42. "The Economic Discussion in Science," *Science Economic Discussion*, 69 (1886). For a discussion of Ely as an exemplar of the "middle way" between individualism and collectivism, see Kloppenberg, *Uncertain Victory*, 207–234. For Ely's collectivist or idealist side, see his laudatory description in 1886 of the "new school" of economics (meaning, the institutionalists) as "plac[ing] society above the individual, because the whole is more than any of its parts." "Ethics and Economics," *Science Economic Discussion*, 54.

43. "Progressive Individualism," 565.

44. See, e.g., T. H. Green, *Lectures on the Philosophy of Kant;* "Liberal Legislation and Freedom of Contract" [1881] reprinted in *The Political Theory of T. H. Green,* 43–74 (John Rodman, ed., 1964).

45. "The Impossibilities of Anarchism," *Fabian Tract No. 45,* at 17 (1891). Hale reproduced the quote in his course materials for the Seminars in Economics, Law, and Politics (1931) and Social Control in Economic Life (1932).

46. See Nicholls, "Positive Liberty, 1880–1914," 116. Charles Forcey summarized Herbert Croly's goal as using Hamiltonian means (state control) to achieve Jeffersonian (individualistic) ends. Croly, *The Promise of American Life,* x. For Croly's version of the argument, see id. at 213–214. The same might aptly be said of most other progressives.

47. For Frank Knight's somewhat excessive criticism of Hale for not taking those problems more seriously, see Book Review, 39 *Virginia Law Review* 871 (1953) (reviewing *Freedom Through Law* (1952)).

48. Letter to Thomas Carver, Nov. 22, 1923, pp. 3–4, Hale Papers, folder 1.

49. Draft ms. (undated) entitled "Invisible Government and Individual Liberty," p. 1, Hale Papers, folder 56.

50. "Bargaining, Duress, and Economic Liberty," 43 *Columbia Law Review* 603, 628 (1943). Max Weber offers a strikingly similar analysis of the problem in a discussion of "Freedom and Coercion" in 2 *Economy and Society,* 729–731 (1968 trans. from 4th German ed., 1956). In a capitalist society, real as opposed to formal contractual freedom is guaranteed only for those with property and hence with the legally guaranteed power to set the terms of exchange. As a result, "[t]he exact extent to which the total amount of 'freedom' within a given legal community is actually increased [over other alternative arrangements] depends entirely upon the concrete economic order and especially upon the property distribution. In no case can it be simply deduced from the content of the law." Id. at 730. Thus, concluded Weber, a shift to a socialist economy, despite the increase in "direct mandatory and prohibitory decrees," might well increase qualitatively and quantitatively the real personal freedom of its participants. Id. at 731. The answer, Weber argued, "cannot be decided, however, by the mere analysis of the actually existing or conceivable formal legal system." Id. It can be decided (he implied) only by social experimentation and empirical study.

51. Twiss, *Lawyers and the Constitution,* 258. The progressive writings embracing this creed are too numerous to catalog. For typical examples, see Ely, *Studies in the Evolution of Industrial Society,* chap. XI; Hobhouse, *Liberalism,* chap. 7.

52. Renewed academic interest in the problem of coercion can probably be traced to Robert Nozick's article on "Coercion," reproduced in *Philosophy, Science and Method,* 440 (Sidney Morgenbesser et al., eds., 1969). For Nozick's and other recent treatments of the problem, see discussion at the end of this chapter.

53. *Democracy and Reaction,* 219 (2d ed., 1909).

54. Green's formative formulation of the distinction between "negative" and "positive" liberty is given in "Liberal Legislation and Freedom of Contract," 51–52. For further discussion of Green's usage of the terms, see later.

55. *Liberalism,* 15.

56. Dewey and Tufts, *Ethics,* 369–373; John Dewey, *The Public and Its Problems,* 86–87 (1927). For other comments pointing out that the case for minimal government was historically contingent, see Green, "Liberal Legislation and Freedom of Contract," 46–48; Hobhouse, *Democracy and Reaction,* 221–225; Seligman, "Continuity of Economic Thought," 9–13; Morris Cohen, "Property and Sovereignty," 13 *Cornell Law Quarterly* 8, 21 (1927); Ely, *Studies*

in the Evolution of an Industrial Society, 22; Walter Rauschenbusch, *Christianizing the Social Order*, 355–356 (1912). In "The Relation of the State to Industrial Action," Henry Carter Adams offered a slightly different version of the argument that the preference for laissez faire was historically contingent. Noting that in England, which had a strong tradition of laissez faire, economists were inclined towards individualism, and that in Germany, which had a strong tradition of state organicism, economists (principally the German Historicists) were kindly disposed towards state action, Adams argued that the philosophical predilection in each case reflected nothing more than a preference for existing arrangements, whatever they might be. Id. at 79.

57. "Liberal Legislation and Freedom of Contract," 72–73.

58. For the standard view among historians that, along with antimonopolism, assertions of the interdependence of all people and obsolescence of "economic man" as an autonomous possessor of property rights constituted one of the strongest strains of progressivism, see Nicholls, "Positive Liberty, 1880–1914"; Kloppenberg, *Uncertain Victory*, 96–97, 171–180, 277–279; 399–401; Daniel T. Rodgers, "In Search of Progressivism," 10 *Reviews in American History*, 113, 124–126 (Dec. 1982). For typical examples, see Henry Carter Adams, "Economics and Jurisprudence," 137, 144–145; Dewey, *The Public and Its Problems*, 155; Ely, *Studies in the Evolution of Industrial Society*, 404–405; Hobson, *The Crisis of Liberalism*, chap. IV; Hobhouse, *Liberalism*, 60; Rauschenbusch, *Christianizing the Social Order*, 421; Ritchie, *The Principles of State Interference*, 11; Herbert Croly, *Progressive Democracy*, chap. IX (1914).

The talk of interdependence can be traced in part to the new social psychology originated by Charles Horton Cooley and strongly evident in the writings of William James, Dewey, Croly, and others, and in part to the new sociology of Lester Ward and Albion Small. For a good overview of Cooley's philosophy and influence, see Price, "Community and Control," 1665–1667. For its influence on J. M. Clark, see Seligman, 1 *Main Currents in Modern Economics*, 202–204 (1962). For a good example of how far "interdependence" had made its way into the consciousness of the educated classes by the first decade of the twentieth century, see Elihu Root, "Experiments in Government and the Essentials of the Constitution–I," 198 *North American Review* 1, 2–3 (July 1913).

59. *The Ethics of Democracy* [1888], 227, 232 (1 Early Works, Jo Ann Boydston et al. eds, 1968).

60. *The Economic Basis of Public Interest*, 59 (1968), paraphrasing John B. Cheadle, "Government Control of Business I," 20 *Columbia Law Review* 438 (1920). For similar comments, see Oliver Wendell Holmes, Jr., Book notice on the Granger cases, 12 *American Law Review* 354 (1878); Thorstein Veblen, *Theory of Business Enterprise*, 274–276, chap. VIII (1915); Hobhouse, 1 *Morals in Evolution*, 367; Dewey, *Ethics of Democracy*, 244. On the need for a new, social notion of individualism and liberty, built on cooperativism, see Barenberg, "Political Economy of the Wagner Act," 1419; Kloppenberg, *Uncertain Victory*, 334–336, 348, 401–403; R. Jeffrey Lustig, *Corporate Liberalism*, 112 (1982); Dewey, *The Public and Its Problems*, 96–98, 126–128, 155–157.

61. For further discussion of public attitudes towards monopolies, see chaps. 3 and 5.

62. For a discussion of the downfall of the traditional common-law injunction, "sic utere tuo ut alienum non laedas" (so use your property so as not to injure others) as a meaningful limitation on government action, see chap. 3.

63. *Liberalism*, 47.

64. *Social Control of Business*, 29 (2d ed., 1939).

65. The phrase is Simon Patten's, commenting in a somewhat different context on David Wells's antiprotectionism. "Wells's Recent Economic Changes," 5 *Political Science Quarterly*

84, 102 (Mar., 1890). See also Dewey, *The Public and its Problems*, 95–96, arguing that nineteenth-century individualists had elevated "the individual" "on high in theory" at the very moment, ironically enough, that he "was in process of complete submergence in fact."

66. Seligman, "Continuity of Economic Thought," 13.

67. *Social Control*, 29.

68. Collini, *Liberalism and Sociology*, 107 n.129.

69. Bk. V, chap. XI, sec. 7.

70. "Liberty of Contract," 460 n.35.

71. "The Relation of the State to Industrial Action," 84, 86, 131.

72. *Social Control of Business*, 151–161.

73. Id., 33.

74. For the view that progressive taxation in particular reflected a "radical break from the liberal creed, a departure resting on the heretical claim that in industrial societies wealth is not a personal but a social product," see Kloppenberg, *Uncertain Victory*, 184.

75. "Liberal Legislation and Freedom of Contract," 51–52. The distinction between "negative" and "positive" freedom was subsequently popularized by Isaiah Berlin in "Two Concepts of Liberty" (1958), reprinted in *Four Essays on Liberty* (1969). In his splendid essay, "Positive Liberty: 1880–1914," David Nicholls helps to locate Green in a comprehensive taxonomy of uses of "liberty" in late nineteenth-century England. The distinction persists in contemporary philosophical literature, and remains critical to framing and defending the libertarian ideal. See, e.g., Eric Mack, "In Defense of 'Unbridled' Freedom of Contract," 40 *American Journal of Economics and Sociology* 1 (1981).

76. *The New Freedom* [1913], 164 (Prentice-Hall, 1961).

77. "On the Different Senses of 'Freedom' as Applied to Will and to the Moral Progress of Man" [1879], II *Works* 308, 323 (3d ed. 1893) reproduced as "The Senses of 'Freedom'" in *The Political Theory of T. H. Green*, 75, 88.

78. "Liberal Legislation and Freedom of Contract," 53.

79. See excerpts from Green's lectures on "The Senses of 'Freedom,'" in particular pp. 75–76 and 84–85.

80. See, e.g., Robert Hale, Book Review of Adler, *The Idea of Freedom*, 59 *Columbia Law Review* 821, 832–833 (1959). For a survey of similar attacks on Green and others who advanced the notion of "freedom [as] self-perfection," see Adler, 2 *The Idea of Freedom: A Dialectical Examination of the Concept of Freedom*, chap. 5 (1958). For Green's heroic efforts to ground his teleological definition of freedom in the more traditional one, see "The Senses of Freedom," sec. 18 at 89–90, arguing that the failure to achieve one's own ideal of self-improvement—of living in accordance with the best one could be—engenders a sense of oppression, due to conflicting wants and impulses, that is the very antithesis of freedom.

81. *The Study of Ethics: A Syllabus*, 4 Early Works 285, (Jo Ann Boydston, ed., 1971). For the parallels between Mill and Green on this score, see John Rodman (ed.), Introduction, *The Political Theory of T. H. Green*, 22, suggesting that what Green did to the notion of freedom, Mill did to the notion of utility when he replaced Bentham's (quantitative) felicific calculus with a qualitative one under which it is relatively clear, at least in Mill's hands, that pushpin did not rank with poetry. For a good overview of the tension between Kantian individualism and social utilitarianism running through progressive thought, see generally Kloppenberg, *Uncertain Victory*, 115–132.

82. Hobhouse, *Liberalism*, 56, 61, 63. For a good summary of the Greenian influences on Hobhouse, arguing that they are far stronger than previously asserted, see Collini, *Liberalism*

and Sociology, 125–128; Kloppenberg, *Uncertain Victory*, 343–346 (also noting Green's influence on Croly and Lippmann).

83. Clark, *Social Control*, 72. See also id. at 59; Adams, "Relation of the State to Industrial Action," 128–133; Croly, *The Promise of American Life*, 22; Ely, "Ethics and Economics," 54; Charles Horton Cooley, *Social Process*, 28–29, 137–143 (1966); Roscoe Pound, "Do We Need a Philosophy of Law?" 5 *Columbia Law Review* 339, 346 (1905). For a discussion of the influence of philosophical idealism on Webb's socialism, see Willard Wolfe, *From Radicalism to Socialism*, 274–278 (1975).

84. Hale, "The Supreme Court and the Contract Clause," 57 *Harvard Law Review* 852, 892 (1944). For the view that appeals to a "commonweal" were a dominant rhetorical strain among American progressives in the first two decades of the century—indeed much stronger (if ultimately less effectual in pursuit of specific ends) than in their New Liberal counterparts in England—see Rodgers, *Contested Truths*, 179–187. On the communitarian strain in American progressive thought, and progressives' faith in "the reality of a common good," see also Price, "Community and Control." There were dissenters from the start, particularly among those with socialist leanings, who tended to regard talk of the common good as merely obscuring underlying class interests. That insight was domesticated and popularized by Charles Beard's 1913 *An Economic Interpretation of the Constitution of the United States*, which revealed the ultimate text of the common good—the Constitution itself—to be nothing more than an excrescence and instantiation of class conflict. In time, the growing tension among progressives over the possibility of defining the "common good" in a pluralist society led many more to abandon the quest entirely. See Edward A. Purcell, Jr., *The Crisis of Democratic Theory* (1973); Rodgers, *Contested Truths*, 176–211. Others were hostile to talk of "the common good" on more pragmatic grounds, arguing that the abstraction, like most others, was ultimately unilluminating. Walter Lippmann's enormously influential *Public Opinion* (1922), for example, suggested that such portentous abstractions like "A National Will" or "Social Purpose" were nothing more than fictions deliberately concocted to alter public opinion, a sentiment echoed with equal force three years later in *The Phantom Public*. The resulting personification of society "as a mind, a soul and a purpose," rather than a collection of disparate individuals with conflicting interests, Lippmann argued, made it impossible to think realistically about improving social life. *The Phantom Public*, 156 (1925).

85. For discussions of the historical importance of Green's notion of "positive freedom," see Nicholls, "Positive Liberty, 1880–1914," 120–127; Kloppenberg, *Uncertain Victory*, 395 (identifying "positive freedom" as the "keystone of progressive theory"). For typical invocations of the trope by British politicians, see Nicholls, id. at 124. For typical invocations by progressive political theorists at the turn of the century, see Kloppenberg, id. at 278–279; Hobson, *The Crisis of Liberalism*, 92–93; Dewey's (and Tawney and Ayres's) "freedom as power" in *Human Nature and Conduct*, 303–313; Roscoe Pound, "Twentieth-Century Ideas as to the End of Law," in *Harvard Legal Essays*, 357, 361–362 (1934); Commons, *Legal Foundations of Capitalism*, 114–121; Ely, *Studies in the Evolution of Industrial Society*, 402–404, 421–422; Croly, *The Promise of American Life*, 180–185. The echoes of Anatole France can be heard throughout the first two decades of the twentieth century. For Hale's obeisance to France, see "Rate Making and the Revision of the Property Concept," 22 *Columbia Law Review* 207, 213 (1922). See also Day's eloquent dissent in Coppage v. Kansas, 236 U.S. at 27, noting the hollowness of liberty without equality.

86. *Les Origines du socialism allamand*, 62 (1903), cited in Kloppenberg, *Uncertain Victory*, 278.

87. Hobhouse, *Liberalism*, 71.

88. "Liberal Legislation and Freedom of Contract," 67–68.

89. *Liberalism*, 41. See also Clark, *Social Control*, 92–93; Jacob Hollander, *Economic Liberalism*, 13–14 (1925); Pound, "Liberty of Contract," 463; Croly, *The Promise of American Life*, 180–185. For a thoughtful discussion of how "positive liberty" was harnessed to the redistributive agenda of the progressives, at the extreme leading to calls for the socialization of all capital, see Kloppenberg, *Uncertain Victory*, 278–283.

90. See, e.g., F. A. Hayek, *The Road to Serfdom*, 25–26, 26n.2 (1944).

91. L. T. Hobhouse, "The Historical Evolution of Property in Fact and Idea," in Hobhouse, *Sociology and Philosophy*, 103 (1966).

92. Id. at 103–104. For an overview of the progressives' usurpation of the "property as personality" argument for their own more radical ends, see Kloppenberg, *Uncertain Victory*, 397–401; Collini, *Liberalism and Sociology*, 31–32. The progressive argument was anticipated not only by Marxian materialism but, as Collini notes, also by ameliorist, nineteenth-century reformer rhetoric about the debilitating effects of poverty. Id. at 31. For typical examples of the progressive argument, see T. H. Green, "Political Obligation," 2 *Works* 526 (3d ed. 1893); Adams, "Economics and Jurisprudence," 154–156; Morris Cohen, "Property and Sovereignty," 13 *Cornell Law Quarterly* 8, 18–19 (1927). The American Legal Realist Walton Hamilton, in a typical progressive move, invoked Locke as an ally across the centuries, arguing that Locke believed that property should serve the interests of personality and liberty, in sharp contrast to the "indigenous American intellectual product" that has reversed the obligation. "Locke made property a means to liberty; a late nineteenth century jurist, Mr. Justice Field, for example, probably made liberty a means to property." "Property— According to Locke," 41 *Yale Law Journal* 864, 877 n.40 (1932).

The struggle between the right and the left over the soul of "property as personality" continues in contemporary literature. Compare, for example, Milton Friedman, *Capitalism and Freedom* (1962), Tibor Machan, *Human Rights and Human Liberties*, 121, 137 (1975), and Fred D. Miller, "The Natural Right to Private Property," in *The Libertarian Reader* 275, 285 (Tibor Machan, ed., 1982), with Margaret Jane Radin, "Residential Rent Control," 15 *Philosophy and Public Affairs* 350 (1986) and William Simon, "Social-Republican Property," 38 *University of California Los Angeles Law Review* 1335 (1991).

93. Whether meeting the argument on its own terms was equally futile is another question. For differing views on whether invocations of constitutional principles like liberty were a mere pretext for judges to enforce their own views of policy, see n.17 earlier and accompanying text.

94. 208 U.S. at 174 (emphasis added).

95. Courts were far more deferential to any claimed legislative intent to further the public welfare in commercial contracts outside the employment area than in the employment area. While acknowledging that police powers could be exercised to protect the health of workers themselves, the courts in *Lochner* and other working conditions cases scrutinized the legislature's claim as to its motive far more skeptically than in any other area. More importantly, courts rejected outright the argument that protecting workers against *economic* injuries resulting from unequal bargaining power was within the state's police powers at all—this, notwithstanding that courts routinely accepted similar justifications for regulation of other commercial contracts, as Justice Holmes repeatedly noted. See *Adair*, 208 U.S. 161; *Coppage*, 236 U.S. 1. For Holmes's comments, see Adkins v. Childrens Hospital, 261 U.S. 525, 567–571 (dissenting) (1923).

96. *Lochner*, *Adair*, and *Coppage* all ultimately turned on the limits of police powers, the equally malleable doctrine of the government's right to regulate interstate commerce, or

both. Holden v. Hardy, 169 U.S. 366 (1898) and Muller v. Oregon, 208 U.S. 412 (1908), two of the more famous cases coming out the other way, turned on the limits of police powers as well. For a general discussion of this accommodationist strategy in progressive legal politics, see chap. 1. For progressives' use of the state's "police powers" in defending regulation of property rights in general, and of public utilities in particular, in the face of a constitutional right to property read into the Fifth and Fourteenth Amendments, see chaps. 3 and 5, respectively.

97. On the former argument, see Ernst, "The Yellow Dog Contract and Liberal Reform," 266–273. Herman Oliphant's version of the argument in his famous brief in IRT v. Green, 131 Misc. 682, 227 N.Y.S. 258 (1928) failed to carry the day. Richberg met with more success in using the argument to support the anti–yellow-dog provisions in the Norris-LaGuardia Act. For a later (legislative) invocation of the proposition that what is good for unions is good for America, this time in conjunction with the NLRA (Wagner Act), see Barenberg, "The Political Economy of the Wagner Act." It was not until 1937 in West Coast Hotel v. Parrish, 300 U.S. 379, that the Supreme Court expressly invoked inequality in the labor market as a rationale for exercise of the police powers.

98. "Law Making by Unofficial Minorities," 20 Columbia Law Review 451. The draft ms., entitled "Economic Nationalism versus Representative Government," is contained in Hale Papers, folder 88. The letter to Fisher, dated Aug. 15, 1912, is contained in Hale papers, mss. folder.

99. 38 Political Science Quarterly 470 (1923).

100. For unpublished versions in his course materials, see materials and outline for Social Control in Economic Life, Hale Papers, folder 39; Legal Factors materials, Columbia Law Library. Other published versions include "Bargaining, Duress, and Economic Liberty"; "Force and the State: A Comparison of 'Political' and 'Economic' Compulsion," 35 Columbia Law Review 149 (1935); "Labor Legislation as an Enlargement of Individual Liberty," 15 American Labor Legislation Review 155 (Dec. 1926).

101. See Seligman, 3 Main Currents in Modern Economics 622 (on Carver's ties to Ely); Link, Woodrow Wilson, 18, on his ties to the others. Carver also contributed to a book of four essays, along with Ely, Ralph Hess, and Charles Leith, called The Foundations of National Prosperity (1917), on various aspects of conservation, including the conservation of human resources.

102. "Coercion and Distribution," 470.

103. Introduction, iii.

104. For Hale's technical attacks on Carver's analysis, see "Coercion and Distribution," 478–494; unpublished draft ms., Part II, reviewing Carver's Essays in Social Justice, in Hale Papers, folder 87. Hale was not alone in his dim view of Carver's work. For letters complimenting Hale on "Coercion and Distribution" and concurring in the view that Carver was (in Edgerton's phrase) a "lamentable muddlehead," see letter from Henry Edgerton, Professor at George Washington University Law School, Dec. 22, 1923, Hale Papers, folder 1; letter from Paul Douglas (of Chicago Business School), Nov. 14, 1923, Hale Papers, mss. folder.

105. Carver's "voting programs," for example, included regulation of monopoly prices, increased taxation of land values, graduated inheritance taxes, and, most significantly, a steeply progressive income tax to raise necessary government revenues. On the progressive income tax, see generally Carver, Principles of National Economy, 645–660. On Carver's role in formulating the case for progressivity on welfare grounds, see chap. 4. Many other

progressives had advocated measures similar to Carver's "balancing up" programs to alter supply and hence prices paid to factors of production. See, e.g., "Socialism and Superior Brains," *Fabian Tract No. 146,* 11 (1909) (proposing that "monopoly revenue" from the provision of scarce, skilled services be eliminated by increasing the supply of talent through increased education).

106. *Principles of National Economy,* 747.

107. "Coercion and Distribution," 478.

108. Letter to Arthur Hadley, Nov. 24, 1923, Hale Papers, folder 1 (citing to a shorter paper Hale submitted to the Academy of Political Science, on which "Coercion and Distribution" is based).

109. "Coercion and Distribution," 474.

110. For similar comments, see Morris Cohen, "Freedom: Its Meaning," in *The Faith of a Liberal,* 163 (1946); Hobhouse, *Liberalism,* 71; Weber, 2 *Economy and Society* 730-731.

111. "Law Making by Unofficial Minorities," 455.

112. Quoted in Eugen V. Böhm-Bawerk, *Capital and Interest: A Critical History of Economical Theory* [sic] [1884], 332 (William Smart, trans., 1890).

113. For the common progressive analogy of managerial to political power, see Barenberg, "The Political Economy of the Wagner Act," 1422, and sources cited therein; Cohen, "Property and Sovereignty," 13. For typical descriptions by Legal Realists and other progressives of the employment relationship as a locus of coercion, see Pound, "Liberty of Contract"; Cohen, "Property and Sovereignty," 12; Frankfurter and Greene, *The Labor Injunction,* 214; Ernst, "The Yellow-Dog Contract," 263-266; Dewey, *Liberalism and Social Action,* 64; Weber, II *Economy and Society* 729-731; Hobhouse, *Liberalism,* 40-41. For similar comments from progressive labor economists, see Neil W. Chamberlain, "The Institutional Economics of John R. Commons," in Dorfman et al., *Institutional Economics* (1963); Ely, *Studies in the Evolution of Industrial Society,* 405-406. For invocation of the rhetoric of unequal bargaining power to defend the Norris-LaGuardia and Wagner Acts, see Barenberg, "The Political Economy of the Wagner Act," 1423-1427. For talk of "unequal bargaining power" from an earlier generation of progressives, see Kloppenberg, *Uncertain Victory,* 181-183 (quoting Green, Sidgwick, and Fouillee); Paul, *Conservative Crisis and the Rule of Law,* 53-60.

114. Cohen's "Property and Sovereignty" is probably the best-known Realist version, summarizing rather than advancing the argument. See also Pound, "Liberty of Contract"; Adams, "Relation of the State to Industrial Action," 94-95, 129-131; Commons, *Legal Foundations of Capitalism,* 47-64, 290-298; Ely, *Property and Contract in their Relations to the Distribution of Wealth,* 603-642.

115. See, e.g., "Our Equivocal Constitutional Guaranties," 39 *Columbia Law Review* 563, 584 (1939); "Law Making by Unofficial Minorities," 453; "Political and Economic Review," 8 *American Bar Association Journal* 707, 708 (1922). See also letter to Carver, Nov. 22, 1923, pp. 3-4, Hale Papers, folder 1, responding to Carver's implication that Hale was a socialist, in part based on Carver's erroneous impression that Hale believed "all laborers are at the mercy of all property owners": "You may not believe it, but I assure you I am not trying to 'make out a case,' [and] that I am quite as ready to admit that labor-incomes are at times excessive as that property-incomes are at times." For a quite similar, formally evenhanded analysis of the coercive effects of the market, see Weber, II *Economy and Society* 729-731.

For hostility from other progressives to craft unionism, the restrictive labor practices of which, it was argued, transferred surplus value from consumers to union members, see Daniel Ernst, "Common Laborers? Industrial Pluralists, Legal Realists, and the Law of Industrial Disputes, 1915-1943," 11 *Law and History Review* 59, 75 n.53 (1993).

116. "Review of *Freedom through Law*," *The Freeman*, 410 (Mar. 9, 1953). Hale's response to the review was published in the Apr. 20, 1953, issue. For similar sentiments in more recent libertarian literature, see, e.g., J. Hospers, *Libertarianism*, 14 (1971); Murray Rothbard, "Society without a State," *Anarchism: Nomos XIX*, 191, 193 (J. Ronald Pennock and John W. Chapman, eds., 1978). See also Milton Friedman, "Freedom Under Capitalism," in *The Libertarian Reader*, 76–77, (T. Machan, ed., 1982), reprinted from Friedman, *Capitalism and Freedom* (1962); Michael Levin, "Negative Liberty," in *Liberty and Equality*, 84, 92–94 (Ellen Frankel Paul, F. D. Miller and Jeffrey Paul, eds., 1985); Jan Narveson, "Equality vs. Liberty: Advantage, Liberty," in *Liberty and Equality*, 33, 59–60, all embracing a version of negative liberty that assumes implicitly or explicitly that the coercive force exercised by the government in the form of regulation, taxation, and other restrictions on economic freedom poses a unique threat to individual freedom.

117. For Max Weber's famous version, the *locus classicus* of the observation for most social theorists who followed, see "Politics as a Vocation" [1919], reprinted in *From Max Weber: Essays in Sociology*, 78 (trans. and ed. by H. H. Gerth and C. Wright Mills, 1946): "[A] state is a human community that (successfully) claims the *monopoly of the legitimate use of physical force* within a given territory." (Emphasis in original.) For an illuminating account of how Weber's own account sought to narrow the broader visions of a state monopoly on coercion offered by Jhering and other nineteenth-century German social theorists, to focus only on physical violence, see James Whitman, "Aux Origines du 'Monopole de la Violence'—et Aux Limites" (draft ms., 1995).

118. "Bargaining, Duress, and Economic Liberty," 616.

119. Union Pac. R.R. Co. v. Pub. Serv. Comm., 248 U.S. 67, 70 (1918). For concurrence with that view, see F. A. Hayek, *The Constitution of Liberty*, 133 (1960); Dawson, "Economic Duress—An Essay in Perspective," 45 Michigan Law Review 253, 267 (1947).

120. "Force and the State" 149–150; "Bargaining, Duress, and Economic Liberty," 606.

121. "Bargaining, Duress, and Economic Liberty," 606.

122. "Our Equivocal Constitutional Guaranties," 565–566.

123. "Bargaining, Duress, and Economic Liberty," 606.

124. For Hale's various attempts to articulate the difference between force "which leaves a choice of evils to a party, and that which leaves him no choice whatever," see "Force and the State," 150; "Our Equivocal Constitutional Guaranties," at 581. For an interesting discussion of coercion by Weber that in many ways parallels Hale's but misses this point about the structure of government coercion, see II *Economy and Society* 729–731. Weber distinguishes government ("authoritarian") coercion, which he argues operates by "direct mandatory and prohibitory controls," from the indirectly coercive force of the market. To the latter, Weber argues, "the statement *'coactus voluit'* [it is his wish, although coerced] applies with peculiar force just because of the careful avoidance of the use of authoritarian forms." Id. at 730. The burden of Hale's argument is that the statement applies equally to government coercion, since what appear to be mandatory controls in fact generally work (as much as market constraints do) as indirect constraints on "voluntary" choice.

125. Unpub. ms. on "Economic Nationalism versus Representative Government," pp. 3–4, Hale Papers, folder 88.

126. See Thomas Grey, "The Disintegration of Property," in *XXII Nomos, Property*, 78–79 (1980). For a typical expression of this central beauty of freedom of contract, see John Chipman Gray, *Restraints on Alienation of Property*, preface viii (2d ed., 1895): "Every one was free to make such agreements as he thought fit with his fellow creatures, no one could

oblige any man to make any agreement that he did not wish, but if a man made an agreement, the whole force of the State was brought to bear to compel its performance. It was a system in which there was no place for privileges . . ." For Spencer's description of the centrality of freedom of contract in the larger scheme of human freedom, see *Social Statics*, Part II, chap. 8 at 165: "Evidently each is free to offer; each is free to accept; each is free to refuse; for each may do these to any extent without preventing his neighbours from doing the like to the same extent, and at the same time. But no one may do more; no one may force another to part with his goods; no one may force another to take a specified price; for no one can do so without assuming more liberty of action than the man whom he thus treats." For Hale's succinct summary of the traditional liberal argument that constitutional rights to property and against involuntary servitude together create an absolute guaranty of individual liberty, see "Our Equivocal Constitutional Guaranties," 564.

127. For conventional statements of this central tenet of the libertarian case for minimal government, see Mill, *Principles of Political Economy*, bk. V, ch. XI, sec. 1; Robert Nozick, *Anarchy, State and Utopia*, ix, 10–12 (1974). For its absorption in the common legal consciousness, see Yick Wo v. Hopkins, 118 U.S. 356, 370 (1886).

128. "Our Equivocal Constitutional Guaranties," 564. For a discussion of the prima facie tort doctrine and other miscellaneous common law doctrines limiting private coercive power, see chap. 3.

129. *Liberalism*, 71.

130. Id., 74.

131. Jeremy Bentham, Principles of the Civil Code, Part I, chap. 1, in I *Works* part II, at 301–302 (1838). A good overview of the evolution of analytical jurisprudence is provided in Joseph Singer, "The Legal Rights Debate in Analytical Jurisprudence from Bentham to Hohfeld," 1982 *Wisconsin Law Review* 975 (1982).

132. "Privilege, Malice, and Intent," 8 *Harvard Law Review* 1 (1894).

133. "Some Fundamental Legal Conceptions as Applied in Judicial Reasoning," 23 *Yale Law Journal* 16 (1913); "Fundamental Legal Conceptions as Applied in Judicial Reasoning," 26 *Yale Law Journal* 710 (1917). For contemporary discussions of Hohfeld's notoriously obscure system and its place in analytical jurisprudence, see Singer, "The Legal Rights Debate in Analytical Jurisprudence from Bentham to Hohfeld," 1049–1059; Horwitz, *Transformation II*, 151–156.

134. "Offer and Acceptance, and Some of the Resulting Legal Relations," 26 *Yale Law Journal* 169 (1917). For Hohfeld's brief discussion, foreshadowing Corbin's argument, see "Fundamental Legal Conceptions," 23 *Yale Law Journal* 49–51.

135. "Privileges of Labor Unions in the Struggle for Life," 27 *Yale Law Journal* 779 (1918); "The Powers of Courts of Equity," 15 *Columbia Law Review* 37–54, 106–141, 228–252 (1915); "The Alienability of Choses in Action," 29 *Harvard Law Review* 816 (1916); "The Alienability of Choses in Action: A Reply to Professor Williston," 30 Harvard Law Review 449 (1917). Cook's memoir of Hohfeld, "Hohfeld's Contribution to the Science of Law," 28 *Yale Law Journal* 721 (1919), was reprinted as a preface to a posthumous volume of Hohfeld's complete work, *Fundamental Legal Conceptions as Applied to Judicial Reasoning*. For Cook's complicated relationship to Hohfeld, see John Henry Schlegel, *American Legal Realism and Empirical Social Science*, chap. 1 (1995).

136. "Fundamental Legal Conceptions as Applied in Judicial Reasoning," 26 *Yale Law Journal* 746–747.

137. "Taxation of Seats on the Stock Exchange," 31 *Yale Law Journal* 429 (1922).

138. For a comprehensive list of Realist writings influenced by Hohfeld, see Singer, "The Legal Rights Debate," 989–991 n.22. John Henry Schlegel's *American Legal Realism* provides the first in-depth study of Hohfeld's connections to other Realists. In addition to those sources listed by Singer, see Clark, *Social Control*, 79–86, which summarizes Hohfeld's system and notes his influence on Corbin, Cook, Commons, and Hale. For Commons's somewhat confused use of Hohfeldianism, spurred by Walter Wheeler Cook's use of it in his article on the *Hitchman* case, see *Legal Foundations*, 91–134, and "Law and Economics," 34 *Yale Law Journal* 371, 375–376 (1925). For Hale's use of Hohfeld, see "Coercion and Distribution," 472; "Law Making by Unofficial Minorities," 452–453; "Ratemaking and the Revision of the Property Concept," 22 *Columbia Law Review* 209, 214 (1922); and notes in Hale Papers, folder 30, on "How Does a Propertyless Person Acquire a Physical Power to Eat?" running through a step-by-step Hohfeldian description of the constraints on transactions to acquire food.

139. For Hohfeld's own aspirations in that direction, see "A Vital School of Jurisprudence and Law: Have American Universities Awakened to the Enlarged Opportunities and Responsibilities of the Present Day?" 1914 *Association of American Law Schools Proceedings*, 76. For a more skeptical view of whether analytical jurisprudence had any practical payoff, see Schlegel, *American Legal Realism*, chap. 1.

140. For Hale's and other Realists' working out of that line of thought, see chap. 3.

141. "Privilege, Malice, and Intent," 5.

142. Commons, "Law and Economics," 374–375. See also Commons, *Legal Foundations of Capitalism*, 78, 107, 149.

143. Letter to Arthur Hadley, Nov. 24, 1923, p. 1, Hale Papers, folder 1.

144. The following description is drawn primarily from "Coercion and Distribution," 472–473. Other versions of the argument can be found in "Bargaining, Duress, and Economic Liberty," 603–606; "Force and the State," 174; "Our Equivocal Constitutional Guaranties," 582–586; "Law Making by Judicial Minorities," 452–453; handwritten notes in folder 30 (n.d.). For a similar argument, see Cohen, "Property and Sovereignty," 12.

145. "Coercion and Distribution," 473.

146. Id.

147. "Bargaining, Duress, and Economic Liberty," 626.

148. On the reciprocity of coercion in every exchange, see "Our Equivocal Constitutional Guaranties," 586.

149. "Law Making by Unofficial Minorities," 452.

150. "Bargaining, Duress, and Economic Liberty," 606.

151. "Law Making by Unofficial Minorities," 452.

152. "Coercion and Distribution," 472.

153. For a similar comment recognizing that the bargaining power of factors of production affected the distribution of income only with respect to surplus value, see J. A. Hobson, *The Industrial System: An Inquiry into Earned and Unearned Income*, vii (1909).

154. "Coercion and Distribution," 472.

155. Id., 477.

156. *Legal Foundations of Capitalism*, 67. For other versions of the argument, see, e.g., Tugwell, *The Economic Basis of Public Interest*, 28–31; John Hobson, *The Economics of Distribution*, chap. VII (1900); Simon Patten, *Theory of Prosperity*, 57–58, arguing that the "power of substitution" usually sets a ceiling on prices long before the consumer's "surplus is exhausted"—that is, long before prices reach their final ceiling, the utility to the consumer measured by the consumer's reservation price.

157. David Zimmerman, identifying the distinction (in standard philosophical terminology) as the difference between the act-token and act-type of offering to enter into a contract at the going market price, sensitively analyzes the different conclusions that one might draw about the coerciveness of wage contracts, depending upon whether one subtracts the act-type, or merely act-token, in analyzing the next best available alternatives. See "Coercive Wage Offers," 10 *Philosophy and Public Affairs* 121, 142–143 (1981).

158. "Bargaining, Duress, and Economic Liberty," 627. Whether one should consider a threat to withhold completely undesired options to be coercive at all was, as Hale noted, to a functionalist merely a semantic question. See Hale, Book Review of Adler, 830–832.

159. "Law Making by Unofficial Minorities," 452–453.

160. Draft comment on June 1916 article by John Bauer on rate regulation, p. 1, Hale Papers, box 21. See also "Force and the State," 174.

161. Hale, Book Review of Adler, 826.

162. "Bargaining, Duress, and Economic Liberty," 626.

163. "Our Equivocal Constitutional Guarantees," 566, 583; "Bargaining, Duress, and Economic Liberty," 626. For further discussion of this point, see chap. 4.

164. "Our Equivocal Constitutional Guaranties," 591; "Coercion and Distribution," 482.

165. "Our Equivocal Constitutional Guaranties," 594; "Bargaining, Duress, and Economic Liberty," 628.

166. "Our Equivocal Constitutional Guaranties," 594.

167. "Force and the State," 199.

168. Letter of Nov. 24, 1923, Hale Papers, folder 1. Hale would have demurred to everything in Carver's charge, except the word "confuse."

169. Steward Machine Co. v. Davis, 301 U.S. 548, 590 (1937). Hale, responding to Cardozo's complaint, acknowledged that his own argument was determinist, in the sense that it asserts that all acts are in some sense coerced, "either because the will to do otherwise is thwarted, or because the will to do the act is itself brought in to existence by compulsion." But it does not follow that one could not or should not distinguish between the two for political purposes. As Hale noted, "Freedom from the former would, to the determinist, be out of the question; freedom from the latter he might well regard as significant in a political context. Whether a particular act is free or coerced in a politically significant sense,"—that is to say, presents an appropriate occasion for political intervention—"then, is a question which the determinist [that is, the Halean] can approach from the same standpoint as the believer in free will." "Our Equivocal Constitutional Guaranties," 581.

170. United States v. Butler, 297 U.S. 1, 81 (1936). For contemporary writings urging some version of this distinction, see Michael D. Bayles, "A Concept of Coercion," in *XIV Nomos, Coercion*, (1972); Bernard Gert, "Coercion and Freedom," in id.; Theodore Benditt, "Threats and Offers," 58 *The Personalist* 382–384 (October 1977); Mack, "In Defense of 'Unbridled' Freedom of Contract"; Nozick, "Coercion." For an interesting critique of these arguments, attempting in part to offer a more naturalistic definition of coercive effects that does not distinguish between threat and offer, see Joel Feinberg, *Harm to Self*, chaps. 23 and 24 (1986).

171. Massachusetts v. Mellon, 262 U.S. 447, 480, 482 (1923). The case concerned the rather arcane and confused legal doctrine known as "unconstitutional conditions," further discussed later.

172. Rex v. Denyer [1926] 2 K.B. 258, quoted in "Bargaining, Duress, and Economic Liberty," 613.

173. "Force and the State," 168–169.

174. "Our Equivocal Constitutional Guaranties," 577–778.

175. "Bargaining, Duress, and Economic Liberty," 613.

176. See "Bargaining, Duress, and Economic Liberty," 613; "Coercion and Distribution," 476. For a contemporary account that relies (not very satisfactorily) on a variant of this distinction to escape the necessity of relying on moral baselines, see Zimmerman, "Coercive Wage Offers," 133–138.

177. "Bargaining, Duress, and Economic Liberty," 614.

178. "Coercion and Distribution," 475–476.

179. Id., 476. See also "Bargaining, Duress, and Economic Liberty," 613, noting that the easy cases for finding a threat impermissibly coercive involved threats or offers to do things that, if done, would be illegal.

180. Vegelahn v. Guntner, 167 Mass. 92, 107 (1896) (dissenting). For Holmes's later acknowledgment that the issue was more complicated, see Silsbee v. Webber, 171 Mass. 378 (1898), discussed in "Bargaining, Duress, and Economic Liberty," 618–619.

181. For Hale's formative analysis of the unconstitutional conditions problem, see "Unconstitutional Conditions and Constitutional Rights," 35 *Columbia Law Review* 321 (1935). For an acknowledgment by a court that a conditional offer of a benefit can be as coercive as a threat of penalty, see U.S. v. Butler, 297 U.S. at 71–72. There has been a resurgence of interest in the problem in recent years in legal circles, building on Hale's early analysis. For good contemporary discussions of the problem, see Kathleen Sullivan, "Unconstitutional Conditions," 102 *Harvard Law Review* 1415 (1989); Richard Epstein, "The Supreme Court 1987 Term: Unconstitutional Conditions, State Power, and the Limits of Consent," 102 *Harvard Law Review* 5 (1988).

182. Felix Cohen, "Transcendental Nonsense and the Functional Approach," 35 *Columbia Law Review* 809, 820 (1935).

183. "Coercion and Distribution," 476. To put the point another way, one cannot deduce a duty to act or not act from the existence of coercion, since the existence itself is deduced from a prior duty. For further comments from Hale on the impossibility of construing adjustments in coercive power as "favoring" one party or the other without a theory of absolute baseline entitlements, see unpub. ms. on "Economic Nationalism versus Representative Government," p. 5, Hale Papers, folder 88. For contemporary acknowledgments that baseline entitlements may determine whether an offer is viewed as "coercive," see Nozick, "Coercion," at 447–453; Mack, "Individualism, Rights and the Open Society," 3. Returning to the classic problem in coercion of how to treat an "offer" to save a drowning man in return for an extortionate payment, Nozick suggests that we can convert a rescuer's "offer" to save into a "threat" not to save unless the stated terms are met, by treating "the normal or expected course of events as one in which a person in a boat who comes by a drowning person, in a situation such as this, saves him." That is to say, we can do so by bestowing on the drowning victim an entitlement to be rescued by bystanders, and imposing a corresponding duty on any bystander to rescue. Id. at 449–450. For a critique of Nozick's argument as begging what Hale rightly perceived to be the central problem in these "necessity" cases—establishing a "just price" for services for which the provider is in a position to extract an exorbitantly high price—see chap. 4.

For contemporary discussions of the "baseline" problem in coercion and other areas that build on or parallel Hale's insight, see Kelman, *Critical Legal Studies*, 103–106, 177–181; Cass Sunstein, *The Partial Constitution*, chap. 3; Cheney C. Ryan, "Yours, Mine, and Ours: Property

Rights and Individual Liberty," in *Reading Nozick*, 323 (Jeffrey Paul, ed., 1981). See also Zimmerman, "Coercive Wage Offers." Zimmerman recognizes the circularity in other of Nozick's distinctions between "coercive" and "noncoercive acts." But he reinscribes it in his own unsatisfactory attempt to give a "nonmoral" account by relying on the distinction between feasance and nonfeasance—the salience of which, as Hale noted, is inevitably grounded in the moral assumption that we usually, although not always, have no duty to act to help others.

184. Letters of Carver to Hale, Nov. 19, 1923, and Dec. 14, 1923, Hale Papers, folder 1. For a similar attempt to distinguish "coerced" from "noncoerced" transactions based on whether the good or service offered was indispensable to the would-be purchaser, see Hayek, *The Constitution of Liberty*, 133–139. Hayek offered the definition to counter the "abuse" of the term to describe "an all-pervasive and unavoidable phenomenon," which he traced back to Hale's "Coercion and Distribution" and Commons's *Institutional Economics* (1934). Id. at 139 and n.6. For other similar definitions of coercion, see Harry Frankfurt, "Coercion and Moral Responsibility," in *Essays on Freedom of Action*, 65, 71–72 (Ted Honderich, ed., 1973); Gert, "Coercion and Freedom," 31.

185. Letter from Hale to Carver, Nov. 22, 1923, p. 3, Hale Papers, folder 1.

186. "Bargaining, Duress, and Economic Liberty," 621. More precisely, cases involving extortionate prices also involve necessity, since the same paucity of alternatives that enables the offeror to extract a price well in excess of cost also makes the offer irresistible. But the claim that an offer is irresistible is obviously different from the claim that it is substantively unfair.

Robert Nozick's well-known article on coercion offers another more recent attempt to help out the necessitous victim of extortionate pricing without plunging the state into the quagmire of fixing a reasonable or just price for the rescuer's services, a task that Nozick suggests is close to intractable. "Coercion," 468–469 n.29. Nozick suggests that this can be done by creating an unconditional right of the drowning victim to be rescued by bystanders and a corresponding duty on any bystander to rescue. As previously noted, in Nozick's scheme, we create such a baseline entitlement to be saved (thereby converting a rescuer's "offer" to save into a "threat" not to save unless stated terms are met) by treating "the normal or expected course of events as one in which a person in a boat who comes by a drowning person, in a situation such as this, saves him." Id. at 449. It is not clear that such a solution would even avoid the problem of fixing a just price, unless Nozick intends the duty to be to save *at no cost* (or perhaps, at most, at a cost of provable out-of-pocket expenses). But even if it did avoid the problem, a moment's reflection would almost certainly persuade Nozick that this solution keeps him out of the just price conundrum only at the cost of entertaining an even greater intrusion of the state on personal liberty: allowing it to impose (on the world at large? only on passersby?) an affirmative duty to act as our neighbors' keepers. Even Hale, in general skeptical of the distinction between negative and affirmative duties, would not have gone that far, believing that making the law "an instrument to enforce general unselfishness" imposed too great a constraint on liberty and required impossible determinations as to *who* bore that duty. See "Prima Facie Torts, Combination, and Non Feasance," 46 *Columbia Law Review* 208, 215 (1946). The common intuition of justice (and one imagines Nozick's on second thought as well) would argue for at most a conditional duty on the would-be rescuer in the boat: he is free not to save the drowning man, consistent with our normal rule against imposing affirmative duties of care on strangers; but *if he chooses to save him*, he is under a duty not to charge more than a fair price for his services. For a passing acknowledgment of this by Nozick elsewhere, see *Anarchy, State, and Utopia*,

179, noting that the Lockean proviso that "enough, and as good" be left for others would not only prevent one person from monopolizing ownership of the water supply; "[m]ore weakly, and messily, it may exclude his charging certain prices for some of his supply." Nozick then drops the doubt: "Thus a person may not appropriate the only water hole in a desert and charge what he will. Nor may he charge what he will if he possesses one, and unfortunately it happens that all the water holes in the desert dry up, except for his." Id. at 180.

187. *Christianizing the Social Order*, 233.

188. See "Our Equivocal Constitutional Guarantees," 577; "Force and the State," 169.

189. "Our Equivocal Constitutional Guaranties," 577.

190. "Coercion and Distribution," 476–477. For Holmes's famous exposition of malice—meaning damage inflicted or threatened solely for the purpose of injuring the plaintiff or bringing the plaintiff to terms—as a basis for distinguishing between permissible and impermissible forms of coercion, see "Privilege, Malice, and Intent."

191. "Force and the State," 153, 165–166. For Hale's examples of instances in which intent was legally determinative, see discussion of the prima facie tort doctrine in chap. 3, and "Unconstitutional Conditions," 358; and more generally "Bargaining, Duress, and Economic Liberty," 606–610. For a suggestive discussion of the role of "motive" in constraining private economic power, through the lens of Holmes's changing views, see Horwitz, *Transformation II*, 130–137.

192. "Force and the State," 152–153. As Hale notes, Holmes himself ultimately conceded that point.

193. "Coercion and Distribution," 477; "Force and the State," 153, 165–166. As Hale explained, responding to Carver's argument that the price that a seller charges for tobacco could be distinguished from the tax that the government levies on its sale on the ground that the government did not produce the tobacco but charges the manufacturer or the dealer only for the privilege of manufacturing or selling, "Whether the owner has rendered a service or not bears only on the question of the justification of the income which he collects, not on whether the process of collecting it was coercive." "Coercion and Distribution," 474.

194. For examples in the contemporary literature that insist on "bad intention" as a prerequisite for coercion for reasons that are implicitly or explicitly related to the economic productivity of the conduct for which payment was demanded, see Nozick, *Anarchy, State and Utopia*, 84–86; Eric Mack, "Nozick on Unproductivity: The Unintended Consequences," in *Reading Nozick*, 169–190 (Jeffrey Paul, ed., 1981); Zimmerman, "Coercive Wage Offers," 137–138.

195. "Coercion and Distribution," 477: "For purposes of ordinary conversation, some other word than coercion may be preferred to describe payments made to a man who makes a sacrifice to 'earn' them."

196. The Fourteenth Amendment declares that "[no] state shall deprive any person of life, liberty, or property, without due process of law." The Fifth Amendment—which, unlike the Fourteenth Amendment, is written in the passive voice—does not literally state that its prohibition is limited to state action: "No person shall . . . be deprived of life, liberty, or property, without due process of law . . ." In practice, however, it has always been construed to apply only to acts by one of the branches of the federal government.

197. For an exploration of the same problem as it arose over the "equal protection" clause of the Fourteenth Amendment, see the discussion of Shelley v. Kraemer in chap. 3.

198. For an acknowledgment that one could not use one's bargaining power to extract concessions that were against public policy, see Justice Day's dissent in Coppage v. Kansas,

236 U.S. at 36–38. For a history of the common-law tort theories employed to enjoin union organizing activities, see Frankfurter and Greene, *The Labor Injunction*, chap. 1. The broadest of these doctrines—the prima facie tort doctrine—held that *any* intentional infliction of harm was tortious unless justified. That standard was broad enough to license courts to strike down virtually any bargaining tactic that they wished. As Hale noted, courts had applied the doctrine to date mostly to unions, but "[i]t is quite capable of being expanded to cover cases of the withholding of jobs or property." "Unconstitutional Conditions," 358.

199. There was a third, and more indirect, consequence of the state action requirement: it raised (or more precisely, stymied one strategy for removing) jurisdictional obstacles to Congress's regulating employment relations. Prior to the Court's expansive reading of the Commerce clause beginning in the late 1930s, it took a restrictive view of Congress's jurisdiction over matters traditionally within the state's police powers. That still left Congress with jurisdiction over federal matters (e.g., working conditions of interstate railroad employees), but relegated the bulk of economic regulation at issue in the 1900s to the 1930s to the jurisdiction of the states, subject to whatever constitutional constraints were imposed by the courts. The enforcement clause in sec. 5 of the Fourteenth Amendment gave Congress "power to enforce, by appropriate legislation, the provisions of [the Fourteenth Amendment]." That meant that *if* private, intrastate economic affairs fell within the purview of the Fourteenth Amendment, Congress could preempt state legislation in the area. In order to conclude that such affairs did fall within the Fourteenth Amendment, however, one would have to embrace both substantive due process and Hale's expansive reading of state action to extend to private exercise of power. Hale makes precisely that argument in "Force and the State," but immediately backs away from its implications: "It is a solution . . . which would make Congress supreme in matters customarily left to the states; however logically the result may follow from the Fourteenth Amendment, it was clearly not foreseen or intended by the framers of it; and there is little present likelihood of its being adopted." Id. at 199.

200. "Law Making by Unofficial Minorities," 451. For a typical Halean assertion that economic power is a form of political power "derived from the political state," see letter to Herbert Morse, Nov. 23, 1951, Hale Papers, folder 71: "Sometimes I have used 'economic power' loosely to distinguish power to coerce other people which is not generally recognized as 'political' from that which is (i.e., power used by government officials). I think both are really political." The argument, a staple of Realist and institutionalist thought, is further discussed in chap. 3. Notable other examples include Cohen, "Property and Sovereignty"; Ely, *Property and Contract in their Relations to the Distribution of Wealth*; Commons, *Legal Foundations of Capitalism*.

201. "Force and the State," 199; "Our Equivocal Constitutional Guaranties," 569, 575–576. For discussion of some of those novel legislative forms, see chap. 3.

202. Id., 576.

203. "Force and the State," 199.

204. Coppage v. Kansas, 236 U.S. at 13. For similar comments explicitly in the labor context, see Adair v. United States, 208 U.S. at 174–175, and Hitchman Coal & Coke Co. v. Mitchell, 245 U.S. at 251.

205. Coppage v. Kansas, 236 U.S. at 16.

206. "[A]ny legislation that disturbs that equality is an arbitrary interference with the liberty of contract which no government can legally justify in a free land." Adair v. United States, 208 U.S. at 175.

207. See Spencer, II *The Principles of Ethics*, 46 (1893); Spencer, *Social Statics*, 121. For other statements of the classic view that common law rules of contract left all individuals as (free) jural equals, see Gray, *Restraints on Alienation*, iii–xii. On the centrality of the principle of jural equality in liberal legal thought, see Robert Gordon, "Legal Thought and Legal Practice in the Age of American Enterprise, 1870–1920," in *Professions and Professional Ideologies in America*, 70, 89–97 (Gerald Geison, ed., 1983). It remains central to the libertarian case against the redistributive state. Perhaps the most famous example is Hayek's "Rule of Law." See Hayek, *Law, Legislation and Liberty, vol. 2: The Mirage of Social Justice*, chap. 9 (1976). But the same argument underlies, in one form or another, virtually all libertarian attacks on the social welfare state, which assert that by interfering with the market distribution of wealth to favor one subclass of citizens over another, the state impermissibly discriminates among its citizens. See, e.g., Nozick, *Anarchy, State, and Utopia*, 167–174; Michael Levin, "Negative Liberty," in *Liberty and Equality*, 87–88 (Ellen Frankel Paul, F. D. Miller, and Jeffrey Paul, eds., 1985); Mack, "In Defense of 'Unbridled' Freedom of Contract," 7.

208. "Transcendental Nonsense and the Functional Approach," 809.

209. 245 U.S. at 258–259. Brandeis, in dissent, pounced on the inconsistency, to argue that "If it is coercion to threaten to strike unless plaintiff consents to a closed union shop, it is coercion also to threaten not to give one employment unless the applicant will consent to a closed non-union shop." 245 U.S. at 271.

210. Lochner v. New York, 198 U.S. at 64; Adair v. United States, 208 U.S. at 172–173; Coppage v. Kansas, 236 U.S. at 12–13.

211. For Hale's and other progressives' elaboration of this argument in attacking the "natural right of property," see chap. 3.

212. "Coercion and Distribution," 478. For other examples of that sentiment from progressives, see Clark, *Social Control*, 162; Hobson, *The Crisis of Liberalism*, 94–95; L. T. Hobhouse, *The Labour Movement*, 94 (2d ed., 1897). Bentham's earlier formulation of the same thought, advocating a pure (Benthamite) sum of unweighted utilities, can be found in Principles of the Civil Code, part I, chap. 1, at 301–302. Hale himself stopped short of that point, acknowledging that some forms of freedom were qualitatively more important than others, and should be weighted accordingly. See Hale's letter to Lon Fuller, Dec. 24, 1954, Hale Papers, box 9, written in response to Fuller's review of *Freedom Through Law*.

213. "Bargaining, Duress, and Economic Liberty," 625–626; "Our Equivocal Constitutional Guaranties," 586–587. For further discussion of Edgeworth's and others' hypothesis of a "declining marginal utility" of wealth and the egalitarian implications that progressives drew from it, see chap. 4.

214. "Bargaining, Duress, and Economic Liberty," 628; "Coercion and Distribution," 481.

215. Quoted in Kloppenberg, *Uncertain Victory*, 399.

216. See Hobhouse, "The Historical Evolution of Property, In Fact and In Idea," 81–106. For a similar, earlier formulation by Sidgwick, see *The Methods of Ethics*, 277 (4th ed. 1890), cited in Kloppenberg, 182, arguing that freedom properly understood implies no "more than [one's] right to non-interference while actually using such things as can only be used by one person at once," not "the right to prevent others from using at any future time anything that an individual has once seized." Hobson revived the Hobhousian distinction twenty years after Hobhouse had popularized it, this time under the rubric of "property versus improperty." By the latter, he meant (roughly) what Hobhouse and others had variously described as property for power, unearned surplus, and irrational gains. See Clarke, *Liberals and Social Democrats*, 267. For further discussion of the distinction, see chap. 4, n.1.

217. "Bargaining, Duress, and Economic Liberty," 619. For the recognition among contemporary scholars that the problem with certain forms of coercion (e.g., blackmail) may lie in the fact that a private party appropriates the leverage of others (the state, private parties who would shun or otherwise punish the blackmailed party if they knew the truth) for his or her private, *unjustified* gain, see James Lindgren, "Unraveling the Paradox of Blackmail," 84 *Columbia Law Review* 670, 701–705 (1984); Symposium, "Blackmail," 141 *University of Pennsylvania Law Review* 1565 (1993).

218. "Bargaining, Duress, and Economic Liberty," 620.

219. Id., 620. For similar observations in the contemporary literature that whether an act is coercive may depend in part on the disproportionality of the return to the "coercer," see Daniel Lyons, "Welcome Threats and Coercive Offers," 50 *Philosophy* 425, 427–428 (1975); Feinberg, *Harm to Self*, 249–253; Jeffrie G. Murphy, "Consent, Coercion, and Hard Choices," 67 *Virginia Law Review* 79, 88–91 (1981).

220. For Holmes's most famous statement on why legislative limits on free speech should be judged harshly, see Gitlow v. New York, 268 U.S. 652, 672–673 (1925) (dissenting). For an illuminating study of progressives' struggle to defend different standards of review for incursions on economic and expressive freedoms, see Mark Graber, *Transforming Free Speech* (1991).

3. The Empty Idea of Property Rights

1. See letter from Hale to Brandeis, June 4, 1916, p. 3, enumerating both objections. Hale Papers, mss. folder.

2. See, e.g., "Coercion and Distribution in a Supposedly Non-Coercive State," 38 *Political Science Quarterly* 482–484 (1923); "Economic Theory and the Statesman," in *The Trend of Economics*, 219 (Rexford Tugwell, ed., 1924); letter to Brandeis, June 4, 1916, Hale Papers, mss. folder, arguing that incentive considerations justified a rule protecting property values to the extent of what owners had to "part with." For typical acknowledgments from other progressives of the importance of incentive considerations, see Benjamin Andrews, "Symposium on the Relation of the State to the Individual," 2 *The Dawn* (Nov. 1890), 297–299; John Dewey, *The Public and Its Problems*, 92 (1927); Richard T. Ely, 1 *Property and Contract in Their Relations to the Distribution of Wealth*, 329–330 (1914); L. T. Hobhouse, *The Labour Movement*, 73–79 (2d ed. 1906).

3. "Economic Theory and the Statesman," 193 n.1, citing to Thorstein Veblen, *The Theory of Business Enterprise*, 272 (1904).

4. For a good summary of the late eighteenth- and early nineteenth-century utilitarian assault on the natural rights view of property, see Richard Schlatter, *Private Property: The History of an Idea*, 239–255 (1951).

5. On the utilitarian arguments for egalitarian redistribution in the late nineteenth and early twentieth centuries, see Benjamin Fletcher Wright, Jr., *American Interpretations of Natural Laws: A Study in the History of Political Thought*, 242–279, 307–326 (1931). For further discussion of the Edgeworthian hypothesis and its implications for income redistribution programs, see chap. 4.

6. See Schlatter, *Private Property*, 255–261, on the Hegelian roots of Greenian idealism. Green's influence on later British progressives is evident in the collection of essays in *Property, Its Duties and Rights* (2d ed. 1915). See also L. T. Hobhouse, *The Labour Movement*, 148–149 (3d ed. 1912); J. A. Hobson, "The Restatement of Democracy" reprinted in *The Crisis of*

Liberalism: New Issues of Democracy, 71–87 (P. F. Clarke, ed., 1974) (1909). For typical American expressions of the "public" or "social" side of private property, see John R. Commons, *Legal Foundations of Capitalism*, 328 (1924) (arguing that the term " 'private business' is a contradiction in terms"); Dewey, *The Public and Its Problems*, 91–93; Ely, *Property and Contract*, 176, 340; Walter Rauschenbusch, *Christianizing the Social Order*, 358 (1915); Theodore Roosevelt, "The New Nationalism" (speech at Osawatomie, Kansas, Aug. 31, 1910), reprinted in 19 *The Works of Theodore Roosevelt*, 10–30 (Hermann Hagedorn, ed., 1925); Edwin R. A. Seligman, *Principles of Economics*, 131–134 (4th ed. 1909).

7. *Property and Contract*, 250. For a similarly defensive attempt to package his own brand of progressivism as "essentially conservative," see Henry Carter Adams, "Relation of the State to Industrial Action," reprinted in *Two Essays by Henry Carter Adams*, 125–129 (Joseph Dorfman, ed., 1969).

8. *The Labour Movement*, 90.

9. Id.

10. Hale's expansive view of the police powers of the state, for example, growing out of his work on public utilities, could be read as an expression of the inherent publicness of property, although it is as easily explainable as a utilitarian (or indeed, even rights-based) response to an interdependent world. In addition, his argument that legal rights can have no meaning except in relation to organized society echoes Green's idealist version of the positivist basis of all rights. See later discussion; Thomas Hill Green, *Lectures on the Principles of Political Obligation*, 45 (1941) (a reissue of Volume II of Green's *Philosophical Works* (1890)).

11. Hale provides an early and uncharacteristically forthcoming declaration to that effect in the opening of the early draft manuscript of *Valuation and Rate-Making*, Hale Papers, folder 49 ("Regulation of Public Service Companies"): "I. General Principles of Distribution. Object of our whole legal system should be not the attainment of certain abstract principles, but the attainment of the utmost welfare of everyone."

12. Frank Chapman Sharp, "The Problem of a Fair Wage," 30 *International Journal of Ethics* 383–384 (1920), an article that Hale included in the Legal Factors materials, provided a straightforward declaration of that program, in a passage that Hale quoted with approval: "[T]hat economic system is just which in its principles of distribution departs from equality so far and only so far as is necessary to supply the spur required to raise production to the maximum desirable." Class notes, Hale Papers, folder 30. For an early statement from Hale going even further in the direction of equality, to a position quite close to the Rawlsian difference principle, see draft manuscript of *Valuation and Rate-Making*, pp. 1–7, Hale Papers, folder 49. After running though the various conditions that produce unequal distributions of income (greater productivity, inheritance, government grants, lower costs, etc.), Hale concludes that the only condition that justifies *not* redistributing wealth to achieve greater equality is incentive-based considerations. When large incomes are necessary to induce performance of valued services, the government should not interfere with the payment of such incomes "merely because the interference will tend to equalize the incomes of rich and poor, if it will make the poor absolutely (tho not relatively) worse off . . . This assumes of course that the interference . . . will result in absolute injury to those at the bottom, which is of course not true in every case." Id. at 7.

13. *Manchester Guardian*, (Feb. 23, 1899), quoted in Peter Clarke, *Liberals and Social Democrats*, 66 (1978).

14. First tenet of the proposed "Constitution of the Society for the Study of National Economy," drafted by Simon Nelson Patten and Edmund James in 1884–1885, reproduced

in Richard T. Ely, *Ground Under Our Feet*, 296 (1938). For a typical insistence from an ardent rent theorist on the need for a more scrupulous separation of individual and social wealth, see Hobhouse, *Liberalism*, 187–188. See also Henry Carter Adams, "Economics and Jurisprudence," reprinted in *Two Essays by Henry Carter Adams*, 156–160; Alfred Fouillée, *La Propriété sociale et la démocratie*, v, 43–45 (1884), quoted in James T. Kloppenberg, *Uncertain Victory: Social Democracy and Progressivism in European and American Thought, 1870–1920*, 183 (1986).

15. E. J. James, "The State as an Economic Factor," in *Science Economic Discussion*, 32 (Richard T. Ely, ed., 1886).

16. See James Tully, *A Discourse on Property: John Locke and His Adversaries*, 62–63 (1980); Roscoe Pound, "The End of Law as Developed in Juristic Thought" 27 *Harvard Law Review* 619 (1914).

17. For a recent, skeptical view, see Tully, *A Discourse on Property*, 49. For an earlier view along the same lines, see Hamilton, "Property—According to Locke." Hamilton argues that the historical Locke invoked the right of private ownership only as a strategic counter to the Stuarts' assertion of absolute royal prerogatives, and was made over into a "prophet of property" by later readers to fit their own justificatory needs. "The men of 'the enlightenment' and of a developing industrial culture,—who always thought of cause as individual and never as social,—looked into Locke's essay, found it good, and read therein their own sense and reason." Id. at 872.

18. Id. at 869.

19. Robert Nozick, *Anarchy, State, and Utopia*, ix (1974).

20. John Maurice Clark, *Social Control of Business*, 73 (2d ed. 1926).

21. For Ely's paraphrase of that argument, see *Property and Contract*, 107.

22. Id., at 107.

23. "The Limitations of Marginal Utility," *Journal of Political Economy* 630 (1909). For similar comments, see Clark, *Social Control of Business*, 73–89; Hamilton, "Property—According to Locke," 872.

24. Jeremy Bentham, *Principles of the Civil Code*, in 1 *The Works of Jeremy Bentham*, 309 (1962). For a thoughtful discussion of the limits of Bentham's and James Mill's positivism, and of whether an alternative theory of natural rights might be deduced from utilitarianism itself, see H. L. A. Hart, *Essays on Bentham: Studies in Jurisprudence and Political Theory*, chap. IV (1982). On Blackstone and Hume, see Robert W. Gordon, "The Elusive Transformation: A Review of Morton J. Horwitz's *The Transformation of American Law, 1870–1960*," 6 *Yale Journal of Law and the Humanities* 153 (1994).

25. By "distribution" Mill did not mean the pricing of factors in production (its customary technical economic meaning)—that is, how the final price paid for any goods or services is divided among the various factors (labor, capital, component parts) that went into its production. Instead, he meant the personal distribution of income among "landowners, capitalists and productive labourers, . . . [the] three classes . . . considered in political economy as making up the whole community." John Stuart Mill, *Principles of Political Economy with Some of Their Applications to Social Philosophy*, bk. II, chap. III, §1, 238 [1848] (1929).

26. Mill, *Principles of Political Economy*, bk. II, chap. I, §1, 201. See also id. at 21. As Mill acknowledged, in the long run, many of these given conditions are subject to change. But in the short run, they determine absolutely the modes of production and hence productivity.

27. Id. at bk. II, chap. I, §1, 200 (footnote omitted). For a thoughtful attempt to put Mill's views on production and distribution in a historical and political context, see Maurice Dobb, *Theories of Value and Distribution Since Adam Smith: Ideology and Economic Theory*, 26–29,

121–136 (1973). As Dobb notes, Mill's insistence on viewing distribution as historically relative and rooted in specific property institutions puts him at odds not only with his classical predecessors but with his marginalist successors as well. The marginalists, with their focus on a "demand-theory of exchange-relationships and a derivation of income-distribution (*via* factor prices) from these exchange-relationships," tilted the emphasis back again to "a portrayal of the economic problem in its essentials as shaped and moulded by universal and supra-historical conditions of any exchange society, whatever its particular social relations, class structure and property-institutions might be." Id. at 26–27. The crucial difference between the classicists and the marginalists, Dobb argues, is that the latter put distributional questions aside not by denying the Millian argument that it was possible to affect income distribution through institutional arrangements, but by putting such questions largely outside the scope of economics altogether. Id. at 172. For further discussion on this point, see later.

28. *Principles of Political Economy*, bk. IV, chap. VI, §2, 749.

29. Id. at bk. II, chap. I, §1, 201. In a passage written years later, of which his progressive heirs were equally fond, Mill traced the evolution of his own thinking on private property from "extreme Benthamism," when "[p]rivate property, as now understood, and inheritance, appeared to me . . . the *dernier mot* of legislation," to the position in which he and his wife regarded "all existing institutions and social arrangements as being . . . 'merely provisional' and welcomed with the greatest pleasure and interest all socialistic experiments by select individuals." *Autobiography*, 230–231, 234 (1873).

30. *Property and Contract*, 62–63. For a similar comment, see Henry Carter Adams, "Economics and Jurisprudence," 150–151.

31. Handwritten notes, Hale Papers, folder 68 (n.d.). For similar comments from other progressives, see Morris Raphael Cohen, *Reason and Law: Studies in Juristic Philosophy*, 185–186 (1950); J. M. Clark, "The Relation Between Statics and Dynamics," in *Economic Essays in Honor of John Bates Clark*, 50 (Jacob H. Hollander, ed., 1927); Ely, *Property and Contract*, 73–74; Walton H. Hamilton and Irene Till, "Property," 12 *Encyclopaedia of the Social Sciences* 529 (Edwin R. A. Seligman and Alvin Johnson, eds., 1933). For a good summary of the "natural rights" view of property as reflected in economics texts at the turn of the century, see Duncan Kennedy, "The Role of Law in Economic Thought: Essays on the Fetishism of Commodities," 34 *American University Law Review* 939 (1985).

32. See letter from Hale to Ordway Tead (an editor at Harpers, then considering publication of *Freedom*), July 10, 1950: "If John R. Commons had not pre-empted the title, the book [*Freedom Through Law*] might be called 'Legal Foundations of Capitalism,' though I hope the discussion is more realistic and less metaphysical than Commons." Hale Papers, folder 84.

33. To that list should probably be added Veblen's *The Theory of Business Enterprise*, Adams's "Economics and Jurisprudence"; and (among the Realists) Roscoe Pound's historical survey of property rights regimes in "The End of Law as Developed in Legal Rules and Doctrines," 27 *Harvard Law Review* 195 (1914), Morris R. Cohen's "The Basis of Contract," 46 *Harvard Law Review* 553 (1933), and Cohen's "Property and Sovereignty," 13 *Cornell Law Quarterly* 8 (1927). Numerous other institutionalist and Realist texts comment at least in passing on the fallacy of a "natural" property regime. See, e.g., Felix S. Cohen, "Dialogue on Private Property," 9 *Rutgers Law Review* 362 (1954); Dewey, *The Public and Its Problems*, 108; Harleigh H. Hartman, *Fair Value: The Meaning of the Term 'Fair Valuation' as Used by Utility Commissions*, 4 (1920). For an overview of progressive and Realist assaults on property rights as a natural category, see Morton J. Horwitz, *The Transformation of American Law*

1870–1960: The Crisis of Legal Orthodoxy, 145–167 (1992) [hereinafter *Transformation II*]. For a thoughtful consideration of Hale's writings on the constitutive role of law in economic distribution, see "The Stakes of Law, or Hale and Foucault!" in Duncan Kennedy, *Sexy Dressing, Etc.* (1993).

34. For Hale's high regard of Clark's *Social Control Through Business*, see letter to Harlan Fiske Stone, Aug. 11, 1926, Stone Papers, Library of Congress.

35. For one version of the argument, see Hale's description of the Legal Factors course, which "will begin with a brief review of the different distributive shares in industry, tracing the recipient's legal ability to claim his share back to two principal sources, (1) benefits from the government at the expense of taxpayers or defendants in legal actions [i.e., vertical grants ab initio and horizontal redistributions in case of conflicts between existing rights], [and] (2) contract rights acquired by some form of bargaining," which are themselves traceable back "to his previous possession of rights against others." Hale Papers, folder 83.

36. Oliver Wendell Holmes, "The Path of the Law," 10 *Harvard Law Review* 458 (1897).

37. *Social Control of Business*, 36 (footnote omitted).

38. 8 *American Bar Association Journal* 707 (1922). For similar comments, see Cohen, "Property and Sovereignty," 8; Hobhouse, *Liberalism*, 189; Lester Ward, "Plutocracy and Paternalism," 20 *Forum* 304–309.

39. Reprinted in *Collected Legal Papers*, 181 (1920).

40. See, e.g., "Contracts for the Benefit of Third Persons," 27 *Yale Law Journal* 1008 (1918); "Discharge of Contracts," 22 *Yale Law Journal* 513 (1913); "Quasi-Contractual Obligations," 21 *Yale Law Journal* 533 (1912); *Corbin on Contracts*, chaps. 2–4 (1952). For a good summary of the seditiousness and influence of Corbin's plodding exposition of this essential Realist insight, see Horwitz, *Transformation II*, 49–51.

41. 46 *Yale Law Journal* 52 (1936).

42. "Our Equivocal Constitutional Guaranties," 39 *Columbia Law Review* 587–588 (1939). The argument seems a bit confused as to the "natural" status of Jones's face. Jones's attachment to his face may make inalienability a physical impossibility (but what about Jones's kidney?) and hence a de facto legal right, but it does not guarantee Jones any legal rights of ownership beyond that. It does not, for example, guarantee him a right of privacy in his face, a right to exploit its likeness for commercial purposes, a right to prevent others from doing so, a right to be free from physical abuse, etc. At the extreme of slavery, it guarantees him no legal rights at all, beyond what physical necessity makes it impossible to deprive him of. Perhaps the unexpressed thought underlying Hale's example is that Jones's physical relationship to his face and to his other bodily parts, *unlike* his incorporeal relationship to his car, carries with it a strong, universally shared, intuition as to certain basic legal rights that ought to go along with it.

43. July 17, 1919, reproduced by Hale in his materials for the Legal Factors seminar. For similar sentiments, see remarks of Senator John Sherman in 1870, advocating repeal of a modest federal inheritance tax that had been in effect since 1862: "Direct devise from a father to a son is so natural a disposition of property that it would not seem to be right to tax it." *Cong. Globe*, 41st Cong., 2d Sess., 4708, quoted in Sidney Ratner, *American Taxation: Its History as a Social Force in Democracy*, 128 (1942).

44. Legal Factors materials, p. 610. To the same effect, see "Labor Legislation as an Enlargement of Individual Liberty," 15 *American Labor Legislation Review* 160 (Dec. 1926); "Our Equivocal Constitutional Guaranties," 590. The argument had been anticipated by Mill in part (as to intestacy and incompetency statutes) in *Principles of Political Economy*, bk.

V, chap. I, §2, 797, in a passage that Hale had excerpted in the materials for his seminars on "Economics, Law and Politics" (hereinafter "ELP") and "Social Control in Economic Life" (hereinafter "Social Control").

45. *Principles of Political Economy*, bk. II, chap. II, §4, 226–227; bk. V, chap. I, §2, 797; bk. V, chap. IX, §§4, 889–897.

46. See Ely, *Property and Contract*, 58–62, 136–137; John R. Commons, *The Distribution of Wealth*, 93 [1893] (reprint Augustus M. Kelley, 1963); Clark, *Social Control of Business*, 78–86, noting the "indefinite possible variations in the 'bundle of rights' which constitutes private property," id. at 73; Cohen, "Property and Sovereignty," 21–22. For anticipation of the argument from a surprising source and to a somewhat different political end, see Christopher G. Tiedeman, "What Is Meant by 'Private Property in Land'?" 19 *American Law Review* 878 (1885). Many of the later Realists rightly attributed the widespread recognition of what "a many-sided and elastic thing property is," as J. M. Clark put it in *Social Control of Business*, 97, to Hohfeld's efforts to decompose abstract, seemingly unitary rights and obligations into their functional component parts. See, e.g., James C. Bonbright, 1 *The Valuation of Property*, chap. 5 (1937); John R. Commons, "Law and Economics," 34 *Yale Law Journal* 375–376 (1925); Arthur L. Corbin, "Comment, Taxation of Seats on the Stock Exchange," 31 *Yale Law Journal* 429 (1922); Hamilton and Till, "Property," 12 *Encyclopaedia of the Social Sciences* 529. For a discussion of the Hohfeldian scheme and its significance to the Realists, see chap. 2.

47. "Bargaining, Duress, and Economic Liberty," 43 *Columbia Law Review* 624 (1943).

48. See chap. 4.

49. 9 *American Bar Association Journal* 810 (1923); 10 *American Bar Association Journal* 259 (1924). For a lucid elaboration of the argument, see Paul H. Douglas, "Elasticity of Supply as a Determinant of Distribution," in *Economic Essays in Honor of John Bates Clark*, 101.

50. 10 *American Bar Association Journal* 259. For a typical example of the laissez-faire position, see von Mises's review of Hale's *Freedom Through Law*, which takes as given the existence of a natural price against which to measure "interventionism" by the state. Ludwig von Mises, "Freedom Is Slavery," 3 *The Freeman* 410 (Mar. 9, 1953).

51. Hale, "Economic Theory and the Statesman," 193.

52. John Maurice Clark, "Distribution," 5 *Encyclopaedia of the Social Sciences* 172 (Edwin R. A. Seligman and Alvin Johnson, eds., 1934).

53. See Hale's letter to Harry Gunnison Brown, Aug. 3, 1921, Hale Papers, folder 5; Hale's unpublished review of Carver, *Essays in Social Justice*, pt. VI, pp. 39–40, Hale Papers, folder 87.

54. See Hale's unpublished review of Carver, *Essays in Social Justice*, Hale Papers, folder 87, pt. VI, pp. 39–40.

55. On the last point, most progressive economists argued that strong unions could affect the elasticity of the supply curve of labor, among other means, by altering the costs to workers of temporarily withholding their labor. See Douglas, "Elasticity of Supply as a Determinant of Distribution," 98–102, for an extremely good discussion of the point. Like most of his contemporaries, Hale was particularly interested in the government's role in determining whether there *would* be strong unions, through the limits that the government set on employer and employee bargaining tactics in such decisions as *Hitchman* and *Coppage*. See chap. 2.

56. As Hale and others noted, the initial distribution of income skews demand for goods in the direction of the tastes of those with the greatest purchasing power, in turn leading society to channel resources into satisfying those tastes, thereby affecting both the supply and

the price of all goods. See "Coercion and Distribution," 492–493. For a good, contemporary discussion of the same point, see Maurice Dobb, *Theories of Value and Distribution Since Adam Smith*, 34–35.

57. For further discussion of this point, see chap. 4.

58. See Hale, "Value and Vested Rights," 27 *Columbia Law Review* 523 (1927); Hale, *Valuation and Rate-Making: The Conflicting Theories of the Wisconsin Railroad Commission, 1905–1917* (1918); Commons, *Legal Foundations of Capitalism*, 83–84. For an account of economists' development of the capitalized value analysis, see Bonbright, 1 *Valuation of Property*, 218–227. For further discussion of its significance in connection with public utilities regulation, see chap. 5.

59. The materials for the Social Control, ELP, and Legal Factors courses touch (among other things) on government payments for services and subsidies, government devices facilitating business (currency, banking, mortgage and corporation laws, enforcement of contracts), labor laws, taxation, restriction on foreign trade, government rationing of economic resources and materials, usury laws, rediscount rates, regulation of utilities, tariff laws, antitrust laws, patent and copyright laws, exclusive franchises, government investments in the infrastructure of the economy (e.g., highways) that reduce transportation rates, the government's role in furnishing information to producers (crop reports, Bureau of Standards), and its role in educating persons for skilled positions.

60. Legal Factors materials, pp. 129–134. For the same argument from Hale transposed to contemporary American labor markets, see 9 *American Bar Association Journal* 810; 10 *American Bar Association Journal* 259; "Minimum Wages and the Constitution," 36 *Columbia Law Review* 629 (1936) (all noting that the equilibrium price for labor was the product, among other things, of the government's failure to distribute land to potential employees so that they could work for themselves). It should be noted, in Thomas Carver's belated defense, that the sort of government intervention that Hale was implicitly advocating here was just a variant of the "balancing up" programs for which he had taken Carver so strongly to task. See chap. 2.

61. "Distribution," 172. To Clark's list should probably be added John A. Hobson's *The Economics of Distribution* (1900), as well as the American sociologist Charles Horton Cooley's work on the market as a social system. The latter had a formative influence on Clark as well as on Walton Hamilton. For Clark's tribute to Cooley, see John Maurice Clark, *Economic Institutions and Human Welfare*, 57 (1957).

62. For similar accounts clearly influenced by Hale, see Clark, *Social Control of Business*, 94, and Bonbright, 1 *Valuation of Property*, 46–53.

Hale at least on occasion distinguished between property and services in this regard, arguing that whereas income from property was the fruit of law-made pressure on nonowners to desist from use without the owner's consent, income from services was the fruit of a law-made decision not to interfere with the natural right to threaten to withhold one's own services. See Hale, "Economic Theory and the Statesman," 215–216. See also handwritten notes on "Laissez Faire," Hale Papers, folder 90 (subsequently dated by Hale as written between 1911 and 1914), for an early, explicit version of the argument. His distinction seems to assume that rules against slavery (but not against use of another's property) have a natural status, the boundaries of which are self-defining. As noted earlier, that very Lockean assumption as to the naturalness of every person's "'property' in his own 'person'" seems at best debatable. But given Hale's own skepticism about the moral distinction between government feasance and nonfeasance, nothing of consequence appears to turn on that assumption. Suggesting that the right to withhold services might be "extralegal" in some sense, Hale nonetheless thought it entirely appropriate for the government to intervene to decrease income from services through wage controls or through efforts to increase the supply of labor, and to tax any remaining rent to inframarginal providers. See 8 *American Bar Association Journal* 708 (1922), and unpublished review of Carver's *Essays in Social Justice*, pt. II, pp. 22–24, in Hale Papers, folder 87. Without recourse, however, to the argument that the "right" to withhold labor was in the first instance a gift of the state, one had to justify such intervention on more frankly utilitarian grounds than in the property context, or by arguing that one is no more entitled (as a matter of justice) to unequal "natural" endowments than to unequal endowments bestowed by the state. Hale felt comfortable with both justifications.

63. "Economic Theory and the Statesman," 217. Similar statements can be found throughout Hale's work. See, e.g., Legal Factors materials, pp. 655–666; handwritten notes on "Conventional Contrast of *Artificial* and *Natural* Economies," p. 2, Hale Papers, folder 39: "'Laissez faire' is not such, but really gov[ernmen]tal indifference to [the] effects of artificial coercive restr[ain]ts, partly grounded on gov[ernmen]t itself."

64. "Property" rules describe those legal remedies (e.g., an injunction against any infringement of rights) that protect an owner's right to withhold property entirely, and hence the lesser-included right to extract the maximum the market will bear in any voluntary exchange. "Liability" rules describe those legal remedies (e.g., monetary payments for tort damages) that compensate after the fact for liquidating an owner's property right nonconsensually. For further discussion of the distinction, see Guido Calabresi and A. Douglas Melamed, "Property Rules, Liability Rules and Inalienability: One View of the Cathedral," 85 *Harvard Law Review* 1089 (1972); Frank I. Michelman, "Pollution as a Tort: A Non-Accidental Perspective on Calabresi's *Costs*," 80 *Yale Law Journal* 647 (1971).

65. "Value to the Taker in Condemnation Cases," 31 *Columbia Law Review* 1 (1931). Hale's analysis in the article was incorporated in the first volume of Bonbright's *Valuation of Property*, 422–426, and Lewis Orgel's definitive treatise on *Valuation Under the Law of Eminent Domain*, 351–407 (James C. Bonbright, ed., 2d ed. 1953), both of which were produced as part of a larger study on valuation overseen by Bonbright, and in which Hale participated. See also Legal Factors materials, pp. 112–114, *Valuation and Rate-Making*, 83 and "Bargaining, Duress, and Economic Liberty," 611 n.16, for different versions of the same argument.

66. Assuming that the property does not have unique value to the owner, the "reproduction cost" would equal the market price at which like property could be purchased. When the property is unique (the traditional assumption as to land) and nonreproducible, Hale's analysis assumes that the owner is entitled to be paid the full intrinsic value. Thus, if the closest comparable parcels of land sell for $100,000 but this particular owner would demand at least $120,000, the owner gets $120,000. In recent practice, however, for evidentiary if no other reasons, courts in eminent domain cases have tended to value the property at the market value of the nearest comparable property—in this example, $100,000. See Richard A. Epstein, "Forward: Unconstitutional Conditions, State Power, and the Limits of Consent," 102 *Harvard Law Review* 5, 62 n.167 (1988). The effect of that shift is simply to deprive the owner of another valuable right bestowed by a property (as opposed to liability) rule of damages, in addition to the right to hold up the government as would-be buyer for its idiosyncratic value: the right to protect the idiosyncratic value to the owner himself. Id. at 62–63. That is not the end of the matter, however. As Hale noted, when the market value is derived from actual sales of like property, the market price may have been inflated by

speculators' anticipation that the taker would want that piece of like property, thereby incorporating the idiosyncratic value to the taker. The court facing such a situation is thus faced with a further decision: whether to deprive the owner of the right to extract that portion of third-party market value reflecting the *erroneous* expectation that idiosyncratic value to the taker would be protected. "Value to the Taker," 2–3. Hale's purpose, one takes it, in raising this further, slightly tortured, twist was not to resolve the theoretical complications but to suggest that they could be multiplied endlessly.

67. Legal Factors materials, pp. 112–113. To the same effect, see Hale, "Value to the Taker," 12–24; *Valuation and Rate-Making*, 83. For an early recognition by the courts that valuations in eminent domain cases excluded the "strategic value" to the taker, see Holmes's decisions in McGovern v. City of New York, 229 U.S. 363, 372 (1913), and Boston Chamber of Commerce v. City of Boston, 217 U.S. 189, 194–195 (1910), both of which are cited in Hale, "Bargaining, Duress, and Economic Liberty," 611 n.16; and United States v. Boston, Cape Cod & N.Y. Canal Co., 271 F. 877, 893 (1st Cir. 1921) and United States v. Chandler-Dunbar Water Power Co., 229 U.S. 53, 79–81 (1913), both of which Hale excerpted in the ELP and Social Control materials.

68. For a succinct statement of this argument, see letter from Hale to Glenn Allen (a former student), June 28, 1954, Hale Papers, folder 71.

69. *Valuation and Rate-Making*, 84.

70. For a discussion of some of the factors Hale considered relevant in resolving it, see Hale, "Value to the Taker," 25–31.

71. 109 Minn. 456, 124 N.W. 221 (1910). For another discussion of *Vincent* by Hale, see "Bargaining, Duress, and Economic Liberty," 610–611. Hale included *Vincent*, along with Ploof v. Putnam, 81 Vt. 471 (1908), and Smith v. Staso Milling Co., 18 F.2d 736 (2d Cir. 1927) (discussed later), in the materials for the 1931 ELP and the 1932 Social Control seminars, drawing out of them substantially the same moral as in the Legal Factors materials. Of torts materials contemporaneous with Hale, two authors discuss *Vincent* and the companion case of Ploof v. Putnam, but neither focuses on the damages issue. See Fowler Vincent Harper, *A Treatise on the Law of Torts*, §60, 140 (1933), and Francis H. Bohlen, "Incomplete Privilege to Inflict Intentional Invasions of Interests of Property and Personality," 39 *Harvard Law Review* 307 (1926).

72. Legal Factors materials, p. 115. For a similar analysis, see "Bargaining, Duress, and Economic Liberty," 611.

73. Legal Factors materials, p. 114.

74. Legal Factors materials, pp. 114–115. For a description of *Vincent* (and the companion case of Ploof v. Putnam) as removing strategic bargaining behavior induced by the provider's monopoly position, see Epstein, "Unconstitutional Conditions," 17–18. As Epstein notes, in cases in which the rescued party has agreed ex ante to pay a monopoly price, under traditional admiralty law, courts reached the same result as in *Vincent* by refusing to enforce the contract ex post, substituting instead their own determination of fair price, taking into account the risk to the salvor and the gain to the rescued ships. Id. at 18–19. That is to say, "[m]odifications of the law of contract [limiting the normal right to have a bargain enforced] parallel those in the law of property." Id. at 18. For Hale's treatment of the salvor cases, see "Bargaining, Duress, and Economic Liberty," 622–623, and following discussion.

75. As Hale noted on a number of occasions, the same issues were raised by nuisance cases like Smith v. Staso Milling Co., a forerunner to the case (more familiar to modern audiences) of Boomer v. Atlantic Cement Co., 26 N.Y.2d 219 (1970). The court in *Smith*

awarded ex post tort damages for pollution, measured by the landowner's actual loss rather than "by what [the landowner] might have exacted from the [polluter] by threatening to cause it to cease operations by enforcing his right to have the pollution stopped." "Bargaining, Duress, and Economic Liberty," 611. The latter amount, as Hale noted, would have included the polluter's sunk costs in its operations. Legal Factors materials, pp. 115–116. For a parallel hypothetical, see May 1951 LF exam, question 1, Hale Papers, folder 32.

76. "Law Making by Unofficial Minorities," 456. As Hale noted, that the current system is the product not of noninterference but rather of blind interference does not make it indefensible. But any such defense would require that blindness works miracles that conscious intervention is incapable of bettering. See handwritten notes on Carver's *Principles*, p. 9, Hale Papers, folder 86.

77. 286 U.S. 73 (1932). The Court found the required state action in the fact that the state had invested the executive committee with the power to proclaim voting qualifications.

78. 295 U.S. 45 (1935). *Grovey* was eventually overruled in Smith v. Allwright, 321 U.S. 649 (1944).

79. Legal Factors materials, p. 514. Hale was referring to the *Civil Rights Cases*, 109 U.S. 3 (1883). For Hale's lengthier, published version of the state action argument, focusing on private racial discrimination, see "Rights Under the Fourteenth and Fifteenth Amendments Against Injuries Inflicted by Private Individuals," 6 *The Lawyers Guild* 627 (1947).

80. Legal Factors materials, p. 512A; "Rights under the Fourteenth and Fifteenth Amendments," 629–630.

81. 334 U.S. 1 (1948). Folder 95 of Hale's papers contains Hale's correspondence on the restrictive covenant cases. Among the items included in the folder are rough drafts of the American Jewish Congress's amicus briefs in Shelley v. Kraemer and McGhee v. Sipes (a companion case to Shelley v. Kraemer consolidated with *Shelley* by the Supreme Court in granting certiorari; a memo from Thurgood Marshall (lead counsel for petitioners in *Shelley*) enclosing a rough draft of the *Sipes* brief with a request for comments; and correspondence with Will Maslow of the American Jewish Congress concerning the enclosed draft brief for petitioners in a post-*Shelley* New York State restrictive covenant case, Dorsey v. Stuyvesant Town Corp., 299 N.Y. 512 (1949). For Hale's analysis of *Shelley* and *Dorsey*, see *Freedom Through Law*, 366–379 (1952).

82. The Court's rationale, as commentators were quick to note, meant that *all* private acts became state action at the moment that courts intervened in the matter in any form. See Comment, "The Impact of Shelley v. Kraemer on the State Action Concept," 44 *California Law Review* 733 (1956), and Herbert Wechsler, "Toward Neutral Principles of Constitutional Law," 73 *Harvard Law Review* 1, 29–31 (1959). The Court disavowed the radical implications of *Shelley* in its subsequent, more cautious formulations of state action doctrine. See Jackson v. Metropolitan Edison Co., 419 U.S. 345 (1974), and Moose Lodge No. 107 v. Irvis, 407 U.S. 163 (1972). Hale, however, no doubt would have gone even further than *Shelley*, holding that *any* private exercise of property rights, whether enforced by self-help in the shadow of the law or enforced through the courts, constituted state action, as it depended on the state's grant of such property rights to begin with. For further discussion of Hale's attempt to contain the implications of such an expansive state action doctrine through other constitutional means, see chap. 6.

83. "Bargaining, Duress, and Economic Liberty," 628. For a similar thought, see Ely, *Property and Contract*, 205. Although conceding that private property was treated as an individual and inviolate right in the eighteenth century, Ely argues that the social side of

property was (necessarily) smuggled in even then through the power of the courts to define the precise scope of property. Id. at 207.

84. "Economics and Jurisprudence," 82, 86.

85. 8 *American Bar Association Journal* 638 (1922).

86. Letter to Ordway Tead, July 10, 1950, Hale Papers, folder 84.

87. Letter to Elliot Cheatham, Nov. 2, 1933, Hale Papers, folder 57, enclosing an outline of a proposed required course (in all likelihood, Legal Factors). Such a discussion, said Hale, requires that lawyers "be acquainted with some of the types of judgments that must be passed—judgments 1st as to the efficacy of particular means to desired ends and as to other possible results of adopting those means, then, second, judgments as to what ends are desirable—value judgments." Id.

88. For a forceful statement of that view from a contemporary (sometime) advocate of natural rights, see Richard A. Epstein, *Takings: Private Property and the Power of Eminent Domain*, 5–6 (1985). For John Marshall's equally strong repudiation of the positive basis of rights and obligations, see Ogden v. Saunders, 25 U.S. 212, 345 (12 Wheat. 135, 219) (1827).

89. *Principles of Political Economy*, bk. II, chap. II, §3, 221. For a survey of late nineteenth-century economics textbooks incorporating a Lockean premise, see James May, "Antitrust in the Formative Era: Political and Economic Theory in Constitutional and Antitrust Analysis, 1880–1918," 50 *Ohio State Law Journal* 270–275 (1989); Kennedy, "The Role of Law in Economic Thought," 955.

90. On the German Historical School, see generally Benjamin B. Seligman, *Main Currents in Modern Economics*, 273–276 (1962). On its influence on late nineteenth-century American economists (many of whom were trained in Germany), see J. Dorfman, "The Role of the German Historical School in American Economic Thought," 15 *American Economic Review* 17–28 (1955); Jurgen Herbst, *The German Historical School in American Scholarship: A Study in the Transfer of Culture* (1965); Dorothy Ross, *The Origins of American Social Science*, 104–113 (1991).

91. *Principles of Political Economy*, bk. II, chap. II, §4, 226–227; bk. V, chap. I, §2, 797; bk. V, chap. IX, §§4, 889–897.

92. Ely, for example, devoted considerable space in the first volume of *Property and Contract* to demonstrating the historically contingent nature of property regimes. His *Studies in the Evolution of Industrial Society* (1906) contains similar observations about the changeability of inheritance regimes to those of Mill, with a more explicit moral. Id. at 279–280. Ely, who as a young man had studied in Germany with Karl Knies, a leading figure in the Historical Movement, subsequently identified Knies as the most important intellectual influence on his own work. He noted in particular the influence of Knies's discussion of property as "an institution undergoing continuous evolution and influencing thereby the distribution of wealth." Remarks by R. T. Ely in "Institutional Economics," 22 *American Economic Review Supplement* 115 (No. 1, 1932) (transcription of a roundtable conference on institutional economics). For Seligman's tour de force effort to locate the history of economic thought in its (contingent) social context, self-consciously as part of the "new movement" of economic historicism, see Edwin R. A. Seligman, "Continuity of Economic Thought," in *Science Economic Discussion*, 1–23 (Richard T. Ely, ed., 1886). The historical attack on property rights can be seen as a part of progressives' broader use of history as an implicit rebuke to any notion of a fixed, or noncontingent, reality, whether idealist or positivist. For a sensitive discussion of that broader trend, see Kloppenberg, *Uncertain Victory*, 107–114. As recent historiography has underscored, however, historicism was not the tool solely of the left.

Figures such as Spencer, Tiedeman, and Cooley employed it to defend existing practice as best adapted to meet current needs. For a thoughtful discussion of this, see Daniel R. Ernst, "The Critical Tradition in the Writing of American Legal History," 102 *Yale Law Journal* 1042–1044 (1993).

93. *Principles of Political Economy,* bk. II, chap. I, §3, 208–209.

94. Id. at bk. I, chap. I, §3, 208.

95. Id. at bk. II, chap. I, §4, 212: "[I]t is giving to those who have; assigning most to those who are already most favoured by nature."

96. See R. H. Tawney, *Equality,* 143–144 (1931); Taussig, 2 *Principles of Economics,* 134–141 (3d ed. 1921).

97. The Legal Factors materials, for example, contain excerpts from Mill, Shaw, Taussig, and others on both points.

98. *Principles of Political Economy,* bk. V, chap. I, §2, 797. Hale quoted the passage in *Freedom Through Law,* 12 n.4, as well as his seminar materials. See also his comments at the 1951 University of Chicago Conference on "The Economics of Mobilization," Hale Papers, folder 59.

99. For contemporary acknowledgments of this central problem with Lockean appropriation, see Nozick, *Anarchy, State, and Utopia* 175–176; Eric Mack, "Distributive Justice and the Tensions of Lockeanism," 1 *Social Philosophy and Policy* 132 (no. 1, 1983); and Richard A. Epstein, "The Utilitarian Foundations of Natural Law," 12 *Harvard Journal of Law and Public Policy* 730–732 (1989). As Epstein notes, it is theoretically unsatisfying and empirically unjustified to dismiss the problem as *de minimis.*

100. Tully, *A Discourse on Property,* 117.

101. *Social Statics,* chap. IX, §4, 136–137 [1850] (D. Appleton & Co., 1890).

102. For Hale's argument that property rights are easily justified only as long as the Lockean proviso holds, see 9 *American Bar Association Journal* 107 (1923). For similar comments, noting that "property is a function of inequality" in the sense of relative scarcity, see Felix S. Cohen, "Transcendental Nonsense and the Functional Approach," 35 *Columbia Law Review* 816 (1935). For Hale's own support of a strict interpretation of the proviso, see handwritten notes on "Laissez Faire," Hale Papers, folder 90 (later dated by Hale between 1911 and 1914), arguing that there is "natural right" to a certain piece of land only (if at all) "where *everyone* has a similar r[igh]t; *not* a r[igh]t to *purchase* land *at owner's terms,* but an [equal]ly valuable right w[ith]out paying for it, over another piece of land." For Hale's argument that the proviso will be met only when "there is equally valuable land open to all, in which cases the ownership of the land itself has no value," see letter to Walter Fisher (Secretary of the Interior), Aug. 15, 1912, Hale Papers, mss. folder, and letter to the Editor of the *New York Globe,* Oct. 23, 1912, Hale Papers, folder 62.

103. Legal Factors materials, pp. 609–610; see also 9 *American Bar Association Journal* 107. In addition, as noted in Thurman W. Van Metre's *Economic History of the United States,* 45–47 (1921), the relevant portions of which Hale excerpted in the Legal Factors materials, ownership of much of the land in the original colonies was dispensed by methods not equally open to all even from the start.

104. Legal Factors materials, p. 610. Hale made substantially the same point in a letter to the Editor of the Harvard Alumni Bulletin, Jan. 16, 1912, using a parable of the gradual usurpation of private property in "some country on Mars." Hale Papers, folder 62.

105. Legal Factors materials, p. 609. For further discussion of scarcity value—in Hale's view, the key problem with any claims to the distributive justice of the market—see chap. 4.

262

Hale's argument has taken on renewed significance as a result of Robert Nozick's recent attempt in *Anarchy, State, and Utopia* to adapt the Lockean proviso to (modern) conditions of scarcity. Nozick argues, in brief, that the spirit of Locke's requirement that "enough, and as good" be left for all others will be satisfied, provided that latecomers are better off in a state where all the available land has already been given to early comers than they would have been in a state where no private property in land has been allowed at all. Such a condition will be met in most civilized societies, Nozick argues, because the institution of private property serves as a (necessary) spur to the community to develop economically to the point at which all members (*including* latecomers) are better off than they would have been without private property. Id., 178–182. Nozick's attempt to rescue the Lockean proviso by relaxing its demands does not, however, answer Hale's essential objection. The fact that *every* member of society (even the propertyless) may gain from a private property regime may be a good utilitarian argument for adopting that regime. But it is hard to see how that fact provides a Lockean (rights-based) argument for allocating any portion of the collective surplus (above the labor actually invested in the land) to the property owners rather than the community at large. Again, a utilitarian argument could supply the missing piece, provided that one believed that the prospect of accruing such future surplus was necessary to motivate the early comers to take and develop the land. But that is just to say that Nozick's argument should be addressed to the children of Bentham (who have, in any event, already indicated general agreement), not those of Locke.

106. On the convergence of opposition to private ownership of land on the left and right, see generally Stefan Collini, *Liberalism and Sociology: L. T. Hobhouse and Political Argument in England 1880–1914*, 102–107 (1979). For the relationship of that opposition to the general rent-theory critique of market distribution, see chap. 4. Of course, private land ownership had its strong defenders, most notably the Liberty and Property Defence League in England, whose propagandistic efforts increased with the growing viability of the land tax movement. See David Abraham, "Liberty and Property: Lord Bramwell and the Political Economy of Liberal Jurisprudence Individualism, Freedom, and Utility," 38 *The American Journal of Legal History* 307–308, 316–319 (1994).

107. See, e.g., Commons, *The Distribution of Wealth*, chap. 4; Ely, *Property and Contract*, 165; Hobhouse, *Liberalism*, 95–98; John Hobson, "A Rich Man's Anarchism," in 12 *Humanitarian* 390–397 (1898), quoted in M. W. Taylor, *Men Versus the State: Herbert Spencer and Late Victorian Individualism*, 248 (1992); Mill, *Principles of Political Economy*, bk. II, chap. II, §6. The classic attack came, of course from Henry George, a matter discussed at greater length in chap. 4.

108. Collini, *Liberalism and Sociology*, 102. For a discussion of the individualist strain in Henry George's land tax proposals, see chap. 4.

109. *Social Statics*, chap. IX, §2, 132, and §10, 143. The solution, Spencer argued, was to turn all land over to a "joint-stock ownership of the public"—i.e., nationalize it—with the difficult matter of compensation to existing landowners to be decided. But, Spencer warned, "In our tender regard for the vested interests of the few, let us not forget that the rights of the many are in abeyance; and must remain so, as long as the earth is monopolized by individuals." Id., chap. IX, §§8–9, 141–142. The importance of Spencer's concession was not lost on the right or the left. See, e.g., Sidney Webb, *Socialism in England*, 80 n.2 (1890). When Spencer realized in the 1880s and 1890s (with the help of broadsides from the Liberty and Property Defence League) that his argument had made him an unwitting ally in a variety of collectivist measures that he abhorred, he recanted, omitting chap. 9 entirely from

263

Social Statics when the book was reprinted in 1892. In its place, he put a qualified defense of private property rights, reiterated the next year in 2 *The Principles of Ethics*, 92, 443–444 (D. Appleton & Co., 1898) (1893). For accounts of Spencer's about-face, see Collini, *Liberalism and Sociology*, 103 and n.109; M. W. Taylor, *Men Versus the State: Herbert Spencer and Late Victorian Individualism*, 246–252 (1992); David Wiltshire, *The Social and Political Thought of Herbert Spencer*, 119–131 (1978). For an interesting response from a legal conservative, attempting to co-opt the Georgian and Spencerian argument by suggesting that our legal system already acknowledged that all land was ultimately owned by the state, see Tiedeman, "What Is Meant By 'Private Property in Land'?" 878.

110. 8 *American Association Bar Journal* 638.

111. Hobson, *The Crisis of Liberalism*, 4 (P. F. Clarke, ed., 1974).

112. Ms. on "Monop[oly] and Privil[ege] Problem," p. 9 (n.d.), Hale Papers, folder 90.

113. See chap. 5.

114. Henry Sidgwick, *The Elements of Politics*, 556 (1891).

115. *Principles of Political Economy*, bk. V, chap. XI, §11, 962–963. Mill went on to state, "To make the concession for a limited time is generally justifiable, on the principle which justifies patents for inventions: but the state should either reserve to itself a reversionary property in such public works, or should retain, and freely exercise, the right of fixing a maximum of fares and charges, and, from time to time, varying that maximum." Id. at 963. See also Mill, "Public Agency or Trading Companies, Memorials on Sanitary Reform . . . including correspondence between Mill . . . and the Metropolitan Sanitary Association" (1851), 19–23. For other descriptions of the charges levied by railroads and public utilities as a tax, see Charles Francis Adams, *Second Annual Report*, Mass. Board of Railroad Commissioners (1871), 38, quoted with approval at Felix Frankfurter, *The Public and Its Government*, 82 (1930); Hartman, *Fair Value*, 68.

116. Hartman, *Fair Value*, 71.

117. Letter from Herbert Knox Smith to Charles P. Howland, 15 April 1910, quoted in Martin J. Sklar, *The Corporate Reconstruction of American Capitalism, 1890–1916: The Market, the Law, and Politics*, 301 (1988). For similar sentiments, see Adams, "Economics and Jurisprudence," 145–147; Commons, *The Distribution of Wealth*, 86–117. The argument was echoed by supporters of the Norris–LaGuardia Act and other prounion measures, who pointed to the state's role in creating the corporate form that allowed employers' centralization of power to justify the state's regulating use of that power under its police powers. See preamble to the Norris–LaGuardia Act and elaborations by Donald Richberg, its chief drafter, both cited in Ernst, "Yellow-Dog Contracts," 272–273.

118. *Liberalism*, 95–96.

119. Hale's position, radical among progressives, did get some unwitting support from Justice Field, dissenting in Munn v. Illinois, 94 U.S. 113, 136 (1876). Field sought to distinguish the price controls upheld in *Munn* (wrongly, in his view) from those imposed under usury laws, by arguing that English common law had prohibited *any* charge for the use of money. Thus, when Parliament intervened to permit the taking of a limited amount of interest, it was conferring a special privilege that it had the right to condition as it saw fit. Id. at 153. Absent some theory as to what baseline rights the state was precluded from prohibiting in the first place (a theory that Field at least did not offer), it is not apparent why the state could not similarly convert limitations on the right to exchange property into conditions on a grant of special privilege by first depriving individuals of the right entirely.

120. For a similar thought, see Mill, *Principles of Political Economy*, bk. II, chap. I, §3, 209: "That all should indeed start on perfectly equal terms is inconsistent with any law of

private property . . ." For Hale's thumbnail sketch of how public recognition of government privilege has progressed from formal monopoly grants, to ownership of property in de facto monopolized industries, to all private property, see handwritten notes beginning "In the past it has been customary to ignore . . ." (n.d., but from internal evidence, evidently written sometime during World War I), Hale Papers, folder 24.

121. Hale, "Labor Legislation as an Enlargement of Individual Freedom," at 157–158.

122. Letter to John Frank, Dec. 8, 1949, Hale Papers, folder 42.

123. *Legal Foundations of Capitalism*, 327.

124. Outline for course on "Government and Industry," pp. 2–3, Hale Papers, folder 39.

125. "Coercion and Distribution," 488.

126. Id.

127. "Economic Theory and the Statesman," 218–219. For comments in a similar vein, see Hale, "Rate Making and the Revision of the Property Concept," 214; Cohen, "Property and Sovereignty," 13.

128. See, e.g., correspondence in Hale Papers, folder 62, including letter to R. S. Hale, Jan. 12, 1912, coming close to arguing that property is theft; and letters to the *New York Globe*, Oct. 23, 1912, and to the editor of Harvard Alumni Bulletin, Jan. 16, 1912, both going over the line. The argument runs through much of Hale's correspondence in 1912. See other letters in Hale Papers, folder 62.

129. Legal Factors materials, p. 611. In the same vein, see also J. M. Clark's hyperbolic paraphrase of the progressive case against natural rights of property (a case for which he had considerable sympathy), ending with "the crowning wrong of the inheritance of the swollen fortunes gained by all the other wrongs, whereby a favored few acquire the hereditary overlordship of great economic principalities, in a country where hereditary overlordships are supposed to be things of the past." *Social Control of Business*, 40.

130. *Principles of the Civil Code*, 1 *The Works of Jeremy Bentham*, 333.

131. *Principles of Political Economy*, bk. II, chap. II, §4, 226–229; bk. V, chap. II, §3, 809.

132. F. Shehab, *Progressive Taxation: A Study in the Development of the Progressive Principle in the British Income Tax*, 198–199, 256–257 (1953).

133. See, e.g., Croly, *The Promise of American Life*, 203–204, 381–385; Richard T. Ely, *Taxation in American States and Cities*, 317–320 (1888); Ratner, *American Taxation*, 235–236; William J. Schultz, *The Taxation of Inheritance*, 98–113, 152–156 (1926); E. R. A. Seligman, "The Theory of Progressive Taxation," 8 *Political Science Quarterly* 220 (1893). For Hale's support of a steep inheritance tax on amounts above whatever "moderate amount" is required as an incentive for "the productive activities of those who leave the property," see Legal Factors materials, pp. 741–742.

134. Ratner, *American Taxation*, 354.

135. Id. at 354–358, 380, 396–399, 419–421, 428–432, 449, 466–471. Fairly modest federal inheritance taxes had been in effect prior to 1916 for brief periods during the 1860s and the Spanish-American War. Id. at 70–77, 128–130, 234–237, 354.

136. "Mellon Declares High Estate Taxes 'Economic Suicide,' " *New York Times*, A1 (Apr. 3, 1924); Andrew W. Mellon, *Taxation: The People's Business*, 123 (1924).

137. Legal Factors materials, p. 611.

138. "Rate Making and the Revision of the Property Concept," 213.

139. Legal Factors materials, p. 611. See also Hale, "Labor Legislation as an Enlargement of Individual Liberty," 160.

140. *Principles of Political Economy*, bk. V, chap. II, §3, 358. See also Spencer, 2 *Principles of Ethics*, 118, arguing that "[c]omplete ownership of anything implies power to make over

the ownership to another." Mill apparently thought better of the statement, omitting it in the third and all later editions of *Principles*, although he left standing similar language in bk. II, chap. II, §4, 226: "[B]equest is one of the attributes of property: the ownership of a thing cannot be looked upon as complete without the power of bestowing it, at death or during life, at the owner's pleasure . . ." Contemporary versions of the argument that ownership of property must necessarily carry with it the right upon death to transfer it to whomever the owner wishes, appear in Nozick's "justice in transfer" rule in *Anarchy, State, and Utopia*, 150–153; Murray N. Rothbard, *For a New Liberty: The Libertarian Manifesto*, 40–41 (rev. ed., 1985); Epstein, *Takings*, 304.

141. *Social Control of Business*, 150.

142. 170 U.S. 283, 300 (1898).

143. "Our Equivocal Constitutional Guaranties," 590.

144. For similar comments, see Ward, "Plutocracy and Paternalism," 304–309.

145. Epstein, *Takings*, 5. For a classic statement of the importance of clear boundaries between rights to the maintenance of a "natural" rights scheme, see F. A. Hayek, 1 *Law, Legislation and Liberty: A New Statement of the Liberal Principles of Justice and Political Economy*, 107 (1973). For similar observations from skeptics as to whether such clear boundaries do exist, see Kennedy, "The Role of Law in Economic Thought," 955; Thomas C. Grey, "The Malthusian Constitution," 41 *Miami Law Review* 21 (1986); Mark Kelman, "Taking *Takings* Seriously: An Essay for Centrists," 74 *California Law Review* 1829 (1986).

146. *Principles of National Economy*, 103–104 (1921). Hale took Carver to task for this simpleminded view of the boundaries of property rights in his review of Carver's book in "Coercion and Distribution," 471–472. Carver, in response, while protesting Hale's ascription of that view to him, simultaneously and apparently unintentionally confirmed its accuracy: "At the bottom of page 471 [in "Coercion and Distribution"] you say, 'Any lawyer could have told [Carver] that the right of property is much more extensive than the mere right to protection against forcible dispossession.' I do not need a lawyer or anybody else to tell me that. I already knew it. But everything else that goes with the right of property consists in definition and limitation. The essentials of the right of property are all contained in the fact of protection against forcible dispossession . . . [P]roperty would exist in its most important and fundamental particulars the moment violence was repressed." Letter from Carver to Hale, Nov. 19, 1923, p. 4, Hale Papers, folder 1.

147. Hale, "Law Making by Unofficial Minorities," 455.

148. Spencer, 2 *The Principles of Ethics*, 46. For a similar formulation, see *Social Statics*, 55 (revised ed. 1892). For the centrality of Spencer's Law of Equal Freedom to individualists in late nineteenth-century England, see Taylor, *Men Versus the State*, 1–4.

149. Typewritten notes (untitled, beginning "The income-distribution-pattern: The laisser faire ideal"), Hale Papers, folder 24.

150. Id.

151. Statements of the minimalist "force and fraud" view of the state's role in enforcing property rights are legion in nineteenth-century writings, from Mill's straightforward presentation of it in *Principles of Political Economy*, bk. II, chap. II, §1, to Thomas Carlyle's derisive characterization of it as amounting to "Anarchy plus the constable." Notable contemporary restatements of the view can be found in Nozick's *Anarchy, State, and Utopia*, Ellen Frankel Paul's *Property Rights and Eminent Domain* (1987), and Epstein's *Takings* and *Simple Rules for a Complex World* (1995). Mill himself expressed skepticism elsewhere in *Principles of Political Economy* as to the self-contained and self-defining nature of the "force and fraud"

exception, noting that state action could be expanded significantly in reliance on those principles. Id. at bk. V, chap. XI, §12.

152. 9 *American Bar Association Journal* 107.

153. Id.

154. "Bargaining, Duress, and Economic Liberty," 603. It is also plausible to imagine a largely self-executing definition of wrongful transgression with respect to physical assaults on one's body, a fact that undoubtedly accounts for the continuing popularity of such examples with advocates of a natural property rights regime. See, e.g., Nozick, *Anarchy, State, and Utopia* 33–35, 171: "My property rights in my knife allow me to leave it where I will, but not in your chest." As Holmes noted, even the most seemingly indefensible physical transgressions against another's person—e.g., slapping another's face merely for the pleasure of it—presents the problem of conflicting liberty interests. Granting the owner the right to prohibit such transgression inhibits the nonowner's liberty, in the form of "[t]he gratification of ill will." But as Holmes also noted, the interests on one side seem so strong, and on the other so weak, as to make the choice to vindicate the owner's right not to be hit seem like no choice at all. See "Privilege, Malice, and Intent," 8 *Harvard Law Review* 1, 5–6 (1894).

155. The classic statement that all injuries to property represent the "joint costs" of noncompatible activities is given in Ronald Coase, "The Problem of Social Cost," 3 *Journal of Law & Economics* 1 (Oct. 1960).

156. Kloppenberg, *Uncertain Victory*, 278. For further discussion of the progressive tropes of interdependence and the resulting problem of "unsocial freedom," see chap. 2.

157. *An Essay on Man*, Epistle IV, 116 (Thomas Tegg, 1815).

158. Legal Factors materials, pp. 44–46.

159. Typewritten notes (beginning "The income-distribution-pattern: The Laisser faire ideal"), Hale Papers, folder 24.

160. 276 U.S. 272 (1928). For later commentaries on the case, see Epstein, *Takings*, 113–114 (conceding that *Miller* presents an extremely difficult case under traditional nuisance law, but arguing that it should have been decided on those grounds nonetheless), and Frank I. Michelman, "Property, Utility and Fairness: Comments on the Ethical Foundations of 'Just Compensation' Law," 80 *Harvard Law Review* 1198–1199 (1967).

161. Miller v. Schoene, 276 U.S. at 279. Hale included the case in the Legal Factors materials. For his endorsement of Stone's argument, see "Mr. Justice Stone and the Constitution," 36 *Columbia Law Review* 368 (1936); handwritten notes (untitled), p. 1, Hale Papers, folder 83; *Freedom Through Law*, 398–399.

162. 276 U.S. at 279.

163. Hale drew heavily on the article, inter alia, in "Prima Facie Torts, Combination, and Non Feasance," 46 *Columbia Law Review* 208–214 (1946), reprinted as chap. 5 of *Freedom Through Law* and in the Legal Factors materials.

164. "Privilege, Malice, and Intent," 5.

165. Id. at 3.

166. Bowen, L. J., in Mogul Steamship Co. v. McGregor, 23 Q.B.D. 598, 613 (1889), cited in Holmes, "Privilege, Malice, and Intent," 3, and Hale, "Prima Facie Torts," 196.

167. "Privilege, Malice, and Intent," 3.

168. Legal Factors, Section II, pp. 25–135 (on the "Economic Significance of Legal Control or Non-control of Private Conduct Harmful to Others"). For J. M. Clark's version of the same argument, see *Social Control of Business*, 93.

169. "Prima Facie Torts," 196; Legal Factors materials, p. 104.

170. "Prima Facie Torts," 196.

171. 236 U.S. 1 (1915).

172. 245 U.S. 229 (1917). The classic Realist critique of *Hitchman* is given in Walter Wheeler Cook, "Privileges of Labor Unions in the Struggle for Life," 27 *Yale Law Journal* 779 (1918). For further discussion of the importance that progressives attached to *Coppage* and *Hitchman,* see chap. 2.

173. "Prima Facie Torts," 198. See also Legal Factors materials, pp. 631–650, including *Coppage,* along with Miller v. Schoene, in a section entitled "The Constitutionality of Legislation Which Deprives Some Persons of Liberty or Property on Behalf of Someone Else's Liberty or Property . . ."

174. "Prima Facie Torts," 200; "Labor Legislation as an Enlargement of Individual Liberty," 159. For the equally scathing attacks by Hale, Holmes, and other progressives on the Court's argument that union boycotts were logically distinguishable from other refusals to deal because the former required an active conspiracy not to deal, see Commons, *Legal Foundations of Capitalism,* 288–297; Hale, Legal Factors materials, p. 96; Holmes, "Privilege, Malice, and Intent," 8–9; Matthew Tobriner, "Equal Protection of the Law," 64 *New Republic* 222 (Oct. 15, 1930).

175. The early twentieth-century literature on the police powers doctrine is extensive, reflecting its political and philosophical importance to progressives. Among the better discussions are Clark, *Social Control of Business,* 171–176; Walter Wheeler Cook, "What Is the Police Power?" 7 *Columbia Law Review* 322 (1907); Edward S. Corwin, "The Basic Doctrine of American Constitutional Law," 12 *Michigan Law Review* 247 (1914); Tugwell, *The Economic Basis of Public Interest,* 4–11 (summarizing various definitions given to the term). As Richard Ely remarked, the "police power[s]" doctrine represented "the peculiarly flexible element in our legal system," and the "possibilities of development" of the doctrine were unlimited. *Studies in the Evolution of Industrial Society,* 417. For a less sanguine recognition of the same potential by conservatives, see Lochner v. New York, 198 U.S. 45, 56 (1905). Ernst Freund, "Police Power" in 2 *Cyclopedia of American Government,* 706–710 (Andrew C. McLaughlin and Albert Bushnell Hart, eds., 1914), and Charles Warren, 3 *The Supreme Court in United States History,* 451–478 (1923), provide a general history of the police powers doctrine.

176. Clark, *Social Control of Business,* 171.

177. Tiedeman, *A Treatise on the Limitations of the Police Power,* viii.

178. Christopher G. Tiedeman, *A Treatise on the Limitations of Police Power in the United States,* vii (1886). Similar sentiments were expressed in Thomas M. Cooley, 2 *A Treatise on the Constitutional Limitations Which Rest Upon the Legislative Power of the States of the American Union,* 1225 (8th ed. 1927), and Justice Waite writing for the majority and Justice Field in dissent in Munn v. Illinois, 94 U.S. at 124–125, 145–148.

179. See Warren, 3 *The Supreme Court,* 466. For an interesting Realist catalog of various government incursions on property rights that were held *not* to be a wrongful confiscation, see Charles Warren, "What Is Confiscation?," 140 *Atlantic Monthly* 246 (1927). Hale heralded Warren's article as a "brilliant and masterly" discussion in "What Is a 'Confiscatory' Rate," 35 *Columbia Law Review* 1047 n.13 (1935).

180. For typical expressions of that principle, see W. Frederick Foster, "The Doctrine of the United States Supreme Court of Property Affected By a Public Interest, and Its Tendencies," 5 *Yale Law Journal* 79 (1895); Ernst Freund, *The Police Power: Public Policy and Constitutional Rights,* 546–547 (1904).

181. Michelman, "Property, Utility and Fairness," 1165.

182. The logical embarrassments of the "benefit" and "harm" distinction have continued to interest contemporary legal scholars. For narrow readings of the police power of the state relying on the harm and benefit distinction, see Paul, *Property Rights and Eminent Domain*, and Epstein, *Takings*. For more skeptical views of the coherence of the distinction, see Michelman, "Property, Utility and Fairness," 1196–1201; Mark Kelman, *A Guide to Critical Legal Studies* (1987); and Kelman, "Taking 'Takings' Seriously," 1839.

183. *Reason and Law*, 186. See also Clark, *Social Control of Business*, 106, noting that the police powers doctrine "represents what the courts will permit the states to do in limiting liberty and altering the rights of private property." For a somewhat more cynical version of the same point, see O. W. Holmes, Book Notice, 6 *American Law Review* 141–142 (1871–1872): "We suppose this phrase [police powers] was invented to cover certain acts of the legislature which are seen to be unconstitutional, but which are believed to be necessary."

184. 19 *The Works of Theodore Roosevelt*, 24.

185. For further discussion of the "police powers" doctrine as applied to rate regulation, see chap. 5.

4. A Rent-Theory World

1. Robert L. Hale, "Bargaining, Duress, and Economic Liberty," 43 *Columbia Law Review* 603 (1943); Hale, "Labor Legislation as an Enlargement of Individual Liberty," 15 *American Labor Legislation Review* 155, 157 (1926). The distinction between property for use and property for exchange (or power) was a commonplace in late nineteenth- and early twentieth-century economic and political discourse, its most notable proponent being Hobhouse. See L. T. Hobhouse, "The Historical Evolution of Property, in Fact and in Idea," in *Property: Its Duties and Rights* (2d ed., 1915), reprinted in Hobhouse, *Sociology and Philosophy*, 83 (1966); Hobhouse, *The Labour Movement*, 95 (3d. ed., 1912). See also John R. Commons, *Legal Foundations of Capitalism*, 10–36 (1924); John Maurice Clark, *Social Control of Business*, 94–100 (2d ed., 1939); 1 Richard T. Ely, *Property and Contract*, 276–288 (1914). The distinction was important as well to those socialists who would have permitted private ownership for use but not for profit by hire. See 2 F. W. Taussig, *Principles of Economics*, chap. 66, §2, at 467–468 (3d ed. rev., 1921). The distinction is an old one; James Kloppenberg traces its origins to Aristotle. See *Uncertain Victory*, 508 n.7 (1986).

2. Hale, "The Constitution and the Price System: Some Reflections on Nebbia v. New York," 34 *Columbia Law Review*, 401–402 (1934). See also Hobhouse, "Historical Evolution of Property," 101–104, which Hale cited to admiringly in "Labor Legislation as an Enlargement of Liberty," 157 n.1, for substantially the same argument; Henry Rottschaefer, "The Field of Governmental Price Control," 35 *Yale Law Journal* 438, 458–460 (1926).

3. The literature on the rise of the regulatory welfare state is voluminous. For good overviews of the American experience, see Sidney Fine, *Laissez Faire and the General-Welfare State* (1956); Calvin Woodard, "Reality and Social Reform: The Transition from Laissez-Faire to the Welfare State," 72 *Yale Law Journal* 286 (1962); Robert L. Rabin, "Federal Regulation in Historical Perspective," 38 *Stanford Law Review*, 1189–1272 (1986). On the rise of the British welfare state, see J. R. Hay, *The Development of the Welfare State in Britain, 1880–1975* (1978); Maurice Bruce, *The Coming of the Welfare State* (1961). For studies focusing on railroad and public utilities regulation, see chap. 5. For recent studies of the judicial response to minimum wage and factory legislation in the 1880s to 1920s, see David P. Currie, "The Constitution in the Supreme Court: 1910–1921," 1985 *Duke Law Journal* 1111, and Herbert Hovenkamp,

269

"The Political Economy of Substantive Due Process," 40 *Stanford Law Review* 379 (1988). Sidney Ratner, *American Taxation*, chaps. 12–13 (1942), provides a good overview of the tax reform movement at the turn of the century.

4. Letter from Professor Henry Rottschaefer of Minnesota Law School to Hale, Oct. 14, 1925, Hale Papers, folder 3.

5. The Court did not clearly differentiate between direct regulation of price and non-price terms of a contract until Adkins v. Children's Hospital, 261 U.S. 525, 553–555 (1923), although one can find numerous suggestions prior to that time that price controls would be subject to much stricter scrutiny than other forms of government regulation. See, e.g., Frisbie v. United States, 157 U.S. 160, 165–166 (1895); Bunting v. Oregon, 243 U.S. 426, 434–435 (1917). See generally Currie, "The Constitution in the Supreme Court," 1129–1131; Roscoe Pound, "Liberty of Contract," 18 Yale Law Journal 454, 485–486 (1910). For other post-*Adkins* decisions singling out direct price regulation for censure, see Wolff Packing Co. v. Court of Industrial Relations, 262 U.S. 522. 544 (1923); Tyson Bros. v. Banton, 273 U.S. 418, 440 (1927); Ribnik v. McBride, 277 U.S. 350, 358 (1928). The claim that the Court in general tolerated nonprice regulations is subject to one important qualification, in the area of labor contracts. Some of the most notorious "freedom of contract" decisions in the first two decades, including the *Lochner*, *Adair*, and *Coppage* decisions, concerned nonprice regulations of labor contracts. As noted in chap. 2, the particular judicial sensitivity to any form of regulation of labor contracts reflects the politically charged nature of the struggle over all labor legislation. As to taxation, the Court put numerous restrictions on the government's authority to single out specific activities for differential taxation. See Hale, *Freedom Through Law*, 271–293 (1952), for a good summary. But with the ratification of the 16th Amendment in 1913, no further serious constitutional challenge was raised to the federal government's right to levy a tax on income.

It is not easy to account for the distinction drawn between price regulation on the one hand, and nonprice regulations or taxation on the other. As Hale noted, as an economic matter the distinction was untenable. Price controls could operate differently from other forms of regulation or taxation in a number of respects (for example, in determining who ultimately bore the government-imposed costs, and in their effect on supply and demand). Those differences were significant to all economists (including Hale) in choosing the optimum form of intervention. But, as Hale noted, the effect on owners in all cases (at least in the first instance) was to reduce profits that they would otherwise have realized in the absence of regulation—in the case of taxation, by raising costs; in the case of regulation of the price and other terms of exchange, by lowering revenues. Hale, "Economic Theory and the Statesman," in *The Trend of Economics*, 191, 209–211 (Rexford G. Tugwell, ed., 1924). A court solicitous of property rights under a due process analysis ought therefore to have been indifferent as between price regulation, nonprice regulation, and taxation, and equally suspicious of all three. Hale was hardly alone in thinking the distinctions incoherent. On the indistinguishability of price and nonprice regulation, see Justice Stone's dissent in Ribnik v. McBride, at 373–374. On the indistinguishability of taxation and other forms of government takings, see Morris R. Cohen, *Reason and Law: Studies in Juristic Philosophy*, 137–138 (1950). The latter point, of course, was made first and most famously by John Marshall in McCollough v. Maryland, 17 U.S. (4 Wheat.) 316, 431 (1819), declaring that "the power to tax [property] involves the power to destroy." Notwithstanding the obvious economic truism of Marshall's dictum, taxation maintained a relatively privileged position in political discourse, resistant to all logical argument. Perhaps the starkest example was Henry George's proposal for a

270

confiscatory "single tax" on land values, which he embraced as an "individualist" alternative to the socialists' proposal for appropriating land, notwithstanding his own acknowledgement that the tax left owners the mere "shell" of ownership and took the "kernel." *Progress and Poverty*, 405 [1891] (Robert Schalkenbach Foundation, 1955). For further discussion of George's argument, see later. Two of the best-known recent libertarian attacks on the welfare state—Robert Nozick's *Anarchy, State, and Utopia* (1974) and Richard Epstein's *Takings: Private Property and the Power of Eminent Domain* (1985)—are both notable, among other things, for embracing the traditional progressive view that taxation should be subject to the same moral and constitutional scrutiny as use and price regulations, departing from progressives only in their conclusions as to whether the three jointly survive that scrutiny.

Courts commonly offered several rationales for distinguishing taxation and nonprice controls from price regulation. None of them (Hale and others argued) was enormously persuasive. First, courts suggested that although all three clearly deprived owners of part of the value of their property, the first two did so merely coincidentally to their intended purpose of raising revenues or preventing harm to others (in both cases, a permissible exercise of the state's police power). See Hale, "Conflicting Judicial Criteria of Utility Rates," 38 *Columbia Law Review* 959, 966–967 (1938); Hale, "Economic Theory and the Statesman," 217–218. But statutes precluding collusion or other monopolistic practices, which were designed to deprive companies of the market power that enabled them to extract monopoly prices, were clearly redistributive in intent. See Hale, *Freedom Through Law*, 416. Only by the most exquisite logic could progressive tax schemes be thought not to be redistributive as well. As Justice Stone noted, dissenting in Tyson v. Banton, 452–453, the singularly harsh treatment given price regulations led to the peculiar result that the Court would sustain any form of regulation *except* direct price regulation as a cure for extortionate prices. Moreover, the argument depended upon the view that redistribution itself was an impermissible goal of government intervention, a view that Hale strenuously resisted.

Second, courts argued that "wages to be paid and received," unlike nonprice terms, go to "the heart of the contract." Adkins v. Children's Hospital, 553–554; see also Tyson v. Banton, 429. That view, as Holmes and Taft suggested in dissent in *Adkins*, would have to be ascribed more to the realm of metaphysics than of economics. Id. at 564, 569–570. Finally, courts argued that price controls, unlike taxation and nonprice regulation, leave the parties with no opportunity to adjust the price term of the bargain to compensate for the costs imposed by regulation. Id. at 554. It is of course true that parties cannot adjust the price term of a contract to compensate for the effects of price regulation, notwithstanding the Court's fifty-year attempt to accomplish just that feat with respect to public utilities rate regulation. See chap. 5. But parties may be in a position to offset price changes with changes in nonprice terms—for example (in the case of minimum wages) by demanding more work per hour or offering fewer nonwage benefits, or (in the case of maximum prices for goods or services) by offering lower quality.

As a historical matter, the relatively harsher treatment accorded rate regulation (at least as compared with taxation) may be explainable, ironically enough, by the fact that courts, although recognizing that taxation would always confiscate property, erroneously believed that it was possible to devise a form of rate regulation that did not. Thus, even though they acknowledged that subjecting taxation to any form of "takings" scrutiny would be futile, the courts labored for some fifty years under the illusion that they could devise some formula for regulating the prices charged by public utilities regulation that would simultaneously reduce rates and preserve the value of the utilities' property. See chap. 5. Walton

Hamilton offered a different but equally unsettling explanation for the Court's inconsistent treatment of rate regulation and taxation, arguing that it may have been the result of Justice Waite's accidental and erroneous transformation of Marshall's dictum ("the power to tax involves the power to destroy") into his own declaration that "the power to regulate is not the power to destroy," Stone v. Farmers' Loan & Trust Co., 116 U.S. 307, 331 (1886), followed by Waite's willingness to let his "more radical colleagues . . . have their way with his rhetoric." "Price—by Way of Litigation," 38 *Columbia Law Review* 1008, 1014 n.12 (1938). Says Hamilton, "[t]he subtlety is that of the Lord Chancellor in W. S. Gilbert's Iolanthe who by inserting a 'not' in a perpetual decree provided the deus ex machina which allowed the action of the play to come to rest. The powers to tax and to regulate rest upon the same constitutional foundations and such a distinction between them has no constitutional warrant." Id.

6. *The Theory of Business Enterprise*, 272 (1904).

7. See chap. 2; Commons, *Legal Foundations of Capitalism*, chap. 4.

8. "Economic Theory and the Statesman," 215.

9. 2 *The Principles of Ethics*, §301 (New York, Appleton, 1893).

10. 2 *The Principles of Sociology*, §568 (New York, Appleton, 1882).

11. "Limits to State Control of Private Business," 1 *Princeton Review* 233, 271 (ser. 4, 1878). For the traditional view of commentators that Locke's labor theory of value is a theory of desert, see also David Miller, "Justice as Property," 22 *Ratio* 1 (1980); Lawrence Becker, *Property Rights*, 43–45 (1977). On the powerful hold of that intuition on the Anglo-American consciousness, see Kenneth Arrow, "Some Ordinalist-Utilitarian Notes on Rawls's Theory of Justice," 70 *Journal of Philosophy* 9 248 (1973); David Ellerman, "On the Labor Theory of Property," 16 *Philosophy Forum*, 293 (1985); Elliot Abramson, "Philosophization Against Taxation: Why Nozick's Challenge Fails," 23 *Arizona Law Review* 753, 759 (1981); Herbert McClosky and John Zaller, *The American Ethos: Public Attitudes Towards Capitalism and Democracy* 226 (1984).

12. John Locke, *Second Treatise of Government*, §31, quoted in slightly different form in Hobhouse, "Historical Evolution of Property," 102. "[W]hatever is beyond this," concluded Locke, "is more than his share, and belongs to others." Id.

13. Locke, *Second Treatise of Government*, §33.

14. Hobhouse, "Historical Evolution of Property," 102. Hobhouse was hardly alone in enlisting Locke as an implicit critic of unlimited property rights in the modern industrial state. James Tully argues that the standard reading of Locke through the early twentieth century was as a proponent of what was at root a *social* theory of property. *A Discourse on Property: John Locke and His Adversaries*, x (1980). Early English and French Socialists had invoked Locke not only (and most obviously) in support of labor's exclusive right to property (see later) but also to argue that such a right should be regulated by need. Id. See Max Beer, *A History of British Socialism*, 101–113 (one vol. ed., 1948); C. H. Driver, "John Locke," in *The Social and Political Ideas of Some English Thinkers of the Augustan Age: A.D. 1650–1750)*, 69, 91 (F. J. C. Hearnshaw, ed., Barnes & Noble, 1950). Progressive political theorists likewise read his work—once translated to modern conditions—as a tacit endorsement of a radical redistribution of wealth along the lines envisioned in the modern welfare state. See, e.g., John R. Commons, *Myself*, 131 [1934] (University of Wisconsin Press, 1963). For Walton Hamilton's attack on what he took to be the wholesale and anachronistic appropriation of Locke's precapitalist defense of property by Smith, Hume, Blackstone, and (in Hamilton's time) J. B. Clark to defend the existing distribution of wealth in their own very different economic worlds, see "Property—According to Locke," 41 Yale Law Journal 864, 870 (1932).

Tully dates the start of the modern reinterpretation of Locke as a champion of a strong regime of private property rights to J. L. Stocks' 1933 article, "Locke's Contribution to Political Theory," in *John Locke: Tercentenary Address* (J. L. Stocks and Gilbert Ryle, eds., 1933). Tully, *A Discourse on Property*, 177 n.6. That reinterpretation culminated in C. B. MacPherson's *The Political Theory of Possessive Individualism: Hobbes to Locke*, 218 (1962). Of the many recent efforts to resurrect Locke as a strong *opponent* of unlimited private property rights, Tully's own book is among the best. See id. at 99–100, 161–170. Although in some respects Tully goes even further than Hobhouse in reading into Locke a social view of property, his analysis generally supports Hobhouse's summary reading given earlier. See also Thomas M. Scanlon, "Liberty, Contract, and Contribution," in *Markets and Morals*, 43, 49–50 (Gerald Dworkin et al., eds., 1977).

15. Hobhouse, "Historical Evolution of Property," 102–103. See also John Stuart Mill, *Principles of Political Economy*, bk. II, chap. 2, §3, at 209 [1848] (1929) (arguing that "proportion between remuneration and exertion" is the "equitable principle . . . on which in every vindication of [the institution of property] that will bear the light it is assumed to be grounded").

16. Hale, "Political and Economic Review," 10 *American Bar Association Journal* 259 (1924); Hale, "Political and Economic Review," 9 *American Bar Association Journal*, 810–811 (1923). For Holmes's similar argument, see Adkins v. Children's Hospital, 570 (dissenting). For Hale's parallel argument in the public utilities context, debunking the suggestion that a fair price could be deduced from what services "are reasonably worth to consumers," see chap. 5.

17. It is frequently ambiguous whether progressives' arguments for protecting incentive incomes rested on utilitarian or rights-based considerations, and Hale was no exception in this regard. See chap. 3, n.2; Legal Factors materials, pp. 592–593. For typical statements looking in both directions, see L. T. Hobhouse, *Liberalism and Other Writings*, 92 (1994); J. A. Hobson, *The Conditions of Industrial Peace*, 63 (1927).

18. For purposes of the entire discussion that follows, costs should be understood to include only out-of-pocket costs, not opportunity costs (meaning the value of the forgone opportunity to sell one's goods to alternative buyers). As Hale noted, it is a "mere truism" that where there are multiple buyers at the same price, the market return to all producers (inframarginal as well as marginal) conforms to opportunity cost, and hence begs the question of whether such a return is justified. Notes on the "Conventional contrast of *artificial* and *natural* economies," p. 2 (under heading "Bargaining incomes are not in 'natural' conformity to costs"), Hale Papers, folder 39.

19. Hale, *Freedom Through Law*, 438; Draft review of H. G. Brown's *The Theory of Earned and Unearned Incomes*, Hale Papers, folder 58.

20. *Science of Wealth*, 82 (1911). Hobson used the term "unproductive" surplus to isolate that portion of the market return, in excess of minimal payments demanded to cover current costs, that was not reinvested in future productive growth. For other statements to the effect that the real controversy reduced to the distribution of the "unproductive" surplus from trade, see Hobson, *The Economics of Distribution*, 16 (1900); Hobhouse, *Liberalism and Other Writings*, 92–96; Charles W. MacFarlane, *Value and Distribution*, pt. I, chap. 5 (1898).

21. "Profit," 12 *Encyclopaedia of the Social Sciences* 480 (1934), reprinted in Fellner and Haley, *Readings in the Theory of Income Distribution*, 533, 546 (1946).

22. This of course assumes that one did not subscribe to Hale's expansive view of state-bestowed privilege as including all property rights. See chap. 3.

23. *The Wealth of Nations*, bk. I, chap. 7, chap. 10, pt. 2 [1776] (Modern Library ed., Random House, 1965).

24. *Principles of Political Economy*, bk. I, chap. 9, §3, at 143–144 (New ed., Longmans, Green and Co., 1929) (9th ed., 1885).

25. Fine, *Laissez Faire and the General-Welfare State*, 335–340; Stefan Collini, *Liberalism and Sociology: L. T. Hobhouse and Political Argument in England, 1880–1914*, 101–102 (1979). For further discussion of the broad support for regulating public utilities, see chap. 5.

26. See Fine, *Laissez Faire and the General-Welfare State*, 338; Martin Sklar, *The Corporate Reconstruction of American Capitalism, 1890–1916*, 34–38 (1988).

27. For a discussion of *Vincent*, see chap. 3.

28. For Hale's correspondence with Carver on this point, see chap. 2. For one of Hale's many uses of the drowning man hypothetical, see Legal Factors materials, p. 593.

29. Hale, "Bargaining, Duress, and Economic Liberty," 624. See also Robert L. Hale, "Commissions, Rates, and Policies," 53 *Harvard Law Review* 1103, 1130 (1940).

30. Hale, "Bargaining, Duress, and Economic Liberty," 624. For a contemporary acknowledgment that the common law solution in duress and necessity cases in effect imposes ad hoc judicial controls on monopoly profits, see Richard Epstein, Foreword, "Unconstitutional Conditions, State Power, and the Limits of Consent" 102 *Harvard Law Review* 4, 17–19 (1988).

31. Hale, "Bargaining, Duress, and Economic Liberty," 624.

32. "Economic Duress and the Fair Exchange in French and German Law" (pt. 2), 12 *Tulane Law Review* 42, 57 (1937). For Hale's parallel comments on the tension in public utilities rate regulation between limiting earnings to what are "generally acknowledged as rightfully belonging to the owners of [unregulated] property" and striving for some more fundamental notion of fairness, see *Valuation and Rate-Making*, chap. 7, §3. See also discussion in chap. 5. For his related comments on setting "reasonable" wages in labor arbitrations, see "Law Making by Unofficial Minorities," 20 *Columbia Law Review* 451, 455 (1920).

33. See letter from Hale to Carver, Nov. 22, 1923, p. 3: "[T]here is no social ground for letting him be enriched for doing a trivial act (of trivial sacrifice, I mean)." Hale Papers, folder 1.

34. "Economic Theory and the Statesman," 191.

35. On the convergence of the two traditions in nineteenth-century thought, see Richard Schlatter, *Private Property: The History of an Idea*, 249 (1951).

36. See letter from Hale to Donald Richberg, Apr. 12, 1922, Hale Papers, folder 6; "Economic Theory and the Statesman," 200–201.

37. "Economic Theory and the Statesman," 201; Hale, "Political and Economic Review," 9 *American Bar Association Journal* 39 (1923); letter from Hale to Donald Richberg, Apr. 12, 1922, Hale Papers, folder 6.

38. 1 *The Valuation of Property*, 409 (1937).

39. *Wealth of Nations*, bk. I, chaps. 6 and 7. For a summary of Smith's "cost of production" theory, see Mark Blaug, *Economic Theory in Retrospect*, 38–39 (4th ed. 1985); Maurice Dobb, *Theories of Value and Distribution Since Adam Smith*, 43–47 (1973).

40. J. E. Cairnes, writing in 1874 to indicate his own dissent from Mill's account, noted that it was, as far as Cairnes knew, "acquiesced in, either expressly or implicitly," by virtually all economists in England and elsewhere. *Some Leading Principles of Political Economy, Newly Expounded*, pt. 1, chap. 3, §2, at 46, §3, at 48 (New York, Harper, 1874).

There is language in both Ricardo's and Smith's accounts suggesting a (one-factor) labor theory of value. That ambiguity, as Eugen Böhm-Bawerk noted, resulted in both accounts' being pressed into service on both sides of the controversy that erupted between Marxian and non-Marxian classicists as to whether all value was created by labor. See *Capital and*

Interest, bk. VI, chap. 3, at 375–380 (London, MacMillan, 1890). Dispute about Ricardo's intent has continued into the twentieth century, with the revival of a pure labor theory interpretation spearheaded by Sraffa's famous Introduction in the 1950s to his edition of 1 *The Works and Correspondence of David Ricardo,* xiii–lxii (1951). Although further exploration of Sraffa's argument is outside the scope of this book, those who are interested can find an able (and sympathetic) exposition of it by his collaborator, Maurice Dobb, in *Theories of Value and Distribution,* chaps. 3 and 9 and passim. For the more traditional reading of Ricardo as proposing a two-factor (capital and labor) cost of production model, see George J. Stigler, "Ricardo and the 93 Per Cent Labor Theory of Value," reprinted in Stigler, *Essays in the History of Economics,* 326 (1965); Stigler, "The Ricardian Theory of Value and Distribution," reprinted in Stigler, *Essays in the History of Economics,* 156, 188–189. Stigler argues that Ricardo's was not an analytic theory of labor value, but merely an empirical one—that is, an empirical prediction that fluctuations in interest rates would have little effect on the relative prices of labor and fixed-capital intensive goods as compared with fluctuations in labor rates. Stigler, "Ricardo and the 93 Per Cent Labor Theory of Value," 333. For agreement with Stigler, see Blaug, *Economic Theory in Retrospect,* 92–96, 114–115. See also Alfred Marshall, *Principles of Economics,* app. I (8th ed. 1930).

41. Smith, *Wealth of Nations,* bk. I, chap. 7. Notwithstanding Smith's assertion that the long-run prices of final products were solely supply-determined, his analysis of equilibrium prices, like that of all the classical economists, rests on an implicit theory of demand that makes it possible (without doing anachronistic violence to the argument) to restate classical value theory in neoclassical terms.

42. Smith never had a complete theory of value, and had no theory of distribution at all. Ricardo came closest to providing the latter in his analysis of land rents, in a fashion that pointed the way to the neoclassical (marginalist) solution to an integrated value theory (price of final goods) and distribution theory (price of factors of production). See Blaug, *Economic Theory in Retrospect,* 298–299; Dobb, *Theories of Value and Distribution,* 66–67.

43. Cairnes, *Political Economy,* pt. I, chap. 3, §3.

44. For the latter, readers should consult Blaug, *Economic Theory in Retrospect;* Dobb, *Theories of Value and Distribution;* Joseph A. Schumpeter, *History of Economic Analysis* (1954); Stigler, *Essays in the History of Economics;* and George J. Stigler, *Production and Distribution Theories* (1941).

45. For Smith's embrace of Malthusianism, see *Wealth of Nations,* bk. I, chap. 8. For Ricardo's, see *Principles of Political Economy and Taxation,* chap. 5, especially at 45–46 and 52–53, chap. 32 *passim* [1821] (Irwin, 1963). Mill's view is (characteristically) somewhat more ambiguous. He purports to embrace Malthusianism as an indisputable truth. At the same time, he injects a note of empirical skepticism, noting that in the forty years preceding 1862 (the year of the 5th edition of Mill's *Principles*), the population of England had decreased while the standard of living and employment steadily increased, and he indicates his faith that education, culture, and an acquired taste for a higher standard of living can teach self-restraint in reproduction. See *Principles of Political Economy,* bk. I, chap. 10, §§2–3, and bk. II, chap. 10.

46. Subsistence wage was defined as that wage necessary to keep population stationary—that is, the wage rate below which workers have no incentive to reproduce. Blaug, *Economic Theory in Retrospect,* 90, 117; Ricardo, *Principles of Political Economy,* chap. 5, at 45.

47. See Smith, *Wealth of Nations,* bk. I, chap. 8, at 68–71; Ricardo, *Principles of Political Economy,* chap. 5, at 46–47.

48. Ricardo, *Principles of Political Economy*, chap. 5, at 47; Stigler, "Ricardian Theory of Value," 164; Schumpeter, *History of Economic Analysis*, 664–665.

49. *Wealth of Nations*, bk. I, chap. 10, pt. I. For Hale's critical discussion of Smith's theory of "equal net advantages," see Legal Factors materials, p. 594. See also Dobb, *Theories of Value and Distribution*, 52–53; Blaug, *Economic Theory in Retrospect*, 46–49. For Ricardo's endorsement of Smith's argument, see *Principles of Political Economy*, chap. 1, §2.

50. Hale's paraphrase, in the Legal Factors materials, p. 594.

51. *The Labour Movement*, 25–31. For a similar analogy from Marshall, arguing that the physical "wear-and-tear" on a miner, as much as on machinery, must be deducted from income in calculating net earnings, see *Principles of Economics*, bk. VI, chap. 5, §6.

52. See later discussion.

53. For the progressive attack on treating the psychic disutility of labor as a cost, see later. For an attack on risk as a true cost of labor, see Herbert Joseph Davenport, *Value and Distribution*, 98–106 (1908).

54. By "Lockean justification," again I do not mean to imply a justification that Locke himself would have accepted, but rather one that seems consonant with the premises of the Lockean theory of property rights. As a historical matter, Locke thought interest defensible, but on grounds that are impossible to square with those premises. In his tract on the origin of loan interest, entitled "Some Considerations of the Consequences of lowering the Interest and raising the Value of Money" (1691), Locke begins with the assertion that "[m]oney is a barren thing, and produces nothing; but by compact transfers that profit, that was the reward of one man's labour, into another man's pocket," in the form of interest. Notwithstanding that description, Locke concludes that interest is justified on the ground that money, when coupled with the industry of the borrower, will produce a return greater than the interest owed on it, just as land "through the labor of the tenant" is able to produce more fruit than the amount of its rent. Thus, Locke concludes, "[b]orrowing money upon use is not only, by the necessity of affairs and the constitution of human society, unavoidable to some men; but to receive profit from the loan of money is as equitable and lawful as receiving rent for land, and more tolerable to the borrower [as it usually leaves him with a greater proportion of profits after payment], notwithstanding the opinion of some over-scrupulous men." Id. at 37, quoted in Böhm-Bawerk, *Capital and Interest*, 45. As Böhm-Bawerk notes, the argument is not a happy one. Locke's assertion that money is productive (at least when combined with the labor of the borrower) may explain the demand for borrowed funds. If one adds a theory of scarcity of supply, it may explain their price as well. But it hardly explains why it is "equitable" in the usual Lockean sense for the lender to retain that price. Locke's own assertion that the payment of interest represents the diversion to capital of a reward that is justly labor's, in return for services that themselves produced nothing, surely suggests that it is not. As Böhm-Bawerk notes, the analogy to land rents seems apt, but only if it leads to the conclusion that neither, not both, is justified under a Lockean regime. Id. at 46.

55. Smith and Mill identified "profit" as including three distinct payments: the wages of management, compensation for risk-bearing, and interest. Smith, *Wealth of Nations*, bk. I, chap. 9, at 97; Mill, *Principles of Political Economy*, bk. III, chap. 23, §1. Under Mill's considerable influence, that definition became standard until the early twentieth century. Schumpeter, *History of Economic Analysis*, 646. But both Smith and Mill treated the wages of management as merely a species of wages, regulated by the general principles of wage theory. As for compensation paid for risk-bearing, Smith treated it in effect as a profit on

a separate insurance business. While assuming it would have to be sufficient to induce those bearing the risk to undertake it, *Wealth of Nations*, bk. I, chap. 9, at 97, Smith offered no theory of "cost" to the capitalist as insurer that would explain (in strictly Lockean terms) his right to the payment. That left interest, which Smith estimated to account for about 50 percent of the total "profit" (including in the denominator, for these purposes, the wages of management). Id. Other classical economists limited the definition of "profits" from the start simply to interest. Blaug, *Economic Theory in Retrospect*, 94. Thus, for all practical purposes, inquiry into the Lockean justification for profits centered on interest.

56. Schumpeter, *History of Economic Analysis*, 646–647.

57. Smith had little to say on the subject of interest rates, beyond the general observation that the natural price of capital, like that of labor, land, and final goods, would be determined by the conditions of supply and demand. Dobb, *Theories of Value and Distribution*, 44. Blaug notes that Ricardo never thought about whether the "waiting" for which interest is paid "is a factor of production that requires a minimum rate of reward to be forthcoming" (on a real cost basis, presumably—clearly a minimum rate of reward would be required on an opportunity cost basis, although it is not clear that Ricardo thought about that either). *Economic Theory in Retrospect*, 93. At the same time, there are comments throughout both *Wealth of Nations* and Ricardo's *Principles* that seem to provide, on the one hand, hints of Senior's "abstinence" theory, and on the other, support for the view that all value is created by labor. The latter view contains more than a hint of Marxist exploitation theory, a point not lost on subsequent readers of Smith and Ricardo. As Böhm-Bawerk noted, "Adam Smith and Ricardo may be regarded as the involuntary godfathers of the Exploitation theory." *Capital and Interest*, 269, 316. For invocations of Smith and Ricardo by subsequent exploitation theorists, see comments throughout id., especially bk. VI.

58. For an excellent summary of the development of supply-side explanations of interest beginning with Senior, see Blaug, *Economic Theory in Retrospect*, 193–195. More detailed accounts of Senior's and Mill's theories can be found in Dobb, *Theories of Value and Distribution*, 104–105, 129–130; Schumpeter, *History of Economic Analysis*, 637–640 (Senior). Böhm-Bawerk, *Capital and Interest*, bk. IV, provides a lively if somewhat partisan account of the development of "Abstinence" theory, including a brief account of the unsatisfactory attempts prior to Senior to offer a justification for interest. Id. at 269–270.

59. *Outlines of the Science of Political Economy*, 185 (George Allen & Unwin, 1938) (6th ed. 1872).

60. Id. at 59. On the development of abstinence theory as an extension of the labor theory of value, see Herbert Joseph Davenport, *The Economics of Enterprise*, 370 n.1 [1913] (1929).

61. Blaug, *Economic Theory in Retrospect*, 193.

62. See *Principles of Political Economy*, bk. II, chap. 2, §1; Id., bk. II, chap. 15, §1, at 405, arguing that "the profits of the capitalist are properly, according to Mr. Senior's well-chosen expression, the remuneration of abstinence," and that (contrary to frequent assumptions) laborers therefore do not have a right to the "whole produce" of their labor; Id., bk. II, chap. 15, §2, arguing that the remuneration required will depend "on the comparative value placed, in the given society, upon the present and the future," which amount will differ widely in different societies. See also id., bk. III, chap. 4, §4.

63. "The revenue arising from a dock, or a wharf, or a canal, is profit in the hands of the *original constructor*. It is the reward of *his* abstinence in having employed capital for the purposes of production instead of for those of enjoyment. But in the hands of his heir it has all the attributes of rent. It is to him the gift of fortune, not the result of a sacrifice." *Outlines of the Science of Political Economy*, 129.

64. *Principles of Political Economy*, bk. II, chap. 2, §1. Although it is not always clear with Mill, here at least he seems to be proceeding as a Lockean and not as a utilitarian. His entire discussion of abstinence focuses on how it fits with an express Lockean justification for property.

65. Id., bk. IV, chap. 4, §3.

66. For the problem of inframarginal savers' surplus implied by Mill's analysis, see later.

67. See, e.g., Edwin Cannan, *A History of the Theories of Production and Distribution in English Political Economy from 1776 to 1848*, 197, 214 (2d ed. 1903).

68. For a survey of early exploitation theories emerging contemporaneously with the development and popularization of Senior's thesis, see Böhm-Bawerk, *Capital and Interest*, bk. VI, chap. 1, at 317–325. On the connection between the two, see id., bk. IV, chap. 2, at 286: "Senior's Abstinence theory has obtained great popularity among those economists who are favourably disposed to interest. It seems to me, however, that this popularity has been due, not so much to its superiority as a theory, as that it came in the nick of time to support interest against the severe attacks that had been made on it. I draw this inference from the peculiar circumstance that the vast majority of its later advocates do not profess it exclusively, but only add elements of the Abstinence theory in an eclectic way to other theories favourable to interest." For similar comments, see Hamilton, "Property—According to Locke," 870.

69. For purposes of this discussion, two things should be kept in mind. First, classical rent theory concerned itself solely with rental payments made for the use of undeveloped land-payments, as Ricardo put it, for "the use of the original and indestructible powers of the soil." It disregarded any payments made in the form of wages or interest to the landlord for labor or capital invested in clearing the land or putting in improvements. Ricardo, *Principles of Political Economy*, chap. 2, at 29; Smith, *Wealth of Nations*, bk. I, chap. 11. As Stigler notes, although Ricardo set this requirement, he frequently ignored it, casually equating rent with the total payments to landlords. "Ricardian Theory of Value," 184. But as an analytic matter, Ricardo's arguments about the source and nature of rent, explicated later, make sense only with regard to that portion of the payments that he carefully isolated in theory, payments for the use of undeveloped land. Second, classical rent theory assumed that the landlord had acquired the land at no cost to himself. Were that not the case, the same analysis would hold but would apply only to the portion of rents that reflected the appreciation of the property over its original cost. The remaining rents, which would have been capitalized in the purchase price, would simply represent a form of interest on fixed capital.

70. On rent as pure surplus to unproductive landlords, see *Wealth of Nations*, bk. I, chap. 6, at 49; Id., bk. II, chap. 5, at 345. For Smith's belief that the amount of rent was price-determined, see id., bk. I, chap. 11, pt. I, at 146 ("High or low wages and profit, are the causes of high or low price; high or low rent is the effect of it").

71. On Smith's view that rents are price-determining, see id., bk. I, chap. 11, at 152. The reconciliation, of course, lies in the fact that rents reflected a real cost to farmers but only an opportunity cost to landlords.

72. For fine overviews of the development of the law of diminishing returns and its relationship to Ricardian rent theory (from which the following description has borrowed liberally), see Blaug, *Economic Theory in Retrospect*, 77–83; Stigler, "Ricardian Theory of Value," 173–197; Daniel H. Buchanan, "The Historical Approach to Rent and Price Theory," in *Readings in the Theory of Income Distribution*, 599, 613; Dobb, *Theories of Value and Distribution*, chap. 3.

73. As Daniel Buchanan noted, technically speaking "[i]t is only when no-rent land is in use that there is an effective extensive margin. Otherwise we have merely another case of the intensive margin." "Historical Approach to Rent," 631 n.66.

74. Ricardo, *Principles of Political Economy*, chap. 2, at 32–33.

75. *Principles of Economics*, bk. VI, chap. 9, §5, at 636 and n.1.

76. Ricardo, *Principles of Political Economy*, chap. 2, at 34–36, chap. 17, at 142.

77. Id., chap. 2, at 34.

78. *The Application of Capital to Land* (1815), reprinted in *A Reprint of Economic Tracts*, 39 (Jacob H. Hollander, ed., 1903).

79. See Ricardo, *Principles of Political Economy*, chap. 2, at 34.

80. For Ricardo's view that rents were pure exploitation of "one class . . . at the expense of another," see id., chap. 2, at 34–35 n.1. Although Smith shared the view that landlords had no Lockean entitlement to rents, he stopped short of condemning land rents outright. David M. Ricci, "Fabian Socialism: A Theory of Rent as Exploitation," 9 *Journal of British Studies* 105, 118 n.52 (1969); Dobb, *Theories of Value and Distribution*, 53. Mill was by far the most vociferous of the three in attacking private ownership of any land rents not directly attributable to the landlord's active improvements to the land. See discussion later.

81. On the belief that only agricultural lands and not urban lands generated rents, see Buchanan, "Historical Approach to Rent," 618–619. On the belief that manufacturing faced constant returns to scale, see West, *Application of Capital to Land*, 12; Ricardo, *Principles of Political Economy*, chap. 17, at 142. In addition to (unnecessarily) limiting the applicability of rent theory in *distribution* theory, the Ricardians' belief in a sharp split between nonaugmentable land and all other infinitely elastic inputs resulted in two theories of *value*. For products produced with labor and capital alone, prices (value) were assumed to derive solely from conditions of supply (costs). For agricultural products, prices were assumed to vary with the scale of output and hence demand. Blaug, *Economic Theory in Retrospect*, 298.

82. On the history of the Corn Laws, see C. R. Fay, *The Corn Laws and Social England* (1932). For a good summary of the influence of the Corn Law controversy of 1813–1815 on West's, Malthus's, and Ricardo's versions of rent theory, see Buchanan, "Historical Approach to Rent," 613–624.

83. "Economic Theory and the Statesman," 191.

84. For late nineteenth-century versions of the "harmonious, just world" to result from free competition, see James May, "Antitrust in the Formative Era: Political and Economic Theory in Constitutional and Antitrust Analysis, 1880–1918," 50 *Ohio State Law Review* 257, 271–275. For Hobhouse's paraphrase of the classical vision, see *Liberalism and Other Writings*, 27–29. The preceding discussion deals only with the second claim—that the free market will achieve distributive justice. For the first claim—that the free market tends to optimize the allocation of resources—see Blaug, *Economic Theory in Retrospect*, 61 (on Smith); James Mill, *Elements of Political Economy*, 125–126 [3d ed. 1844] (Kelley, 1963).

85. See, e.g.. John Bates Clark, *Capital and Its Earnings*, 34 and n.1 [1888] (Garland, 1988).

86. See George J. Stigler, "Bernard Shaw, Sidney Webb, and the Theory of Fabian Socialism," 103 *Proceedings of the American Philosophical Society* (1959), reprinted in Stigler, *Essays in the History of Economics*, 268, 275–276. On the decline of agricultural land rents in England, see Robert J. Thompson, "An Inquiry into the Rent of Agricultural Land in England and Wales During the Nineteenth Century," 70 *Journal of the Royal Statistical Society*, 587 (1907), cited in Stigler, "Bernard Shaw, Sidney Webb," 275.

87. The argument that site values were a social and not an individual creation was a frequent fixture in progressive writings throughout the late nineteenth century and the

early twentieth century. For the Fabian version of the argument, see Sidney Webb, Fabian Tract No. 30, *The Unearned Increment* (1891) and Sidney Webb, Fabian Tract No. 7, *Capital and Land* (1888). For the New Liberals' version of the argument, see Hobhouse, *Democracy and Reaction*, 232–233 (2d ed., 1909); Hobhouse, *Liberalism and Other Writings*, 46–47 (endorsing a Georgian land tax as a solution); Hobson, "The Influence of Henry George," *Fortnightly Review*, Dec. 1897, reprinted in *The Development of Economic Thought* 330, 337–338 (H. W. Spiegel, ed., 1952); and Collini, *Liberalism and Sociology*, 104–107, and sources cited therein. Hale's unpublished writings contain frequent assertions to the effect that site value (like all other scarcity value) is a social creation. For a particularly strident version, see his handwritten draft beginning "With the increased discontent of masses of the people. . .," in Hale Papers, folder 24.

88. For a typical Millian attack on the injustice of land rents, see *Principles of Political Economy*, bk. V, chap. 2, §5, at 818. For Mill's role in reviving criticism of private ownership of land, which had died down after the repeal of the Corn Laws, see Stigler, "Bernard Shaw, Sidney Webb," 274; Collini, *Liberalism and Sociology*, 103–104. For an account of his increasingly radical antilandlord position, see Willard Wolfe, *From Radicalism to Socialism: Men and Ideas in the Formation of Fabian Socialist Doctrines, 1881–1889*, 52–65 (1975).

89. *Principles of Political Economy*, bk. V, chap. 2, §5, at 818. As Mark Blaug notes, the early marginalists Walras and Wicksteed proposed substantially the same result as Mill, but to be reached by nationalizing property and paying full compensation. *Economic Theory in Retrospect*, 85. Assuming that property values did not decrease thereafter, the effect would be identical to preserving private ownership of property and leaving untaxed all increments in value as of the present, but subjecting any future increments to a 100 percent tax. It should be noted that under either version of the land tax, the expected (ex ante) value of the tax was zero. The value of the land at the time that (under Mill's proposal) the cutoff valuations were made or (under Walras and Wicksteed's proposal) that the land was taken for just compensation would reflect the present value of all future expected increments in value. Mill recognized that fact. See *Principles of Political Economy*, bk. V, chap. 2, §5, at 819. But he failed to see that it meant that a tax on inframarginal rents from future increments in value would be positive only if the market had systematically underestimated future growth at the time the cutoff valuation was made. Walras in fact made just that assumption, positing that rents would continually rise in a growing economy (and implicitly that the market would continually fail to anticipate that growth). See Blaug, *Economic Theory in Retrospect*, 88. For a similar difficulty with an analogous proposal by Hale for nationalizing future increments in the value of public utilities, see chap. 5.

90. Blaug, *Economic Theory in Retrospect*, 85. P. S. Atiyah, *The Rise and Fall of Freedom of Contract*, 641–644 (1979), describes all the various land-tax bills enacted in England in the twentieth century as complete failures, if not outright counterproductive.

91. *Progress and Poverty* contains the most complete statement of George's single-tax proposal. For a more concise version by George, see "A Single Tax on Land Values" (1890). For a brief and thoughtful summary and critique of the economic assumptions behind George's proposal, which Blaug calls "thirty years out of date the day it was published," see Blaug, *Economic Theory in Retrospect*, 84–85.

92. *Progress and Poverty*, 404.

93. Id. at 405.

94. On the strange confluence of individualist and collectivist attacks on private owner-ship of property in the late nineteenth century, see chap. 3. For a sensitive reading of George

280

that identifies both strands, see Hobson, "The Influence of Henry George," 330–340. For the view that George's support for a land tax was more a reflection of extreme individualism than of collectivism, see Collini, *Liberalism and Sociology*, 33, 103. That view gets support from George himself, who strongly repudiated socialism, defending capitalists' right to profit and interest on their capital. The view was shared by a number of progressives, who saw George as only a limited ally. See, e.g., Hobhouse, *Liberalism and Other Writings*, 45; 1 Richard T. Ely, *Property and Contract in Their Relations to the Distribution of Wealth*, 255–256 and 260–261 n.8; Dorothy Ross, "Socialism and American Liberalism: Academic Social Thought in the 1880's," 11 *Perspectives in American History* 5, 48–49 and n.75.

At the same time, the prospect that a tax confiscating the "unearned increment" in land, however much it might follow from individualist principles, would be but the first of many assaults on the sanctity of private property rights, led many individualists including Spencer to repudiate it. See chap. 3; David Abraham, "Liberty and Property: Lord Bramwell and the Political Economy of Liberal Jurisprudence Individualism, Freedom, and Utility," 38 *The American Journal of Legal History* 288, 316–319 (1994). In addition, George himself supported a confiscatory land tax as much because of the consequentialist belief that it was the best means of eradicating poverty as because of the conviction that private ownership of site values was indefensible under an individualist view of rights. *Progress and Poverty*, bk. V, chap. 2. As one might expect, the programmatic implications of that belief—as one sympathetic observer put it, that poverty was not due to weakness of character but "was an evil preventable by State action"—made George's program far more palatable to the progressive successors of Mill than to the individualist heirs of Spencer. Kirkup, *History of Socialism*, 369–370 (5th ed., 1913).

95. On the public appeal of the single-tax movement in the United States in the late nineteenth century, see Charles Albro Barker, *Henry George*, chap. 17 (1955). On George's equally great appeal in England, see Hobson, "The Influence of Henry George," 330–340; Roy Douglas, "God Gave the Land to the People," in *Edwardian Radicalism: 1900–1914*, 148, 149 (A. J. A. Morris, ed., 1974) (arguing that *Progress and Poverty* was "[w]ithout exaggeration . . . one of the dozen most influential books written in the nineteenth century"); Elwood P. Laurence, *Henry George in the British Isles*, pts. 1 and 2 (1957) (describing George's triumphal lecture tours beginning in 1882). It was on one of these tours in 1882 that Shaw accidentally drifted into a London hall and heard one of George's lectures on behalf of the single tax, which he subsequently credited for his conversion to the cause of radical economic reform. See Archibald Henderson, *George Bernard Shaw: Man of the Century*, 215–216 (1956).

96. Barker, *Henry George*, 429–430, 565–567, 582. See generally Steven B. Cord, *Henry George: Dreamer or Realist?* (1965), for an account of the reaction of four generations of economists to George. Commons supported a "farmers' single tax" in Wisconsin. Barker, *Henry George*, 634. For one of the few books by an economist supporting a modified version of the single tax, see Henry Gunnison Brown, *The Theory of Earned and Unearned Incomes* (1918). Hale, in a review of the book that was apparently never published, noted that it "should disprove once [and] for all the shallow myth that no economist has ever favored the single tax." A short version of the review, which Hale sent to Brown on August 5, 1920, is contained in the Hale Papers, folder 26, and a longer version in folder 58.

97. On the lack of legislative accomplishments through 1916, see Arthur Nichols Young, *The Single Tax Movement in the United States*, 285–287 (1916).

98. See 1 Bonbright, *Valuation of Property*, 457, on the influence of the single-tax movement on high assessments of vacant land. The single-taxers also remained a significant pressure

group in the pre-1914 British parliaments that considered and ultimately adopted a Millian land tax. See later. John Hobson also credits George with having spurred numerous other land-related reforms not analytically linked to the single-tax proposal, including movements to preserve public rights, protect tenants' rights, and impose various restraints on alienation of land. "The Influence of Henry George," 338–339.

99. For an excellent discussion of the relationship of George's arguments to the "Socialist Revival" of the 1880s, see Wolfe, *From Radicalism to Socialism*, 79–93. Barker, *Henry George*, 621–635, and Ransom E. Noble, Jr., "Henry George and the Progressive Movement," 8 *American Journal of Economics and Sociology* 259 (1949), both provide a good overview of the Georgian influence on Progressive-Era reformers. For George's influence on other progressives, see John R. Commons, "A Progressive Tax on Bare Land Values," 38 *Political Science Quarterly* 41 (1908); Commons, "The Single Tax in Theory and Practice," 10 *The Public* 1205 (1908). For his influence on Fabian socialists and New Liberals, see Sidney Webb, *Socialism in England*, 21 [2d ed., 1893] (Gower, 1987); Edward R. Pease, *The History of the Fabian Society*, 20–21 (1916).

100. "The Influence of Henry George," 332.

101. Letter from Hale to Philip Wells, Oct. 29, 1912, Hale Papers, folder 65. See also Hale, "Political and Economic Review," 9 *American Bar Association Journal* 107 (1923) (arguing for a tax on urban land rents as a minimum gesture towards equality).

102. See letter to Harvard Alumni Bulletin, Jan. 16, 1912; letter to the Editor of the *New York Globe*, Oct. 23, 1912; letter to the Editor of the *Herald*, Oct. 24, 1912; and letter to Learned Hand, Oct. 27, 1912, all contained in the Hale Papers, folder 62. All of the foregoing defend the single-taxers against the accusation that confiscation of private property is theft, using the (soon to be) familiar Halean argument that private property is a governmental grant of special privilege to hold up the rest of the community. Given Hale's contemporaneous criticism of the single-tax proposals, however, Hale's early support is probably better read as defending the government's right to attach unearned income in any form that it sees fit than as endorsing the particular approach that the single-taxers advocated. For Hale's list of the practical reasons that one might not want to tax the unearned increment in land, without committing himself one way or the other, see "The 'Physical Value' Fallacy in Rate Cases," 30 *Yale Law Journal* 710, 724 (1921).

103. See chap. 5.

104. See Hale's letter to *The Freeman*, a Georgian publication (n.d., never published), Hale Papers, folder 62, describing himself as an "apostate from the single tax," and sharply criticizing the simplemindedness of the single-taxers' belief (encapsulated in the credo that "man is a land animal") that only income from land, not capital, was unjustified. See also letter to the *New Statesman*, Sept. 2, 1913, folder 62, and "Current Political and Economic Review," 8 *American Bar Association Journal* 638–639 (1922) to the same effect. For similar critiques of George for failing to extend his analysis of land rents to all other incomes, see 1 Ely, *Property and Contract*, 255–256, 260 n.8; Hobson, "The Influence of Henry George," 334–336.

105. On the implicit role of supply in marginalist accounts of price, see later. It is perhaps worth noting here the debt of Hale's theory of coercion (discussed in chap. 2) to the marginal utility revolution. When Hale says, "[a]ll incomes, in the last analysis, whether derived from ownership of property or from personal services, are not 'products' created by the recipients; they are payments derived from the rest of the community by the exertion of some sort of pressure," he is merely restating the lessons of marginalism in the language

282

of politics. Value is not created by the cost of production. It is created by marginal demand, and extorted by suppliers by means of a threat to withhold what others demand except on payment of an amount up to that value. For Hale's express acknowledgment that the *magnitude* of the incomes that one can extract by the threat not to produce depends on the marginal value of what one would produce, see letter to Henry Rottschaefer, Nov. 5, 1925, Hale Papers, folder 3.

106. For a detailed technical discussion of marginal productivity theory, see Blaug, *Economic Theory in Retrospect*, chap. 11. The respective roles of Clark, Wicksteed, and Wicksell in its development are discussed in Stigler, *Production and Distribution Theories*, chaps. 10, 11, and 12.

107. Blaug, *Economic Theory in Retrospect*, 299. For Wicksteed's demonstration that Ricardian rent theory is analytically equivalent to marginal productivity theory, see *The Co-ordination of the Laws of Distribution* [1894] (rev. ed., 1992). For Marshall's version of marginal productivity theory, see *Principles of Economics*, bk. VI, chap. 1.

108. Blaug, *Economic Theory in Retrospect*, 136.

109. Id. at 136, 425–427; Stigler, *Production and Distribution Theories*, 326–327. For a description and critique of Clark's version of marginal productivity theory, see id. at 302–308. For an excellent summary of the development of the Clarkian argument as an extension of Ricardian rent theory, see Paul H. Douglas, "Elasticity of Supply as a Determinant of Distribution," in *Economic Essays Contributed in Honor of John Bates Clark*, 71–73 (Jacob H. Hollander, ed., 1927); Charles A. Tuttle, "A Functional Theory of Economic Profit," in *Economic Essays*, 321, 331–333. For Clark's own acknowledgment that he was playing off Georgian rent theory, see *The Distribution of Wealth*, viii (New York, MacMillan 1899).

110. *Co-ordination of the Laws of Distribution*, 55.

111. The shift from supply-side to demand-side explanations of price was less absolute than the preceding statement would suggest. All economists from Smith on understood market prices to be in some sense equilibrating supply and demand. Just as some form of demand curve was necessarily implicit in Smithian classical value theory (see Blaug, *Economic Theory in Retrospect*, 39–44; George J. Stigler, "The Development of Utility Theory," in Stigler, *Essays in the History of Economics*, 66, 69–70), so also some form of supply curve was necessarily entailed in marginalist value and distribution theory, although it tended to be submerged in early (pre-Marshallian) presentations. Thus, the shift was in one sense just a shift in emphasis, reflecting different beliefs as to the relative importance of supply and demand in determining prices. The differences, however, could be significant. The strongest demand-driven versions of marginalism (e.g., the Austrians' theory of value) tended to reduce the practical significance of supply almost to nothing, by assuming that "one started from *given* supplies of productive factors, whose 'services' entered into the exchange-process by commanding a 'hire price.'" Dobb, *Theories of Value and Distribution*, 170; Douglas, "Elasticity of Supply," 75–76. That is to say, they implicitly assumed to exist the only state of facts under which demand will unilaterally determine factor prices: that supply of factors is perfectly inelastic (that is, not responsive to changes in prices that they fetch) within the relevant range. For Hale's argument to that effect, see "Economic Theory and the Statesman," 197–199. As Blaug has noted, that simplifying assumption might lead "[a]n unkind critic [to] say that neoclassical economics indeed achieved greater generality [than classical economics], but only by asking easier questions." *Economic Theory in Retrospect*, 299.

At least in the case of labor, the assumption of short-run inelasticity was empirically doubtful. As Marshall noted, it ignored the possibility that even a fixed population of workers could expand supply by expanding the number of hours that they worked or the intensity of their labor. *Principles of Economics,* bk. VI, chap. 2, §2, at 527 n.2. As Paul Douglas noted, the assumption also ignored the possibility that the reservation price of the existing supply of labor could be increased by such extraneous measures as unionization, strike funds, etc. "Elasticity of Supply," 99. In any event, argued Douglas, the assumption of inelasticity was testable by empirical research that (as of 1927) no one had yet undertaken. Id. at 117–118.

112. Blaug, *Economic Theory in Retrospect,* 136.

113. Stigler, "Ricardian Theory of Value," 185; see also Blaug, *Economic Theory in Retrospect,* 295, to the same effect.

114. "Political and Economic Review," 9 *American Bar Association Journal* 39 (1923). For Hale's other versions of the argument, see "Economic Theory and the Statesman," 201; letter from Hale to Donald Richberg, Apr. 12, 1922, Hale Papers, folder 6. As Marshall noted, this conventional formulation of the argument, which implied that rents accrued to those factors that were *superior to* other (presumably marginal) factors, was somewhat misleading. It was not the existence of inferior resources per se, but rather the natural scarcity of such resources, that generated rents. *Principles of Economics,* bk. V, chap. 8, §6, at 412, chap. 9, §5, and chap. 10, §2, at 428–429. Indeed, as Marshall noted, the existence of inferior resources, rather than raising the rents of better agents, in fact lowers them over what would be obtainable with no alternative sources of supply at all. Id., bk. VI, chap. 9, §5, at 424. For Hale's more precise formulation of the problem, see later.

115. *Principles of Economics,* app. K, §1.

116. "Economic Theory and the Statesman," 216.

117. Blaug, *Economic Theory in Retrospect,* 296–297, 428, provides a good summary of the operation of the "equimarginal principle" in both marginal utility and marginal productivity theories. On its theoretical significance, see Joseph A. Schumpeter, *Ten Great Economists from Marx to Keynes,* 126 (1951), arguing that "the historical importance of the utility and marginal utility theory of Jevons, Menger and Walras rests mainly upon the fact that it served as the ladder by which these economists climbed up to the conception of general economic equilibrium." On the political implications of general equilibrium analysis, see T. W. Hutchison, *A Review of Economic Doctrines, 1870–1929,* 283 (1953).

118. *Ten Great Economists,* 123–124. For an early, eloquent attack on the institutionalists for turning their back on the only method that could foster scientific progress in economic theory, see Arthur T. Hadley, "Economic Laws and Methods," in *Science Economic Discussion* 92–97 (The Science Company, 1886).

119. The Fabians were a notable exception, in general embracing with enthusiasm the marginalists' claims for the allocative efficiency of the market. For a typical Fabian statement to that effect, see Sidney Webb, "The Rate of Interest and the Laws of Distribution," 2 *Quarterly Journal of Economics* 188, 194–197 (1888).

120. The core of Veblen's attack is contained in "Professor Clark's Economics" in Veblen, *The Place of Science in Modern Civilisation and Other Essays,* 180 (1919), and "The Limitations of Marginal Utility," in Veblen, *The Place of Science,* 231. See also "Why Is Economics Not an Evolutionary Science?" in Veblen, *The Place of Science,* 56.

121. "The Limitations of Marginal Utility," 240.

122. For a good description of Clark's static state and its close relationship to Marshall's shorter-run and longer-run normals, see John Maurice Clark, "John Maurice Clark on J. B. Clark," in *The Development of Economic Thought,* 592, 602–605. Clark's static model was meant

to describe the economic equilibrium that would result if change and progress were stopped and if the equilibrating forces in the economy were allowed to operate until an imaginary equilibrium was reached. Clark expressly excluded from his static model five principal types of dynamic change: that population, capital, technology, and consumers' desires are increasing or improving, and that "[t]he forms of industrial establishments are changing: the less efficient shops, etc., are passing from the field, and the more efficient are surviving." *Distribution of Wealth*, 56. But he also implicitly excluded from consideration the effect of legal regimes, income distribution, the social construction of preferences, and a host of other factors that would have to be included in the sort of comprehensive model of a dynamic world that Clark himself envisioned as a counterpart to his statics. Although Clark briefly explored the dynamic system in *Essentials of Economic Theory* (1907), his most famous and extended work was based on his static state assumptions.

John Maurice Clark, with an abundance of filial tact, suggested that his father's great contribution was in constructing a static theory that could serve as a "stepping-stone" to a more realistic dynamics. "The Relation between Statics and Dynamics," in *Economic Essays*, 46. Veblen (a one-time student of J. B. Clark's at Carleton College) was more skeptical that the dynamics J. B. Clark envisioned could undo the damage that his static state had inflicted, arguing that in Clark's conception of it, "The 'dynamic' condition is essentially a deranged static condition: whereas the static state is the absolute perfect, 'natural' taxonomic norm of competitive life." "Professor Clark's Economics," 190. That view of Clark's work gets some support from J. B. Clark himself, who expressed the belief that "[t]he actual form of a highly dynamic society hovers relatively near to its static mode, though it never conforms to it." *Essentials of Economic Theory*, 195. On Veblen's relationship to Clark, see Hutchison, *Review of Economic Doctrines*, 262. Despite their profound philosophical disagreements and the vitriol with which Veblen was wont to put his side of the matter, the two remained lifelong friends.

123. Veblen's *The Theory of the Leisure Class* (New York, MacMillan, 1899) provided the most famous and durable attack on the psychological underpinnings of marginal utility analysis. By demonstrating the inherent manipulability and interdependence of consumer preferences, Veblen hoped (among other things) to undercut claims both that individual preferences were given and that they were morally significant. If the subjective value of, say, diamonds, could evaporate the moment that their possession was no longer conspicuous but common, what normative weight ought to be given the satisfaction of that preference? For an incorporation of Veblen's critique in a mainstream economics text, see 1 Taussig, *Principles of Economics*, 126–127. A. C. Pigou implicitly relied on Veblen's analysis of interdependent preferences in arguing for a progressive income tax, reasoning that to the extent that the utility of wealth derives from invidious comparisons with one's economic and social rivals, a steep tax on the wealthy reducing absolute but not relative status would decrease aggregate utility little. *A Study in Public Finance*, 90–92 (3d rev. ed., 1962).

124. See, e.g., "The Limitations of Marginal Utility," 233 ("It is characteristic of the [marginal utility] school that wherever an element of the cultural fabric, an institution or any institutional phenomenon, is involved in the facts with which the theory is occupied, such institutional facts are taken for granted, denied, or explained away."). On the tendency of the marginal utility school to take for granted property, contract, and other "natural" rights, see id. at 235–236.

125. Id. at 232.

126. "Professor Clark's Economics," 193.

285

127. See chap. 2.

128. For a general overview of contemporary attacks on the psychological assumptions of the rational maximizing model of neoclassical economics, see Herbert Hovenkamp, "The First Great Law and Economics Movement," 42 *Stanford Law Review* 993, 1049–1051 (1990). Pieces of the argument can be found in J. M. Clark, "Economics and Modern Psychology" (pts. 1 and 2), 26 *Journal of Political Economy* 1, 136 (1918); Wesley C. Mitchell, "The Backward Art of Spending Money," 2 *The American Economic Review* 269 (1912); Wesley C. Mitchell, "Human Behavior and Economics: A Survey of Recent Literature," 29 *Quarterly Journal of Economics* 1 (1914); 1 John R. Commons, *Institutional Economics*, 74 (1934); Marshall, *Principles of Economics*, bk. III, chap. 2 (giving his own version of conspicuous consumption); Hobhouse, *The Theory of Knowledge*, 59 (New York, MacMillan, 1896); J. A. Hobson, *The Social Problem*, 67 (1902); Arthur Twining Hadley, *Economics: An Account of the Relations Between Private Property and Public Welfare*, 69–70 (New York, Putnam, 1896); Walter Lippmann, *Public Opinion*, 7–32 (1922); Thurmond W. Arnold, *The Folklore of Capitalism*, 58–70 (1937); Herbert Croly, *Progressive Democracy*, 194–200 (1914); Frank Hyneman Knight, *The Ethics of Competition and Other Essays*, chaps. 1 and 2 (1935); Frank Hyneman Knight, "The Limitations of Scientific Method in Economics," in *The Trend of Economics*, 229, 262–263.

129. *Social Process*, 316 (1918). For further discussion of the new social psychology of Charles Horton Cooley, William James, John Dewey, and others, which insisted on the "essentially social" nature of individuals' values and desires, see chap. 2. For a good overview of the arguments of Hobhouse, Croly, and other political theorists that individual preferences were social products, see Kloppenberg, *Uncertain Victory*, 329–331. As Kloppenberg notes, the fact that experience was "essentially social," as Croly put it, led progressives to conclude that "the choices of the individual, although voluntary, are not expressions of the sort of pure individuality cherished by liberal theorists." Id. at 330.

130. See Blaug, *Economic Theory in Retrospect*, 353. For an early argument in favor of the switch from "pleasure to desire," see Irving Fisher, "Mathematical Investigations into the Theory of Value and Price," 9 *Transactions of the Connecticut Academy of Arts and Sciences*, 1–124 (1892); Irving Fisher, "Is 'Utility' the Most Suitable Term for the Concept It Is Used to Denote?," 8 *American Economic Review* 335 (1918). For a discussion of the conservative political motivations for and implications of that switch, see Robert Proctor, *Value-Free Science?* 189–193 (1991).

131. "Distribution," 5 *Encyclopaedia of Social Sciences* 167 (1931), reprinted in *Readings in the Theory of Income Distribution*, 58, 67.

132. *Preface to Social Economics*, 113 (1936).

133. The discrepancy between private choice and social welfare was pursued chiefly by A. C. Pigou in *Economics of Welfare* (4th ed., 1932), although, as J. M. Clark noted, the germ of the idea can be found in Mill's *Principles of Political Economy*. "J. M. Clark on J. B. Clark," 598–599. For versions of the argument from American progressives, see Henry Carter Adams, "Relation of the State to Industrial Action," 1 *Publications of the American Economic Association* 465 (1887), reprinted in *Two Essays*, 59, 70–72 (J. Dorfman, ed., 1969); John R. Commons, *The Distribution of Wealth*, 61; Richard T. Ely, *An Introduction to Political Economy*, 98–100 (1893); Davenport, *Value and Distribution*, 558–559 and n.3; Clark, *Social Control of Business*, 108–111; C. E. Ayres, *The Theory of Economic Progress* (2d ed., Schocken Books, 1962). For a thoughtful summary of the difficulty and importance of developing a theory of social value distinct from property value, see 1 Bonbright, *Valuation of Property*, 195–198.

134. *Economics of Enterprise*, 391.

135. 1 *Valuation of Property*, 196.

136. For a summary of this proposition, the so-called "Fundamental Theorem of Welfare Economics," see Amartya Sen, *On Ethics and Economics*, 34–35 (1987). A more extensive account can be found in Kenneth J. Arrow and F. H. Hahn, *General Competitive Analysis* (1971).

137. For an overview of the progressives' embrace of the egalitarian implications of Edgeworth's analysis, see Hovenkamp, "The First Great Law and Economics Movement," 1000–1002. For its incorporation in the arguments for a steeply progressive income tax, see later. In more technical terminology, the progressives' argument was that to say that the market automatically achieves Pareto optimality is to say only that it will make the most efficient use of resources *given* an initial distribution of wealth. The statement says nothing about whether that outcome is superior or inferior to different Pareto-optimal outcomes that could be achieved with different initial distributions. If Edgeworth was right in thinking that an additional increment of money would generate far more utility in a poor person's hand than in a rich one's, even a Pareto suboptimal state following a radical redistribution of wealth from the rich to the poor could well dominate, in welfare terms, a Pareto optimal state leaving entitlements where they currently were.

138. Robbins's formative attack on so-called interpersonal utility comparisons is contained in *An Essay on the Nature and Significance of Economic Science*, 136–143 (2d ed., 1935). Robbins's argument, in brief, was that we can assert with certainty that aggregate utility will be maximized by equalizing wealth only if we know *both* (i) that the marginal utility of money declines for every person in inverse relation to their wealth, *and* (ii) that money has the same *absolute* utility to every person of equal wealth (that is, we all have identical utility functions). Even if the first proposition were true, Robbins argued, given the impossibility of making interpersonal utility comparisons, we could never prove the second. For a discussion of the political salience of Robbins's attack, see Proctor, *Value-Free Science?*, 189–194. In the last twenty years, Robbins's assumption has come under serious attack in the work of Amartya Sen, John Harsanyi, and others. For an extensive bibliography of writing on the controversy, see Sen, *On Ethics and Economics*, 30 n.2.

139. Hale adhered to the typical progressive view that Edgeworth's hypothesis about the declining marginal utility of money was correct, and argued (on strictly utilitarian grounds) for a radically egalitarian redistribution of income, subject only to incentive considerations. See, e.g., "Economic Theory and the Statesman," 209; outline for Ec. 320 sec. C., "Function of Prices in Apportioning Production to the Needs of Different Consumers," Hale Papers, folder 36; unpub. review of Carver's *Essays*, pt. II, pp. 16–17, Hale Papers, folder 87. Once it was recognized that "[a] rich man will ordinarily be willing and able to pay far more for a product than a poor man, without desiring it any more intensely," Hale argued, it is clear that the market "is but a crude method of estimating net social gain or loss . . ., and one whose fallibility should be fully recognized." "Commissions, Rates, and Policies," 1140–1141.

Hale's unpublished notes, all in the Hale Papers, contain numerous comments in passing on the rift between choice and individual or aggregate utility, again reflecting the general progressive critique. See, e.g., handwritten notes in folder 83; comments in draft ms. on "Defects of the Marginal Utility Measure of Service," box 21, noting the problems of negative externalities as well as of self-defeating choices; handwritten notes on Carver's *Principles of National Economy*, p. 1, folder 86; unpublished review of Carver's *Essays in Social Justice* in folder 87.

140. Hale Papers, box 21. The manuscript is undated. However, in a letter to Harry Gunnison Brown, dated Aug. 3, 1921, Hale Papers, folder 5, Hale commented on his own

"elaborate but unreadable attempt," written "some six years ago" but never submitted for publication, disputing the assumption that the "natural" market achieves allocative efficiency, on the ground that it at most reflects the preferences of marginal consumers and producers only, leaving open the possibility that an "artificial" rechanneling of resources may capture others as well. The reference almost surely is to this manuscript. Hale argues that under some hypothetical demand curves, by altering the relative prices of two "competing" goods (through a subsidy or tax imposed on only one of the two) to favor that good, the purchase of which will generate higher potential inframarginal surplus, the government could increase aggregate consumer surplus. The argument is almost certainly wrong, at least without a number of heroic assumptions. But it is interesting for its early sensitivity to the effects of taxes on consumer surplus under different demand functions—an issue about to become salient in the optimal tax literature. It is interesting as well in filling out Hale's obsession with inframarginal surplus, here focusing on efficiency rather than equity considerations.

141. For a brief overview of the pre-Marxian exploitation theorists, see Dobb, *Theories of Value and Distribution*, 137–141. For more detailed accounts, see Böhm-Bawerk, *Capital and Interest*, bk. VI, chaps. 1 and 2; Alexander Gray, *The Socialist Tradition, Moses to Lenin*, 267–296, 332–351 (London, 1946).

142. For a brief survey of American and English economists' reaction to Marx following the first wave of marginalist analysis, see Dobb, *Theories of Value and Distribution*, 141–142. Böhm-Bawerk, while more respectful than most of the intellectual seriousness of Marx's enterprise, was typical in dismissing his descriptive theory of interest as utterly unfounded. *Capital and Interest*, bk. VI, chap. 3.

143. Jevons's development of marginal utility analysis predates any knowledge of Marx's work. See Dobb, *Theories of Value and Distribution*, 166–167. On the other hand, as noted before, exploitation theories based on a labor theory of value were in the air at least since the 1820s. Moreover, the growing hold of Marx's version of exploitation theory might well explain why marginal utility analysis found ready acceptance in some quarters, even if it does not explain its original development. For such a suggestion, see "J. M. Clark on J. B. Clark," 605.

144. 1 *Principles of Economics*, v–vi (1st ed., 1890).

145. A good summary of Clark's argument, its influence, and the adverse reaction that it engendered can be found in 2 Seligman, *Main Currents in Modern Economics*, 311–328. See also Hutchison, *A Review of Economic Doctrines*, 253–262; Blaug, *Economic Theory in Retrospect*, 426–428. For an account of the young Clark's socialist sympathies, see Ross, "Socialism and American Liberalism," and Dorothy Ross, *The Origins of American Social Science*, 102–109 (1991). For an account of the evolution of Clark's apologetics between the writing of *The Philosophy of Wealth* (1886) and its full-blown presentation in *The Distribution of Wealth* (1899), see John F. Henry, "John Bates Clark and the marginal product: An historical inquiry into the origins of value-free economic theory," 15 *History of Political Economy* 375 (1983). For a (naturally) more sympathetic portrayal of Clark, playing down the conservative implications of his later work, see "J. M. Clark on J. B. Clark," 593–612. For J. M. Clark's critique of the theory of distributive justice embedded in productivity theory, not naming his father as its chief expositor, see *Social Control of Business*, 62–63.

146. *Distribution of Wealth*, 3, 9.

147. *Id.* at 8.

148. On the relationship of Clark's marginal productivity theory to Marxian critiques of capitalism, see Henry, "John Bates Clark and the marginal product"; Ronald L. Meek,

"Marginalism and Marxism," 4 *History of Political Economy*, 499, 503 (1972); Schumpeter, *History of Economic Analysis*, 870; Clark, "J. M. Clark on J. B. Clark," 610. As J. M. Clark stated, "The marginal theories of distribution were developed after Marx; their bearing on the doctrines of Marxian socialism is so striking as to suggest that the challenge of Marxism acted as a stimulus to the search for more satisfactory explanations." "Distribution," 5 *Encyclopedia of the Social Sciences* 167 (1931), reprinted in *Readings in the Theory of Income Distribution*, 58, 64–65. For a similar acknowledgment by Francis A. Walker that the bearing of his early work on marginal productivity to the "socialist assumption that profits are but unpaid wages is too manifest to require exposition," see "The Source of Business Profits," 1 *Quarterly Journal of Economics* 265, 288 (1887).

149. See, e.g., *Distribution of Wealth*, 4–9, 323–324 n.1.

150. Id. at 4.

151. Id. at 3. For an earlier statement to the same effect, see J. B. Clark, "The Law of Wages and of Interest," *Annals of the American Academy of Political and Social Science* 43 (1890).

152. *Social Justice without Socialism*, 34–36 (1914).

153. See, e.g., Stigler, *Production and Distribution Theories*, 297 (dismissing the normative side of Clark's analysis—his "naive productivity ethics"—as of dubious merit, regrettably providing "a made-to-order foil for the diatribes of a Veblen"); Schumpeter, *History of Economic Analysis*, 869–870; T. N. Carver, "Clark's Distribution of Wealth," 15 *Quarterly Journal of Economics* 578 (1901); Davenport, *Value and Distribution*, 440 n.2; Lionel Robbins, *The Evolution of Modern Economic Theory*, 19–20 (1970); Frank H. Knight, *Risk, Uncertainty and Profit*, 109–110 [1921] (Midway Reprint ed., Univ. of Chicago Press, 1985). See generally 2 Seligman, 2 *Main Currents in Modern Economics*, 325–326.

154. 2 Seligman, *Main Currents in Modern Economics*, 327. On the influence of Clark's apologetics, see also Ross, *Origins of American Social Science*, 178–179. Hamilton, "Property— According to Locke," 870 n.12, notes that the "cruder notions" inherent in marginal productivity theory, of which professional accounts like Clark's were a refinement, "were matters of faith to business men at the end of the century," and that the theory was still prevalent in many college economics textbooks at the time of his writing in 1932.

155. Blaug, *Economic Theory in Retrospect*, 425–426. See Hobson, *Economics of Distribution*, 144–148; Walter M. Adriance, "Specific Productivity," 29 *Quarterly Journal of Economics* 149, 157–158 (1915); Davenport, *The Economics of Enterprise*, 146–150; Henry Carter Adams, "Economics and Jurisprudence," 2 *Economic Studies* 1 (1887), reprinted in *Two Essays*, 137, 156–160. For a later exchange between Hobson and Carver on this point, see J. A. Hobson, "Marginal Units in the Theory of Distribution," 12 *Journal Political Economy* 449 (1904); T. N. Carver, "The Marginal Theory of Distribution," 13 *Journal of Political Economy* 257 (1905); J. A. Hobson, "The Marginal Theory of Distribution: A Reply to Professor Carver," 13 *Journal of Political Economy* 587 (1905). For Marshall's criticism that appears to be going to the same point (without identifying Clark by name), see *Principles of Economics*, bk. VI, chap. 1, §7, at 518.

156. *Theory of Business Enterprise*, 291.

157. "Economic Theory and the Statesman," 198. For a similar critique of Carver's version of Clarkian apologetics, see Hale's unpublished review of Carver's *Essays*, pt. II, Hale Papers, folder 87.

158. It should be noted that the Marxian socialist critique of capitalism was not a strict Lockean one. That is, the argument that labor was entitled to the full market value of all goods that it helped produce was *not* based on the assumption that such value merely

compensated labor for the sacrifice entailed in working. Indeed, the very fact that there was "surplus" value at all (above and beyond what labor minimally required to work) to divert to capitalists refuted the argument that value equaled the sacrifice of labor. Rather, it was based on the assumption that, as between two parties (labor and capital), one of whom generates all the value inherent in commodities and the other of whom generates none, justice argues for distributing that value entirely to the former. (As Shaw noted in a slightly different context, the argument does not consider a third possibility: that any value in excess of sacrifice ought to be distributed to the consumer, directly in the form of lower prices or indirectly in the form of taxation. See G. B. S. Larking, "Who Is the Thief?," Letter to the Editor, *Justice*, Mar. 15, 1884, at 6, reprinted in *Bernard Shaw and Karl Marx: A Symposium, 1884–1889*, 1 (Richard W. Ellis, ed., 1930). However, in an economy of only workers, the two schemes would differ only in their distribution *among* workers.) Thus, the Marxian argument, like Clark's, is based on imputed productivity, not sacrifice; and Clark's refutation of Marx's underlying factual assumption as to labor's relative share in the production of value would (if true) dispose of the Marxian critique.

159. "Professor Clark's Economics," 203. For similar critiques, see Veblen, "Industrial and Pecuniary Employments," 2 *Publications of the American Economic Association* 190 (3d ser., 1901); Marshall, *Principles of Economics*, bk. VI, chap. 1, §8, at 519; Hamilton, "Property—According to Locke," 870; Tunell, "Valuation for Rate Making and Recapture of Excess Income," 35 *Journal of Political Economy* 725, 769 (1927); Taussig, *Principles of Economics*, chap. 66, §4, at 477.

160. *Value and Distribution*, 440 n.2.

161. It is perhaps worth noting that the condition that would have to hold for costs to coincide with price—complete elasticity of supply—is in opposition to the implicit assumption of complete *in*elasticity on which a pure demand-driven model of short-run prices depends. See n.111.

162. See generally Blaug, *Economic Theory in Retrospect*, 313–314. For Marshall's insistence that the disutility of labor governs the short-run supply of labor, see *Principles of Economics*, bk. VI, chap. 2, §2. For Marshall's incorporation of it in measuring "workers' surplus," see id., app. K, §1, at 831.

163. "Economic Theory and the Statesman," 216.

164. *Value and Distribution*, 82–83.

165. "Doctrinal Tendencies—Fetter, Flux, Seager, Carver," 14 *Yale Review* 300, 315–316 (1905). Davenport's argument can be illustrated by the following example. Worker A, destitute, is "willing" to forgo an additional hour of leisure for wages of $1. Worker B, a millionaire, is not "willing" to forgo an additional hour of leisure for less than $1,000. All other things (besides wealth) being equal, the most plausible explanation for this disparity is surely not that A values an additional hour of leisure one thousand times less than B, but that she values a marginal dollar of income one thousand times more. That is, at the lowest income levels, the disutility of starvation (or to put it another way, the high utility of money in warding off starvation) will dominate the reservation price. At higher income levels, at which the marginal utility of an additional dollar is very low, the disutility of forgoing leisure will dominate the reservation price. If the sole question were preserving incentives for A and B to work given current distributions of wealth, the reason for the disparities in reservation prices would be irrelevant. But from a Lockean perspective, the situation seems troubling, as it suggests that in taking the reservation price as reflecting the "cost" of labor, we are overstating B's cost relative to A's. The obvious answer seems

to be that, if B's sacrifice is the same as A's, so also is his reward, measured by the utility of the money in his hands. That is to say, if we assume that one hour of leisure has the same absolute value to A and B, then the minimum monetary equivalent that each will demand for relinquishing it ($1 in A's case, $1,000 in B's) must have the same absolute (subjective) value as well. The answer seems dispositive, taking the initial distribution of wealth as given. But it raises further questions as to the justice of so taking it, and thereby treating A (at the extreme with a "bundle" of goods at the end of the day equal to 8 hours of leisure and $16) and B (at the extreme with a "bundle" equal to 23 hours of leisure and $1,000) as enduring equal sacrifice for equal reward.

166. *Principles of Economics*, app. K, §1, at 831.

167. Id. For an interesting development of this point, arguing that the development of human capital ought to be treated as an overhead cost, compensable by society to the extent that it is not adequately compensated in the wage contract, see John Maurice Clark, *Studies in the Economics of Overhead Costs*, 361–364 (1923).

168. Marshall, *Principles of Economics*, bk. VI, chap. 4, §2, at 560–561.

169. *Principles of Political Economy*, bk. II, chap. 14, §1, at 388. Jevons, resorting to somewhat less casual empiricism in refuting Malthus's iron law, showed that wages in England varied from 10 to 40 shillings a week in different parts of the country, with no sign that they were tending towards convergence. *The Theory of Political Economy*, 269 (5th ed., 1965).

170. Marshall, *Principles of Economics*, bk. VI, chap. 5, §7, bk. VI, chap. 8, §8, at 623–624. For Marshall's reservations about extending the Ricardian law of rent in such fashion, see "Wages and Profits," 2 *Quarterly Journal of Economics* 218, 223 (1888).

171. *Principles of Political Economy*, bk. II, chap. 1, §4, at 212.

172. Legal Factors materials, pp. 593–594.

173. See Marshall, *Principles of Economics*, bk. VI, chap. 5, §§1,2,3.

174. Cairnes, *Political Economy*, pt. I, chap. 3, §5, at 65–68. For Mill's presentation of Cairnes's theory of noncompeting groups in embryonic form, see *Principles of Political Economy*, bk. II, chap. 14, §2, at 391–393. For similar comments, arguing that for many of the most highly paid forms of labor, "each individual more or less constitutes a market of his own, drawing monopoly rents," see Hobson, *Economics of Distribution*, 225–226 (1900).

175. 2 Taussig, *Principles of Economics*, chap. 47, §§3,4,5.

176. "Economic Theory and the Statesman," 216.

177. Most economists assumed that the supply price of labor rose for each additional hour of labor because of the increasing psychic costs of forgoing leisure and the diminishing marginal utility of income. For Marshall's version of the argument, see *Principles of Economics*, app. K, §1, at 830 ("a worker . . . derives a *worker's surplus*, through being remunerated for all his work at the same rate as for that last part, which he is only just willing to render for its reward; though much of the work may have given him positive pleasure").

178. See Clark, *Distribution of Wealth*, 124–125. Clark's theory of capital, set forth in his 1888 monograph, *Capital and Its Earnings*, is ably summarized in Frank A. Fetter, "Clark's Reformulation of the Capital Concept," in *Economic Essays*. For the most part modern economics, following Clark's lead, has abandoned the idea that land is an economically unique commodity, treating it simply as a species of concrete capital, defined to include all fixed instruments and materials of production. See Blaug, *Economic Theory in Retrospect*, 82–83. As Fetter notes, Clark's reworking of capital theory to lump land with other forms of fixed capital was self-consciously in reaction to Henry George's single-minded campaign against land rents. Clark hoped that by showing that pure capital invested in land was

economically indistinguishable from that invested in any other means of production, he could demonstrate that it ought to have "the same rights [there] that elsewhere belong to it." *Capital and Its Earnings,* 66, quoted in Fetter, "Clark's Reformulation of the Capital Concept," 144. Although Clark hoped that his unified theory of capital goods would undermine the singular critique of land in Georgian rent theory, the theory could as easily be used to extend the Georgian critique to all capital goods—precisely the result in the Fabian and later progressives' version of rent theory. See later discussion.

179. "Economic Theory and the Statesman," 202.

180. For Hale's acceptance of that view, see id. at 201–203; "Rate Making and the Revision of the Property Concept," 22 *Columbia Law Review* 209, 214 (1922). For the same view from other progressives equally hostile as a general matter to "unearned incomes," see Hobhouse, *The Labour Movement,* 121–122; Brown, *Earned and Unearned Income,* 250. Hobson's *Economics of Distribution* 230–232, 247–254, provides a particularly interesting and spirited defense of Senior, bemoaning Marshall's wrong decision to compromise Senior's point by "substituting 'waiting' for 'abstinence.'" See also J. A. Hobson, *Veblen,* 69–70 (1936) (gently criticizing Veblen for failing to recognize that postponing present consumption constitutes a real "cost"). The Fabians should probably be counted as an exception. Although their position on interest is hard to pin down, on balance they appear closer to the (Marxian) socialist view of it as pure surplus than to the progressive view. See, e.g., Sidney and Beatrice Webb, *A Constitution for the Socialist Commonwealth of Great Britain,* xii, 80; Sidney Webb, Fabian Tract No. 233, *Socialism and Fabianism,* 4 (1930).

181. G. A. Kleene, "Productive Apparatus and the Capitalist," 31 *Journal of Political Economy* 1, 19 (1923). Hale included the article in the ELP and Social Control materials, and elsewhere described it as "very significant." "Economic Theory and the Statesman," 203 n.1. For a more general acknowledgment that the right to interest depends on the right of private property, see 2 Taussig, *Principles of Economics,* chap. 40, §7, at 49–50. For a proposal to curtail those rights sharply in the case of inherited wealth by a steep inheritance tax, thereby transferring the right to interest on that capital to the community, see Hobhouse, *The Labour Movement,* 117–122.

182. Hale Papers, folder 58, pp. 6–7.

183. Of course, if (as in Hale's example) the conditions placed on savings are significantly more onerous than those placed on current spending, the mere fact that we have formally burdened both options will not prevent "owners" from opting in large numbers to spend instead of to save—a problem not presented by Kleene's example of forced investment through taxation. But that is a matter going to utilitarian considerations, not questions of right (and one that on a utilitarian basis Hale was inclined to take seriously, as his last comment suggests).

184. *Kapital und Arbeit,* 110 (Berlin, 1864), quoted in Böhm-Bawerk, *Capital and Interest,* 276.

185. *Value and Distribution,* 258–260.

186. Frank Taussig, developing the same argument, noted that many of the poorest savers are willing to save at low or possibly zero interest rates not because they mind deferring consumption less (in any absolute sense) than do marginal savers, but because they feel compelled to accumulate a bare minimum for future retirement needs irrespective of the current interest rate. Indeed, if their future needs are fixed and can be met only out of current income, the lower the interest rate, the *greater* the amount they will have to set aside to meet that need. 2 *Principles of Economics,* chap. 68, §5, at 517. For Marshall's argument to the same effect, see *Principles of Economics,* bk. IV, chap. 7, §9. Taussig's argument—in

modern terminology that poor savers may be inframarginal because of income effects rather than substitution effects—is analogous to the argument in n.165 made with respect to wages, and it invites the same response. Person A, fearing that she will be destitute in later life, is willing to set aside $100 of current income for as little as 1 percent interest. Person B, expecting to have ample income in his later years, will not set aside $100 for less than 10 percent interest. By comparing only the nominal value of their respective reservation prices, we are (as Taussig implies) understating A's sacrifice relative to B's. But we are also understating her reward relative to B's, measured by the utility of each incremental dollar of future wealth in their respective hands. As with the problem of wages, the response seems dispositive, taking the distribution of expected future wealth as given. As with wages, though, the response raises serious questions about the justice of so taking it. Taussig acknowledged as much in proposing as a solution that a progressive tax be levied only on large property incomes. On the assumption that most large property holders were inframarginal savers but that the converse was not necessarily true, the result would be to limit the tax to savers that were *both* inframarginal and wealthy. But the justification for such a tax scheme cannot rest on rent theory (which would seek to reach *all* inframarginal savers, poor and rich alike). As Taussig frankly acknowledged, it must rest instead on the straightforward social welfarist view that "great inequalities in wealth are undesirable, and should be lessened . . . so far as other consequences equally undesirable for the community can be avoided." 2 *Principles of Economics*, chap. 68, §5, at 517.

187. *Value and Distribution*, 46–47. See also Davenport, *Economics of Enterprise*, 366.

188. *Economics of Enterprise*, 361–362.

189. *Value and Distribution*, 49.

190. *Economics of Enterprise*, 376 n.1. Davenport's argument was not without a possible response. Proponents of an abstinence justification for interest could have conceded that Davenport was right as a descriptive matter that the "pain" of abstinence was no more than an opportunity cost, but argued that that was sufficient to entitle a saver to interest. A saver's ownership of $100 in capital gives her the right to consume it currently, retaining the full value of whatever pleasure that affords her. By agreeing to relinquish that right for one year only in exchange for (say) 10 percent interest, she has declared that for her, *for whatever reason*, the right to consume $100 currently is equivalent in value to the right to consume $110 next year. If she had an absolute right to the first "bundle" of goods ($100 of present consumption), so also she should have a right to the second equivalent "bundle" ($110 of consumption next year) for which she exchanges it. Under that line of argument, it is irrelevant what absolute value the marginal saver puts on the two options. It matters only that they are (in her view) equivalent. The response, however, gives up any distinct claim on behalf of abstinence theory, in favor of the broader claim that any right (here, the right to consume one's wealth currently) necessarily carries with it a subsidiary right to one's reservation price for relinquishing the right, *whatever the reason for that price*. Thus, the argument—in effect equating efficiency with equity concerns—subsumes Senior's abstinence argument, along with any other explanation for the existence of a positive supply price for capital, as it holds true irrespective of the ground for preferring present to future consumption. That economy of explanation, however, is achieved at the cost of whatever moral weight that the Seniorian rhetoric of sacrifice lent the cause. For an exploration of this and related problems with treating abstinence from current consumption as a true cost, in the context of the contemporary debate over the fairness of exempting all returns to capital from taxation, see Barbara Fried, "Fairness and the Consumption Tax," 44 *Stanford Law Review* 961, 967–976 (1992).

191. For rare dissents from progressives, see Hobhouse, *The Labour Movement*, 122–123; Hamilton, "Property—According to Locke," 869–870; Commons, 2 *Institutional Economics*, 500–506; Simon Patten, *Theory of Dynamic Economics*, pt. IX (1892). See also David I. Green, "Pain-Cost and Opportunity-Cost," 8 *Quarterly Journal of Economics* 218 (1894). Among mainstream economists, Irving Fisher concurred in the view that labor (at least when "disagreeable") reflects the only true cost of production, but distanced himself on other grounds from the socialist conclusion that interest was therefore morally unjustifiable. *The Theory of Interest*, 20–24, 486–487, 539–541 (1930).

Lassalle's skepticism about whether saving entailed any sacrifice for the rich was frequently echoed (albeit in more subdued tones) in the latter part of the nineteenth and the early part of the twentieth centuries, among centrist and progressive economists alike. See, e.g., Böhm-Bawerk, *Capital and Interest*, 277 (quoting Lassalle with approval); 2 Taussig, *Principles of Economics*, chap. 68, §5, at 517. One could read these comments as denying that *any* wealthy saver (even the marginal one) endures any sacrifice. If so, the comments clearly indicate dissent from the view that "sacrifice" should be equated with incentive costs. But the more likely intent, at least for the postmarginalists, was simply to suggest that most saving by the wealthy is *inframarginal*.

192. Marshall, *Principles of Economics*, bk. VI, chap. 6, §3, at 587. For Marx's own sketchy dismissal of abstinence theory, suggesting that saving for the purpose of productive investment is automatic (and hence costless), see 1 *Capital*, pt. VII, chap. 24, §3 [1867] (Modern Library, 1934). Shaw's rejoinder to Marx—that if the provision of capital were truly costless, capitalists would compete with each other to supply it until they drove the cost of capital to zero—demonstrated conclusively the existence of a positive supply price, at least assuming no scarcity of supply relative to demand. But it said nothing about the moral right to that reservation price.

193. Kleene's article, "Productive Apparatus and the Capitalist," supplied one dissenting note on the latter proposition. John Hobson provided another and more famous one in his proto-Keynesian argument that underconsumption and not undersavings was the cause of economic stagnation. On Hobson's underconsumption theory and its influence on Keynes, see 1 Seligman, *Main Currents in Modern Economics*, 221–238.

194. On supply-side versus demand-side theories of interest, see generally Blaug, *Economic Theory in Retrospect*, 498–506; Böhm-Bawerk, *Capital and Interest*, bk. IV, chaps. 1–3.

195. "Economic Theory and the Statesman," 202–203. For a dissenting view, see J. A. Hobson, *Economics of Unemployment*, 51–53 (1922).

196. "Economic Theory and the Statesman," 203.

197. "Economic Theory and the Statesman," 203. For a similarly skeptical view of the feasibility of separating inframarginal from marginal savers, see Hobson, *Economics of Distribution*, 251–252.

198. Marshall, *Principles of Economics*, app. H.

199. "Economic Theory and the Statesman," 197–198. For the assumption that the law of diminishing returns applies to production of all kinds, see Clark, *Distribution of Wealth*, 208; Edwin R. A. Seligman, *Principles of Economics*, §88 (4th ed. rev., 1909); Marshall, *Principles of Economics*, bk. IV, chap. 3, §7, at 168–169.

200. For a good summary of the Marshallian distinction, see Blaug, *Economic Theory in Retrospect*, 374–376.

201. *Principles of Economics*, bk. V, chap. 9, §3, at 420–421, §5, at 424.

202. See id., bk. V, chap. 15, §3, at 499.

203. Blaug, *Economic Theory in Retrospect*, 375–376. Or, to put it another way, in the long run all industries tend towards the constant cost curve that Smith et al. envisioned, because in the long run, all costs are variable.

204. "Economic Theory and the Statesman," 200–202. See also letter from Hale to Donald Richberg, Apr. 12, 1922, Hale Papers, folder 6, and typewritten notes (n.d.) beginning "When a governmental body regulates price," Hale Papers, folder 24, sketching the same argument.

205. Henry Rottschaefer to Hale, Oct. 14, 1925, Hale Papers, folder 3.

206. Hale to Henry Rottschaefer, Nov. 5, 1925, p. 2, Hale Papers, folder 3.

207. See, e.g., Hobhouse, *Democracy and Reaction*, 231–233; *Liberalism and Other Writings*, 45–47.

208. Hale to Rottschaefer, Nov. 5, 1925, Hale Papers, folder 3.

209. For a typical use of the term "rent" to cover all cases in which the price that an owner can obtain "bears no necessary relation to the cost of any effort of his own," see Hobhouse, *Liberalism and Other Writings*, 46.

210. For a discussion of the centrality of rent theory to early Fabianism, see Ricci, "Fabian Socialism." See also Stigler, "Bernard Shaw, Sidney Webb;" Wolfe, *From Radicalism to Socialism*, chaps. 5 and 6; Peter Clarke, *Liberals and Social Democrats*, 30–33 (1978); Collini, *Liberalism and Sociology*, 61–66. For the Fabians' own acknowledgment of the importance of rent theory to them, see Sidney Webb, Introduction to *Fabian Essays in Socialism*, xvii (G. Bernard Shaw, ed., 1931); Shaw, *Fabian Essays*, 183 ff.

211. A brief account of the Hampstead meetings by one of the participants can be found in Pease, *History of the Fabian Society*, 64–65. For a somewhat fuller account of the meetings and their influence on the development of Fabian rent theory, see Clarke, *Liberals and Social Democrats*, chap. 2; Wolfe, *From Radicalism to Socialism*, 178–181.

212. Wallas to E. R. Pease, 10 January 1916, Wallas Papers 10, quoted in Clarke, *Liberals and Social Democrats*, 31. Shaw's lively account of his own somewhat slower but no less total conversion to marginalism is given in his memorandum "On the History of Fabian Economics," reprinted in Pease, *History of the Fabian Society*, app. I. "[T]he upshot," concluded Shaw, "was that I put myself into Mr. Wicksteed's hands and became a convinced Jevonian . . . Accordingly, the abstract economics of the Fabian Essays are, as regards value, the economics of Jevons." Id. at 261. For one of Sidney Webb's many declarations of intellectual independence from Marxian socialism, see *Socialism in England*, 84–85. See also Stigler, "Bernard Shaw, Sidney Webb," 269–273; Wolfe, *From Radicalism to Socialism*, 178–180, 206–211.

213. Webb, "The Rate of Interest." See also Bernard Shaw, Fabian Tract No. 146, "Socialism and Superior Brains," 11, 14 (1909). As Stigler notes, the analogy between labor and land was closer than that between capital and land in one respect at least: rents to labor and land are attributable to natural differences in quality (of people and acres) that are unlikely to be completely eliminated under any social system. "Bernard Shaw, Sidney Webb," 280. For Webb's acknowledgment that his "law of three rents" was influenced by Francis Walker's revisionist doctrine of rent, see "The Rate of Interest," 188–189.

214. Sidney Webb, Fabian Tract No. 69, *The Difficulties of Individualism*, 9 (1896). As Wallas stated, "We therefore came in to the [Fabian] Society ready-made Anti-Marxists, and at once began that insistence on the Ricardian Law of Rent as applied to Capital and ability, as well as to Land which made William Morris say 'These Fabians call their noddles their Rents of Ability.'" Ms. review of Pease's *History of the Fabian Society*, quoted in Clarke, *Liberals and Social Democrats*, 32.

215. For sarcastic Fabian attacks on land rents, see Sidney Webb, Fabian Tract No. 15, *English Progress Towards Social Democracy*, 12 (1890) ("[T]he earth may be the Lord's, but the fulness thereof must, inevitably, be the landlord's"), and Stewart D. Headlam, Fabian Tract No. 42, *Christian Socialism*, 13 (1892) ("[E]very salmon which comes up from the sea might just as well have a label on it, 'Lord or Lady So-and-So, with God Almighty's compliments' "). Stigler suggests that the Fabians' desire to extend the Georgian indictment of land rents to capital and labor might have reflected their own uneasiness about the viability of a reform movement based solely on land rents, which in fact accounted for a very small portion of income in late Victorian England. See Stigler, "Bernard Shaw, Sidney Webb," 275–276.

216. *Principles of Political Economy*, bk. V, chap. 2, §5, at 817–818.

217. See, e.g., L. T. Hobhouse, "The Ethical Basis of Collectivism," 8 *International Journal of Ethics*, 137 (1898); Clarke, *Liberals and Social Democrats*, 51 (on Hobson's rejection of Marxian value theory).

218. Good summaries of the pervasiveness of Fabian rent theory in the works of Hobson and of Hobhouse can be found in Collini, *Liberalism and Sociology*, 61–66; Clarke, *Liberals and Social Democrats*, 45–54. See also A. M. McBriar, *Fabian Socialism and English Politics: 1884–1914* (1962); Hutchison, *Review of Economic Doctrines*, 124–125, 128 (on Hobson). For a typical example, see Hobhouse, *The Labour Movement*, chap. 4, which is straight Marshallian economics with a Fabian moral. For a good overview of the influence of rent theory on all of the so-called New Liberals, both in their individual work and in the editorial policy of *The Nation*, the British weekly that they jointly edited, see Clarke, *Liberals and Social Democrats*, 108–118. As Collini notes, Hobson and Hobhouse were reluctant from the start to acknowledge their debts to Fabian rent theory. That reluctance grew as the Fabians became more unpopular, and as the New Liberals (including Hobson and Hobhouse) found themselves increasingly at odds with the Fabians over the Fabians' support of the Boer War, their growing preoccupation with social efficiency, and their tendency to dismiss any claims on behalf of individualism as no more than a "form of outdated sentimentality" that obstructed the cause of economic improvement. *Liberalism and Sociology*, 63 nn.70,77. For Hale's dissent from the last of these, a familiar criticism of the Fabians, see his review of Sidney and Beatrice Webb's *Constitution for the Socialist Commonwealth of Great Britain* (1920), 45 *The Survey* 514 (1921). On the growing disenchantment of progressives with Fabianism, see generally Collini, *Liberalism and Sociology*, 71–78; Clarke, *Liberals and Social Democrats*, 54–61; and McBriar, *Fabian Socialism*, 46n.

219. Hobhouse, *The Labour Movement*, 76–78 (1st ed., 1906). Hobson's first fully developed version of his rent theory of distribution is contained in *The Economics of Distribution* (1900), although the key elements appear as early as 1891 in his article on "The Law of Three Rents." Collini, *Liberalism and Sociology*, 63 n.70. For a later version, see Hobson, *The Industrial System: An Inquiry into Earned and Unearned Income* (1909). His proposal for constructing a tax system based on rent theory is contained in *Taxation in the New State* (1919). Hobson coined the term "improperty" to mean property acquired for power, or as part of unearned surplus or irrational gains, reserving the term "property" for earned wealth. See *Property and Improperty*, 39–40 (1937).

220. On the continuing influence of Georgian land taxers on pre-1914 Parliaments, see H. V. Emy, *Liberals, Radicals and Social Politics*, chap. 6 (1973).

221. Clarke, *Liberals and Social Democrats*, 115. For details of the tax reform measures adopted in the 1907 and 1909 Liberal budgets, see the following discussion and F. Shehab,

Progressive Taxation, 248–255 (1953). For the New Liberals' lobbying efforts surrounding the 1907 and 1909 Budgets, see Clarke, *Liberals and Social Democrats,* 109–118. Hobhouse recorded his own view that the 1909 Budget was a triumph for rent theorists in *The Labour Movement,* 118–119. See also Hobhouse, *Liberalism and Other Writings,* 47, suggesting that "[t]he great Budget of 1909 had behind it the united forces of Socialist and individualist [i.e., Georgian] opinion."

222. *The Nation,* May 8, 1909, cited in Clarke, *Liberals and Social Democrats,* 115. As Clarke notes, when in September 1909 Winston Churchill gave a speech defending the budget, he did so in terms that were pure Hobson. The "new attitude of the State" towards wealth, Churchill declared, shall be to ask not only "How much have you got?" but also "How did you get it?" *Liberalism and the Social Problem,* 377 (1909), cited in Clarke, *Liberals and Social Democrats,* 117.

223. On the Fabians' influence on the Labour Party platform in its early years, and influence more generally on the emerging British welfare state, see Ricci, "Fabian Socialism," 119–121, and sources cited therein. Ricci argues that the almost total disappearance of rent-theory rhetoric from Fabian writings after 1920 does not signal its rejection, but rather its wholesale incorporation into Labour party politics. The principal legislative achievements of the Labour party—national health service, a comprehensive program of social insurance, steeply progressive taxation, nationalization of important industries—he argues, were all "predicated upon a socialist rationale borrowed in the party's formative years from early Fabianism, rent-theory Fabianism." Id. at 120.

224. See Walter J. Blum and Harry Kalven, Jr., *The Uneasy Case for Progressive Taxation,* 65 n.162 (1953). On the federal level, an "earned income" credit was in effect from 1924–1931 and from 1934–1941, ranging from 10 percent to 25 percent of the tax due on "earned" (generally, wage) incomes up to a ceiling ranging from $10,000 to $30,000. However, as certain amounts of unearned income were presumed to be earned income for these purposes, the differential effects of the credit were relatively modest. In addition, at least some adherents supported the credit on grounds unrelated to the moral worthiness of "earned income." See, e.g., Andrew W. Mellon, *Taxation: The People's Business,* 56–57 (1924).

225. See, e.g., *Christianizing the Social Order,* 222–234, 337–338, 346 (1915).

226. Walter Lippmann, *Drift and Mastery,* chap. 6 (1985), contains a lengthy and somewhat muddled diatribe against unearned wealth, lumping it with all inefficiencies of modern life as the source of "the Social Surplus," and suggesting in passing that inheritance taxes and drastically progressive income taxes be used to tap it. See also Herbert Croly, *The Promise of American Life,* 369–371, 381–385 (1963) (supporting an inheritance tax and a graduated tax on unearned surplus of quasi-monopolistic enterprises). For the *New Republic* crew's postwar enthusiasm for the New Liberal/Labour program, see Paul F. Bourke, "The Status of Politics 1909–1919: *The New Republic,* Randolph Bourne and Van Wyck Brooks," 8 *Journal of American Studies* 171, 172 (1974). Unlike the New Liberals, both Lippmann and Croly were more given to asserting generally the need for sweeping social change than to offering particular proposals, and they clearly repudiated the Fabian brand of social engineering. Lippmann's friendship with and admiration for Graham Wallas, documented in William E. Leuchtenburg, "Walter Lippmann's *Drift and Mastery,*" in *Drift and Mastery,* 1, came only after Wallas distanced himself from Fabian politics in later years. See Bourke, "The Status of Politics," 180–181. For a telling criticism of the ultimately conservative cast of reform rhetoric from Lippmann, Croly, and the *New Republic,* see Kenneth McNaught, "American Progressives and the Great Society," 53 *Journal of American History* 504, 515–517 (1966).

227. See Henry Carter Adams, "Suggestions for a System of Taxation," 1 *Publications of the Michigan Political Science Association* 60 (1894); Rexford G. Tugwell, *The Economic Basis of Public Interest*, 32 (1968); Simon N. Patten, *The Theory of Prosperity*, chap. 2 (1902); Patten, *Theory of Dynamic Economics*, 148–153; Patten, "The Scope of Political Economy," 2 *Yale Review* 264, 271–272 (1893). On Sidney Webb's connection to Seligman, Ely, and other American progressives, see Ross, "Socialism and American Liberalism," 30, 50, and sources cited therein. In addition, an earlier group of marginalists had invoked the language of rent theory to argue that the "unearned increment" was going to labor. See Walker, "Source of Business Profits," 277–278; Jacob H. Hollander, "The Residual Claimant Theory of Distribution," 17 *Quarterly Journal of Economics* 261, 270 (1903).

228. For Ely's early support for various proposals for taxing the unearned increment in land values, see *Outlines of Economics*, 363–365, 643–645 (rev. ed., 1908); *Taxation in American States and Cities*, 264–268 (New York, Crowell, 1888); "Land, Labor and Taxation" (pts. 1–6), 39 *Independent* 1541, 1571, 1608, 1646, 1680 (1887), 40 *Independent* 5 (1888). He also supported socializing the "unearned increment" accruing to natural monopolies. See *Socialism: An Examination of Its Nature, Its Strength and Its Weakness, with Suggestions for Social Reform*, 262–278 (New York, Crowell, 1894). On his later repudiation of rent theory, see Seligman, *Main Currents in Modern Economics*, 617–618.

229. 2 *Institutional Economics*, 805–833.

230. For a summary of this strand of Commons's thought, see Mary O. Furner, "The Republican Tradition and the New Liberalism," in *The State and Social Investigation in Britain and the United States*, 171 (Michael J. Lacey and Mary O. Furner, eds., 1993).

231. *The Distribution of Wealth*, 249 (1893).

232. *Legal Foundations of Capitalism*, 65–67. For discussion of Commons's analysis, see chap. 2. Mary Furner argues that Commons's distribution theory was influenced by the neo-Ricardian law of three rents, as well as by his reaction to John Bates Clark. Furner, "Knowing Capitalism: Public Investigation and the Labor Question in the Long Progressive Era," in *The State and Economic Knowledge*, 258 n.22 (Mary O. Furner and Barry Supple, eds., 1990).

233. Draft letter to the editor of the New Statesman, Sept. 2, 1913, Hale Papers, folder 62. For another, slightly later, declaration of faith in rent theory, see "The 'Physical Value' Fallacy," 722.

234. See Beer, *History of British Socialism*, pt. I, chap. 5, at 58, pt. II, chap. 2, at 101–102, 112–114, pt. IV, at 210 n.2; Driver, "John Locke," 90–91.

235. *Principles of Political Economy*, bk. V, chap. 2, §5, at 817–818. For similar comments insisting on the public origins of, and hence public right to, private surplus, see Hobhouse, *Democracy and Reaction*, 232–234; Hobhouse, *Liberalism and Other Writings*, 46–47; Hobson, *The Industrial System*, 218–219; Hobson, "Influence of Henry George," 337–338; Henry George, *Progress and Poverty*, 93–94; "The Constitution of the Society for the Study of National Economy," drafted by Simon Nelson Patten and Edmund James in 1884–1885, reproduced in Richard T. Ely, *Ground Under Our Feet*, app. III (1938); Adams, "Economics and Jurisprudence," 159–160; Edmund James, "The State as an Economic Factor," in *Science Economic Discussion*, 24, 32 (1886); Albion Small, "Scholarship and Social Agitation," 1 *American Journal of Sociology* 564, 571–578 (1896). Some such affirmative argument for the public's right to the surplus was needed, in addition to the argument against private right, to counter the argument (as one contemporary commentator has put it) that "[i]t is not so much that the producers *deserve* the product of their labors. It is rather that no one else does. . ." Lawrence C. Becker, *Property Rights: Philosophic Foundations*, 41 (1977).

236. Sidney and Beatrice Webb, *Constitution for the Socialist Commonwealth*, xii.

237. For Hobson's comments lauding Fabian rent theory for repudiating all earlier variants of rent theory that had erroneously assumed only one residual claimant, see "Influence of Henry George," 336.

238. See, e.g., Sidney Webb, Fabian Tract No. 5, *Facts for Socialists*, 12–13 (J. F. Oakeshott, ed., 1887) (arguing that what is popularly known as "class war" is in fact conflict that stems from the efforts of rentiers to retain their monopolistic hold over land, capital, and ability); Hobson, *The Science of Wealth*, 82 ("The only true bone of contention, the only valid cause of conflict between capital and labour, land, ability, is the unproductive surplus"); Commons, *Distribution of Wealth*, 249. See also J. A. Hobson, *Work and Wealth: A Human Valuation*, 276–277 (1914) (arguing that capital and labor were in harmony with respect to entitlements to "the productive surplus," the only source of discord being over division of "the unproductive surplus"). For Hobhouse's desire to forge a theory of just property rights that would appeal to the "hearts and intellects" of the propertied as well as the propertyless classes, and the warm reception that the theory got from other progressives, see Collini, *Liberalism and Sociology*, 144.

239. See chap. 2.

240. *The Nation*, Apr. 27, 1907, quoted in Clarke, *Liberals and Social Democrats*, 111.

241. See Shaw, Address to the Liberal Club, reprinted in *The Metropolitan Magazine*, Dec. 1913, at 9. Hale included excerpts of the address in the Legal Factors and Social Control materials, along with a somewhat critical review by Lewis Mumford in *The New Republic*, July 4, 1928, p. 177, of Shaw's expanded version of the same argument in *The Intelligent Woman's Guide to Socialism and Capitalism* (1928). While sharing Shaw's contempt for the traditional liberal arguments that *what* society ought to be equalizing was opportunity and not income, Hale ultimately sided with the New Liberals against Shaw in believing that the *extent* of such programs had to be limited by due regard for effort.

242. See Letter to the Editor, *The Nation*, May 17, 1913, at 268, 269, arguing that Hobhouse's proposal to "distribute income in rewards to exertion" was defeated by the impossibility of devising a measure for exertion. As to Hobhouse's suggestion that "time and piece-work," although rough, might be serviceable measures (*The Nation*, May 24, 1913, at 312), Shaw responded, "Mr. Hobhouse's notion that two hours' work means twice the exertion of one hour's work is the notion of a bricklayer; and as Mr. Hobhouse is not a bricklayer, I cannot imagine how he came to entertain it." Letter to the Editor, *The Nation*, May 31, 1913, at 350. Since Shaw was prepared to guarantee the same income to those who demonstrably did no work at all, however, the argument, though relevant to a Hobhousian scheme that purported to take account of effort, seems beside the point to Shaw's. A good summary of the Shaw-Hobhouse exchange—which was prompted by Shaw's address to the Liberal Club—can be found in Collini, *Liberalism and Sociology*, 134–136.

243. On the latter point, to Hobhouse's argument against the justice and prudence of supplying a "man with an income throughout his life whether he works or idles" (Letter to the Editor, *The Nation*, May 24, 1913, at 312), Shaw responded with his characteristic blend of flippant ridicule and deadly seriousness: "His refusal to work is not the end of the world. You can shame him; you can kick him; you can wait until he gets tired of idling or succumbs to the English horror of not doing what everybody is doing—of being eccentric, in short. You can even kill him, if you think the matter serious enough. Or you can support him in idleness, as we support so many nowadays. You can do fifty sensible and amiable things. Why should you do the one hopelessly silly, cruel, and disastrous thing [of throwing

him back into poverty], only to find an idle tramp on your hands after all?" Letter to the Editor, *The Nation*, May 31, 1913, at 350, 351.

244. Hale's comprehensive list of the possibilities included eliminating restraints on competition; reducing prices; increasing prices charged to recipients of large incomes (for the benefit of other patrons of the company charging the price); taxing excess income; and stimulating competition with the recipient of the large income, among other means by the government's educating competitors and loaning them capital. Handwritten notes on "Government Control in Industry," p. 2 ("Methods of Redistributing the Excess Incomes"), Hale Papers, folder 39.

245. Hobson, *Economics of Distribution*, 360.

246. See, e.g., Webb, *Socialism in England*, 126. For a more recent defense of inframarginal surplus along similar lines, see Hayek, 2 *Law, Legislation and Liberty: The Mirage of Social Justice*, 76–77 (1976).

247. Letter to Donald Richberg, Apr. 12, 1922, Hale Papers, folder 6. For further discussion of both points, see chap. 5.

248. See, e.g., 1 Taussig, *Principles of Economics*, 492 (1st ed., 1911); Adams, *Science of Finance*, 335 (1898); Thomas Carver, *Principles of National Economy* (1921).

249. See "Economic Theory and the Statesman," 217, for Hale's statement of this fundamental difference between taxation and rate regulation.

250. For Hale's explicit acknowledgment of the problem and his support of a land tax, in part because (unlike price regulation) it treated the injury as befalling all nonprivileged classes in general, see letter to *The New Statesman*, Sept. 2, 1913, Hale Papers, folder 62. See also draft mss. in folder 88 ("Economic Discrimination and Internationalism" and "Economic Nationalism versus Representative Government") noting that agreement about how much of an owner's income shall be taken from him still leaves open the question, "How much of this shall go into the public treasury, how much into the hands of his employees, and how much into the pockets of his customers?" The question, Hale argued, cannot be resolved by any general principle, but only by "some rule of expediency."

251. As Hale acknowledged, that response merely pushes the problem back one level, to justifying the redistributive transfer of income to those "by whom it will also be 'unearned.'" "Economic Theory and the Statesman," 219. As Hale hints here, and elsewhere expressly states, the justification for that transfer cannot be found in rent theory. It must be found in some broader theory of distributive ethics, which is collectivist in nature. For the same acknowledgment, see Hobhouse, *Liberalism and Other Writings*, 97–98.

It might be objected that the second step renders rent theory superfluous. If the reason to raise revenues is to redistribute wealth in accordance with collectivist aims, why bother justifying the initial levy on individualist (rent theory) grounds at all? The answer is that rent theory provides the Lockean justification for treating some portion of privately held wealth as public property. Once that wealth is public, individual rights pose no barrier to spending it in accordance with a collective vision of the common good. In this sense, the individualist rationale offered by rent theorists for expropriating property can be separated from the collectivist uses to which that property is put in a way in which Hale (rightly) argues that the essentially collectivist "ability to pay" or "minimum sacrifice" criteria for taxation cannot. See later discussion.

252. For a history of progressive tax legislation in the late nineteenth and early twentieth centuries in England and the United States, see Edwin R. A. Seligman, *Progressive Taxation in Theory and Practice*, 40–45, 101–118 (1908) (summarizing both countries through 1908);

Shehab, *Progressive Taxation*, 189–209; H. V. Emy, "The Impact of Financial Policy on English Party Politics before 1914," 15 *Historical Journal* 103 (1972); Ratner, *American Taxation*, chaps. 11–15.

253. Blum and Kalven's *The Uneasy Case* remains the most comprehensive presentation and critique to date of the arguments for progressivity. While not expressly historical in focus, the book provides an excellent summary of late nineteenth- and early twentieth-century arguments. Seligman's *Progressive Taxation in Theory and Practice* covers the period through 1907 in more depth, although with somewhat less theoretical sophistication. Many of Blum and Kalven's points were anticipated in skeletal form in Henry C. Simons, *Personal Income Taxation*, 3–29 (1938).

254. *The Communist Manifesto*, 30 [1848] (International Publishers, 1948).

255. Wagner's "socialist theory of progression" is discussed critically in Seligman, *Progressive Taxation*, 129–132. For a more sympathetic treatment, see Simons, *Personal Income Taxation*, 15–16, and Blum and Kalven, *The Uneasy Case*, 71 n.176.

256. See, e.g., J. R. McCulloch, *A Treatise on the Principles and Practical Influence of Taxation and the Funding System*, 142 (1845); Seligman, *Progressive Taxation*, 141.

257. *Principles of Political Economy*, bk. V, chap. 2, §6 (on land rents); id., §7, at 822 (on inheritance).

258. See, e.g., Mill, *Principles of Political Economy*, bk. V, chap. 2. §3; Benjamin Taylor, "The Income Tax," 206 *Quarterly Review* 331, 335 (1907); J. R. McCulloch, "On the Complaints and Proposals Regarding Taxation," 57 *Edinburgh Review* 143, 164 (1833); Seligman, *Progressive Taxation*, 131. At least some of those who opposed egalitarianism as a motive for taxation (Seligman being a notable example) were perfectly happy to see it result from a progressive scheme justified on nonegalitarian grounds. See Seligman, "The Theory of Progressive Taxation," 8 *Political Science Quarterly* 220, 222 (1893); Taylor, "The Income Tax," 335.

259. For discussions of the "benefit" and "equal sacrifice" theories, see Seligman, *Progressive Taxation*, 150–228; Blum and Kalven, *The Uneasy Case*, 35–45.

260. For support for the latter view, on the ground that "a person who commands more of the resources of society will also gain proportionately more from what the government has contributed," see Hayek, *The Constitution of Liberty*, 316.

261. For Mill's version, see *Principles of Political Economy*, bk. V, chap. 2, §2. For Sidgwick's, see *Principles of Political Economy*, 518–533, 566–571 (2d ed., 1887). For a summary of subsequent tax theorists who adhered to an "absolute sacrifice" definition of equal sacrifice, see Blum and Kalven, *The Uneasy Case*, 43 n.110.

Mill's theory of just taxation is notoriously ambiguous. It is clear that Mill supported a proportionate tax on all earned incomes above subsistence level. It is less clear why. The most consistent inference that one can draw from his discussion in *Principles of Political Economy* is that he supported a proportionate tax because he believed that it would result in an equal absolute sacrifice from all taxpayers, once the declining marginal utility of money was taken into account. See, e.g., his discussion of exemptions and abatements, bk. V, chap. 2, §3, at 806–807. But there are suggestions as well in *Principles* that he supported a proportionate tax because he believed that it would result in the minimum sacrifice for all taxpayers (see later), and (more ambiguously) because he believed that it would result in a proportionate sacrifice for all taxpayers. Moreover, whichever of the three interpretations is correct, since Mill equated "sacrifice" with subjective disutility, his support of a proportionate tax to distribute sacrifices in the desired fashion depended on his assumptions about the utility of money. That fact was not lost on Mill's later progressive followers, who argued that Mill had rejected comprehensive progressivity not on principle, but merely on the strength of an (as it turned out) erroneous empirical assumption that the law of diminishing marginal utility held true over only a rather limited range of incomes. That reading gained more than a little support from the revisions Mill made in the 1852 (3d) edition of *Principles*. He deleted references to schemes to "tax the larger incomes at a higher percentage than the smaller" as a "mild form of robbery," and to proportional taxes as the fairest standard of "real equality," inserting in their place the statement merely that "Whether the person with £10,000 a year cares less for £1000 than the person with only £1000 a year cares for £100 . . . does not appear to me capable of being decided with the degree of certainty on which a legislator or a financier ought to act." Id. at 807. In fact, Mill's inconsistent pronouncements on the issue of taxation, like many other inconsistencies in *Principles*, suggest that his "monarchical influence" over his contemporaries (as Bagehot put it in his obituary of Mill) was due at least in part to the fact that most people could find in *Principles* whatever they were looking for. As Hobhouse noted, that need not be construed as an insult. See *Liberalism and Other Writings*, 51–52.

262. See Blum and Kalven, *The Uneasy Case*, 40. Although tax theorists in the last century have universally assumed that sacrifice should be measured by the utility of money, that conclusion is by no means inevitable. One could measure sacrifice instead, for example, by the hours that one must work to cover one's tax liability to the state, a standard that would produce a proportionate tax, at least on earned income. See id. at 59 n.148. One could also measure sacrifice simply by dollars relinquished, a standard that would obviously produce the steeply regressive head tax. Contrary to the general view, the choice to measure sacrifice by the utility of money rather than by its face value is neither obvious nor distributively neutral. It rejects the normal "market" measure of sacrifice—nominal price exacted—in favor of subjective disutility, which is (by hypothesis) correlated inversely with the initial distribution of wealth. Thus, it could fairly be argued, that choice smuggles in through the back door the distributive concerns that it has ostentatiously barred at the front. It does so not, as in proportionate or marginal sacrifice, by exacting an absolutely greater sacrifice from the rich (see later), but by measuring absolute sacrifice in accordance with a standard that has distributive objectives built into it.

263. See id. at 42; Blaug, *Economic Theory in Retrospect*, 336–338.

264. The somewhat confused history of "proportionate sacrifice" theory is summarized in Blum and Kalven, *The Uneasy Case*, 41–44. The earliest clear exposition and defense of "proportionate sacrifice" was given by the Dutch economist Cohen-Stuart, in *A Contribution to the Theory of Progressive Taxation* [1889] (Ms. trans. Te Velde, University of Chicago Libraries, 1936). Proponents of "proportionate sacrifice" have generally assumed that a tax scheme built on that principle would be nonredistributive in nature, and hence would not violate individualist entitlements to wealth. See, e.g., Blum and Kalven, *The Uneasy Case*, 43–44. The assumption is open to doubt. Blum and Kalven, like Cohen-Stuart before them, rest their argument on the fact that under a "proportionate sacrifice" formula, all taxpayers are "equally worse off" after taxes, *as measured by "the relative distribution of satisfactions among taxpayers."* Id. at 44 (emphasis added). But one could as easily argue that taxpayers will be "equally worse off" only when they are deprived of equal amounts of satisfaction—a notion of "worseness" that would obviously favor absolute sacrifice as the distributively neutral solution. The choice between the two measures thus boils down to a choice between absolute well-being and relative well-being as the salient characteristic of one's pretax position to which one holds an entitlement. There seems no obvious normative reason for preferring one choice over the other.

265. As Cohen-Stuart demonstrated, it is possible to construct declining marginal utility curves for which, under a proportionate sacrifice theory, regressive taxes would result for some portion of the curve. See Seligman, *Progressive Taxation,* 218–222; F. Y. Edgeworth, "Minimum Sacrifice versus Equal Sacrifice," in 2 *Papers Relating to Political Economy,* 234, 239–240 (1925). However, the curves that would satisfy that condition are sufficiently improbable that as a practical matter, they are generally disregarded. See Blum and Kalven, *The Uneasy Case,* 43 n.109.

266. See Seligman, *Progressive Taxation,* 222; Edgeworth, "The Pure Theory of Taxation," in 2 *Papers Relating to Political Economy,* 63, 116–117; Blum and Kalven, *The Uneasy Case,* 45.

267. Carver's version of the argument was initially presented in "The Ethical Basis of Distribution and Its Application to Taxation," 6 *Annals of the American Academy* 79 (1895), and subsequently elaborated in "The Minimum Sacrifice Theory of Taxation," 19 *Political Science Quarterly* 66 (1904). Edgeworth developed his version of the argument in two essays, "The Pure Theory of Taxation," and "Minimum Sacrifice versus Equal Sacrifice." Pigou is the name most closely associated with the argument in the twentieth century. See, e.g., *Study in Public Finance,* pt. II, chaps. 4 & 5; Pigou, *Economics of Welfare.* For a good summary of the development of the equimarginal principle, see Blum and Kalven, *The Uneasy Case,* 49–52; Shehab, *Progressive Taxation,* 199–209.

The notion that taxes should be set to minimize their total disutility was not new with Carver or Edgeworth. Most of the early marginalists, including Jevons, Wicksteed, and Marshall, considered the possibility that the declining marginal utility of money would mandate that incomes be equalized on utilitarian grounds. Bentham had anticipated the argument in *Principles of the Civil Code,* pt. I, chap. 13, in 1 *The Works of Jeremy Bentham,* 13 (1859). So also had Mill, in a passage that has been endlessly debated. Beginning by advocating "equal sacrifice" as the only just rule of taxation, Mill thus concludes: "As a government ought to make no distinction of persons or classes in the strength of their claims on it, whatever sacrifices it requires from them should be made to bear as nearly as possible with the same pressure upon all, *which, it must be observed, is the mode by which least sacrifice is occasioned on the whole.*" *Principles of Political Economy,* bk. V, chap. 2, §2, at 804 (emphasis added). As innumerable commentators have since noted, Mill's equation of "equal" and "minimum" sacrifice is obviously erroneous. It also leaves ambiguous whether (as a normative matter) Mill embraced the former merely as a means of achieving the latter, or the latter merely as a happy by-product of the former. Edgeworth, in an attempt to rescue Mill from logical error and simultaneously resolve his loyalties in favor of minimum sacrifice, suggested the possibility that *"equal sacrifice* [was] but a corrupt reading" from the start for *"equi-marginal sacrifice."* See "The Pure Theory of Taxation," 115.

268. Carver, "The Minimum Sacrifice Theory"; Carver, *Principles of National Economy,* 644–660 (1921).

269. "Coercion and Distribution," 487. See also Hale's unpublished draft review of Carver's *Essays in Social Justice,* pt. II, 11–14, Hale Papers, folder 87. For similar observations, see Edgeworth, "The Pure Theory of Taxation," 103; Pigou, *Study in Public Finance,* 57–58. Hale leveled a parallel criticism at Seligman and other "ability to pay" tax theorists for artificially segregating the burdens imposed by taxation from those entailed in the residual distribution of wealth, and thereby robbing the "ability to pay" theory "of any value as a theory of justice." Unpublished review of Carver's *Essays in Social Justice,* id. at 13; "Coercion and Distribution," 485–488; "Economic Theory and the Statesman," 217.

Hale argued (persuasively, I think) that at least in the case of the "ability to pay" theorists, the motivation for segregating the tax and expenditure side of public finance was to maintain the illusion that tax policy was "aloof[] from the problems of the propriety of distribution": "If the distribution of wealth is faulty, they say in effect, correct it in some other manner; taxation is difficult enough as it is, without raising more difficulties as to distribution. Therefore, forget the faults of distribution when levying taxes, but make each person pay, as nearly as is practical, according to his ability to pay. The result will be, it is true, to diminish the rich man's income by a greater amount than that taken from the poor man's; but since someone has to bear the burden, it is better that those best able to should bear the most." Id. at 217–218. As Hale suggested here and elsewhere, the illusion is without any substance.

270. "The Pure Theory of Taxation," 104. Sidgwick retreated from an early form of minimum sacrifice theory to the "equal sacrifice" principle, when he realized that "if the [former] principle of addressing inequalities is applied at all, any limit to its application seems quite arbitrary." *Principles of Political Economy,* bk. III, chap. 7, §1, at 520, and bk. III, chap. 8, §7, at 567.

271. Edgeworth concluded that the optimal tax, taking into account incentive effects, might well be a degressive one—that is, a progressive tax on lower incomes and a proportionate tax on higher incomes. "The Pure Theory of Taxation," 109–112. Carver was somewhat more optimistic that the result would be an at least moderately progressive tax throughout most income brackets. See "Minimum Sacrifice Theory," 79; "Ethical Basis of Distribution," 94–97. For Hale's support for moderating progressivity for incentive reasons, see, e.g., his draft review of Carver's *Essays,* pt. II, at 11, Hale Papers, folder 87. Indeed, Hale would have gone even further than Carver and Edgeworth, taking into account the possibility that for any given wealth distributed, the psychological cost of reducing the settled expectations of the rich may exceed the benefit to the poor. "Coercion and Distribution," 488.

272. See Edgeworth, "The Pure Theory of Taxation," 102–103 (arguing, in an interesting variant of the modern-day Rawlsian appeal to ex ante self-interest, that since no one can expect in the long run to obtain a larger than average share of the total welfare, even a self-interested person will conclude that in the long term, the "maximum sum-total utility corresponds to [his] maximum individual utility"); Pigou, *Study in Public Finance,* chaps. 4 and 6 (defending equimarginal sacrifice as "equal sacrifice" among individuals of different taxable capacity).

273. Edgeworth, "The Pure Theory of Taxation," 100–101, 103; Pigou, *Economics of Welfare,* pt. iv, chap. 9, at 715–717. For the suggestion that political support for Edgeworthian utilitarianism itself is rooted in egalitarianism, see Blum and Kalven, *The Uneasy Case,* 55.

274. For a discussion of Robbins's attack, see earlier. For a generally sympathetic summary of the other attacks on the empirical assumptions necessary to translate equimarginal sacrifice theory into a workable tax scheme, see Blum and Kalven, *The Uneasy Case,* 56–63.

275. For support for a tax targeting rents on this ground, see Hobson, *The Economics of Distribution,* 315; Hobson, *Taxation in the New State,* pt. I, chap. 2; H. J. Davenport, "The Formula of Sacrifice," 2 *Journal of Political Economy* 561, 570–571 (1894); Mill, *Principles of Political Economy,* bk. V, chap. 2, §3, at 808.

276. *Liberalism and Other Writings,* 97. See also Mill, *Principles of Political Economy,* bk. 1, chap. 1; Hale, "Economic Theory and the Statesman," 220: "Since [such] incomes . . . are special benefits conferred by the government, it follows that failure to tax those incomes completely away is to confer special favors on that class." The clearest defense of a rent-theory-based scheme of redistributive taxation was given by Hobson in *The Industrial System.* For a discussion of Hobson's argument, see Freeden, "J. A. Hobson as a New Liberal

Theorist," 34 *Journal of the History of Ideas* 421 (1973), and P. F. Clarke, Introduction to J. A. Hobson, *Crisis of Liberalism*, ix (P. F. Clarke, ed., 1974). For a particularly clear statement from progressives embracing both the utilitarian and rights-based justification for progressive taxation, see *Towards a Social Policy*, 123–124, quoted in Collini, *Liberalism and Sociology*, 118 n.172. See also Patten, *Theory of Dynamic Economics*, 148–153.

277. See, e.g., Hobhouse, *Liberalism and Other Writings*, 95; Hobson, *The Industrial System*, 231–232. For Hale's support of a 100 percent tax on inheritances above the minimum amount necessary to induce lifetime savings by would-be bequeathers, see draft review of Brown's *Earned and Unearned Incomes*, Hale Papers, folder 58.

278. See, e.g., 2 Taussig, *Principles of Economics*, 516–517, which Hale excerpted in the ELP and Social Control materials; and sources previously cited.

279. That is, one would have to assume that few savers were marginal, and that most inframarginal savers had a reservation price close to zero. For the widespread acceptance of "abstinence" as a real cost of saving, see earlier.

280. See n.242.

281. See Clarke, *Liberals and Social Democrats*, 110–111; Shehab, *Progressive Taxation*, 246–250. The solution was endorsed by at least some of the New Liberals. See, e.g., Hobhouse, *Democracy and Reaction*, 233.

282. On the New Liberals' move towards progressivity as the solution to the problem of "unearned income," see Collini, *Liberalism and Sociology*, 117–119, 133–134; Clarke, *Liberals and Social Democrats*, 111, 113–115. The report of the 1907 Select Committee of Taxation supported graduated rates (in addition to differentiation on the basis of source of income). That policy was enacted in the "super-tax" on incomes over £5,000 a year imposed in Lloyd George's 1909 Budget, and graduated rates on higher earned incomes imposed in his 1914 Budget. See Shehab, *Progressive Taxation*, chaps. 13 and 14.

283. *Economics of Distribution*, 332. See also Hobson, *Taxation in the New State*, viii (1913). Hobhouse, defending the 1909 budget, acknowledged that "the distinctions drawn are not perfectly scientific, but they are the best rough-and-ready approximations that have yet been made on this side to a form of taxation tending to relieve steady industry at the expense of good fortune." Leader, *Manchester Guardian*, Dec. 13, 1909, quoted in Collini, *Liberalism and Sociology*, 134. For a similar admission and defense, see Hobson, *The Conditions of Industrial Peace* 85 (1927). For Taussig's more detailed but ultimately still speculative attempt to defend a progressive tax on interest as the best means to isolate "saver's rent," see 2 *Principles of Economics*, chap. 68, §5, at 516–517.

284. Hobhouse, *Liberalism and Other Writings*, 96–97; Hobhouse, *The Labour Movement*, 123 n.1.

285. See Collini, *Liberalism and Sociology*, 131–133. As Clarke notes, "It is a recurrent difficulty in Hobsonian economics that some such supposition is in the end always necessary." *Liberals and Social Democrats*, 52. For Hobson's own skepticism about the "hypothesis that unearned surplus varies directly and closely with the size of the income," see *The Industrial System*, 239–240.

286. Draft typescript entitled "Regulation of Public Services Companies," pp. 1–2 (section entitled "General Principles of Distribution"), Hale Papers, folder 49. The draft, which is dated 1914–15, appears to be an early draft of *Valuation and Rate-Making*. Hale's argument assumes that the supply curve is identical to costs that should be counted as relevant for purposes of rent theory, and further assumes that ex ante miscalculations by producers as to expected revenue will in the aggregate cancel out.

287. Unpublished review of H. G. Brown's *The Theory of Earned and Unearned Incomes*, p. 1, Hale Papers, folder 58.

288. On the former, Hale hand-copied the following passage from Mark Twain's *A Connecticut Yankee in King Arthur's Court*, lampooning the fairness of a head tax: "If you take a nation of 60,000,000 where average wages are $2 per day, 3 days' wages taken from each individual will provide $360,000,000 and pay the government's expenses. In my own day, in my own country, this money was collected from imports, and the citizen imagined that the foreign importer paid it, and it made him comfortable to think so; whereas, in fact, it was paid by the American people, and was so equally and exactly distributed among them that the annual cost to the $100-millionaire and the annual cost to the sucking child of the day laborer was precisely the same—each paid $6. Nothing could be equaller than that I reckon." Hale Papers, folder 58.

289. Untitled typescript on rate regulation of public utilities (beginning "It is surprising that so little interest . . ."), 1 (n.d., but from internal evidence, appears to be an early draft of *Valuation and Rate Making*), Hale Papers, box 21.

290. Hale to Learned Hand, Oct. 27, 1912, p. 2, Hale Papers, folder 62.

291. Untitled typescript on rate regulation of public utilities, p. 1, Hale Papers, box 21.

5. Property Theory in Practice

1. The 1887 Interstate Commerce Act that created the ICC had arguably bestowed upon the ICC power to set maximum rates. The Court in Interstate Commerce Commission v. Cincinnati, N.O. & T.P. Ry. Co, 167 U.S. 479 (1897), however, ruled that the ambiguity was fatal. Its decision in effect limited the ICC's powers only to recommending rate changes that the railroads could voluntarily adopt. In the 1906 Hepburn Act, Congress finally unambiguously granted the ICC power to set maximum rates upon complaint of a shipper.

The breathtakingly brief summary of railroad rate regulation provided in the text elides an enormously complicated and much debated history. For present purposes, in which railroad rate regulation is relevant mainly as a forerunner of public utilities regulation and as a testing ground for legal doctrine subsequently extended to public utilities as well, this brief account may suffice. For fuller accounts of the Granger movement and other state rate regulatory efforts that followed, see Solon Justus Buck, *The Granger Movement* (1913); George H. Miller, *Railroads and the Granger Laws* (1971); Robert L. Rabin, "Federal Regulation in Historical Perspective," 38 *Stanford Law Review* 1189, 1197–1206; Grover G. Huebner, "Five Years of Railroad Regulation by the States," 32 *Annals of the American Academy of Political and Social Science* 138 (1908). State regulatory commissions typically took one of two forms: the so-called "weak" commission, with power only to investigate and recommend rates, and the so-called "strong" commission, with power to mandate rates. For an account of the states' largely ineffectual efforts prior to the Granger movement to regulate railroad rates or profits by provisions inserted in railroads' charters, see Miller, *Railroads and the Granger Laws*, 30–31. The classic treatment of railroad regulation under the ICC is I. L. Sharfman's five-volume study, *The Interstate Commerce Commission: A Study in Administrative Law and Procedure* (1931–1937). Ari Hoogenboom and Olive Hoogenboom, *A History of the ICC* (1976), and Stephen Skowronek, *Building a New American State: The Expansion of National Administrative Capacities, 1877–1920*, 150–162, 248–284 (1982), provide good, contemporary treatments. Gabriel Kolko's *Railroads and Regulation* (1965) spawned a substantial revisionist history of railroad regulation, arguing that the ICC functioned largely to protect railroads' interests. A summary of the revisionist literature can be found in Skowronek, *Building a New American State*, 125-131, and Hoogenboom and Hoogenboom, *History of the ICC*, 191-195, which also give a good overview more generally of the scholarly literature on the ICC.

2. G. Lloyd Wilson et al., *Public Utility Regulation*, 15-20 (1938); I. Leo Sharfman, "Commission Regulation of Public Utilities: A Survey of Legislation," 53 *Annals of the American Academy of Political and Social Science* 1, 3-4 and n.2, 9-11, 14-16 (1914). There were sporadic efforts to control utilities' prices prior to 1907 by direct state legislation. See Louis Cox, "The Regulation of Public Utilities, Other than Railroads, by State Administrative Commissions," 20 *Kentucky Law Journal* 133, 141-144 (1931).

3. The extent to which British and American legislatures in earlier periods had sought to regulate prices was a matter of much dispute at the time, with progressives typically arguing that such statutes were far more common than generally thought. See, e.g., Breck P. McAllister, "Lord Hale and Business Affected with a Public Interest," 43 *Harvard Law Review* 759, 767 (1930); "State Regulation of Prices under the Fourteenth Amendment," 33 *Harvard Law Review*, 838-839 (1920); Edward A. Adler, "Business Jurisprudence," 28 *Harvard Law Review* 135, 146-147 (1914); New State Ice Co. v. Liebmann, 285 U.S. 262, 305-306 (1932) (Brandeis, J., dissenting); Young B. Smith et al., *Cases on Public Utilities*, 1-3 (2d ed. 1936).

4. On the central role of public utilities and railroad rate regulation in litigation over price controls, see Henry Rottschaefer, "The Field of Governmental Price Control," 35 *Yale Law Journal* 438, 439-443 (1926); 3 Charles Warren, *The Supreme Court in United States History*, 463 (1922); Albert N. Merritt, *Federal Regulation of Railroad Rates*, 160-161 (1907).

5. Felix Frankfurter, *The Public and Its Government*, 83 (1930).

6. For Hale's use of the horizontal/vertical distinction, see "The Constitution and the Price System: Some Reflections on Nebbia v. New York," 34 *Columbia Law Review* 401, 424-425 (1934).

7. Letter to Frank Haigh Dixon, Apr. 8, 1922, Hale Papers, folder 6.

8. Letter to Brandeis, June 4, 1916, Hale Papers, mss. folder. For other comments indicating Hale's dim view of the competence of the Court (and indeed the legal profession in general) to deal with economic questions, see "Economic Theory and the Statesman," in *The Trend of Economics*, 191, 213-214 (Rexford G. Tugwell, ed., 1924); Letter to Harlan Fiske Stone, June 29, 1929, Hale Papers, mss. folder: "The Supreme Court seems to me at a pretty low ebb just now. Except for you and Holmes and Brandeis, there is no Justice really equipped to deal with constitutional questions having any economic aspect. . . They have that dangerous combination of ignorance with assurance that they are right."

9. See, e.g., letter from N. T. Guernsey to the editors of *American Bar Association Journal*, and the editors' none-too-pleased response to Hale, in Hale Papers, folder 74. For a similar, charged exchange between James C. Bonbright and Judge William L. Ransom, see Bonbright, "Value of the Property as the Basis of Rate Regulation," 2 *Journal of Land & Public Utility Economics* 276 (1926), and Ransom, "Comments upon Professor Bonbright's Article," 2 *Journal of Land & Public Utility Economics* 281 (1926).

10. 22 *Columbia Law Review* 209, 213 (1922). Similar statements indicating the importance of public utilities regulation as a testing ground for more general controls on property rights can be found throughout Hale's writings on public utilities. See *Valuation and Rate-Making*, 148-149 (1918); "Non-Cost Standards in Rate Making," 36 *Yale Law Journal* 56, 65-67 (1926); letter to Learned Hand, Oct. 27, 1912, Hale Papers, folder 62; letter to Lesley Ames, Jan. [27?], 1915, Hale Papers, folder 25, stating that some of the issues he was dealing with in *Valuation and Rate-Making* are "questions which might come up if regulation were to be used more seriously as a tool for correcting the evil results of unlimited property rights."

11. "Economic Theory and the Statesman," 214.

12. Letter to Brandeis, June 4, 1916, p. 4, Hale Papers, mss. folder. Hale did go on to suggest that the Justices might use the pulpit that they had, at least in *dicta*, to "enlighten the bar and the law schools on the functions of property; law students have to read and try to understand, at least, the opinions of Supreme Court Justices—and if any of these are radical it is about the only radical thought they become acquainted with." Id., pp. 4–5.

13. Letter to Richmond Weed, June 3, 1942, Hale Papers, folder 12.

14. "Rate Making and the Revision of the Property Concept," 215. See also *Valuation and Rate-Making*, 137, 148–149, and *Freedom Through Law*, 535 (1952).

15. "Rate Making and the Revision of the Property Concept," 216.

16. For comments on the Granger movement, see "The Potter Act at Washington," 9 *American Law Review* 212, 235 (1875). For counsels' anticommunist rhetoric in *Munn* and companion cases, see Charles Fairman, "The So-called Granger Cases, Lord Hale, and Justice Bradley," 5 *Stanford Law Review* 587, 640–641, 644–645, 647–651 (1953), and Benjamin R. Twiss, *Lawyers and the Constitution*, 86–87 [1942] (Russell & Russell, Inc. 1962).

17. "Property and the Supreme Court," *New York Tribune*, quoted in 3 Warren, *The Supreme Court*, 304.

18. John Norton Pomeroy, "The Supreme Court and State Repudiation—The Virginia and Louisiana Cases," 17 *American Law Review* (1883), quoted in 2 Warren, *The Supreme Court*, 582–583. For a summary of the popular reaction to Granger legislation and the decision in *Munn* as representing a step towards socialism, see 3 Warren, *The Supreme Court*, 303–305. See also Maurice Finkelstein, "From Munn v. Illinois to Tyson v. Banton: A Study in the Judicial Process," 27 *Columbia Law Review* 769, 777 (1927).

19. Edmond E. Lincoln, "The Control of Return on Public Utility Investments," 6 *American Economic Review* 869, 873 (1916).

20. 1 *Publications of the American Economic Association* 471 (1887).

21. Benjamin G. Rader, *The Academic Mind and Reform*, 88–91, 224–225 (1966). For the suggestion that the later Ely was a captive of utility industry interests, see id. at 208–213. Other progressives who supported municipal ownership of utilities and other natural monopolies included Walter Rauschenbusch and Edward Bellamy (the latter supporting it as part of a program to nationalize all business and industry). See Rauschenbusch, *Christianizing the Social Order*, 435–440 (1912), and *Christianity and the Social Crisis*, 386–389 [1907] (Robert D. Cross ed., Harper Torchbooks 1964); Bellamy, *Equality*, 330–339, 406–409 (1897) and "The Programme of the Nationalists," 17 *Forum* 6 (1894). Proposals to nationalize public utilities had much wider support among European progressives. See James T. Kloppenberg, *Uncertain Victory: Social Democracy and Progressivism in European and American Thought, 1870–1920*, 255–257 (1986).

22. In 1888, only about a dozen states allowed municipalities to own gasworks, and all electric and streetcar companies were privately owned. Morton Keller, *Affairs of State*, 340–341 (1977). In 1900, only 26 of 981 cities had municipal gasworks, and only 13 percent of urban electric systems were publicly owned. Morton Keller, *Regulating a New Economy: Public Policy and Economic Change in America, 1900–1933*, 56 (1990). By 1932, roughly 97 percent of electric output was generated by privately owned power plants. Wilson et al., *Public Utility Regulation*, 524. For a summary of municipally owned utilities as of 1936, see id., 521–525. Railroads were briefly nationalized in late 1917, to prevent bankruptcy and to meet the exigencies of the war, but reverted to private control in 1920. Skowronek, *Building a New American State*, 276–283. By way of contrast, in 1928, roughly two-thirds of all electric power and 40 percent

of gas in Great Britain were produced by municipally owned companies. Marshall E. Dimock, "British and American Utilities: A Comparison," 1 *University of Chicago Law Review* 265, 267 (1933).

23. "The Trusts, the People, and the Square Deal," *Outlook* 649, 654 (1911). For other comments from progressives that were meant to allay the widespread fear that public control of utilities was the first step towards public ownership of all private industry, see 2 F. W. Taussig, *Principles of Economics*, 434–435 (3d ed. 1921); Wilson et al., *Public Utility Regulation*, 546–547.

24. See, e.g., John Bauer, "The Control of Return on Public Utility Investments," 31 *Political Science Quarterly* 260, 285 (1916); Donald R. Richberg, "A Permanent Basis for Rate Regulation," 31 *Yale Law Journal* 263, 276 (1922); *N.Y. State Commission on Revision of the Public Service Commissions Law, Report of Commissioners*, 1 (1930), quoted in Frankfurter, *The Public and Its Government*, 94. Henry Carter Adams, defending the ICC on similar grounds, stated that if the ICC "succeeds, we may look for a solution of all the vexed industrial problems in harmony with the fundamental principles of English liberty. If it fails, there is nothing for the future of our civilization but the tyranny of socialism." Thomas G. Craig and H. C. Adams, "Discussion of the Interstate Commerce Act," *Publications of the Michigan Political Science Association* (May 1893), 143.

25. "Rate Making and the Revision of the Property Concept," 216.

26. See Martin J. Sklar, *The Corporate Reconstruction of American Capitalism, 1890–1916*, 228–297 (1988). For a more skeptical view of the reformist thrust of such legislation, see Gabriel Kolko, *The Triumph of Conservatism*, 133–138, 261–267, 280–281 (1963); James Weinstein, *The Corporate Ideal in the Liberal State: 1900–1918*, 74–91 (1968); Robert H. Wiebe, *Businessmen and Reform*, 79–85 (1962).

27. Federal Power Commission v. Hope Natural Gas Co., 320 U.S. 591 (1944).

28. 169 U.S. 466 (1898).

29. Charles C. Marshall, "A New Constitutional Amendment," 24 *American Law Review* 908, 931 (1890).

30. There are a number of fine studies of *Munn* and the "affected with a public interest" criterion that it suggested. See especially Fairman, "The So-called Granger Cases"; Walton H. Hamilton, "Affectation with Public Interest," 39 *Yale Law Journal* 1089 (1930); McAllister, "Business Affected with a Public Interest"; Harry Scheiber, "The Road to *Munn*: Eminent Domain and the Concept of Public Purpose in the State Courts," in 5 *Perspectives in American History*, 329 (Donald Fleming and Bernard Bailyn, eds., 1971); Stephen A. Siegel, "Understanding the *Lochner* Era: Lessons from the Controversy over Railroad and Utility Rate Regulation," 70 *Virginia Law Review* 187, 194–215 (1984). For a discussion of *Munn's* reception, see 3 Warren, *The Supreme Court*, 303–311. For summaries of the various interpretations given to its legal standard, see Rexford G. Tugwell, *The Economic Basis of Public Interest*, 38–42 (1922); Charles W. McCurdy, "Justice Field and the Jurisprudence of Government-Business Relations: Some Parameters of Laissez-Faire Constitutionalism, 1863–1897," 61 *Journal of American History* 970, 995–998 (1975); Siegel, "Understanding the *Lochner* Era," 199–207; Rottschaefer, "Governmental Price Control," 443–447; Dexter Merriam Keezer and Stacy May, *The Public Control of Business*, 97–120 [1930] (Arno Press 1973). Hale's version of the confusing history of the "affectation with a public interest" doctrine from *Munn* to *Nebbia* is given in "The Constitution and the Price System," and *Freedom Through Law*, 402–429.

31. Munn v. Illinois, 125–126.

32. For the standard interpretation that Waite (and Justice Bradley, from whom Waite likely got the cite to Lord Hale) quoted Lord Hale merely to deck out the police power doctrine in ancient lineage so as to "make new legislation congenial," see Felix Frankfurter, *The Commerce Clause Under Marshall, Taney and Waite*, 86–87 [1937] (Peter Smith 1978), and Hamilton, "Affectation with Public Interest," 1092–1097.

33. Rottschaefer, "Governmental Price Control," 448–450. For further discussion, see chap. 4, n.5.

34. See Williams v. Standard Oil Co., 278 U.S. 235, 239 (1929); Hamilton, "Affectation with Public Interest," 1091–1092; Rottschaefer, "Governmental Price Control," 443–451. For the argument that *Munn* itself had announced a more stringent standard for price regulations, see Justice Lamar's dissent in German Alliance Insurance Co. v. Kansas, 233 U.S. 389, 424–428 (1914). *Non*price regulations, in contrast, were usually upheld without any inquiry into whether the businesses in question were "affected with a public interest." There were, however, some notable (indeed, notorious) exceptions involving the nonprice terms of labor contracts, in which the Court struck down regulations, although again without any inquiry into the "affectation" question. Lochner v. New York, 198 U.S. 45 (1905); Adair v. United States, 208 U.S. 161 (1908); Coppage v. Kansas, 236 U.S. 1 (1915). As noted in chap. 4, n.5, the judicial hostility to nonprice regulation of labor contracts reflects, in significant part, the politically charged nature of the struggle over all labor legislation.

35. Rottschaefer, "Governmental Price Control," 447, 450–451.

36. 291 U.S. 502 (1934). In the first three decades after *Munn*, a more liberal interpretation of the "affectation" requirement prevailed, with the Court's generally upholding the price regulations that it reviewed. Beginning in the 1920s, a more conservative Court, taking a narrower view of the doctrine, invoked it increasingly to strike down price controls. For a brief overview of the changing fortunes of the doctrine, see Hamilton, "Affectation with Public Interest," 1097–1103.

37. 262 U.S. 522, 535 (1923).

38. People ex rel. Annan v. Walsh, 22 N.E. 682 (N.Y. 1889) (Peckham, J., dissenting). *Annan* was initially unreported, and then subsequently appended to the later case of People v. Budd, 22 N.E. 670 (N.Y. 1889), in which Judge Gray, dissenting along with Peckham, reiterated much of Peckham's argument.

39. Thomas M. Cooley, "Limits to State Control of Private Business," 1 *Princeton Review* 233, 252–253 (ser. 4, 1878) (written directly in response to *Munn*); Thomas M. Cooley, *Constitutional Limitations*, 736–739 (5th ed. 1883); Christopher G. Tiedeman, *A Treatise on the Limitations of Police Power in the United States*, 233–234 [1886] (Da Capo Press 1971). While conceding the legislature's right to regulate formal monopolies, Cooley and Tiedeman both argued that the right did not extend to the sort of "virtual" (i.e., de facto) monopoly at issue in *Munn*, in which a business occupied the field by superior industry and without the aid of special privileges, leaving all others at liberty under the law to compete with that business if they so desired. Cooley, "Limits to State Control," 268–269; Tiedeman, "Limitations on Police Power," 234–238.

40. The Slaughterhouse Cases, 83 U.S. 36, 48 (1873) (reporter's synopsis of plaintiff's oral argument). For the almost universal support of the government's right to regulate businesses operating under special grants of privilege, see Michael Les Benedict, "Laissez-faire and Liberty: A Re-Evaluation of the Meaning and Origins of Laissez-Faire Constitutionalism," 3 *Law and History Review* 315–322 (1985); Siegel, "Understanding the *Lochner* Era," 204–207; Sklar, *Corporate Reconstruction*, 34–38. As noted in chap. 3, that view found strong support

from Mill, Sidgwick, and other nineteenth-century liberals. For an amusing description of the "evangelical" overtones in which the courts described exemption from competition as a "dedication" or "consecration" of property to the public interest, see Walton H. Hamilton, "Price—By Way of Litigation," 38 *Columbia Law Review* 1008, 1019 (1938). The "consecration," Hamilton notes drily, apparently "has been the removal of the business from the tumultuous course of events to the monastic retreat of a closed industry."

41. Wolff Packing v. Court of Indus. Relations, 534–535.

42. Munn v. Illinois, 132.

43. McAllister, "Business Affected with a Public Interest," 768. See also Gustavus H. Robinson, "The Public Utility Concept in American Law," 41 *Harvard Law Review* 277, 278–279 (1928).

44. Adler, "Business Jurisprudence," 146–158; John B. Cheadle, "Government Control of Business," 20 *Columbia Law Review* 438, 550–578 (1920); Smith et al., *Public Utilities*, 1–3.

45. Argument of John Jewett, counsel for the defendants in Munn v. Illinois, 37, quoted in Fairman, "The So-called Granger Cases," 634.

46. McAllister, "Affected with a Public Interest," 774.

47. For discussion of that expansive view, see chap. 3.

48. Tyson & Bros. v. Banton, 273 U.S. 418, 438 (1927).

49. Munn v. Illinois, 141. For a discussion of Field's position in *Munn*, see McCurdy, "Justice Field," 995–998.

50. Budd v. N.Y., 549, 551. Brewer's reference is, of course, to Edward Bellamy's *Looking Backward*, and the influential, utopian socialist vision that it proffered. See also Justice Lamar's dissent in German Alliance v. Kansas, 420. Chief Justice Waite himself recognized that "[t]he great difficulty in the future will be to establish the boundary between that which is private, and that in which the public has an interest." Letter from Waite to James Sheldon (Mar. 30, 1877), quoted in C. Peter Magrath, *Morrison R. Waite: The Triumph of Character*, 187 (1963).

51. Munn v. Illinois, 131–132. As has been frequently noted, the grain elevators in *Munn* were a peculiar occasion to justify regulation by the presence of monopoly, given that there were no significant economic or technical barriers preventing other companies from operating competing grain elevators. The choice to single them out as fit objects of government regulation likely rested on political rather than economic grounds, reflecting their political salience in the Granger movement. James R. Nelson, "The Role of Competition in the Regulated Industries," 11 *Antitrust Bulletin* 1, 7–8 (1966), quoted in 2 Kahn, *The Economics of Regulation*, 118 n.10 (1971). For the persuasive argument that Waite never intended monopoly status to be a prerequisite to regulation, see McAllister, "Business Affected with a Public Interest," 769–770.

52. German Alliance v. Kansas, 411–415; Wolff Packing v. Court of Indus. Relations, 538; Block v. Hirsh, 256 U.S. 135, 156 (1921).

53. Southwestern Bell v. Public Serv. Comm'n, 262 U.S. 276, 291 (1923) (Brandeis, J., concurring).

54. Budd v. New York, 545; Williams v. Standard Oil, 240. The Court unambiguously rejected monopoly status as a prerequisite for regulation in Brass v. North Dakota ex rel. Stoeser, 153 U.S. 391, 403 (1894); German Alliance v. Kansas, 410.

55. Tyson v. Banton, 451–452 (Stone, J., dissenting).

56. Id. at 439–440.

57. New State Ice v. Liebmann, 274; Washington ex rel. Stimson Lumber Co. v. Kuykendall, 275 U.S. 207, 211–212 (1927). As J. M. Clark noted, one could argue that all businesses met that criterion. *Social Control of Business*, 177 (2d ed. 1939).

58. Weems Steamboat Co. v. People's Steamboat Co., 214 U.S. 345, 356–358 (1909); Louisville & N.R.R. Co. v. West Coast Naval Stores Co., 198 U.S. 483, 500 (1905).

59. Tyson v. Banton, 451.

60. Tyson v. Banton, 446. Holmes's view had changed little from the way that he had expressed it when *Munn* was first decided. See Book Notice, *United States Reports, Supreme Court*, 12 *American Law Review*, 354–355 (1878).

61. Finkelstein, "From Munn v. Illinois to Tyson v. Banton," 770. For similar comments, see Hamilton, "Price—By Way of Litigation," 1019; Robert L. Hale, "Does the Ghost of Smyth v. Ames Still Walk?," 55 *Harvard Law Review* 1116, 1131 (1942); Adler, "Business Jurisprudence," 146.

62. Cooley, *Constitutional Limitations*, 737–739.

63. W. Frederic Foster, "The Doctrine of the United States Supreme Court of Property Affected by a Public Interest, and Its Tendencies," 5 *Yale Law Journal* 49, 76–77 (1895). On the fight over reading *Munn* to cover all "virtual monopolies," see Siegel, "Understanding the *Lochner* Era," 201–207.

64. *The Economic Basis of Public Interest*, chaps. 6 and 7 [1922] (Augustus M. Kelley 1968). For a similar suggestion, see Holmes, Book Notice, 354.

65. Tyson v. Banton, 451–452. See also Ribnik v. McBride, 359–360 (Stone, J., dissenting). Stone's interpretation of the "affected" test in his *Tyson* and *Ribnik* dissents closely tracks Clark's description in *Social Control* of the broadened Tugwellian test, a fact that Clark himself noted in the second edition of *Social Control*, 178 and n.3. It seems likely that Stone's language was indebted at least in part to Clark. Hale had sent Stone the first edition of Clark's book when it came out in 1926 with a strong endorsement, and Stone reported to Hale that he "read it with greatest interest," and purchased a copy for his own library. Letter from Hale to Stone, Aug. 11, 1926, and letter from Stone to Hale, Oct. 23, 1926. Both are contained in Harlan Fiske Stone Papers, Library of Congress, box 15, Robert L. Hale folder.

66. *Social Control of Business*, 300–301 (1st ed. 1926). For Clark's exposition of the economic factors that made regulation desirable, and that (he argued) many so-called competitive industries shared with public utilities, see his *Studies in the Economics of Overhead Costs*, 11–15 (1923).

67. Hamilton, "Affectation with Public Interest," 1107–1109. For a Georgian (single-tax) proponent's related attack on conservatives for their inability to see that market failure was not limited to monopolistic industries, see Harry Gunnison Brown, "Railroad Valuation and Rate Regulation," 33 *Journal of Political Economy* 505, 518 (1925). Justice Brandeis went even further in his famous dissent in *New State Ice*. Arguing that even perfectly competitive markets produced wasteful investment and destructive business cycles of overinvestment and depression, Brandeis insisted that regulation was needed to correct excessive competition as much as its absence altogether. New State Ice v. Liebmann, 306–311 (Brandeis, J., dissenting). The view, not surprisingly, was a conventional one during the Depression. See, e.g., the voluminous list of cites at id. at 309 nn.51–55.

68. Harleigh H. Hartman, *Fair Value: The Meaning and Application of the Term "Fair Valuation" as Used by Utility Commissions*, 235–236 (1920).

69. John R. Commons, *Legal Foundations of Capitalism*, 328 (1924). For other statements questioning the distinction between public and private businesses, see Henry Carter Adams,

"Economics and Jurisprudence," *Science Economic Discussion* 90 (The Science Company, 1886), and Adler, "Business Jurisprudence," 158.

70. *Legal Foundations of Capitalism*, 327.

71. "Rate Making and the Revision of the Property Concept," 212. See also 2 Taussig, *Principles*, 405–407. Hale credited Taussig's treatment of the "affectation" issue in *Principles* with influencing his own views on the subject. See letter to Taussig, May 23, 1934, Papers of Frank Taussig, Harvard University Archives.

72. "Price—By Way of Litigation," 1019.

73. Edwin R. A. Seligman, *Principles of Economics*, 131–134 (4th ed. 1909). See also Henry Carter Adams, "The Corporation Financier and Commercial Education," *Michigan Alumnus*, Dec., 1902, 92, quoted in Joseph Dorfman, *Introduction* to *Two Essays by Henry Carter Adams*, 49 (Joseph Dorfman, ed., 1954); Tugwell, *The Economic Basis of Public Interest*, 12; Commons, *Legal Foundations of Capitalism*, 327 (noting that what is signified by the term "public utility" is in part that "the business is a peculiar public *disutility* and is therefore sorted out for special restraint"). Harleigh Hartman economically embraced both justifications in stating that all property rights are derived from "social arrangements sanctioned by the state with a view to the general welfare." *Fair Value*, 4.

74. For the use of the "interdependence" argument to justify the progressive assault on atomistic liberty interests, see chap. 2. For its use in justifying broad government powers to regulate prices, see Adler, "Business Jurisprudence," 158.

75. *On Liberty*, 87–88, 94–95 [1859] (Elizabeth Rapaport ed., Hackett Publishing 1978).

76. *Social Control*, 176–180.

77. Id. at 180 n.1.

78. *Fair Value*, 71. For a strong endorsement of that view with respect to railroads, see Chicago, M. & St. P. Ry. v. Minnesota, 134 U.S. 418, 461 (1890) (Bradley, J., dissenting). For a similar argument with respect to public utilities, see Brandeis's famous concurrence in Southwestern Bell v. Public Serv. Comm'n, 290–291. For the view that the advantages that the state bestowed on public utilities extended far beyond formal franchises, in the aggregate "shed[ding] considerable doubt upon the 'naturalness'" of public utilities and other so-called natural monopolies, see Horace M. Gray, "The Passing of the Public Utility Concept," reprinted in *Readings in the Social Control of Industry*, 280, 283–284 and n.1 (American Economic Association, ed., 1942). The argument made here with respect to utilities had clear philosophical ties to the nineteenth-century "public trust" doctrine, which recognized a residual, nonalienable public right in waterways and submerged lands. For a discussion of the doctrine, see Carol Rose, "The Comedy of the Commons: Custom, Commerce, and Inherently Public Property," 53 *University of Chicago Law Review* 711 (1986).

79. On the significance of the public's role in creating the economic and social infrastructure that made exploitation of property profitable, see chap. 3. On the normative implications of demand-driven prices, see chap. 4. For a suggestive discussion of the "odd Lockeanism" by which one might derive the public's right to share in the value of property from its social role in creating that value, see Rose, "The Comedy of the Commons," 766–774.

80. Munn v. Illinois, 124–125.

81. Foster, "The Doctrine of the United States Supreme Court," 79–80. The charge that *Munn* was socialistic, argued Foster, would be true if (as Justice Brewer had suggested in *Budd*) the case held that whenever a business became sufficiently prosperous to benefit the public, "the public might claim an interest in it to the detriment of the owner." But the true meaning of *Munn*, Foster concluded, is that "the public interest was not created by the *benefit* derived from the business but by the *injury* resulting from it." Id. at 79.

82. Book Notice, 354.

83. For further discussion of this, see chap. 2.

84. 8 *Harvard Law Review* 1 (1894).

85. For an explication of this central difficulty with defining the scope of the "police power," see chap. 3.

86. For typical expressions of the widespread conviction that industry structure was tending toward monopoly, see, e.g., John B. Clark, *The Philosophy of Wealth* (1894), and Arthur Burns, *The Decline of Competition*, 522–589 (1936). For the argument that it was tending toward "monopolistic competition," see chap. 1.

87. 291 U.S. 502 (1934).

88. Id. at 529–532.

89. Id. at 533, 536.

90. Letter of May 31, 1934, Hale Papers, folder 10.

91. "The Constitution and the Price System," 424. Stone, thanking Hale for taking the trouble in the article "to remind people that there were some of us to whom the doctrine announced in *Nebbia* v. *New York* was not a novel one," added, "I confess that I could never have a hope for such a sweeping repudiation of the *Tyson* case and those like it." Letter from Stone to Hale, June 5, 1934, Hale Papers, mss. folder.

92. On the codes of fair competition authorized by the National Industrial Recovery Act and their implementation under the National Recovery Administration (NRA), see Ellis Hawley, *The New Deal and the Problem of Monopoly*, chaps. 1, 3, and 7 (1966). The NRA codes were ultimately struck down as unconstitutional in 1935 in the famous *Schecter Poultry* decision, but on other grounds than those removed by the Court in *Nebbia*. Schecter Poultry Corp. v. United States, 295 U.S. 495. In practice, the NRA codes resulted generally in self-regulation of industry rather than government control. See Hawley, *Problem of Monopoly*, 55–66, and sources cited therein. However, as Alfred Kahn noted, that "does not alter the fact that the National Recovery Administration represented during its short lifetime a further blurring of the distinction between the competitive and public utility sectors." 1 *The Economics of Regulation*, 10 (1970).

93. Gerard C. Henderson, "Railway Valuation and the Courts," 33 *Harvard Law Review* 1031, 1051 (1920).

94. Munn v. Illinois, 134. Explicating that holding in 1915, Hale argued that two possible constitutional theories could underlie it: that the company's right to charge the unregulated rate is a privilege and not a right, and hence in regulating it, the state does not deprive the company of private property at all; or that the regulation is a deprivation of property to which the company had a legal right, but the deprivation is with due process within the meaning of the Fourteenth Amendment, because it is within the proper scope of the state's police power. Letter to Lesley Ames, Jan. [27?], 1915, Hale Papers, folder 25. See also letter to Frank Stevens (counsel to New York Central Lines), Oct. 27, 1914, Hale Papers, folder 49, expanding on the latter theory. For similar formulations, see Clark, *Social Control*, 304; 2 James C. Bonbright, *The Valuation of Property*, 1093–1094 (1937).

95. John W. Cary, Brief and Argument, pp. 3–4, Peik v. Chicago & N.W.R.R., 94 U.S. 164 (1877).

96. Chicago, M. & St. P. Ry. v. Minnesota. The earlier decisions foreshadowing that holding were Spring Valley Water Works v. Schottler, 110 U.S. 347, 354–55 (1884); Stone v. Farmers' Loan & Trust Co., 116 U.S. 307, 331 (1886); Dow v. Beidelman, 125 U.S. 680, 689 (1888).

97. 169 U.S. 466 (1898).

98. Stone v. Farmers' Loan, 331. For the suggestion that the Court in *Smyth* misinterpreted Chief Justice Waite's intent in *Stone,* see Fairman, "The So-called Granger Cases," 663–666.

99. Smyth v. Ames, 526. For similar language, see id. at 525.

100. Id. at 546–547.

101. Pub. L. No. 400, §19a, 37 Stat. 701 (1913); Pub. L. No. 66–152, 41 Stat. 456 (1920). Both Acts mandated that the ICC undertake a massive valuation project to determine (under the *Smyth* criteria) the "fair value" of all property held by such companies. The valuations were to be used by the ICC to set rates for all railroads and (under the 1920 Act) to implement the so-called "recapture clause," which mandated that railroads earning more than a 6 percent annual return on their "valuation" pay half of the excess into a fund administered by the ICC to benefit less prosperous railroads. By the time of the 1920 Act, the railroads were in serious financial trouble, and Congress intended the 1920 Act in part to help them by giving the ICC authority to set minimum as well as maximum rates. Both the statutorily mandated "fair value" rate base and the recapture clause were finally repealed by the Emergency Railroad Transportation Act of 1933. For an excellent summary of the 1913 and 1920 Acts, see George G. Tunell, "Value for Rate Making and Recapture of Excess Income," 35 *Journal of Political Economy* 725, 728–731 (1927). See also Wilson et al., *Public Utility Regulation,* 156–161; 2 Bonbright, *Valuation of Property,* 1105–1108; Hale, *Freedom Through Law,* 524–526; Stuart Daggett, *Principles of Inland Transportation,* 584–606, 826–849 (rev. ed. 1934). For further discussion of the valuations undertaken by the ICC pursuant to the Acts, see later.

102. Discussions of the fair value controversy by progressive economists include John Bauer and Nathaniel Gold, *Public Utility Valuation for Purposes of Rate Control* (1934); 2 Bonbright, *Valuation of Property,* 1092–1094, 1108–1110 (drawing on Hale); Clark, *Social Control,* 305–335; Henry White Edgerton, "Value of the Service as a Factor in Rate Making," 32 *Harvard Law Review* 516 (1919); Edwin C. Goddard, "The Evolution of Cost of Reproduction as the Rate Base," 41 *Harvard Law Review* 564 (1928); Hamilton, "Price—By Way of Litigation"; Hartman, *Fair Value;* Henderson, "Railway Valuation and the Courts," 902–910, 1031–1057; Richberg, "A Permanent Basis." For a more recent historical account, see Siegel, "Understanding the *Lochner* Era," 224–259.

103. Henderson in his own early and influential writing in the area, "Railway Valuation and the Courts," 1032 n.4, identifies Hale's *Valuation and Rate-Making,* along with Robert H. Whitten's *Valuation of Public Service Corporations,* §57 (1913), as formative works. For other praise of Hale from fellow economists in the public utilities field, see James C. Bonbright, *Principles of Public Utility Rates* 33 n.7, 79 n.12, 164 n.4, 183 n.14 (1961), and Irston R. Barnes, *The Economics of Public Utilities Regulation* 402 (1942).

104. Hale's many attacks on *Smyth* include Smith et al., *Public Utilities,* 635–641; "Commissions, Rates, and Policies," 53 *Harvard Law Review* 1103, 1128–1132 (1940); "The Constitution and the Price System," 424–425; Noel T. Dowling et al., "Mr. Justice Stone and the Constitution," 36 *Columbia Law Review* 351, 372–379 (1936); "Non-Cost Standards in Rate Making"; "Pseudo-Protection of Property in Rate Cases," 24 *Michigan Law Review* 166 (1925).

105. For typical statements to this effect, see *Valuation and Rate-Making,* 35–42; "Commissions, Rates, and Policies," 1128–1130; "What Is a 'Confiscatory' Rate?," 35 *Columbia Law Review* 1045, 1051 (1935). For similar statements from other progressives, see Clark, *Social Control of Business,* 303–304; 1 Bonbright, *Valuation of Property,* 122; Southwestern Bell v. Public Serv. Comm'n, 310 (Brandeis, J., concurring). See also Hadley, "Meaning of Valuation," 177.

106. Letter to James Parker Hall, Hale Papers, folder 2.

107. Letter of June 4, 1916, Hale Papers, mss. folder.

108. "The 'Physical Value' Fallacy in Rate Cases," 30 *Yale Law Journal* 710 (1921).

109. 2 *Valuation of Property*, 1097.

110. Smyth v. Ames, 547.

111. "Commissions, Rates, and Policies," 1129–1130; "Economic Theory and the States-man," 195; *Valuation and Rate-Making*, 16 n.1; "Utility Regulation in the Light of the Hope Natural Gas Case," 44 *Columbia Law Review* 488, 526–527 (1944). See also 2 Bonbright, *Valuation of Property*, 1156–1163. For Hale's analogous arguments debunking the claim that a minimum wage law would compel the purchase of labor at higher than its value to employers, see chap. 3.

112. *Valuation and Rate-Making*, 17 n.1.

113. Ms. on "Defects of the Marginal Utility Measure of Service" [undated], Hale Papers, box 21. See also *Freedom Through Law*, 438.

114. Hale, "Economic Theory and the Statesman," 194. For a case invoking the "value of the service" criterion, see San Diego Land & Town Co. v. National City, 174 U.S. 739, 757 (1899). The ICC similarly invoked "value of service" in its early years as the principal criterion for railroad rate-setting, while ignoring it in practice. See M. B. Hammond, *Railway Rate Theories of the Interstate Commerce Commission*, 9–13 (1911).

115. For Hale's observations on the malleability of "market value" in the eminent domain context, see chap. 3.

116. For typical statements from economists on the circularity of the "fair value" rule in *Smyth*, see Arthur T. Hadley, "Meaning of Valuation," 175; George G. Tunell, "Value for Taxation and Value for Rate Making," 20 *Proceedings of the National Tax Association* 263, 266–268 (1928); 1 Taussig, *Principles*, 112–113; 2 Bonbright, *Valuation of Property*, 1082, 1167 (quoting Hadley's comment that he could recall but one economist who agreed with the courts in accepting "value" as the measure of the rate base, and that economist was dead); Richberg, "A Permanent Basis," 264; Henderson, "Railway Valuation and the Courts," 902, 910, 1051, 1055. Bonbright credits Fetter and Irving Fisher with having developed in the early 1900s the theoretical justification for using capitalized earning stream as a measure of value, albeit long after it had become a customary technique for appraisers. 1 *Valuation of Property*, 218. J. M. Clark traces capitalized earning theory back still earlier to H. C. Adams. *Social Control of Business*, 281.

117. Los Angeles Gas & Elect. Corp. v. Railroad Comm'n, 289 U.S. 287, 305 (1933).

118. Smyth v. Ames, 546–547.

119. For Hale's speculation on why both values might have been ignored, see *Freedom Through Law*, 477. The most obvious reason for ignoring the current market value of all outstanding securities was that such value generally equaled the worth of the company. Thus, using it to measure "fair value" led to the same circular result as did using the exchange value of the company. The Court itself approved ignoring the market value of securities in subsequent cases. See *Minnesota Rate Cases*, 230 U.S. 352, 440 (1913).

120. Letter to Frank Stevens, Oct. 27, 1914, p. 4, Hale papers, folder 49. For a more charitable view of Harlan's execution of his unenviable task of "establishing a dialectical harmony among a group of incompatibles," see Hamilton, "Price—By Way of Litigation," 1017 n.22.

121. "Rate Making and the Revision of the Property Concept," 210.

122. Hadley, "Meaning of Valuation," 173. For Prouty's early support of a valuation project, see Hoogenboom and Hoogenboom, *History of the ICC*, 66.

123. Hamilton, "Price—By Way of Litigation," 1017.

124. "Protecting Property and Liberty, 1922–1924," 40 Political Science Quarterly 404, 406–407, 410 (1925). For other criticisms in the same vein, see Goddard, "Fair Value of Public Utilities," 22 *Michigan Law Review* 652, 671 (1924); James C. Bonbright, "Progress and Poverty in Current Literature on Valuation," 40 *Quarterly Journal of Economics* 295, 307–310 (1926); Henderson, "Railway Valuation and the Courts," 1031.

125. Letter to Hon. John B. Winslow, Chief Judge, Wisconsin Supreme Court, Sept. 14, 1918 (enclosing a copy of *Valuation and Rate-Making*), Hale Papers, folder 2. For other statements from Hale on the Court's fundamental confusion between fact-finding and policy-making, see *Valuation and Rate-Making*, 35; "Pseudo-Protection of Property," 170; "Utility Regulation in the Light of Hope," 496. For similar remarks from other commentators, see 1 and 2 Bonbright, *Valuation of Property*, 116, 1081, 1167; Hadley, "Meaning of Valuation," 176–177; Southwestern Bell v. Public Serv. Comm'n, 295–296 (Brandeis, J., concurring).

126. Henderson, "Railway Valuations and the Courts," 911.

127. "Price—By Way of Litigation," 1018 (footnote omitted).

128. For an astute, contemporaneous review of the Columbia project that captures its significance, see Hamilton, "Price—By Way of Litigation."

129. 1917 memo from Charles Prouty to the ICC, quoted in Tunell, "Value for Rate Making and Recapture of Excess Income," 751 (emphasis omitted). Prouty added, "I doubt if any definition can ever add to this description of the thing itself."

130. " 'Fair Value' Merry-Go-Round, 1898 to 1938," 33 *Illinois Law Review* 517, 518 (1939). For other statements by Hale of this central fallacy of *Smyth*, see "Conflicting Judicial Criteria of Utility Rates—The Need for a Judicial Restatement," 38 *Columbia Law Review* 959, 967–968 (1938); *Valuation and Rate-Making*, 23.

131. Smyth v. Ames, 545–546.

132. 295 U.S. 662, 671 (1935). Roberts's opinion occasioned a strong dissent by Stone, concurred in by Cardozo and Brandeis and unanswered by Roberts. For typical other cases using eminent domain language, see Stone v. Farmers' Loan & Trust, 335; San Diego Town & Land v. National City, 756–757; Willcox v. Consolidated Gas, 41; Minnesota Rate Cases, 452; McCardle v. Indianapolis Water Co., 272 U.S. 400, 411 (1926); Railroad Comm'n v. Pacific Gas Co., 302 U.S. 388, 402–403 (1938) (Butler, J., dissenting). For Walton Hamilton's argument that the Court first "stumbled" into the eminent domain analogy in Chicago, M. & St. P. Ry. v. Minnesota, 465, see "Price—By Way of Litigation," 1013–1015.

133. As Gerard Henderson noted, the implicit change in identity of the party required to pay compensation was just one of the problems with the analogy never plumbed by its proponents. "Railway Valuation and the Courts," 906. For a similar criticism, see Hartman, *Fair Value*, 66.

134. *Valuation and Rate-Making*, 20.

135. "Utility Regulation in the Light of Hope," 489.

136. "Mr. Justice Stone and the Constitution," 372–373, "Public Utility Valuation," 9 *American Bar Association Journal* 392 (1923). Indeed, Hale argued, not only would no reduction be permitted. None would be required, since by hypothesis, current earnings would always constitute a fair return on current market value. *Valuation and Rate-Making*, 20. For invest-ments made after reduced rates were announced, a reduction raised no fairness concerns, as the price that investors would be willing to pay would reflect the new (lower) expected earnings. For precisely that reason, however, it was doubtful whether reducing rates by regulatory fiat would have any effect whatsoever on the rate of return to new investment. For further discussion of this issue, see later.

137. "Rate Making and the Revision of the Property Concept," 211. See also Hale, "What Is a 'Confiscatory' Rate?," 1049. For other critiques pointing out the logical circularity of an eminent domain analysis, see Henderson, "Railway Valuation and the Courts," 1031–1032 (crediting Hale in *Valuation and Rate-Making* and Whitten with having exposed it); Hartman, *Fair Value*, 63; Bauer and Gold, *Public Utility Valuation*, 21–22; Richberg, "A Permanent Basis," 265; Bonbright, "Current Literature on Valuation," 307–308 and n.5 (citing to Hale and Henderson).

138. For arguments in support of the eminent domain analogy from counsel to railroads and public utilities, see Tunell, "Value for Rate Making," 733–749; William L. Ransom, "Some Aspects of the Valuation of Private Property for Public Uses," 2 *Journal of Land and Public Utility Economics* 1–16 (1926); Hale, *Valuation and Rate-Making*, 23 (citing to the argument of Frank Stevens, acting as counsel to the New York Central Lines). Stevens's position represented an about-face from the days when he was Chairman of the New York State Public Service Commission. In that former capacity, he had argued that the Court must have meant by "fair value" something other than exchange value, as exchange value would preclude any regulation at all. Hale, commenting on that about-face, wrote the following: "To Stevens, as Public Service Commissioner, [the words of Smyth v. Ames] prove . . . that the court could not have meant exchange value. To the same Stevens, as counsel for the New York Central Railroad, they prove that it could not have meant anything else." "The 'Physical Value' Fallacy," 714 n.14. For Hale's more scathing comments in private, see later.

139. "Conflicting Judicial Criteria," 968.

140. "An Apology and a Reply to Mr. Maltbie on Valuation," 10 *American Bar Association Journal* 60, 61 (1924).

141. "Utility Regulation in the Light of Hope," 490. For the typical incomplete analogies to eminent domain to which many commentators resorted, which purported to apply eminent domain principles while expressly permitting some reduction in earnings, see Frederic G. Dorety, "The Function of Reproduction Cost in Public Utility Valuation and Rate Making," 37 *Harvard Law Review* 173, 178 (1923). As Bonbright astutely observed, "when we say that so-called 'evidence of value' is often a better basis of valuation than value itself, we mean that, in many legal appraisals, the law is verbally wrong in stating that the object is to determine what the property is really worth, and that it tacitly corrects this error by accepting one of the proffered items of evidence—say, original cost, or depreciated replacement cost—as constituting a better legal standard than would the most accurate estimate of the value of the property." 1 *Valuation of Property*, 122.

142. Smyth v. Ames, 546–547.

143. Railroad Comm'n v. Pacific Gas, 403 (Butler, J., dissenting).

144. More precisely, it would equal the *lower* of the replacement cost of the assets minus an allowance for accrued depreciation, or the capitalized value of the anticipated earnings of the assets in this or another business. (The latter limit assumes that no one would pay more for assets than such assets can earn.) See Dorety, "Function of Reproduction Cost," 184–186. For further discussion of the development and significance of the reproduction cost standard, see later.

145. For an account of the Court's slow progress towards a reproduction cost interpretation of *Smyth* from 1898–1926, see Goddard, "Fair Value," 654–666; Hartman, *Fair Value*, 99–105, 119–124; Bauer and Gold, *Public Utility Valuation*, 53–55, 63–103. For the Court's subsequent decisions backing off any definitive measure of fair value, see id., 105–109. Some

progressive commentators valiantly argued as late as 1925 that all of the Court's support for reproduction costs was consistent with an actual cost standard, an argument taken up by Justice Brandeis in his concurrence in Southwestern Bell v. Public Serv. Comm'n, 298–299, 309–310. See Bauer and Gold, *Public Utility Valuation*, 71–74. But the Court's unambiguous embrace of reproduction costs in McCardle v. Indianapolis Water put such arguments to rest. For discussions of *McCardle*, see Bauer and Gold, *Public Utility Valuation*, 98–103; Donald R. Richberg, "Value—By Judicial Fiat," 40 *Harvard Law Review* 567 (1927). At the other extreme, for the view (not shared by most historians of the period) that the Court from the start intended *Smyth* to impose a reproduction cost standard, see Siegel, "Understanding the *Lochner* Era," 225–232. For the standard progressive view that the Court tilted toward a reproduction measure of fair value following World War I because such a measure had come to favor utilities as a result of high inflation, see Powell, "Protecting Property and Liberty," 409–410.

146. As Hale noted, in a world of perfect competition and perfect mobility of capital, the fair market value of the company (equal to capitalized earnings) would tend to approximate the reproduction costs of physical assets, since any return in excess of that amount would attract new capital until the return was driven down to a fair return on replacement costs. See *Freedom Through Law*, 481. However, the fact that utilities were *not* competitive industries, because of the existence of natural or legal monopolies, was what created the need for regulation to begin with. It was to be expected, then, that the market value of the company (with unregulated rates) would exceed the replacement cost of its physical assets.

147. Id. at 483.

148. A third—good will (that is, the competitive advantage that a business derived from friendly customer relations)—was generally ignored, on the ground that there could be no good will in a monopoly, whose customers had no alternative source of supply. For Hale's critique of that argument, which he thought dubious, see "Does the Ghost of Smyth v. Ames Still Walk?," 1123. For a good summary of the treatment of all three, see 2 Bonbright, *Valuation of Property*, 1142–1151, and articles cited therein; Hale, "Utility Regulation in the Light of Hope," 491–492.

149. See generally Hale, *Freedom Through Law*, 486–493; 2 Bonbright, *Valuation of Property*, 1146–1151. Courts at least occasionally took it to mean the entire value of the company as a going concern, in excess of the value of its physical assets. See McCardle v. Indianapolis Water, 413–415. For Hale's summary of the Court's obfuscations on the meaning of "going concern" value, see "Does the Ghost of Smyth v. Ames Still Walk?," 1123–1125.

150. For an example of the self-canceling calculations that such a standard would call for, see Hale, *Valuation and Rate-Making*, 53 n.2. For Hale's description of Butler's Los Angeles Gas v. Railroad Comm'n dissent as proposing just such a ludicrous exercise, see "Does the Ghost of Smyth v. Ames Still Walk?," 1126–1127, and "Utility Regulation in the Light of Hope," 492.

151. Willcox v. Consolidated Gas, 44–48.

152. Cedar Rapids Gas Light Co. v. Cedar Rapids, 223 U.S. 655, 669–670 (1912).

153. United Rys. and Elec. Co. v. West, 280 U.S. 234, 258 (1930) (Brandeis, J., dissenting) (citation omitted). See also McCart v. Indianapolis Water Co., 302 U.S. 419, 433 (1938) (Black, J., dissenting); 2 Bonbright, *Valuation of Property*, 1143–1145; Hartman, *Fair Value*, 71, 190–193.

154. 2 Orgel, *Valuation Under the Law of Eminent Domain*, 116–118 (2d ed. 1953).

155. Georgia Railway and Power Co. v. Railroad Comm'n, 262 U.S. 625, 632 (1923) (Brandeis, J.).

156. 304 U.S. 470, 479 (1938) (citation omitted). Butler had anticipated his argument in *Denver* in his dissent in Los Angeles Gas v. Railroad Comm'n, 324–326.

157. Hale's commentaries on the case include "'Fair Value' Merry-Go-Round"; "Utility Regulation in the Light of Hope," 492–493; "Does the Ghost of Smyth v. Ames Still Walk?," 1127–1128; *Freedom Through Law*, 493–497. Hale probably read into the decision a more definitive position than Butler intended. At least in retrospect, the decision reveals something closer to the usual confusion of half-articulated and contradictory impulses evident in most Court opinions construing *Smyth*.

158. "Utility Regulation in the Light of Hope," 492.

159. As Hale notes, even under eminent domain proceedings, the government could confiscate without compensation that portion of the value of property attributable to unlawful practices. *Freedom Through Law*, 495 n.91. Thus, by analogy to eminent domain, to the extent that the value of a utility's property resulted from its ability to charge unlawfully high rates, the government could lower the rates without depriving the owner of any of its (lawful) property. The problem, obviously, is with the assumption that the rates charged by a utility prior to reduction *were* unlawful. See id.; "Commissions, Rates, and Policies," 1105–1108.

160. "Utility Regulation in the Light of Hope," 492–493.

161. "Does the Ghost of Smyth v. Ames Still Walk?," 1129.

162. For Holmes's dislike of rate cases, see his letter to Harold J. Laski (Apr. 18, 1924), in 1 *Holmes-Laski Letters*, 610 (Mark DeWolfe Howe, ed., 1953). For a more telling anecdote revealing Holmes's distaste for the technical economic problems that Brandeis reveled in, see Alpheus Thomas Mason, *Brandeis: A Free Man's Life*, 578 (1946). For Holmes's praise of Brandeis's handling of rate cases, see his letter to Laski (Feb. 22, 1929) in 2 *Holmes-Laski Letters*, 1135. Notwithstanding his disinclination to take on *Smyth* directly, Holmes's characteristic hostility to judicial intervention in regulatory decisions is evident in Denver v. Denver Union Water Co., 246 U.S. 178, 195 (1918) (dissenting), and Louisville v. Cumberland Tel. and Tel., 225 U.S. 430, 436 (1912).

163. Letter of June 4, 1916, Hale Papers, mss. folder.

164. Galveston Elec. Co. v. Galveston, 258 U.S. 388 (1922). Brandeis sent a copy of his opinion in *Galveston* to Hale on Apr. 14, 1922, writing, "I hope you will not think that the enclosed has added to the mountain of error." Hale Papers, mss. folder. It is a safe bet that Hale thought it did. Other rate cases in which Brandeis silently acquiesced in opinions purporting to apply *Smyth* include Lincoln Gas and Elec. Co. v. Lincoln, 250 U.S. 256 (1919), and Newton v. Consolidated Gas Co., 258 U.S. 165 (1922).

165. Hale Papers, mss. folder.

166. Southwestern Bell v. Public Serv. Comm'n, 292, 310.

167. Id. at 295.

168. Id. at 312.

169. Id. at 290–291. Although Brandeis does not credit Hale (or indeed anyone else) for his critique of *Smyth*, indirect evidence suggests that the critique was at least partly indebted to Hale. In its general thrust and a number of particulars, the critique closely follows two of Hale's articles that Hale had sent to Brandeis: "The 'Physical Value' Fallacy in Rate Cases" and "Rate Making and the Revision of the Property Concept." The first article, which Hale sent to Brandeis on Aug. 23, 1921, Brandeis cited in *Southwestern Bell* for its critique of reproduction costs and in the *Galveston* case for its definition of "prudent investment." Hale sent the second article to Brandeis on Apr. 3, 1922, in the letter in which

320

he urged Brandeis to repudiate *Smyth* in dissent. Hale Papers, mss. folder. The article was included in Brandeis's court papers bearing on the *Southwestern Bell* case. Louis D. Brandeis Papers, Harvard Law School, Part I, Reel 14. Among the many verbal parallels, perhaps the most significant is Brandeis's telltale reference to "unearned increment," one of only two uses of that politically loaded phrase by the Supreme Court, and one of few occasions in which it was invoked by any court as an argument *for* regulation. (As Hale notes, courts and commissions, associating the phrase, thanks to Henry George, with appreciation in land values, often invoked it to argue *against* confiscating increments in land value, as distinct from intangible values. "The 'Physical Value' Fallacy," 727–731.) The phrase, central to Hale's defense of actual prudent costs, appears repeatedly in both articles.

170. "Conflicting Judicial Criteria," 976.

171. For typical praise for Brandeis's concurrence, see Powell, "Protecting Liberty and Property," 407–410. Hale praised the opinion repeatedly in print, and remarked in a letter to Justice Stone that J. M. Clark's discussion of "fair value" in *Social Control of Business* was "as good as Brandeis's concurring opinion in the Southwestern Bell case, which I intend as very high praise." Letter of Aug. 11, 1926, Stone Papers, Library of Congress.

172. Letter of Jan. 20, 1926, Hale Papers, mss. folder. The pending case was McCardle v. Indianapolis Water.

173. The Hale Papers at Columbia University and the Stone Papers, Library of Congress, box 15, Robert L. Hale folder, together include about 25 letters between Stone and Hale from 1926 through 1939 dealing with rate regulation issues.

174. HFS to Hale, Feb. 6, 1926, Hale Papers, mss. folder. A copy of the letter also appears in the Stone Papers, Library of Congress.

175. See, e.g., McCardle v. Indianapolis Water, 421–425 (Brandeis, J., dissenting) (with Holmes not joining); United Rys. v. West (Brandeis and Stone, JJ., each dissenting); Los Angeles Gas v. Railroad Comm'n (Brandeis and Stone, JJ., silently acquiescing in a majority decision upholding a rate reduction under *Smyth*); Dayton Power and Light Co. v. Public Utils. Comm'n, 292 U.S. 290 (1934) (Cardozo, J.); Columbus Gas and Fuel Co. v. Public Utils. Comm'n, 292 U.S. 398 (1934) (Cardozo, J.); West v. Chesapeake and Potomac Tel., 680 (Stone, J., dissenting). Probably the most famous example of the trio's attempt to circumvent *Smyth* was the 1929 decision in St. Louis and O'Fallon Ry. Co. v. United States, 279 U.S. 461 (1929). For further discussion of *O'Fallon*, see later. The general strategy of paying lip service to *Smyth* did not, however, prevent the three from taking occasional oblique swipes at the rule. See, e.g., St. Louis and O'Fallon Ry. v. United States, 503–505; United Rys. v. West, 279–280; West v. Chesapeake & Potomac Tel., 689–690. On the wavering of the Court during the 1930s, see 2 Bonbright, *Valuation of Property*, 1098–1102; Hale, "Utility Regulation in the Light of Hope," 491–493.

176. See, e.g., Los Angeles Gas v. Railroad Comm'n; Lindheimer v. Illinois Bell Tel. Co., 292 U.S. 151 (1934); Dayton Power and Light v. Public Utils. Comm'n, 292 U.S. 290 (1934); Railroad Comm'n v. Pacific Gas. The last decision in particular reveals the Court's marked shift since the late 1920s, when it decided St. Louis & O'Fallon Ry. v. United States. The case presented the same issue as *O'Fallon*. In both cases, the rate-setting commissions, while purporting to take into account reproduction costs, derived a valuation figure closely tied to historic costs, a standard that they appeared to support on policy grounds. Although a majority of the Court in *O'Fallon* had reversed the valuation on that ground, there were only two votes for reversal in *Pacific Gas*—Butler and McReynolds.

177. Letter of May 31, 1934, Hale Papers, folder 10. Hale closely tracked the Court in a series of articles throughout the 1930s for signs that it had left *Smyth*'s "fair value" doctrine

behind. See, e.g., "The New Supreme Court Test of Confiscatory Rates," 10 *Journal of Land and Public Utility Economics* 307 (1934); "Conflicting Judicial Criteria"; " 'Fair Value' Merry-Go-Round."

178. "Does the Ghost of Smyth v. Ames Still Walk?," 1140.

179. McCart v. Indianapolis Water, 423, 441 (Black, J., dissenting). Black was the lone dissenter in the case. Stone was horrified by Black's boldness in taking on *Smyth* directly in *McCart*, when the issue had not been raised by counsel and the case had been disposed of by an unsigned (per curiam) opinion, from which dissents were rare in Court tradition. At the same time, Stone thought Black's analysis quite strong—indeed, so strong that he expressed doubt that Black himself had written it—and sought unsuccessfully to have the case reargued or at least delayed to allow himself time to reconsider his own reluctant support of the per curiam decision. Letter from Harlan Fiske Stone to Charles Evans Hughes (Dec. 30, 1937), quoted in Alpheus Thomas Mason, *Harlan Fiske Stone: Pillar of the Law*, 468 (1956).

180. Frankfurter had taught a public utilities course for many years at Harvard Law School, and had advised Roosevelt (when governor of New York and later President) on problems of public utilities holding companies. See Liva Baker, *Felix Frankfurter*, 43, 88, 103, 175–179 (1969). Although chiefly interested in other aspects of public utilities regulation, he embraced the standard progressive critique of the "fair value" rule in *Smyth*. See, e.g., *The Public and Its Government*, 101–104. Hale's personal connection with Frankfurter dates back to 1927, when he joined Frankfurter's campaign to get the convictions of Sacco and Vanzetti overturned. See chap. 1.

181. 307 U.S. 104, 122–123 (1939).

182. Stone was as dismayed by Frankfurter's brashness as he had been by Black's in *McCart*. He urged Frankfurter in a private memo not to take on *Smyth* headlong "until we have a case where the issue is raised and unavoidable," and expressed concern that raising it in *Driscoll* would simply harden support on the Court for *Smyth*. Memo from Harlan Fiske Stone to Felix Frankfurter (Apr. 13, 1939), quoted in Mason, *Harlan Fiske Stone*, 482–483. Frankfurter held firm, stating that he felt strongly about his point. Memo from Felix Frankfurter to Harlan Fiske Stone (Apr. 14, 1939), quoted in H. N. Hirsch, *The Enigma of Felix Frankfurter*, 237 n.58 (1981).

183. 315 U.S. 574, 602 (1942).

184. The opinion, which appears to be largely Douglas's handiwork, cites (inter alia) to two Hale articles that laid out the central fallacies of *Smyth*, in language closely tracked in the concurrence: "Conflicting Judicial Criteria of Utility Rates" and " 'Fair Value' Merry-Go-Round." Federal Power Comm'n v. Pipeline, 603.

185. Stone, writing for the Court, upheld the rate reduction in question, but in terms that appeared to leave *Smyth* intact. Given Stone's 1939 statement to Frankfurter that he thought it inadvisable to denounce *Smyth* until the votes were in hand to overrule it, Stone's reticence may simply reflect his belief that (with Frankfurter's change of heart) his own vote would still leave the anti-*Smyth* forces one vote shy of a majority. Frankfurter, even more surprisingly, given his strong denunciation of *Smyth* three years earlier in *Driscoll*, wrote separately to support Stone and to endorse, wholly gratuitously, the judiciary's right to review the substantive fairness of utility rate regulation. Federal Power Comm'n v. Pipeline, 609–610. It is not entirely clear what impelled Frankfurter's change of heart from *Driscoll* to *Natural Gas Pipeline* and, two years later, the *Hope Natural Gas* case. The change may reflect Frankfurter's genuine deference to Congress, which Frankfurter read (in *Pipeline*)

as having intended a meaningful level of judicial review under the Natural Gas Act and (in *Hope*) as having incorporated, by its failure to repudiate, the Court's substantive due process analysis in pre-*Smyth* cases. More likely, however, the change reflects Frankfurter's growing personal animosity toward Douglas, Murphy, and (most of all) Black, whose unanticipated intellectual independence and growing influence on the Court infuriated Frankfurter. For a study of the deteriorating relations between Frankfurter and Black from 1939 to the mid-1940s, see James F. Simon, *The Antagonists*, 105–129 (1989). The latter explanation is borne out by Frankfurter's need to write a separate concurrence at all, to "correct" Black et al. on their account of legal history, which (as Hale correctly noted) did not materially differ from his own. See "Does the Ghost of Smyth v. Ames Still Walk?," 1134 n.42. It is also borne out by the vituperative tone of both decisions.

186. See "Does the Ghost of Smyth v. Ames Still Walk," 1130. Correspondence with Frankfurter concerning Hale's article is contained in the Hale Papers, mss. folder.

187. "Does the Ghost of Smyth v. Ames Still Walk?," 1137.

188. Id. at 1140, quoting Driscoll v. Edison Light, 123 (Frankfurter, J., dissenting).

189. Federal Power Comm'n v. Hope Natural Gas Co., 320 U.S. 591, 601–602 (1944).

190. Goddard, "Fair Value of Public Utilities," 781. Most often, the factors averaged were historic and reproduction costs of the physical assets. See Hale, *Freedom Through Law*, 479, and 2 Bonbright, *Valuation of Property*, 1091. Bonbright notes that decisions tended not merely to split the difference between the two measures (which would too obviously reveal the compromise nature of the venture) but rather to fix on some more eccentric point between them. Id.

191. 2 Bonbright, *Valuation of Property*, 1104. For similar cynical views of the extent to which rate determinations were detached from the analysis mandated by *Smyth*, see Bauer, "Return on Public Utility Investments," 263–264; Bauer and Gold, *Public Utility Valuation*, 103; Hale, *Valuation and Rate-Making*, 99–100; Henderson, "Railway Valuation and the Courts," 912.

192. 2 *Valuation of Property*, 1143.

193. Brandeis in *Southwestern Bell* stated that as of 1923, the Court had passed on the validity of rates under *Smyth* only twenty-five times; and that of those cases, in no instances in which the commission had set rates after a full hearing did the Court reverse them as too low. Southwestern Bell v. Public Serv. Comm'n, 297 n.8. The two most notable cases of mutiny, provoking two famous reversals, were *Southwestern Bell* itself and the *O'Fallon* case. In both cases, the commissions directly questioned the relevance of reproduction costs, and adopted measures of "fair value" suspiciously close to actual prudent costs.

194. Southwestern Bell v. Public Serv. Comm'n, 308.

195. Tunell, "Value for Rate Making," 730. Charles Prouty, the director of the Valuation Project, was no fan of *Smyth*, and embraced the standard critique of its circularity and incoherence. For most of Prouty's tenure, the ICC avoided any direct confrontation over *Smyth*. The typical ICC valuation reports recited in ceremonial fashion the factors to be assessed under *Smyth*, but never revealed the method of calculation used to arrive at a final figure. In the series of valuations culminating in *O'Fallon*, the ICC grew more indiscreet about its disregard of *Smyth*, finally provoking a direct rebuff from the Court. See id., and 3B Sharfman, *The Interstate Commerce Commission*, 221–255.

196. Goddard, "Fair Value of Public Utilities," 778–780; Vanderblue, "Railroad Valuation by the Interstate Commerce Commission," 299; Edgerton, "Value of the Service," 516.

197. St. Louis and O'Fallon Ry. v. United States.

198. 3A Sharfman, *The Interstate Commerce Commission*, 42–43. For a detailed discussion of the Valuation Project, see id. at 95–319.

199. Bauer, "Return on Public Utility Investments," 266–267.

200. The case of Newton v. Consolidated Gas, for example, was under almost continuous consideration for twenty years. Goddard, "Fair Value of Public Utilities," 778 n.63. In a case involving the Chicago telephone company, the Court finally enforced a rate reduction order eleven years after it was first issued. See Smith v. Illinois Bell Tel. Co., 282 U.S. 133 (1930), appeal dismissed, 283 U.S. 808 (1931), and Lindheimer v. Illinois Bell Tel. For other telling cases, see Frankfurter, *The Public and Its Government*, 95–106, describing the first eleven years of the dispute over New York telephone rates, not yet resolved as of 1930, and McCart v. Indianapolis Water, 423–424 (Black, J., dissenting), in which Justice Black protested against a decision to remand the case, given its already protracted history.

201. Hale, "The 'Physical Value' Fallacy," 717.

202. Henderson, "Railway Valuation and the Courts," 1033.

203. For the classical economists' belief in a long-run "natural" value, converging with the costs of production, and the marginalists' refutation of it, see chap. 4. For an astute description of the professional rift between lawyers and economists over the fallacy of "fair value," and the roots of that fallacy in the classical notion of a "normal" or "just" price, see 2 Bonbright, *Valuation of Property*, 1081–1084. See also Siegel, "Understanding the *Lochner* Era," 243–250.

204. "Utility Regulation in the Light of Hope," 490.

205. Letter to Powell, June 13, 1916, Hale Papers, box 10 (correspondence on *Valuation and Rate-Making*). See also Hale, "The 'Physical Value' Fallacy," 710, noting that "[t]o the unsophisticated, . . . a reduction of rates to the point where they yield a fair return on [physical value] seems to squeeze out ruthlessly whatever 'water' there may be in the property. To reduce them further is thought to be not only unconstitutional, but unthinkable—it is to fly in the face of some 'physical' law as immutable as the law of gravitation (in pre-Einstein days)." For the argument that the "old" reified view of property as a tangible thing to which rights attach was in fact a relatively modern development, see Walton H. Hamilton and Irene Till, "Property," 12 *Encyclopaedia of the Social Sciences* 529 (Edwin R. A. Seligman and Alvin Johnson, eds., 1934).

206. For Bonbright's interpretation of the *Smyth* controversy along these lines, see 2 *Valuation of Property*, 1169–1171, citing to Cohen's "brilliant essay," "Transcendental Nonsense and the Functional Approach," 35 *Columbia Law Review* 809 (1935), and Jerome Frank's *Law and the Modern Mind* (1930). See also Commons, *Legal Foundations of Capitalism*, 18. Siegel, "Understanding the *Lochner* Era," and McCurdy, "Justice Field," 973–974, offer a thoughtful interpretation of *Smyth* along the same lines. As Siegel suggests, there is some irony in the fact that the politically progressive result in *Munn* (setting no limits on the extent of regulation permissible) rested on the retrograde, verbalist vision of property as a thing with inherent value. Siegel, "Understanding the *Lochner* Era," 211–212.

207. Munn v. Illinois, 141.

208. "Railway Valuation and the Courts," 1056.

209. Henderson, "Railway Valuation and the Courts," 913. For similar statements from Hale, see "'Fair Value' Merry-Go-Round," 518.

210. "The Meaning of Valuation," 179.

211. Nebbia v. New York, 536.

212. Hartman, *Fair Value*, 81–82.

324

213. Hadley, "The Meaning of Valuation," 179.

214. Hale, "Does the Ghost of Smyth v. Ames Still Walk?," 1131.

215. Smyth v. Ames, 489–493, 498–502; Hamilton, "Price—By Way of Litigation," 1016–1018.

216. From 1913–1920, prices rose 150 percent. During the 1920s, they stabilized at a level about 75 percent higher than prewar prices. Following the economic collapse of 1929, prices for the first time fell to a prewar level, making a reproduction cost standard once again attractive to proregulatory forces. Siegel, "Understanding the *Lochner* Era," 234 n.206.

217. "Fair Value of Public Utilities," 658.

218. For a summary of the shifting support for reproduction and historic costs, see Goddard, "Fair Value of Public Utilities," 654–658, 669–670; Bauer and Gold, *Public Utility Valuation*, 53, 74–76, 103–104; Hamilton, "Price—By Way of Litigation," 1015–1018.

219. Tunell, "Value for Rate Making," 738–739. For Walton Hamilton's comments on the irony that Bryan and Butler—worlds apart in political philosophy—should be joined in an unwitting partnership here, see "Price—By Way of Litigation," 1017 n.24.

220. Among the supporters were Charles Prouty of the ICC, Harry Gunnison Brown, Willard J. Graham, and F. G. Dorety, counsel to Great Northern Railway. See Tunell, "Value for Rate Making," 752–755 (on Prouty); H. G. Brown, "Rate Base for Railroad and Utility Regulation," 34 *Journal of Political Economy* 479 (1926); Willard J. Graham, *Public Utility Valuation* (1934); Dorety, "Function of Reproduction Cost."

221. Hale, "The 'Physical Value' Fallacy," 714–715.

222. See H. G. Brown, "Railroad Valuation and Rate Regulation"; Dorety, "The Function of Reproduction Cost," 187–188; Graham, *Public Utility Valuation*. See also 2 Bonbright, *Valuation of Property*, 1086–1088, summarizing Brown and others' position in support of reproduction costs.

To the extent that the efficiency justification for a reproduction cost standard focused on the demand side, it had validity, although, as discussed later, most economists in the subsequent generations abandoned it in favor of setting prices equal to the long-run incremental cost of supplying the new (marginal) consumer. In practice, the chief difference between the two was that the latter excluded that portion of the value of existing assets that reflected sunk capital investments. 1 Kahn, *Economics of Regulation*, 65–66, 109–111. To the extent that the proponents of a reproduction cost over actual cost rate base were concerned with supply-side efficiency (that is, with not distorting investment decisions), their concern was misplaced. Any rate base would attract adequate new capital, provided only that the market could adjust the price of the investment to reflect the lower expected return. For further discussion of this problem, in the context of Hale's and others' attempts to manipulate the return to new investment, see later.

223. See Brown, "Railroad Valuation and Rate Regulation," 508–510; 1 Kahn, *Economics of Regulation*, 110.

224. A partial list of supporters include John Bauer, *Effective Regulation of Public Utilities* (1925); Bauer and Gold, *Public Utility Valuation*, 63–66; Bonbright, "The Economic Merits of Original Cost and Reproduction Cost," 41 *Harvard Law Review* 593 (1928); Clark, *Social Control of Business*, 308; Edgerton, "Value of the Service," 520–522; David Friday, "An Extension of Value Theory," *Quarterly Journal of Economics* 197 (1922); Goddard, "Fair Value of Public Utilities," 783–785; Hartman, *Fair Value*, 86–88; Henderson, "Railway Valuation and the Courts"; Powell, "Protecting Property and Liberty," 408–409; Richberg, "A Permanent Basis," and "Value—By Judicial Fiat"; I. Leo Sharfman, *The American Railroad Problem,*

301–304 (1921); Robert H. Whitten, "Fair Value for Rate Purposes," 27 *Harvard Law Review* 419 (1914). For the view that the majority of economists supported actual prudent costs as of 1937, see 2 Bonbright, *Valuation of Property*, 1085. For the irregular use of "cost of service" for railroad rate setting in the early years of the ICC, see Hammond, *Railway Rate Theories*, 170–185. Among judges, Brandeis was of course the most famous exponent of a cost rate base. For a rare expression of skepticism from a progressive about the utility of either actual costs or reproduction costs as an all-purpose formula, see Hamilton, "Price—By Way of Litigation," 1024–1025. Hamilton ultimately leaned towards actual prudent costs, but only as "the lesser of two irrelevancies." Id. at 1025.

225. See "Notes on Conventional Contrasts of Artificial and Natural Economies," (n.d.), folder 39 (stating that both concerns had to be taken into account); letter to H. F. Stone, June 29, 1929, indicating his respect for "*some* arguments, like Dorety's, for reproduction cost." Hale Papers, mss. folder.

226. For his early, equivocal support for a reproduction cost rate base, see *Valuation and Rate-Making*, 29–30; correspondence with Thomas Reed Powell in the summer of 1916, Hale Papers, box 10.

227. See "The 'Physical Value' Fallacy." Hale's change of heart was prompted by a friendly critique the year earlier in Henderson's "Railway Valuation and the Courts," 1048–1050, which (as Hale wrote to Henderson) "freed my mind . . . from the 'physical value' incubus." Letter of May 4, 1921, Hale Papers, folder 5. While crediting Hale's "valiant attempt" in *Valuation* to come up with a measure of exchange value independent of earnings, Henderson argued that Hale had failed, providing (by way of proof) a very Halean analysis of how the hypothetical exchange price of physical assets would change under different assumptions. "Railway Valuation and the Courts," 1048–1050.

228. 2 Bonbright, *Valuation of Property*, 1088; Clark, *Social Control of Business*, 306–308.

229. 2 Bonbright, *Valuation of Property*, 1088–1089. For a list of the typical methods for estimating reproduction costs, see Charles F. Phillips, Jr., *The Economics of Regulation*, 241–242 (rev. ed. 1969). For an eloquent description of the folly of estimating the cost of rights for which there was no market at all, see McCart v. Indianapolis Water, 432–433 (Black, J., dissenting). Indeed, the unreliability of regulatory determinations under such a standard, it was feared, would pose an additional financial risk for which investors would demand a premium. 2 Bonbright, *Valuation of Property*, 1085–1086.

230. On the difficulties of administering a reproduction cost standard, see 2 Bonbright, *Valuation of Property*, 1086–1089; 1 Kahn, *Economics of Regulation*, 109–114; Richberg, "Value—By Judicial Fiat," 570–572; Whitten, "Fair Value for Rate Purposes," 427–429; Southwestern Bell v. Public Serv. Comm'n, 292–294 (Brandeis, J., concurring). That actual costs, unlike reproduction costs, could provide a stable rate base was a primary reason that most commissions and at least some progressive economists supported it. See Bauer and Gold, *Public Utility Valuation*, 74–76; 2 Bonbright, *Valuation of Property*, 1085–1086.

231. *Valuation and Rate-Making*, 137.

232. Hale, "Rate Making and the Revision of the Property Concept," 211.

233. For Hale's general rent-theory attack on the distributive justice of the competitive market, see chap. 4.

234. "Utility Regulation in the Light of Hope," 526–527.

235. For Hale's support of an excess profits tax as the optimal solution in most markets, see "Utility Regulation in the Light of Hope," 525–559; *Valuation and Rate-Making*, 15; "Non-Cost Standards in Rate Making," 66–67. For support for that solution from other progres-

326

sives, see Bonbright, "Current Literature on Valuation," 303–306. For the now conventional view that an actual cost standard (to the extent it deviates from reproduction costs) will cause distortions even in so-called noncompetitive markets, by mispricing services relative to other, competing alternative uses of resources, see 1 Kahn, *Economics of Regulation*, 65–66, 109–111.

236. Under the Transportation Act of 1920, the ICC was instructed to set uniform rates for competing railroads, on the basis of aggregate "fair value" of property for the whole group, so as to avoid congestion on low-cost lines and discriminatorily higher prices for those customers forced to use other lines. To the extent that the rates so set generated a return for any given railroad in excess of 6 percent of its "fair value," one half of the excess was to be paid into a revolving fund to be administered by the ICC to fund loans to weaker railroads. Wilson et al., *Public Utility Regulation*, 158–159. The Court, upholding the excess profits tax in Dayton-Goose Creek Ry. Co. v. United States, 263 U.S. 456, 484 (1924), noted that railroads were no worse off than if rates had been lowered *before* collection. For typical expressions of enthusiasm from progressives for the recapture clause, see Bonbright, "Current Literature on Valuation," 305, and Hale, "Non-Cost Standards in Rate Making," 66–67.

237. *Freedom Through Law*, 531. Bonbright noted that Hale was one of the few commentators who recognized the need to separate the problems of controlling profits and controlling rates. "Current Literature on Valuation," 306 n.9. Interestingly, in his earliest discussion of the problem, Hale suggested a third alternative to dispose of utilities' excess profits: a "compulsory wage increase" to their employees. *Valuation and Rate-Making*, 15. The suggestion that some of capital's earnings should be redistributed to labor was hardly surprising, coming from a progressive in 1918. But as Shaw noted, it did not necessarily follow as a matter of progressive rent theory, since labor—already receiving compensation for its own sacrifices—might be supposed to have as little right to capital's excess earnings on top of that as capital does itself. Hale dropped the suggestion in subsequent discussions, consistent with his and other rent theorists' general position that, at least as an analytical matter, rent theory did not necessarily pit capital against labor. For further discussion, see chap. 4.

238. "Utility Regulation in the Light of Hope," 526–527 (quoting Dayton–Goose Creek Ry. v. United States, 484).

239. Dayton–Goose Creek Ry. v. United States, 484.

240. On the railroad recapture clause, see, e.g., Homer Bews Vanderblue and Kenneth Farwell Burgess, *Railroads: Rates—Service—Management*, 331–332 (1923), dismissing the clause as an unfairly discriminatory application of the doctrine of Henry George. On a cost rate base, see, e.g., Hadley, "The Meaning of Valuation," 175, tracing the movement for a cost rate base back to George.

241. For use of "unearned increment," see, e.g., Brandeis's defense of actual prudent costs in Southwestern Bell v. Public Serv. Comm'n, 312 (concurring). For a particularly value-laden use of the language of Lockean sacrifice as the basis on which the public should pay for service, see Bauer, "Control of Return on Public Utility Investments."

242. Letter of Oct. 27, 1914, Hale Papers, folder 49. The strong tone of the letter may be partially explained by the fact that Stevens, in his earlier incarnation as Chairman of the New York Public Service Commission, had been a progressive ally on these matters.

243. Letter of Sept. 18, 1918, Hale Papers, folder 2.

244. For one of Hale's accounts of the problems, see, e.g., "Economic Theory and the Statesman," 204–209.

327

245. For Hale's discussion of some of the complexities involved, see *Valuation and Rate-Making*, 141–148; *Freedom Through Law*, 518–523; "Utility Regulation in the Light of Hope," 503–517.

246. On the administrative problems of ascertaining "prudence," see Hamilton, "Price—By Way of Litigation," 1024.

247. *Freedom Through Law*, 529–530. As Hale noted, the solution borrowed the strategy of the railroad recapture clause, which permitted railroads to retain one-half of excess profits. Variants of that solution were built de facto into the regulatory process by the time lag in adjusting rates to reflect excess profits. They were also formally incorporated in many systems, which (following the suggestion of Hale and others) allowed some deviation around a target "reasonable" rate of return. For further discussion of the disincentive problem, see later.

248. One of Hale's earliest statements in support of vested rights under a Georgian single-tax scheme is contained in a letter to *The Herald*, Oct. 24, 1912, Hale Papers, folder 62: "I am quite ready to admit at the start that those who in good faith have invested in land have some claim to consideration regardless of whether the institution of private property in land is just or unjust; and if we conclude that such ownership is unjust, then before abolishing the institution, some form of compensation must be paid to present owners." For a more general statement that there are two possible justifications for "property incomes"—providing incentives for production and protecting vested rights—see Hale's notes for an economics seminar, Hale Papers, folder 30.

249. Bauer, "Return on Public Utility Investments"; Bonbright, "Current Literature on Valuation," 297–302; "The Bauer-Bonbright Proposal for the Revision of the New York Public Service Commission Law and Its Constitutionality," 30 *Columbia Law Review* 548 (1930). For Hale's support of the plan, see letter to Prof. Harbeson, July 10, 1942, Hale Papers, folder 12, and *Freedom Through Law*, 508–509. A number of other progressive economists supported the compromise plan, including Sharfman, *The American Railroad Problem*, 301–305, and Clark, *Social Control of Business*, 381. As Hale remarked, fashioning a compromise with vested rights "necessarily requires a somewhat arbitrary decision, and there is no use pretending to be very scientific about it." Letter to Frank Haigh Dixon, Apr. 27, 1922, Hale Papers, folder 6. For one of the few detailed descriptions of the compromise that Hale might use, see Letter to *The Globe*, Oct. 23, 1912, Hale Papers, folder 62, arguing that the return on current value should be protected for the greater of the life of the holder or twenty-five years, in the form of an annuity paying out interest on that value for that term. See also *Freedom Through Law*, chaps. 15–16. Hale recognized that any compromise that protected the value of existing investments in excess of cost would inevitably give a windfall to original investors who still held securities purchased at a price below their value at the time of regulation. Id. at 512. As discussed further later, he failed to realize, however, that by protecting existing investments, he deprived a cost rate base of its only expected source of gain for the state.

250. Vanderblue and Burgess, *Railroads*, 331–332. See also *Valuation and Rate-Making*, 134–139.

251. "The 'Physical Value' Fallacy," 725.

252. Robert Hale, Book Review, 24 *Columbia Law Review* 215, 218 (1924).

253. "The 'Physical Value' Fallacy," 725.

254. Id. at 725.

255. "Rate Making and the Revision of the Property Concept," 214–215.

328

256. Id. at 213.

257. Arthur Twining Hadley, *Economics*, 92–93 (1896).

258. Hadley, "The Meaning of Valuation," 178–179.

259. See Hartman, *Fair Value*, 78; Hale, "The 'Physical Value' Fallacy," 713–714.

260. As of 1967, 28 state commissions (including the District of Columbia) were commonly using actual costs, while 12 used a hybrid of actual and reproduction costs ("fair value"). S. Doc. No. 56, 90th Cong., 1st Sess. 37 (1967). See also 1 and 2 Arthur Anderson and Co., *Return Allowed in Public Utility Rate Cases*. For more recent studies indicating that prices are set so that revenue will equal operating expenses plus current depreciation, plus a "reasonable" return on the rate base, equal to actual depreciated capital investment, see MacAvoy, *The Regulated Industries and the Economy*, 27, 33 (1979).

261. Sympathy to rent-theory arguments for a cost rate base is most evident in two-tier pricing schedules that some regulatory commissions have instituted in times of escalating prices, with old, more cheaply produced goods receiving a lower price, and new, more expensive ones receiving a higher one. One notable example was the two-tier pricing adopted in the 1960s by the Federal Power Commission for the field price of natural gas. For a discussion of the FPC's policy, see 1 Kahn, *Economics of Regulation*, 42 n.55, 68 n.14, and sources cited therein.

262. For an early, influential study concluding that regulation made no significant difference in average electricity rate levels through 1937, see George J. Stigler and Claire Friedland, "What Can Regulators Regulate? The Case of Electricity," *Journal of Law and Economics*, Oct. 1962, 1. For a summary of some of the literature on regulatory effectiveness and a more agnostic conclusion, see 2 Kahn, *Economics of Regulation*, 109–112, 328. For other studies coming to pessimistic conclusions for the 1940s through 1960s for both electricity and natural gas, see MacAvoy, *The Regulated Industries and the Economy*, 35–39, and cites therein, arguing that in most regulated industries, regulation either failed to reduce prices below unregulated levels, or did so only by keeping them below costs, thereby discouraging needed investment.

263. In the 1930s, a number of municipalities moved to acquire or start up public utilities. See "Municipalities in Competition with Private Business: The Effect upon Governmental Powers," 34 *Columbia Law Review* 324 (1934). The federal power policy enacted in Roosevelt's first term had as its cornerstone increased public ownership of electric projects. To that end, the government funded a number of federal power projects, provided federal aid to municipalities to construct local power plants, and encouraged states to remove any legal barriers to publicly owned power plants. The program was not meant to supplant private ownership, but instead to provide an alternative to regulatory commissions for disciplining price and service. As David Lilienthal put it with respect to the most famous of these ventures, the TVA, one purpose was to provide an independent "'yardstick' by which to measure the fairness of the rates of private utilities," and to regulate those rates "not by quasi-judicial commissions but by competition." D. E. Lilienthal, "Business and Government in the Tennessee Valley," 172 *Annals of the American Academy of Political and Social Science* 46, quoted in Wilson et al., *Public Utility Regulation*, 430. For a summary of federal power projects under way as of 1937, see Wilson et al., *Public Utility Regulation*, chap. 16. For a summary of the federal funds that the WPA gave to municipalities during Roosevelt's first term to construct electric and gas facilities, see id. at 536–537. 2 Kahn, *Economics of Regulation*, 104–106, provides an overview of government-owned utilities as of the mid-1960s. For studies showing mixed results of publicly owned utilities at controlling costs and prices, see Michael A. Crew and Paul R. Kleindorfer, *Economics of Public Utility Regulation*, 161–162 (1986), and cites therein.

329

264. For that conventional view, see, e.g., Richard Schmalensee, *The Control of Natural Monopolies* (1979); Edward E. Zajac, "Toward a Theory of Perceived Economic Justice in Regulation," Bell Laboratories Economic Discussion Paper No. 235, (Jan. 1982), bemoaning the fact that "the public find[s] it so hard to accept principles [that efficiency should be paramount in regulation] that are so obvious to trained economists"; Edward E. Zajac, *Fairness or Efficiency* (1978). For a somewhat more sympathetic view of using pricing policies for distributive ends, see 1 Kahn, *Economics of Regulation*, 67–69; J. de V. Graff, *Theoretical Welfare Economics*, 171 (1957).

265. As noted before, most of Hale's contemporaries thought that the optimally efficient pricing strategy for the government was to set prices to generate a fair return on reproduction costs (the costs of reproducing the most efficient set of assets that could deliver the service in question). By the next generation, most economists concluded that the optimally efficient strategy was instead to set prices at marginal cost—that is, the incremental cost of supplying services to the marginal consumer. See Mark Blaug, *Economic Theory in Retrospect*, 601–608 (4th ed. 1985); 1 Kahn, *Economics of Regulation*, 65–75; Harold Hotelling, "The General Welfare in Relation to Problems of Taxation and of Railway and Utility Rates," 6 *Econometrica* 242 (1938). For a variety of reasons, including the difficulty of ascertaining marginal costs and the fact that over the long run, marginal costs tend to converge with full costs, historic costs are generally regarded as a reasonably good approximation of long-run marginal costs. For further discussion of this issue, see Blaug, *Economic Theory in Retrospect*, 600–608; 1 Kahn, *Economics of Regulation*, chs. 3, 4, and 7; and Crew and Kleindorfer, *Economics of Public Utility Regulation*, 13–14.

266. For the more extreme view that the costs of regulation probably exceed the efficiency gains even in the case of monopolies, see Richard A. Posner, "The Social Costs of Monopoly Regulation," 83 *Journal of Political Economy* 807, 818–819 (1975); Richard A. Posner, "Natural Monopoly and Its Regulation," 21 *Stanford Law Review* 548 (1969); Michael A. Crew and Paul R. Kleindorfer, "Governance Costs of Rate-of-Return Regulation," 141 *Journal of Institutional and Theoretical Economics* 104 (1985).

267. This is in contrast to human capital, for which people attach nonmonetary values to particular occupations, making different occupations only partial substitutes for one another. As a consequence, in theory it would be possible to levy a tax on particular occupations in which one suspected a high level of inframarginal labor without necessarily driving all workers to other occupations.

268. Frank H. Knight offered essentially this criticism of cost rate bases in his review of *Freedom Through Law*, noting that "someone must somehow pay for the extra 'risk' resulting." 39 *Virginia Law Review* 871, 878 n.10 (1953). As Arthur Hadley noted, Georgian land tax schemes posed the same problem, by capping the returns to good locational choices while leaving investors fully exposed to bad ones. The effect, argued Hadley, would inevitably be to dry up investment in land. Hadley, "The Meaning of Valuation," 178. For a similar argument from H. G. Brown, an otherwise adamant single taxer, leading him to conclude that it was futile to impose price controls only on railways or other public utilities to capture the unearned increment in their land, see "Railroad Valuation and Rate Regulation," 513–515.

Hale recognized the difficulty, but failed to see its full implications, believing that some risk-adjusted rate of return could be found that would decrease the aggregate return to utilities' investors while still attracting capital. See "The 'Physical Value' Fallacy," 726–727; *Valuation and Rate-Making*, 106–108, 142–147; *Freedom Through Law*, 513–514. In fact, however, that would be true only if investors' ex ante estimates of the expected value of inframarginal

330

rents that they would be stripped of under cost-based regulation systematically underestimated actual performance. That is to say, investors would continually have to think that they were giving up less, in relinquishing the right to enjoy the possible future appreciation in their assets, than they in fact were. Absent the possibility of such chronic market failure, no regulatory tampering with expected yields to utilities' shareholders could affect the risk-adjusted yield to new capital and at the same time attract new capital. The distributive effect of instituting a cost-based system for public utilities or any other isolated industry would therefore be limited to windfall gains and losses to old capital. 1 Kahn, *Economics of Regulation*, 110, 115–116.

269. For a discussion of the abstinence argument and of Hale's and other progressive economists' somewhat surprising assent to it, see chap. 4.

270. On the difficulties with abstinence theory, see chap. 4. Smith had assumed, at least as to human capital, that the willingness to assume risk was a real sacrifice for which people were entitled to compensation. For a contemporary exploration of whether risk assumed in investments of financial capital should be treated as a relevant sacrifice for Lockean purposes, see Barbara Fried, "Fairness and the Consumption Tax," 44 *Stanford Law Review* 961, 985–995 (1992).

271. This conclusion assumes, as would almost certainly be the case, that at least some portion of the tax is ultimately borne by investors, not shifted to consumers through higher-priced goods and services.

272. See F. P. Ramsey, "A Contribution to the Theory of Taxation," 37 *Economic Journal* 47 (1927).

273. See chap. 4, n.164. For the parallel, although somewhat more complicated, argument in the context of savings decisions, see chap. 4, nn.185,186.

274. See, e.g., Bruce Ackerman, "Regulating Slum Housing Markets on Behalf of the Poor: Of Housing Codes, Housing Subsidies and Income Redistribution Policy," 80 *Yale Law Journal* 1093 (1971); Phillip Weitzman, "Economics and Rent Regulation: A Call for a New Perspective," 13 *New York University Review of Law and Social Change* 975 (1984–1985); and Mark Kelman, "Regulation v. Taxation: Constitutional and Prudential Considerations" (unpub. ms., 1997).

275. One example is limited-equity housing co-ops, like the Mitchell-Lama projects in New York State, which allow people to capture the (appreciating) use value of apartments for as long as they wish to live in them, but which prohibit them from cashing out that appreciation on exchange. William H. Simon's "Social-Republican Property," 38 *UCLA Law Review* 1335 (1991), explores similar schemes and advocates for a somewhat more complex set of ends to limit people's ability to cash out the value of their interests in housing and business enterprises. For another interesting example, see Rosemary J. Coombe, "Author/izing the Celebrity: Publicity Rights, Postmodern Politics, and Unauthorized Genders," 10 *Cardozo Arts and Entertainment Law Journal* 365 (1992), which argues against creating a "right to publicity" that permits celebrities to monopolize the commercial value of their own fame, on the ground that the fame is a socially generated surplus.

6. Conclusion

1. Among the defenses of strong private property rights and minimal state regulation in the recent libertarian revival are Richard A. Epstein, *Takings: Private Property and the Power of Eminent Domain* (1985); Richard A. Epstein, *Simple Rules for a Complex World* (1995);

J. Hospers, *Libertarianism* (1971); Robert Nozick, *Anarchy, State, and Utopia* (1974); Ellen Frankel Paul, *Property Rights and Eminent Domain* (1987); Bernard H. Siegan, *Economic Liberties and the Constitution* (1980); essays in *Public Choice and Constitutional Economics* (James D. Gwartney and Richard E. Wagner, eds., 1988). Recent philosophical literature on the problem of coercion, which dates to Nozick's 1974 article on "Coercion," is discussed in chap. 2.

2. See, e.g., Richard A. Epstein, *Bargaining with the State* (1993); Seth F. Kreimer, "Allocational Sanctions: The Problem of Negative Rights in a Positive State," 132 *University of Pennsylvania Law Review* 1293 (1984); Kathleen M. Sullivan, "Unconstitutional Conditions," 102 *Harvard Law Review* 1415 (1989).

3. See, e.g., Samuel Scheffler, "Natural Rights, Equality, and the Minimal State," *Canadian Journal of Philosophy* (March 1976), reprinted in *Reading Nozick: Essays on Anarchy, State, and Utopia*, 148-168 (Jeffrey Paul, ed., 1981).

4. See, e.g., Amartya Sen, *Inequality Reexamined* (1992), and Martha Nussbaum, "Aristotelian Social Democracy," in *Liberalism and the Good* (R. Bruce Douglass, Gerald R. Mara, and Henry S. Richardson, eds., 1990).

5. See, e.g., Herbert Wechsler, "Toward Neutral Principles of Constitutional Law," 73 *Harvard Law Review* 29-31 (1959).

6. See, e.g., Rendell-Baker v. Kohn, 457 U.S. 830 (1982); Jackson v. Metropolitan Edison Co., 419 U.S. 345 (1974). On the evisceration of the state action doctrine, see generally Laurence H. Tribe, *American Constitutional Law*, 1688-1720 (2d ed. 1988).

7. On the struggles of progressives like Louis Brandeis, John Dewey, Ernst Freund, Learned Hand, and Zechariah Chafee to vindicate a broad vision of "free speech" while limiting constitutional protection for economic liberties, see Mark A. Graber, *Transforming Free Speech: The Ambiguous Legacy of Civil Libertarianism*, chaps. 3 and 4 (1991).

8. For attacks on an absolutist version of the first amendment for ignoring disparities in material wealth that assure disparities in access to costly forms of speech, see J. M. Balkin, "Some Realism About Pluralism: Legal Realist Approaches to the First Amendment," 1990 *Duke Law Journal* 375 (1990); Owen M. Fiss, "Social Structure and the State," 71 *Iowa Law Review* 1405 (1986); Graber, *Transforming Free Speech*, 184-227; Frederick Schauer, "The Political Incidence of the Free Speech Principle," 64 *University of Colorado Law Review* 935 (1993); Cass Sunstein, *Democracy and the Problem of Free Speech*, 17-20 (1993). On hate speech, see Mari J. Matsuda et al., *Words That Wound: Critical Race Theory, Assaultive Speech, and the First Amendment* (1993). On pornography, see Catherine A. MacKinnon, *Only Words* (1993). For general comparison of the stakes in government regulation of economic affairs and speech, see Kathleen M. Sullivan, "Free Speech and Unfree Markets," 42 *UCLA Law Review* 949 (1995).

9. Among academic writers, the leading proponents of a broad reading of the takings clause are Epstein, *Takings*, Paul, *Property Rights and Eminent Domain*, and Siegan, *Economic Liberties and the Constitution*. For a sample of the criticism spawned by Epstein's proposal to treat most forms of regulation or taxation as a taking, see Symposium on Richard Epstein's *Takings*, 41 *University of Miami Law Review* 1 (1986). Epstein's position has recently gotten a nod from the political world, in the legislative proposal contained in the Republicans' 1994 "Contract with America" to require government compensation for all environmental regulation that reduces the value of property by more than 10 percent, and in similar proposals now before a number of state legislatures. The courts themselves have shown little inclination to embrace a radically expansive reading of "takings" as a constitutional matter, with jurisprudence in the area largely mired in balancing tests and the physicality

of the taking itself. The most celebrated recent takings cases, Dolan v. City of Tigard, 114 S.Ct. 2309 (1994); Lucas v. South Carolina Coastal Council, 505 U.S. 1003 (1992); Nollan v. California Coastal Comm'n, 483 U.S. 825 (1987); and First English Evangelical Lutheran Church v. County of Los Angeles, 482 U.S. 304 (1987), are at best modest nudges in the direction of a more expansive definition of "regulatory takings."

10. "Rights Under the Fourteenth and Fifteenth Amendments Against Injuries Inflicted by Private Individuals," 6 *The Lawyers Guild* 627, 630 (1947).

11. Hale suggests that when an owner's private actions do not involve any matter of high public importance, "state action cannot be regarded as arbitrary, however arbitrary the whim of the owner." Not being arbitrary, it is therefore constitutionally valid. "Rights Under the Fourteenth and Fifteenth Amendments," 630. But it is perfectly clear (as Hale acknowledges) that were the state itself to bar someone from entering a private home or the state's property on grounds of race, a court would conclude that the state was violating the Fourteenth Amendment, without inquiring whether the state's act implicated matters of public importance. Thus, some independent constitutional principle is needed to explain why private parties as state actors are given more latitude to discriminate than is the state itself. A modern-day Hale could perhaps find that principle in the discriminator's own constitutional right to privacy, which (one could argue) must be weighed against others' Fourteenth Amendment rights not to be discriminated against. When privacy interests are greatest (for example, in picking the guests invited into one's home) and the cost to the discriminated-against party relatively slight, one could argue that the former constitutional interest ought to dominate the latter.

12. See, e.g., C. Edwin Baker, "The Ideology of the Economic Analysis of Law," 5 *Journal of Philosophy and Public Affairs* 3 (1975); Mark Kelman, *A Guide to Critical Legal Studies,* chap. 4 (1987); Mark Kelman, "Taking *Takings* Seriously: An Essay for Centrists," 74 *California Law Review* 1829 (1986); Duncan Kennedy and Frank Michelman, "Are Property and Contract Efficient?," 8 *Hofstra Law Review* 711 (1980); Duncan Kennedy, "Cost Benefit Analysis of Entitlement Problems: A Critique," 33 *Stanford Law Review* 387 (1981). For another critique of law and economics for lapsing into its own version of formalism, see Elinor Ostrom, *Governing the Commons: The Evolution of Institutions for Collective Action* (1990).

13. "Privilege, Malice, and Intent," 8 *Harvard Law Review* 1, 5–6 (1894).

14. For Nozick's own uneasiness about private rights to de facto monopoly profits, see *Anarchy, State, and Utopia,* 179–180, and "Coercion," in *Philosophy, Science, and Method: Essays in Honor of Ernest Nagel,* 468–469 n.29 (Sidney Morgenbesser, Patrick Suppes, and Morton White, eds., 1969). See also Epstein, *Simple Rules for a Complex World,* 85–86, for a similar concern. For critiques of Nozick for his inconsistent or undefended treatment of surplus value, see Barbara Fried, "Wilt Chamberlain Revisited: Nozick's 'Justice in Transfer' and the Problem of Market-Based Distribution," 24 *Philosophy and Public Affairs* 226 (1995), and Eric Mack, "Nozick on Unproductivity: The Unintended Consequences," in *Reading Nozick,* 169–190. The so-called "liability rule" that Nozick uses to compensate dissenters for their loss in being forced into the minimal state, for example, in effect allows the dominant "protective agency" to usurp the surplus value that dissenters could have extracted in voluntary contractual negotiations to enter into that state. See Mack, id. Nozick's "weak form" of the Lockean proviso has precisely the same effect. It permits first-comers to take scarce resources, provided that they can show that later generations are at least as well off as they would have been in a world without private property. But that weak form allows first-comers to expropriate all of the surplus value inherent in those resources, stripping later generations of the share that a strict reading of Locke's proviso of "enough, and as good" would seem to require.

15. See Epstein, *Takings,* 162–166, 172–175, 332–333.

INDEX